INFORMATION
SECURITY SCIENCE

INFORMATION SECURITY SCIENCE

MEASURING THE VULNERABILITY TO DATA COMPROMISES

CARL S. YOUNG
Managing Director and Chief Security Officer,
Stroz Friedberg LLC

ELSEVIER

AMSTERDAM • BOSTON • HEIDELBERG • LONDON
NEW YORK • OXFORD • PARIS • SAN DIEGO
SAN FRANCISCO • SINGAPORE • SYDNEY • TOKYO

Syngress is an imprint of Elsevier

SYNGRESS.

Syngress is an imprint of Elsevier
50 Hampshire Street, 5th Floor, Cambridge, MA 02139, United States

Notices
Knowledge and best practice in this field are constantly changing. As new research and experience
broaden our understanding, changes in research methods, professional practices, or medical treatment
may become necessary.

Practitioners and researchers must always rely on their own experience and knowledge in evaluating
and using any information, methods, compounds, or experiments described herein. In using such information or methods they should be mindful of their own safety and the safety of others, including parties
for whom they have a professional responsibility.

To the fullest extent of the law, neither the Publisher nor the authors, contributors, or editors, assume
any liability for any injury and/or damage to persons or property as a matter of products liability,
negligence or otherwise, or from any use or operation of any methods, products, instructions, or ideas
contained in the material herein.

Library of Congress Cataloging-in-Publication Data
A catalog record for this book is available from the Library of Congress

British Library Cataloguing-in-Publication Data
A catalogue record for this book is available from the British Library

ISBN: 978-0-12-809643-7

For information on all Syngress publications
visit our website at https://www.elsevier.com/

Working together
to grow libraries in
developing countries

www.elsevier.com • www.bookaid.org

Publisher: Joe Hayton
Acquisition Editor: Brian Romer
Editorial Project Manager: Anna Valutkevich
Production Project Manager: Mohana Natarajan
Designer: Mark Rogers

Typeset by Thomson Digital

To my remarkable sisters,
Diane Uniman and Nancy Young

Contents

I

THREATS, RISK AND RISK ASSESSMENTS

1. Information Security Threats and Risk

2. Modeling Information Security Risk

II

SCIENTIFIC FUNDAMENTALS

3. Physics and Information Security

4. Electromagnetic Waves

5. Noise, Interference, and Emanations

III

THE COMPROMISE OF SIGNALS

6. Signals and Information Security

V

THE PHYSICAL SECURITY OF INFORMATION ASSETS

14. Physical Security Controls

15. Data Centers: A Concentration of Information Security Risk

Epilogue   359

Biography

Carl S. Young is an expert in information and physical security risk management. He is currently a Managing Director and the Chief Security Officer at Stroz Friedberg, an international security risk consulting firm. He is the former Global Head of Physical Security Technology at Goldman Sachs as well as a former Senior Executive and Supervisory Special Agent at the FBI. He was also a consultant to the JASON Defense Advisory Group. Mr. Young is the author of *Metrics and Methods for Security Risk Management* (Syngress, 2010), and *The Science and Technology of Counterterrorism* (Butterworth-Heinemann, 2014) as well as numerous journal publications. In 1997 he was awarded the President's Foreign Intelligence Advisory Board (PFIAB) James R. Killian Award by the White House for significant individual contributions to US national security. Mr. Young received undergraduate and graduate degrees in mathematics and physics from the Massachusetts Institute of Technology.

Foreword

All new innovations bring positive and negative consequences for users and society at large. This has been true of the development and broad deployment of alternating current a century ago, and mass vehicular and air transportation, right through to the nuclear age. We enjoy the benefits of these platforms for economic productivity and advancement as well as social interaction, but at the same time in the hands of bad actors, all these represent existential threats to society.

The Internet and electronic communication have come into the public consciousness only over the past 20 years. And perhaps they represent a new frontier in providing benefits to society, by reducing what economists call search and transaction costs. They also bring about the ability to reach and improve the lives of many people in developing economies.

At the same time the extreme networking and electronic interconnection that underpins our day-to-day lives has provided for an extraordinary amount of vulnerability; whether it be through data breaches of corporate networks or the compromise of wireless communication means, cyber threats seem potentially limitless when the tools are put in malicious hands. These threats are also limitless because they are very scalable and rely on the weak underbelly of our basic market economy, which competes on the basis of convenience and speed, often sacrificing security.

This book examines in the most comprehensive fashion how to think about vulnerabilities in a scientific way, the only approach that fully and objectively can determine how to go about identifying, understanding, and rooting out vulnerabilities. It is both wide ranging and looks at each potential vulnerability with a strict scientific mindset to help all readers determine how best to maximize the benefits of interconnection in the Internet age, while at the same time minimizing the downside so as to gain the benefits all societies have come to expect.

Michael Patsalos-Fox
CEO, Stroz Friedberg,
Former Chairman of the Americas,
McKinsey & Co.

Preface

Despite its name, the commercial success of the computer derives from its effectiveness as a communications tool rather than as a machine that *computes*. Humans are arguably obsessed with communication so any device that enables the exchange of information is likely to be popular.

To be sure, information technologies such as the telephone, the television, and the computer *cum* Internet have had transformational effects on society. People who were previously isolated suddenly had unprecedented access to individuals outside their immediate surroundings. In addition, they were now almost immediately aware of events that occurred beyond their immediate environment. Notwithstanding possible correlations between social media and bad grammar, the positive effects of communication technologies cannot be disputed.

Yet not all communications are meant for public consumption. Unauthorized access to information is a problem when the whole point of these technologies is to facilitate the seamless exchange of data. To complicate matters, we are a species that also craves convenience, and convenience and security are often incompatible. In fact, the need for convenience drives much of the information security risk within organizations today.

Although attacks on networks are the focus of typical security strategies, other modes of attack on information assets deserve attention. For example, unauthorized access to visual and audible information is commonplace in many business settings with the potential for significant losses. In addition,

electronic devices radiate compromising energy that can be remotely detected under the right conditions. State-sponsored adversaries have both the incentive and the resources to conduct such attacks thereby obviating the need to intrude on the network and largely eliminating a concern for detection.

This book analyzes the vulnerability to information compromise via a variety of attack methodologies. Many of these are surprisingly low-tech, which substantially increases the risk to many organizations. There is also a strong physical basis for many information security risk scenarios that is not generally appreciated by information security professionals. Quantitative details related to these scenarios are included for those so inclined, but the principal intent is to convey the underlying principles that govern the operational limits on attacks and the effectiveness of countermeasures.

Such principles are essential to estimating the vulnerability to information compromise. In addition, techniques borrowed from various scientific disciplines are presented. These can provide unique insights into security risk as well as yield meaningful risk metrics that have eluded practitioners or at the very least have been difficult to formulate.

To that end, the book is divided into five Parts, and each Part is further divided into Chapters. These are briefly described as follows.

Part I recounts the fundamentals of threats, risk, and risk assessments. These concepts represent the foundation of security risk management, and must be understood in order to rigorously assess information security risk.

- Chapter 1 discusses the concepts of threat and risk. In particular, the risk factor is introduced. Risk factors for various threats and attack vectors are highlighted throughout the text since they are essential to formulating an effective security risk management strategy.
- Chapter 2 explains some of the quantitative tools that are useful in developing simple models of information security risk. Basic functions are described along with concepts pertaining to scale, growth, decay, and rates of change.

Part II provides the scientific background required to analyze the various attack scenarios presented in later chapters.

- Chapter 3 discusses mechanical and electromagnetic energy, which are encoded with information to yield signals. Topics include waves and wave motion, energy, power, resonance, diffraction, and point sources of radiating energy.
- Chapter 4 introduces electromagnetic signal fundamentals to include fields, flux, and Maxwell's equations. The latter are the expressions that govern all electromagnetic phenomena, and therefore explain the mechanisms for information loss.
- Chapter 5 focuses on the generation of electromagnetic emanations in electronic circuits. These emanations are the targets of information compromise in remote attacks. Various sources of noise are discussed, and, as the name implies, are fundamental to the signal-to-noise ratio, *the* critical security parameter in remote attacks on signals.

Part III describes the essential features of attacks on electromagnetic signals, audible signals, and visual images pursuant to information compromises. The relation between information theory and information security is also discussed.

- Chapter 6 introduces topics related to the compromise of electromagnetic signals. The process of modulation transforms energy into signals and thereby conveys information. Risk factors for signal compromises are discussed as well as a high-level review of signal averaging, which is essential to detecting signals in noisy environments. Fundamental concepts of information theory are investigated, which leads to a discussion on the relationship between information theory and information security.
- Chapter 7 analyzes methods to remotely detect emanations from electronic devices. Achieving an adequate signal-to-noise ratio is the Holy Grail for an attacker. A number of variables that affect this ratio are discussed.
- Chapter 8 discusses various countermeasures to attacks that target electromagnetic emanations. These measures principally include shielding and grounding. Fortuitous losses caused by intervening objects that reflect, diffract, and absorb incident electromagnetic energy are also reviewed in some detail and various models of propagation loss are presented. Both intrabuilding and interbuilding signal propagation scenarios are discussed.
- Chapter 9 focuses on optical attacks. The vulnerabilities associated with remote, unauthorized viewing of computer monitors, whiteboards, and keyboards are considered. Such attacks can be conducted using a simple telescope. The resolution limit for a given telescope objective lens and viewing distance is

set by diffraction, which establishes the threshold on vulnerability. An optical attack using photon counting rather than imaging is also described.

- Chapter 10 provides the fundamentals of attacks on audible information. Speech-borne vibrations of molecules in air and/or various materials that support acoustic propagation produce an audible signal that, under certain conditions, can be remotely detected. As in any real-life scenario, noise plays a significant role in determining the operational limits for a given attack scenario. Both airborne and structure-borne scenarios are described as well as the effect of intervening objects that reflect, diffract, and absorb acoustic energy.

Part IV delves into the vast territory of information technology risk. The scale and complexity of security vulnerabilities associated with applications, databases, protocols, operating systems, etc., preclude a meaningful treatment of security in a single reference. In addition, technologies are ephemeral, and vulnerabilities eventually become less relevant over time. But the culture-driven processes that affect the use of these technologies persist long after a machine or software application is decommissioned.

Therefore a unique approach is adopted, which avoids discussions of specific security technologies. Instead, simple statistical measurements of data derived from standard sources of vulnerabilities are specified that lead to enterprise-level information security metrics. These lead to inferences about root causes of information security risk as well as provide a common language on risk that can facilitate meaningful dialogue between technologists and nontechnical management.

- Chapter 11 discusses the principal sources of risk factors for information security: business practices, security

governance, information technology implementation, user behavior, and the physical security of information assets. The nexus between risk-based policies and standards to security risk metrics is also highlighted. Finally, the role of organizational culture is discussed since it can strongly affect risk factors for information compromise.

- Chapter 12 describes various measurements and resulting metrics that can yield insights into the root causes of information technology risk. These metrics can be used to measure effectiveness of underlying risk management processes. Statistical correlation measurements are also used to examine trends in time series of vulnerabilities. Such measurements enable Tier ratings of high-level security controls as defined in the NIST Cybersecurity Framework.
- Chapter 13 presents a variety of specialized information security risk models, measurements, and metrics. Some of these are unique to information security but others have been borrowed from other science and engineering disciplines. The use of the Markov process and Fourier analysis is particularly noteworthy given their use in many other contexts. These methods are suggested here as a means of identifying risk-relevant behaviors within large and/or complex data sets, for example, firewall logs.

Part V is devoted to the physical security of information assets. This topic is often overlooked in traditional treatments of information security risk. However, physical security represents an important source of risk factors since physical security technologies protect critical information assets. In addition, these devices are networked, and therefore are potentially vulnerable to direct compromise in addition to facilitating attacks against the network more broadly.

- Chapter 14 focuses on physical security controls. These include authenticating identity, verifying authorization, and assessing organizational affiliation. The successful implementation and integration of these controls is central to a physical security strategy, which itself is a key element of a comprehensive information security strategy. A discussion of Technical Security Countermeasures is included since organizations rely on these methods to address industrial espionage threats but are generally unable to assess its effectiveness.
- Chapter 15 investigates some of the key security issues affecting data centers. Data centers present an increasing concentration of information security risk. This risk is driven by the popularity of virtualization and the general trend in Cloud computing. A high-level physical security strategy for data centers is presented along with physical security–related vulnerabilities associated with virtualization.

The effects of a high-energy electromagnetic pulse generated in proximity to a data center are also analyzed in this chapter. Such a discussion may seem incongruous in a text on information security until the impact of this terrorist-type threat is analyzed more thoroughly.

Finally, the objectives in writing this book are twofold: The first is to offer a unique reference on information security attacks. Some of these do not receive much attention but nevertheless represent legitimate threats to many organizations. The good news is that effective countermeasures are easily implemented once the physical limits imposed by Mother Nature are understood.

The second objective is to bring the worlds of science and security closer together by elaborating on their many areas of intersection. Achieving this objective is not so easy because distinct populations inhabit each world, and differences in vocabulary, background, culture, and education have traditionally limited meaningful interactions. This book attempts to bridge these gaps, and thereby encourage the inhabitants of each world to discover and appreciate each other's contributions.

> In this electronic age we see ourselves being translated more and more into the form of information, moving toward the technological extension of consciousness.
>
> *Marshall McLuhan*

Source: Mcluhan M. Understanding media: the extensions of man. Critical ed. Gordon WT, editor. Gingko Press, CA, USA; 2003. p. 85.

Acknowledgments

For someone who makes a living at defining metrics, I am remarkably inadequate at estimating the magnitude of contributions by others to this book. Thankfully a quantitative assessment is not required here, but suffice it to say that each of the following individuals provided the inspiration, knowledge, and/or support that made this book possible.

Although they have been recognized previously, I must reiterate the significant and sometimes intangible contributions made by my parents, Dr. Irving Young and Dr. Geraldine Young. A politician once famously remarked that some people think that because they landed on third base they believe they hit a triple. Without the support of my parents I would not have made it to the ballpark.

Specific individuals have profoundly influenced the way I look at security issues and therefore shaped my thinking about this diverse field over many years. Fortunately, I continue to be the beneficiary of their knowledge, experience, and friendship. These individuals include Robert Bryant, Dr. David B. Chang, Robert Grubert, Christopher Hogan, James A. King, Michael McDevitt, David J. Murphy III, Roger Pike, and J. Martial Robichaud.

Risk management and risk managers can assume many forms. Physicians are not necessarily identified in this way, but that is precisely their role. My father has been fortunate to be in the care of a cardiologist, Dr. Donald Haas of Abington Hospital in Abington, PA, who exemplifies the best qualities of a risk manager and caregiver. My family and I are extraordinarily grateful for his expertise and the personal attention he has given my dad. There is no question Dr. Haas is largely responsible for the quality of life my dad now enjoys and the happiness we derive from this as a result.

Jean Gobin at Stroz Friedberg provided both content and ideas in this book. Specifically, he made significant contributions to the section on Fourier transforms applied to security data, the password cracking analysis, and the section on virtual environments. Jean is a brilliant engineer, and my company and I are fortunate to be able to draw on his talent and creativity.

Kate McManus (aka "Ms. Hudson Market") at Stroz Friedberg provided some of the graphics in this book as well as helped formulate the metrics related to the root causes of information technology risk. Kate possesses a keen aesthetic sense and strong technical know-how, and she is a significant individual contributor to the visual presentation of the security risk metrics presented in this book.

Eileen Murphy is my Executive Assistant at Stroz Friedberg. Her competence and effectiveness has helped in writing this book as well as getting things accomplished more generally. She has been a silent partner in this endeavor, and I am grateful for her important if behind-the-scenes contributions.

This past year has had its challenges and without personal support I would not have mustered the motivation to produce this book. Lisa Maass, Fran Davis, and Ruth Steinberg, whom I have known since college and kindergarten, respectively, provided me with the candid advice that only the best of friends can offer. I am grateful for the decades of love and attention they have shown me.

Dr. Peter Rocheleau volunteered for the dubious honor of editing this tome. Peter is an intellectual's intellectual who possesses a keen eye for both detail and thematic enhancement. If this book is successful in achieving its stated objectives, it will largely be due to his insights and encouragement.

Some people contribute to projects in ways that do not often get recognized. In particular, individuals who make it possible to work in a comfortable environment deserve more explicit acknowledgment. To that end, Sadie Torres has been diligent in reducing the "entropy" in my office and thereby reversing the effects of my chaotic ways. I am appreciative of her daily efforts that have contributed to a more productive work environ-ment as well as for the authentic Cuban food she sometimes brings to the office. Muchas gracias Señora.

The publishing experience can seem similar to Dante's Nine Circles of Hell if the publisher and author are not resonant to borrow a term from physics. Fortunately I benefitted significantly from my association with three bona fide editing professionals at Elsevier. Specifically, Anna Valutkevich, Editorial Project Manager, Mohanambal Natarajan, Senior Project Manager, and Brian Romer, Senior Acquisitions Editor, understood what I was trying to achieve and helped me to achieve it. I am extremely appreciative of their efforts.

Finally, for more than a year Dr. Donna Gill has provided masterful collaboration on the piano and elsewhere. Despite her modesty, I believe there is no one who performs the Brahms Intermezzo Op. 117 better than she, a true metric of artistic achievement and sensitivity. I am grateful for her efforts in support of this book as well as in many other facets of my life.

THREATS, RISK AND RISK ASSESSMENTS

Information Security Threats and Risk

INTRODUCTION

Information Security Risk

This book is about estimating the vulnerability to unauthorized access to information by individuals with malicious intent. Attack scenarios range from simple visual observations of white boards or computer monitors and conversation overhears to sophisticated compromises of radiating electromagnetic signals. Many of these scenarios can be modeled using well-established physical principles that provide insights into the magnitude of the vulnerability to information security threats.

Such estimates may appear straightforward, but there are many scenarios of concern and the spectrum of vulnerabilities is broad. This is evident from the following examples:

- electromagnetic signals leaking from a computer located in a country known to sponsor information security attacks against foreign companies;
- a wireless network in the vicinity of a drive-by hacker with one of the network access points promiscuously radiating signal energy to the street;
- sensitive conversations that can be overheard by occupants of another floor in a multitenant office building;
- white boards, keyboards, and computer monitor screens in the direct line-of-sight of distant buildings;
- employees informally conversing on a company balcony while surrounded by properties of unknown control/ownership;
- information technology (IT) networks and systems that communicate via the Internet.

Traditional texts on information security and indeed most organizations often focus on the last bullet. In fact, entire departments are routinely dedicated to network security. It is no secret that the exploitation of IT vulnerabilities has increased in recent years, and the criticality of IT infrastructure demands a disproportionate share of attention. As a consequence, other attack vectors have been ignored despite the fact that they may be simpler to execute and could have equally significant impact.

The historical evidence suggests that IT risk deserve special attention. But despite that attention, traditional security risk management strategies have arguably been less than effective.

Notably, these strategies include numerous and varied security controls. In fact, there is often an abundance of IT security data derived from these controls. But it is not clear such data are yielding insights into risk on a strategic level.

Indeed, IT risk managers are sometimes overwhelmed with data that are intended to identify the risk of information loss. But such data are traditionally used in support of tactical remediation efforts. Problems often recur because such remedies are inherently narrow in scope. Sometimes this abundance of data actually blinds organizations to the most significant risk factors for information compromise, which include business practices, security governance, physical security of information assets, and user behavior in addition to poor or inappropriate IT implementation.

One phenomenon that contributes to the ineffectiveness of current security strategies is the difficulty in quantifying IT risk. Why is this so difficult? The reasons are threefold:

- IT security incidents typically result from the confluence of related issues. The contributions of each issue can vary and it can be difficult to assess their relative magnitudes.
- Robust statistics on actual IT incidents are either nonexistent or not particularly helpful in assessing risk.
- Controlled experiments to determine the effectiveness of risk mitigation in IT environments are difficult to conduct.

The result is an absence of useful models pertaining to IT risk. So it is not easy to rigorously confirm the effectiveness of a particular security strategy.

The problem is exacerbated by the fact that IT protocols and systems have antagonistic objectives: ensuring data security and facilitating communication. To be sure, facilitating communication invites risk. In fact, the very existence of a network is a risk factor for information compromise. Despite continued efforts to ensure data security, these technologies spawn new vulnerabilities each day. The popularity of the Internet in conjunction with well-advertised attacks on systems drives the nearly singular focus on technology as both the culprit and the cure for information security ills.

Information security risk scenarios can admittedly be complex with interrelated elements. In many cases this complexity precludes the formulation of reliable risk models. Finally, the diversity of attackers and their respective motives makes precise statements on the likelihood of a future incident difficult if not impossible.

Information Security in a Routine Business Scenario

The following example illustrates the variety of information security issues that are relevant to even routine business scenarios. Consider an everyday meeting between individuals in a conference room. This event is likely repeated thousands of times each day around the world. Meeting attendees use the gifts provided by Mother Nature to generate, detect, and process acoustic energy in the form of speech.

What is the level of assurance that the acoustic energy will be confined to that conference room and not be overheard by individuals in other parts of the building? For example, acoustic energy propagating within the conference room might couple to building structural elements and be heard by individuals in an adjoining room or even another floor.

Moreover, if the conference room contains a device that enables individuals in remote locations to join the meeting, for example, devices manufactured by Polycom, the information security risk profile clearly changes. Telephones and telephone-enabled technologies are used to intentionally transmit acoustic energy beyond a particular room. Many of these devices are Internet Protocol (IP)–based, and are therefore potentially vulnerable to network-based attacks.

Any electronic device that transmits audible information must first convert acoustic energy into electromagnetic energy pursuant to long-distance transmission. The electromagnetic energy is transmitted via physical channels such as wire, optical fiber, and/or the atmosphere. However, a conversion to electromagnetic energy certainly does not confer immunity from signal compromise, but it does change the methods required to implement an attack.

Suppose further that a conference room targeted by an attacker contains a computer. The meeting organizer is using the computer to display confidential material to attendees in the room via a large monitor. He or she is also sending a PowerPoint presentation to remote attendees via the Internet. The computer is therefore being used to share the information with unseen audiences around the world. Visible displays of the presentation and electronic transmissions of data via the Internet offer adversaries a variety of attack vectors especially if an attacker owns the local communications infrastructure.

In addition, the conference room might be viewable to passers-by in the office hallway. Many modern conference rooms resemble large fishbowls that are located in well-trafficked office areas. These scenarios would provide opportunities for discreet information compromises. In addition, the same image that simultaneously appears on monitors around the world might be visible to passers-by in those distant venues as well.

White boards and computer monitors frequently display images within the direct line-of-sight of other buildings.[1] Such images can be viewed from significant distances with relatively inexpensive equipment. Even reflected images can be viewed in this manner given the appropriate physical conditions. Moreover, remote observation of visible information is much simpler than a network attack yet can yield information of comparable value.

This section concludes by asking the reader to now consider how the risk profile for the conference room scenario might change if someone with malicious intent had physical access to that room prior to a meeting. Many of the standard information security controls used to protect information would be undermined. The consequence is that now physical security controls could play an outsized role in ensuring information assets are secure from so-called "insider" threats. This scenario is an excellent example of the confluence of physical and information security risk, a recurring theme in this text.

Vulnerability to Signal Detection

Although quantitative estimates of information security risk are often desired, certain security scenarios are more amenable to such analyses than others. In particular, signal energy that is either intentionally or unintentionally radiated obeys well-known physical laws

[1]A visible image results from the reflection or direct transmission of energy within the visible portion of the electromagnetic spectrum. The intensity of background light, which lowers the contrast required to discern individual symbols, constitutes noise in this context.

that are formulated in terms of risk factors such as distance and time. Characterizing a threat in terms of these risk factors forms the basis for a quantitative model of vulnerability.

Let us be more specific about what is meant by a signal. A signal is a form of energy that is changed or "modulated" and thereby encoded with information. In other words, the process of modulation results in the transformation of mere energy into energy with information content.[2] A rigorous definition of energy is provided in Chapter 3. For now it is enough to know that both modulated and unmodulated energy obey the laws of physics. And it is modulated energy that is the target of attackers, and therefore provides the impetus to implement security controls.

Critical issues in estimating the vulnerability to signal compromise are the sources of ambient noise or interference and the physics of energy propagation within materials. Signals exist as either mechanical or electromagnetic energy, and each behaves quite differently depending on the material in which they propagate. The nature of these energy–matter interactions significantly affects the vulnerability to audible, visible, and electromagnetic signal compromises.

Environmental features in the path of propagation will affect the signal intensity and thereby impose detection limits as a function of distance. Developing a model for signal propagation that accounts for all risk-relevant features, that is, the risk factors, is critical to understanding the vulnerability component of risk for a given threat.

The physical nature of signals suggests that they should be detectable by some type of sensor. Furthermore, it would be reasonable to assume that these sensors are designed to detect specific forms of energy. In fact, it is the signal intensity that evokes a response by the sensor. Therefore the signal intensity in conjunction with the noise intensity is almost always the key to successfully estimating the vulnerability to information loss.

An attacker with physical proximity to a signal source could potentially detect and reconstruct that signal assuming the signal power is sufficiently greater than the ambient noise power within the signal bandwidth.[3] Moreover, signal energy is inherently promiscuous, and is agnostic to the identity of the individual attempting to detect it.

For example, if a Wi-Fi network is used to access the Internet, the signal is vulnerable to detection by both authorized users *and* an attacker sniffing for network traffic. A Wi-Fi signal carries risk if it is assumed to be undetectable in areas outside an organization's physical span of control and this assumption is part of a defensive strategy.

Although strong encryption (eg, WPA2-PSK) is now incorporated into the 802.11 wireless protocols to address this vulnerability, weaker forms of encryption are still prevalent (eg, WEP). In one ethical hacking exercise, my company exploited this exact vulnerability to gain access to a corporate network. In addition, unauthorized users can use other techniques to

[2]This statement is admittedly ambiguous due to differences in the meaning of "information." The colloquial use of the term refers to any data that convey meaning. The information theoretic interpretation, which will be investigated more thoroughly in Chapter 6, is the uncertainty or diversity associated with an alphabet or source of symbols. To illustrate the distinction, if I have a digital transmitter broadcasting all 1's, this is information in the colloquial sense. But the signal conveys no information in the information theoretic sense as explained in the same chapter. However, either interpretation works in this context if it is specified that modulation creates "content" rather than information.
[3]The effect of encryption is neglected here, which will not influence signal detection but is designed to thwart signal reconstruction if detected.

spoof the system and thereby connect to the network. Signal detection is a necessary precursor to signal reconstruction, so awareness of the risk factors that affect the vulnerability to detection should be top of mind.

Although quantitative estimates of vulnerability are useful, understanding the parameters that affect signal propagation at a high level is often sufficient. Qualitative insights can enable the identification of relevant security controls and thereby inform a risk management strategy. For those interested in more detail, references that offer more complete treatments of specific topics on security risk are provided throughout this text.

Assessing the Root Causes of Information Security Risk

A comprehensive assessment of the vulnerability to information compromise requires visibility into the root causes of information security risk. To that end, most texts on information security focus on technology when identifying issues requiring remediation.

An exclusive focus on technology ignores organizational issues that drive information security risk but are manifest as technology problems. In fact and as noted earlier, a virtual avalanche of information is generated by security technology controls. These controls can be effective in identifying tactical issues but the broader risk associated with security data so derived can be difficult to interpret pursuant to identifying systemic security problems.

Specifically and as mentioned previously, the principal sources of information security vulnerabilities in organizations are as follows:

- business practices
- a lack of security governance
- IT implementation
- the physical security of information assets
- user behavior

Business practices are inexorably linked to the organizational culture where the former is a by-product of the latter. In fact, it is not an exaggeration to say that the culture establishes the security posture in any organization, and reflects the outcome of the security–convenience dialectic that is being played out every day.

A lack of security governance is arguably driven by organizational culture as well. A lax approach to developing and enforcing information security policy follows from a culture of permissiveness or where creativity is encouraged on every level. In particular, a lack of well-designed security policies and standards correlates with a proliferation of information security vulnerabilities.

Although the previous discussion might seem to suggest otherwise, IT implementation is clearly a source of risk factors for information compromise. Poor implementation of technologies used to store, process, and/or transmit confidential information contributes to the overall risk profile of an organization, and must be addressed on both a tactical and a strategic level, but not to the exclusion of other sources of risk.

User behavior is deserving of scrutiny in identifying root causes of information security risk. User behavior in this context includes the history of websites visited, electronic access privileges (eg, Windows user, local administrator, domain administrator), physical access system privileges, history of internal resources accessed, and password complexity.

A user risk profile consisting of these risk factors enables a relative risk ranking of users, and thereby focuses monitoring and/or remediation efforts. Moreover, security perspectives at both the user and the device level provide a multidimensional view of risk, and thereby facilitate more effective risk management strategies.

The Physical Security of Information Assets

The physical security of information assets is relevant to the threat of information compromise and therefore represents an important source of vulnerabilities. Understanding the risk profile of data centers is particularly germane given the concentration of assets therein. The risk is driven principally by the use of virtualization and the related trend in using Cloud storage and computing resources.

Physical security is an area often neglected in traditional treatments of information security. This is unfortunate since the physical security strategy in data centers greatly affects the overall information security risk profile. The most obvious implication of a breakdown in a physical security device is that it increases the vulnerability of specific information assets to compromise. If that device malfunctions due to equipment failure or a network attack, those assets are less protected and therefore at an increased vulnerability to compromise.

In fact, physical security technologies can themselves be a vector for network attacks since most of these devices are IP-enabled and communicate via a local area network and/or the Internet. If a digital video recorder, network video recorder, card reader, or CCTV camera itself was compromised via an attack against its operating system or firmware, it could jeopardize that specific device as well as the network at large. The emphasis in this text will be on strategic security risk rather than the detailed workings of specific physical security technologies. Such technology has been addressed in many other texts [1].

Although nearly all organizations depend on networked devices to communicate and access confidential information, a surprising reliance on paper documents persists in many of these same organizations. The storage and transport of physical media containing confidential information presents surprisingly vexing security challenges, perhaps because organizations focus on network security and therefore neglect what appear to be more pedestrian threats.

Finally, network-based attack vectors against physical security devices and the details associated with remediation methods, for example, network isolation, application whitelisting, and signal encryption, will not be addressed in this book. This decision is again consistent with the fact that many other texts address such issues in exhaustive detail. Attempts at doing so here would potentially vitiate the treatment of security topics that are not typically discussed elsewhere yet can contribute significantly to an organization's information security risk profile.

The Likelihood Component of Information Security Risk

Measuring the vulnerability component of risk is necessary but not sufficient to develop a comprehensive view of information security risk. Assessing the likelihood of occurrence of a future threat incident clearly must be a factor in decisions on risk management. If a future incident is deemed unlikely relative to other threats, then resources might be better applied elsewhere.

The challenge is to evaluate the potential for incident occurrence if historical evidence of security incidents is rare or conditions vary significantly in time. This condition often reflects reality. So how should a Chief Information Security Officer (CISO) or decision maker proceed in such circumstances?

There at least two methods to evaluate the likelihood component of information security risk: (1) perform statistical analyses of security incidents that relate to threat risk factors (this contrasts with attempting to count and analyze actual threat incidents, which, as noted earlier, is often not feasible) and (2) perform statistical analyses of threat incidents that can be modeled as random variables.

Risk factors will be discussed in detail later in this chapter, but the definition is introduced now given its relevance and importance: A risk factor for a specific threat is a feature that increases the magnitude of one or more components of risk for that threat. How are risk factors applicable to measuring the likelihood of a future information security threat incident?

In the absence of actual security incidents, analyzing incidents that relate to a threat risk factor offers a viable alternative. Since by definition a risk factor increases the likelihood, impact, or vulnerability to a threat incident, logic dictates that numerous incidents that relate to a risk factor are indicative of an increased potential and/or vulnerability to such an incident.

An example might be to analyze the number of incidents of unauthenticated access to restricted areas via piggybacking, etc. The successful circumvention of physical access controls to gain access to sensitive areas can yield relevant metrics on the quality of physical security even if such assets have not been compromised as a result. Successful password cracking is another example of where measuring a risk factor, for example, weak authentication, is indicative of the vulnerability to an actual incident.

If threat incidents are believed to occur randomly, it is possible to perform specific statistical analyses, and such a condition accounts for the second method of estimating the likelihood component of risk. If threat incidents can be legitimately considered random variables, well-understood statistical methods can be used to provide a quantitative estimate of the likelihood of occurrence.

It may seem ironic, but random processes confer a degree of certainty to inherently uncertain processes. This is because the standard deviation, which represents the uncertainty about the mean of a probability distribution, is specified for various distributions of random variables. For example, the probability that a given value selected from a normal distribution of values is within a standard deviation of the mean is proportional to the square root of the total population in the distribution.

Unfortunately or not, information security threat incidents that can be modeled as random variables are rare. Nevertheless, certain threat incidents might be amenable to such a model if only to provide crude estimates of risk. Chapter 13 details a method that enables estimates of vulnerability using this type of probabilistic approach. Therefore it can be helpful to be familiar with these methods and to apply them appropriately if judiciously.

INFORMATION SECURITY RISK

Understanding the distinction between a threat and a risk is a prerequisite for effectively communicating a risk management strategy. It is important because although threats and risk are closely related, they are not equivalent. Threats are the entities or conditions that cause harm, and therefore should be the focus of attention in a risk management strategy.

Evaluating the risk associated with a threat provides the impetus for going forward with security solutions as well as the requirements for those solutions. Security professionals should therefore address threats by evaluating the risk they present to their respective organizations. The following definition of a threat is fit-for-purpose, although there can arguably be many variations on a similar theme:

> A threat is any entity, action or condition that results in harm, loss, damage and/or a deterioration of existing conditions.

Given this definition, the spectrum of potential information security threats is quite broad. Threats to organizations might include thieves intent on stealing money, state-sponsored entities attempting to access company-proprietary or classified government information, and groups seeking to embarrass adversaries by exposing confidential information for political or economic gain.

It is this diversity of threats and their respective methods that drives the breadth of security risk mitigation measures. However, no organization can apply every possible mitigation method in equal measure without near-infinite resources. What is needed is a means of prioritizing threats in order to strategically apply remediation, which is precisely the point of a security risk assessment.

In that vein, a critically important role of the security professional is to identify the threats of highest concern (read: highest "risk"). This activity should be followed by measures that reduce his or her organization's vulnerability to those threats within the constraints imposed by budgets. Indeed, it is the finiteness of available resources that makes prioritization of remediation efforts a necessity.

So now that threats have been defined more precisely, what exactly is risk? All threats are described by a fundamental characteristic called risk, which is a set of three components as follows:

- *the impact or importance of a threat incident*
- *the likelihood or potential of a future threat incident*
- *the vulnerability or potential loss due to a threat incident*

These components collectively define the risk associated with a threat. In fact, risk can be notionally represented by an "equation" that is expressed as a product of the individual components as follows:

$$\text{Risk (threat)} = \text{impact} \times \text{likelihood} \times \text{vulnerability} \tag{1.1}$$

(1.1) should be read as, "The risk associated with a given threat equals the product of its impact, the likelihood of its occurrence, and the vulnerability to loss or damage."

For now, suffice it to say that assessing the magnitude of the vulnerability component of risk, that is, the loss, damage, or exposure to a threat incident, is the basis for many of the analyses in this book.

Importantly, the risk associated with a threat is not immutable, and the magnitude of each component can vary significantly depending on circumstances. Context is crucial in assessing risk. In fact, a security assessment is merely an abstraction without context. If one were to provide a high-level if formal job description of a security professional, it is to evaluate the risk associated with the spectrum of distinct and impactful threats in light of scenario-specific parameters.

Identifying the spectrum of distinct and impactful threats is the progenitor of every security strategy. This task sounds simple, but determining what constitutes an impactful threat can be quite subjective and even controversial.

For example, some might argue that religion and television represent dangers to society. Yet many individuals, even intelligent ones, believe quite the opposite. With respect to distinctness threats that are seemingly different can actually be functionally equivalent in terms of the required risk mitigation. However, there is a test for distinctness that will be explained in the discussion on risk factors.

Analogies with the medical profession are often useful when thinking about concepts in security. Security threats are equivalent to diseases in medicine, and risk mitigation measures are analogous to therapies. Most reasonable people would agree that diseases make people worse off. So unless you are a bit sadistic, hearing that a relative, friend, or associate is afflicted with a disease would probably be unwelcome news.

In medicine identifying the need for risk management is usually relatively easy. Patients display symptoms that are manifestations of some condition. Remedies are sometimes prescribed as a prophylactic measure based on one's exposure to a microorganism, a genetic predisposition to an ailment, or some *risk factor* for a particular disease.

Once a disease or precondition has been identified, patients pay physicians (and insurance companies) to prescribe therapies. Such therapies often take the form of a drug. The effectiveness of that therapy will of course depend on the correctness of the diagnosis, but will also relate to each individual's physiological makeup since no two people are identical.

But fortunately people are biologically similar, or at least similar enough, and that fact is the key to the large-scale effectiveness of many therapies. If one believes otherwise, there should be a separate anatomy and physiology textbook for each person on earth.

Experiments can be conducted that leverage the similarity of humans such that the action of a specific therapy can be isolated from other variables, and thereby lead to a conclusion on cause and effect. The process leading to the approval of a new drug, which includes testing hypotheses on effectiveness, is typically quite protracted, and expensive.

First, experiments are conducted on animal models that use a control group to isolate the effect of a single variable, namely the drug in question. Researchers attempt to establish a causal link between the disease and the palliative effects of the drug while observing potential side effects. The type of animal is chosen because their physiological response can be extrapolated to humans.

Once the animal studies have concluded, and it is clear that the drug had the intended result without obvious harmful side effects, human trials can commence. So-called "double-blind" experiments are designed to eliminate bias where a statistically significant trial population is divided into control and test groups.[4]

Following the human trials and assuming a positive outcome, the drug is approved for general use by the Federal Drug Administration (US). As an aside, the average cost of research and development for a prescription drug is estimated to be $2.558 billion [2]. The point

---

[4]Double blind means that the identities of both the control and experimental groups are unknown to the study participants.

is that medical threat scenarios benefit from significant testing of hyptotheses relating cause and effect.

Contrast this with security scenarios. In general, threat incidents are relatively rare, and, importantly, there is often considerable variation in conditions that undermines the ability to isolate a variable under test.

One can simulate attacks on networks and applications. That is the point of conducting penetration tests. Such simulations will provide a degree of confidence in the resilience of specific security controls. But this is not the IT equivalent of a drug that confers broad immunity. The operational model, which consists of the user environment, is too complex, ephemeral, and varied.

INFORMATION SECURITY RISK ASSESSMENTS

In general, comprehensive assessments of information security risk are required to establish a thorough understanding of the risk factors affecting an organization. Furthermore, such assessments must be made with respect to risk-based policies and standards in the absence of useful statistics on incidents. Adopting a process to rigorously assess the risk associated with information security threats is essential to developing a coherent information security risk management strategy [1,3].

Since the essence of security is to mitigate the effect of threats, all estimates of risk should begin with identifying the spectrum of distinct threats. Threats were defined previously, but what is meant by "distinct" in this context?

Distinctness implies a set of characteristics that distinguishes one threat from another. Characterizing threats under general headings such as "terrorism," "street crime," and "hate crime" may be useful for sociologists and politicians, but it is not particularly helpful in developing a risk management strategy. So how *does* one specify that a given threat is distinct from another and why does it matter to a risk assessment strategy? These questions will be answered following a brief digression on risk.

Recall (1.1) was introduced as an operational definition of risk and was formulated in terms of three components, likelihood, vulnerability and impact. This was somewhat hyperbolically referred to as the Fundamental Expression of Risk. However, it is not a true mathematical equation because each component in (1.1) appears to have equal magnitude and this condition is not true in general.

One important feature to notice about this expression is that if a single component is zero, there is no risk. The implication is that if there is no risk, the threat being evaluated does not exist for all practical purposes. Put another way, absent one or more components of risk, a given threat is simply not *threatening*.

In addition, the notion of "cost" broadly defined is missing from (1.1). Although cost is not a fundamental component of risk *per se*, it plays an important role in real-world decisions on security.

For example, it is not uncommon to encounter security risk scenarios where the magnitude of one component of risk is significant but remediation is cost prohibitive. Therefore, despite the assessed risk no action is taken to address it. The cost associated with risk mitigation is a reality associated with real-world risk management processes that would not appear in a strictly academic view.

Although a measurement of risk is ideal, it is not always possible to provide a quantitative estimate. The reality is that a qualitative view of each component is sometimes the best option available. The good news is that such a view is often sufficient to make a meaningful decision on risk mitigation. Moreover, a sophisticated security risk manager understands when quantitative measurements of risk will yield meaningful results and when it is futile to even try.

With that background, the risk assessment process can now be described, and, in particular, the critical role of risk factors in developing an effective risk management strategy. As noted earlier, the first step in a security risk assessment is to identify the spectrum of impactful and distinct threats to an organization. In order to address the question of threat distinctness, the crucially important concept of a "risk factor" must be reintroduced and defined as follows:

> *A risk factor is a feature, characteristic or condition that enhances one or more components of risk for a specific threat or mode of threat implementation. It is the spectrum of risk factors that drive the required mitigation methods.*

The logic associated with risk factors as the basis for risk management is compelling to the point of appearing circular: If risk factors are those features that enhance one or more components of risk for a given threat, then addressing all the risk factors is required in order to effectively manage that threat.

A medical analogy is again illustrative. Consider the threat of cardiovascular disease. Some well-known risk factors for this threat are high blood pressure, obesity, a high concentration of certain types of cholesterol in the blood, smoking, lack of exercise, being male (or a postmenopausal female), diabetes, and a family history of cardiovascular disease.

These risk factors were determined through large population studies that enabled scientists to correlate the presence of a risk factor with the likelihood of a future threat incident. In other words, people had varying rates of heart attacks based on the number and magnitude of one or more risk factors.

The likelihood of a future threat incident increases by some quantifiable amount with each additional risk factor, an artifact of the plethora of data established over years of studying relatively homogeneous models such as humans. In other words, the more risk factors displayed by a patient, the higher is the likelihood he or she will suffer a heart attack in a specific interval of time.

The risk increases with the duration of the time interval under consideration.[5] An individual who displays all of the significant risk factors would likely be a candidate for aggressive medical therapy as determined by a bona fide medical risk manager, for example, a cardiologist.

A Venn diagram can be used to illustrate the intersection of risk factors, a condition that would amplify the likelihood component of risk for the threat of heart attacks as shown in Fig. 1.1.

---

[5]One way to think about the increasing risk associated with lengthening time intervals is to consider the limiting cases of time intervals, that is, $t = 0$ and $t = $ infinity. The likelihood of an event in an interval of 0 s must be zero. At the other extreme, in an infinite time interval the probability of an event would approach unity. For intermediate intervals the probability of an event is proportionate to the duration of that interval. However, recognize that this relationship between likelihood of occurrence and time interval duration might not be linear since the cumulative effect of risk factors could be exponentially increasing with time.

I. THREATS, RISK AND RISK ASSESSMENTS

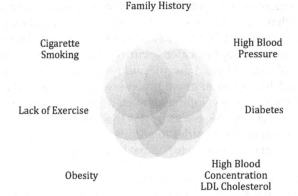

FIGURE 1.1   Intersection of risk factors for the threat of cardiovascular disease.

A similar diagram can be created for any threat. Physical security threats are illustrative of the utility of such diagrams. Consider the threat of vehicle-borne explosive attacks by anti-Western elements against the headquarters of an international bank. Risk factors for this attack might include the following:

- the country where the facility is located;
- the iconic status of this particular facility or the bank in general (in other words, a symbolic association with Western culture and/or a particular government);
- the historical use of this mode of attack by groups of concern;
- the proximity of the facility to vehicular traffic.

Note that the first three risk factors enhance the likelihood component of risk for this threat while the last one enhances the vulnerability component of risk. Understanding the nature of the contribution to risk for a given risk factor is important in managing the risk associated with each impactful and distinct threat. For example, reducing the profile of a company or facility would affect the potential for attack, but would do nothing to reduce the vulnerability or the potential damage/loss should an attack occur.

Fig. 1.2 illustrates the Venn diagram for the set of risk factors associated with a given target and relative to this threat. If all of these risk factors existed for a given target, the risk is enhanced relative to a target that possessed less risk factors.

To further illustrate this important point, if the impactful threats were groups concerned about the global hegemony of fast food corporations, the likelihood component of risk might be significantly altered from the anti-Western terrorists noted earlier. In that case the security strategy might not include this threat as a priority for remediation.

The long-awaited answer to the question of what makes one threat distinct from another can now be presented. Simply put, any two threats are equivalent if the type and magnitude of their respective risk factors are identical. Conversely, if their risk factors differ in either type or magnitude, the two threats are distinct and each threat must be addressed separately as part of a risk mitigation strategy.

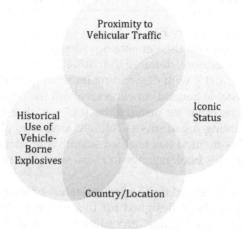

FIGURE 1.2   Risk factors for vehicle-borne explosive attacks by anti-Western groups.

This test for distinctness has a very practical implication. Namely, threats can be logically grouped according to their risk factors. In addition, simultaneously addressing the risk factors will effectively manage all of the threats with risk factors in common. Note that if one risk factor is not addressed, it means at least one vulnerability exists for each threat to which that risk factor applies.

The key to an effective risk mitigation strategy is to address all the risk factors for each distinct and impactful threat. A graphic that depicts the risk management process is captured in Fig. 1.3 [3].

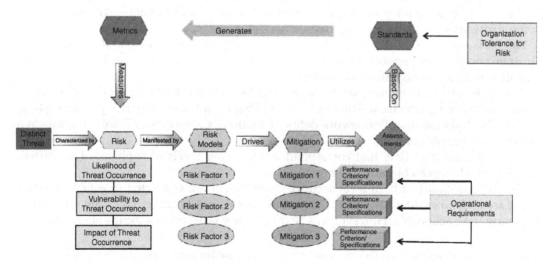

FIGURE 1.3   The security risk management process.

ORGANIZING INFORMATION SECURITY RISK ASSESSMENTS

Organizing an information security risk problem is often a useful initial step in assessing risk. In particular, establishing and then analyzing categories with common features facilitates coherent analyses. Furthermore, defining individual units according to specific features that are categorized in a hierarchy with descending levels of granularity can reveal patterns or themes. These patterns enable general conclusions about the organization as a whole.

Many descriptive sciences organize information this way. For example, biologists have created a hierarchy for all living organisms as follows: kingdom, phylum, class, order, family, genus, and species.[6] This method has enabled scientists to identify evolutionary trends. Presumably anyone reading this book belongs to *Homo sapien* the human genus and species, respectively.

Since organizing a problem according to specific features has applicability to many disciplines, formal methods have been designed for this purpose. Specifically, a so-called *dichotomous key* delineates a group of "things" according to a hierarchy of functionality or some other feature/characteristic. Why is this approach helpful to security risk analyses?

Organizing threats according to a hierarchy of features they have in common facilitates the identification of common forms of mitigation. Such an approach enables the development of a comprehensive and coherent risk management strategy since one can associate general modes of attack with specific mitigation measures.

Following this alignment of general features with mitigation, additional details might drive specific mitigation requirements that deviate from the general case. Unfortunately, sometimes the tendency is to initially focus on details, which is more likely to result in missing the big picture, which in this case translates to missing a particular risk factor.

There are a number of ways to construct a dichotomous key for security threats. One might begin by identifying the spectrum of attack vectors for a given threat. For example, if terrorism is the general threat of concern, one might first want to specify a hierarchy of attacks. Again, the purpose of such a hierarchy is to highlight common risk factors that are addressed by the same mitigation measure. A graphic for one version of a dichotomous key for information security attacks is shown in Fig. 1.4.

Fig. 1.4 is not an exhaustive exposition of the possible modes of attack. It is intended to illustrate one of many possible organizational schemas. Other versions could be constructed according to different organizational criteria.

Although not a dichotomous key *per se*, the NIST Cybersecurity Framework is illustrative of the benefits of a hierarchical structure in addressing complex security risk problems [4].

The NIST Cybersecurity Framework defines Functions, Categories, and Subcategories in a hierarchy of security controls.

It also defines four Tiers that correspond to increasing levels of sophistication: Partial, Risk-Informed, Repeatable, and Adaptive.

The five Functions or high-level security controls that are evaluated to establish a Tier rating are as follows: Identify, Protect, Detect, Respond, and Recover. These are admittedly too coarse to be actionable. However, this 50,000-ft. view is useful as a means of organizing a

---

[6]The phrase "King Philip came over for good soup" is a pneumonic used to assist in recalling the hierarchy of organisms.

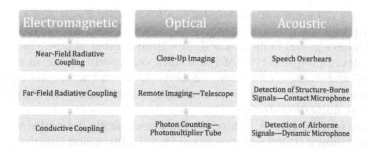

FIGURE 1.4 Abbreviated dichotomous key for information security attacks.

risk-based information security strategy. Metrics to rate specific NIST Tiers are suggested in Chapter 12.

Importantly, the NIST Cybersecurity Framework is not prescriptive, and therefore does not dictate requirements for specific controls. Equally if not more importantly it is not a checklist, which is what makes it adaptable to risk-based security assessments. Rather, it is intended to facilitate assessments of the processes required to assess information security risk *in context.*

Therefore, it enables risk-based decisions based on an organization's sophistication in implementing security controls rather than merely checking that such controls exist. It also facilitates addressing threats in a consistent manner across business units.

For example, one well-known information security threat is the covert exfiltration of confidential information via an IT network. Using the NIST Framework it is a relatively simple process to evaluate the maturity of a security strategy with respect to this threat.

Table 1.1 shows an indicative if high-level and incomplete analysis of this threat using the NIST Framework. Analyses of subcategories/controls relative to NIST Tier criteria are missing. But it illustrates how a NIST-based risk assessment might be organized.

TABLE 1.1 Abbreviated Assessment of the Vulnerability to Covert Data Exfiltration Using the NIST Cybersecurity Framework

Function	Risk-Relevant Category	Analysis of Risk-Relevant Subcategories/ Controls	NIST Tier
Identify	Risk Assessments	Virtual Network Model/Simulation and External Penetration Test Results	Partial
Protect	Network Segregation	Firewall Rule Set	Risk-Informed
Detect	Automated Tools	Data Leakage Prevention (DLP)	Repeatable
Respond	Incident Response (IR)	IR Team, Plan, and Exercises	Adaptive
Recover	Recovery Planning, Communications	Assignment of Recovery Team Roles and Responsibilities, Established and Redundant Communication Protocols/ Channels	Risk-Informed
Overall Assessment/ Tier			Risk-Informed

This exercise may not seem particularly fruitful for a single threat and a small organization. But security professionals are often required to assess threats and the risk they present to organizations that have global footprints and/or a large number of business units.

Furthermore, developing this type of framework can be invaluable in identifying risk-relevant "themes" that emerge from disparate data sources and across stove-piped business units. Once such a framework exists, it is a relatively short journey to identify a coherent, enterprise-level risk mitigation strategy.

There are at least four critical risk factors that must be explicitly delineated within a security risk framework as follows: (1) the sensitive/confidential information (affects the impact component of risk), (2) the business units that use that information (affects the vulnerability component of risk), (3) the modes of information usage/management/access by each unit (affects the likelihood and vulnerability component of risk), and (4) where the sensitive/confidential information exists within the organization (affects the vulnerability component of risk).

Table 1.2 captures these risk factors for a generic academic organization to illustrate the basic assessment methodology.

TABLE 1.2   Analysis of Risk Factors for the Threat of Information Compromise

	Human Resources	Finance Department	Records Management	Fund Raising	Health Department
Sources of Confidential Information	Employee Records (PII)	Social Security Account Numbers	Student Records (PII)	Donor Information	Patient Information
Key Information Storage Resources	File Shares, Central Application	File Shares, Central Application	File Shares, MySQL Database	Bespoke Application	File Shares
Mode of Information Storage and Transmission	Email	Email	Email	Email	Email
Mode of Information Destruction	Manual Purging	Manual Purging	N/A	Manual Purging	Manual Purging
Document Management	Office Storage	Office Storage	Central Archive Storage	Office Storage, Manual Destruction	Office Storage, Manual Destruction
Physical Security Risk Factors	Physical Keys with No Access History	Physical Keys with No Access History	N/A	Physical Keys with No Access History	Physical Keys with No Access History
Technology Risk Factors/ Vulnerabilities	Low-Entropy Passwords for Key Information Assets; Open Network Access to Data Sources	Low-Entropy Passwords, IT Equipment Not Centrally Managed; Open Network Access to Data Sources	Low-Entropy Passwords, Noncurrent Version of Databases; Open Network Access to Data Sources	Low-Entropy Passwords, Extranet Connections; Open Network Access to Data Sources	Low-Entropy Passwords, Extranet Connections; Open Network Access to Data Sources
Specific Authentication, Authorization, and Access Privilege Risk Factors	Manual Assignment and Removal of Access Privileges for File Shares	Manual Assignment and Removal of Access Privileges for File Shares	Manual Assignment and Removal of Access Privileges for File Shares	Manual Assignment and Removal of Access Privileges for File Shares	Manual Assignment and Removal of Access Privileges for File Shares

High-level security themes that emerge from Table 1.2 are as follows:

1. There is a concentration of information security risk. In other words, a small number of applications are used to manage confidential information across the enterprise.
2. An inherently insecure method (email) is used to transmit confidential information across the enterprise and outside the organization.
3. Manual processes are used to facilitate access privilege assignment and removal for file shares.
4. Low-entropy passwords exist. In other words, a limited diversity of possible password constructions for critical assets exists.
5. Mechanical locks and keys are used to secure paper documents. No physical access history is available as a result.

Once these themes on risk are specified, it becomes easier to determine a comprehensive strategy for remediation. In addition, identifying other risk factors provides justification for implementing compensating controls. In the example discussed earlier one might consider using two factors as a means of authentication to access the most critical applications if other vulnerabilities cannot be addressed.

Importantly, intersections of risk factors are apparent from this analysis thereby establishing priorities for remediation. For example, file shares that (1) contain high-impact information, (2) require weak passwords for authentication, and (3) are accessible from the Internet would likely be a priority for remediation.

Any attacker who gained internal access to the network, often accomplished via social engineering, would have little difficulty accessing high-impact information assets and subsequently exfiltrating the information contained therein.

This type of analysis can be done for any security organization. The key is to be precise about the threats, identify the critical information assets and their locations, and determine the spectrum of risk factors that enhance the vulnerability to the relevant attack vectors.

GENERAL RISK FACTORS FOR THE COMPROMISE OF SIGNALS

Information security threats can exploit vulnerabilities in IT protocols, intercept signals with encoded information, or steal a physical object that stores information. This section will focus on general threats and risk factors associated with threats to signals.

Estimating the magnitude of vulnerability for information security threats can be complex, and will vary according to the specific threat under evaluation. However, simple if approximate models exist for electromagnetic and acoustic signals because they obey well-understood physical principles. Therefore, quantitative estimates of vulnerability can be made and thereby enable mitigation strategies.

Moreover, developing a model of signal behavior and the associated risk facilitates analyses of a spectrum of threat scenarios. The result enables more fulsome estimates of vulnerability as well as the general effectiveness of risk mitigation. For example, establishing a model for signal intensity in terms of the distance from a radiating source enables an estimate of the vulnerability to signal interception by an attacker at *any* location.

Five risk factors affect the vulnerability component of risk for the compromise of signals:

1. the form of signal energy (electromagnetic or mechanical);
2. the intervening materials between the radiating source and the point of detection;
3. the physical proximity of a radiating source and the point of detection;
4. the signal bandwidth and the magnitude of ambient noise across that bandwidth;
5. the sophistication of the attacker.

Consider risk factor number three. If the vulnerability to unauthorized signal detection happens to vary strongly with distance from a radiating source of signal energy, it would be prudent to maximize the distance between potential adversaries and the signal source in accordance with this model.

Such insights are admittedly not particularly profound. The real challenge is to determine at what distance the signal becomes invulnerable to detection. Understanding the precise dependence of signal intensity on distance plus the magnitude of the ambient noise power enables such a determination. This and similar estimates represent the essence of the information provided in this book.

A simple graphic depicting the high-level risk factors for threats to radiated signals is shown in Fig. 1.5. More detailed risk factors for the compromise of radiating signals are presented in Chapter 6.

Finally, it is useful to create a holistic view of an information security risk assessment that tells the complete risk story from threats to remediation. It is also helpful to visualize the process depicted in this linear view since the issues are somewhat self-explanatory when presented this way, and therefore helps facilitate decisions on mitigation.

Table 1.3 illustrates this format for an abbreviated assessment. Note that it is organized according to (1.1). In addition, the cost of remediation is included, which facilitates security decisions.

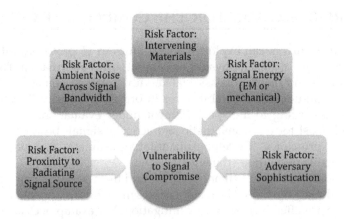

FIGURE 1.5   Risk factors for threats to radiated signals.

TABLE 1.3 Risk Assessment Summary Table

Principal Information Security Threat to the Organization	Risk Factors for Likelihood	Risk Factors for Vulnerability	Threat Impact	Remediation and Cost
Hacktivists seeking to steal personally identifying information (PII) for identity theft	Significant Internet Presence and Links to High-Profile Individuals	1. Open Network Architecture 2. Weak Authentication for Critical Systems	Information Compromise Leading to Reputational Damage and/or Regulatory Fines	1. Internal Firewall and Routing Tables 2. Two-Factor Authentication on Critical Systems Estimated Cost = $1 Million

Risk (threat) = likelihood × vulnerability × impact cost of remediation.

ESTIMATING THE LIKELIHOOD COMPONENT OF RISK

This book admittedly focuses on the vulnerability component of security risk to the exclusion of the other two components, likelihood and impact. This somewhat parochial view is not intended to trivialize the importance of these other components. In fact, assessing the impact associated with the compromise of information should be the first step in determining a set of proportionate security controls. Nonimpactful threats should generate minimal follow-up. Highly unlikely threats might warrant similar levels of inattention.

To be precise, the vulnerabilities analyzed in this text do not cause an incident. For example, it would be technically incorrect to claim that poor physical security controls at a facility increase the likelihood of a physical attack.

However, it would be correct to say that if an attack does occur, such vulnerabilities enhance the likelihood of its success and resulting loss/damage. Recognize that the likelihood of a future incident, which is the type of likelihood specified by (1.1), and the likelihood that such an incident will be successful are two different phenomena.

The impact component of risk is by definition organization-specific. Intellectual property and other proprietary information, personnel records, company strategies, etc., will vary based on each organization's mission, objectives, composition, and/or legal/regulatory requirements. Therefore, it is not particularly useful to discuss this component at length except to point out the overall criticality of determining if such information exists, where it is located, and the impact to the organization were it to be compromised.

On the other hand, the likelihood component of risk warrants additional discussion. The concept of likelihood is not well understood by security professionals and is a perennial source of confusion, which further motivates the following discussion. One theory why this misunderstanding exists is that it stems from the colloquial use of the term "likelihood" coupled with a misunderstanding of probability and statistics.

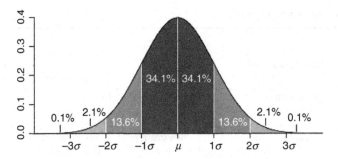

FIGURE 1.6   The normal or Gaussian distribution.

There is a very specific condition that must be satisfied in order to make precise statements about the likelihood of a future security incident. Namely, the incident in question must be a random variable and the outcomes are distributed according to a stochastic (probabilistic) process.

Ironically, the implication of being a random variable is that although the probability of guessing the value of a future event is completely unpredictable, the probability of guessing the value of one event from a distribution of events is quantifiable. Moreover, the predictability improves for larger numbers of events. This phenomenon will be explained later.

Qualitatively, a random event is where the value of the outcome of that event cannot be determined in advance. Yet the spectrum of possible outcomes for a random process can be quite prescribed. For example, in rolling a pair of dice or flipping a coin there is no way to know the value of a specific outcome a priori but the likelihood of any given roll or flip is known exactly. Moreover, flipping a coin or rolling a die 1 million times will generate predictable distributions of outcomes. This seemingly simple condition has profound implications to assessing risk under certain conditions.

A sufficiently large number of randomly occurring events will ultimately yield a normal distribution of outcomes that are dispersed about a mean or average value. The normal distribution density function $g(x)$ for a random variable x is given by Eq. (1.2)[7]:

$$g(x) = \frac{1}{\sqrt{2\pi}} e^{-(1/2)x^2}$$
(1.2)

Crucially, the likelihood that a specific number of events have a certain value can be determined from this distribution. For example, by definition 68.2% of the outcomes of a normal distribution will occur within one standard deviation of the mean. The standard deviation specifies the dispersion or uncertainty about the mean of a distribution. The magnitude of the dispersion, which corresponds to some number of standard deviations about the mean, is the same for any normal distribution.

Fig. 1.6 is a graphic depicting a normal probability distribution of some population of events or things, and the fraction of the population corresponding to one, two, and three

[7]To arrive at a specific value for x requires integrating the density function from minus infinity to that number.

standard deviations about the mean, μ.[8] Note that these fractions and corresponding standard deviations are the same for any normally distributed random variable.

It is readily apparent from Fig. 1.6 that 68.2% of the distribution of values falls within one standard deviation of the mean, 95.4% of the distribution of values falls within two standard deviations of the mean, and 99.8% of the population distribution falls within three standard deviations of the mean.

The importance of the normal distribution to every field of science and to security risk management in particular cannot be overstated. Reference is made to this distribution throughout this text, and its properties will be invoked when discussing the Probability of Protection method in Chapter 13.

The normal distribution is not the only distribution that applies to random variables. The Poisson distribution is another worthy of mention. It is used to model discrete, randomly occurring events and is predicated on three assumptions[9]:

1. The probability of one event occurring in a time interval, $\Delta\tau$, is proportional to $\Delta\tau$ when $\Delta\tau$ is very small.
2. The probability that more than one event occurs in the time interval $\Delta\tau$ is negligible when $\Delta\tau$ is very small.
3. The number of events that occur in one time interval is independent of the number of events that occur in another nonoverlapping time interval.

One useful property of the Poisson distribution is that the mean and the standard deviation are the same value. The probability density function for Poisson distributions is given by Eq. (1.3) where λ is the arrival rate, k is a specific number of events, e is Euler's number, that is, 2.71828..., and $k!$ is "k factorial" or $k \times (k-1) \times (k-2) \times (k-3)$, etc.:

$$P(k;\lambda) = \frac{(\lambda)^k e^{-\lambda}}{k!} \qquad (1.3)$$

The expression yields the probability that k events occurs in a given time interval assuming a constant event arrival rate λ.

The normal and Poisson distributions are related. In fact, for a sufficiently large number of events, a Poisson distribution morphs into a normal distribution. Fig. 1.7 is a graphic depicting the Poisson distribution for different mean values.[10]

Poisson distributions involve randomly occurring, discrete events that adhere to the three assumptions noted above. Examples of such processes include radioactive decay and photon counting. Chapter 9 discusses photon counting in the context of an optical attack on information assets.

A simple example of the use of the Poisson distribution is illustrative. Suppose one was developing a crude packet detector for a 1-Gb/s Ethernet interface in order to detect nascent denial-of-service attacks. Let us assume that packet arrival at the Ethernet interface is a random variable and obeys Poisson statistics as dictated by the three conditions noted earlier.

[8]http://www.srh.noaa.gov/bro/?n=2009event_hottestjuly.
[9]https://www.cis.rit.edu/class/simg713/Lectures/Lecture713-07.pdf.
[10]http://earthquake.usgs.gov/learn/glossary/?term=Poisson%20distribution.

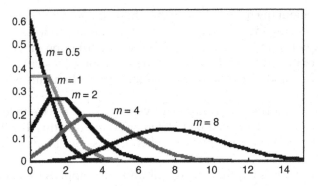

FIGURE 1.7   Poisson distributions with different means.

Suppose further that our detector counts packets in a given time interval t where a mean packet arrival rate λ is known for that link. However, the packet-forwarding rate for this size Ethernet link is assumed to be 1 packet/s (p/s).[11] If the detector is sized to expect the mean packet arrival rate, what is the probability the detector will see precisely 10 packets in a 5-s interval?

The Poisson density function is given by (1.3), and the calculation yields a probability of about 2%. The probability the detector would see less than or equal to 10 packets, that is, the cumulative risk, is about 99%. Therefore, if the detector registers significantly more packets in a 5-s time interval, it should register an alert since this behavior is not representative of normal system conditions.

The standard deviation of both normal and Poisson distributions is proportional to the square root of the sample size, N. What is the implication to estimating N to a specific level of precision?

The standard deviation, σ, is proportional to $\sqrt{N}$, where N is the sample size. Suppose it is mandated that the standard deviation of a distribution be one-tenth the sample size or $N/10$. This condition coupled with the dispersion about the mean associated with normal distributions determines the sample size that is required to achieve this level of precision.

Specifically,

$$\sigma = \sqrt{N} = \frac{N}{10}$$

Therefore,

$$\sqrt{N} = \frac{N}{10} \quad \text{or} \quad N = 100$$

---

[11]The actual packet-forwarding rate for a 1-Gb/s Ethernet link is between 81,274 and 1,488,096 p/s because the number of bytes/packet varies. However, the numbers have been scaled way back to facilitate a simple calculation, which hopefully will not diminish its instructive value.

Suppose the standard deviation is now specified such that it can be no greater than one-hundredth the value of N. This specification would require that $N = 100^2$ or 10,000.

Now in order to achieve 10 times that precision or $N/1000$, N must equal $(1000)^2$ or 1,000,000. From these examples one can generalize that the required precision scales as the square of the sample size.

So statements on the certainty of a specific outcome can be made for distributions of random variables. More specificity regarding the probability that a particular outcome is within a certain distance from the mean can be achieved for distributions with larger sample sizes. *However, such statements are valid only for distributions of random variables.*

To be clear, information security events do not occur randomly in the same way that some physical processes do such as in the production of photons in radioactive decay. To complicate matters, security incidents are relatively rare, and the conditions associated with each incident will vary. This is what makes it difficult to establish a probability distribution of security incidents versus loss. Other industries have created such distributions and one in particular is worth analyzing in some detail.

Investment banks are required to calculate and report their so-called Value at Risk (VaR), which drives their requirement to maintain capital reserves. The VaR is a broadly adopted metric in the banking industry. It corresponds to the probability of loss on a specific portfolio of financial exposures.

For a given portfolio, the time horizon and the p(VaR) is defined as a threshold loss value, such that the probability that the loss on the portfolio over the given time horizon exceeds this value is p. This model assumes so-called mark-to-market pricing, and no trading in the portfolio [5].

For example, if a portfolio of stocks has a 1-day, 10% VaR of $1 million, there is a 0.10 probability that the portfolio will fall in value by more than $1 million over a 1-day period assuming no trading. Alternatively, a loss of $1 million or more on this portfolio is expected on 1 out of 10 days.

Conversely, trading losses over a 1-day period would be expected to be less than $1 million 90% of the time. Clearly financial institutions are incentivized to reduce the amount of money held in reserve since more funds would be available for generating revenue. So the method used to calculate VaR has implications to the bottom line.

For financial institutions the capital reserve calculation is subsumed under the general heading of "Operational Risk." Fig. 1.8 shows a loss distribution curve specifying the portions of the curve corresponding to the Expected Loss, Unexpected Loss, the Extreme Loss, and VaR [6].

Establishing such a curve is the Holy Grail for security risk assessments. Unfortunately it is often elusive in security contexts because precise statements on incident probability versus loss are not so easy to determine. In addition, the value of information is not like the price of bananas, coffee, gold, machinery, equities, fixed income products, etc. Even financial institutions struggle with VaR, because large if infrequent losses (i.e., "tail events") are difficult to model.

Some types of losses are difficult to quantify in security contexts. As a trivial example, the electronic compromise of a 911 (999 in Britain) calling system might result in the loss of 10 lives because of slow response times by emergency services. Where would the magnitude of that loss appear on the VaR curve?

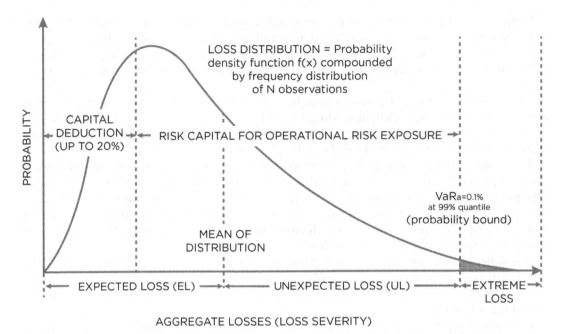

FIGURE 1.8   Loss distribution approach (LDA) for operational risk under the New Basel Capital Accord.

In addition, the same type of attack can result in wildly dissimilar outcomes for a given organization based on slightly different controls or network configurations. Attacks might result in only embarrassment because the objective of the attacker was not to steal information, yet large losses could have been easily sustained if the attackers were so inclined.

The applicability of VAR to real-world security scenarios is questionable for reasons previously cited and should be subject to significant scrutiny before its adoption [7].

The earlier discussion is not meant to imply that meaningful assertions about the *relative* likelihood of a future security incident are not possible. For example, the likelihood of an attempted denial-of-service attack against a high-profile institution such as a bank would likely be higher than for a relatively unknown Mom and Pop store.

In general, information security attacks against specific organizations are more likely because of the existence of specific risk factors such as their Internet presence, the value of the information they store, their political profile, and affiliations with specific individuals or entities. One can therefore safely say the *potential* for a future security incident is increased relative to other organizations based on one or more of these risk factors.

One might argue that there is an increased potential for attack based on Internet activity alone. In fact, the very existence of network connectivity might be considered a risk factor for information compromise since sharing information is the very objective of a network. Moreover, anything that facilitates sharing increases the vulnerability to compromise.

One should not interpret the foregoing discussion as an excuse to ignore the likelihood component of risk in conducting information security risk assessments. If one managed to obtain data from a statistically significant sample of organizations relative to parameters such as network configurations, infrastructure, and the nature of existing security controls during successful attacks, one could make meaningful statements on the vulnerability as a function of scenario-specific parameters.

For example, a statement such as "60% of all successful computer system intrusions occurred when relevant account passwords were 10 characters or less in length" might be useful in developing a security strategy. This statistic would not necessarily demonstrate cause and effect, but it represents a strong correlation, and therefore should give a security risk manager plenty of food for thought.

It is true that certain attackers are known to exploit vulnerabilities merely because they are able to do so and do not necessarily have a reason for targeting a specific entity. However, in general, various risk factors such as those noted earlier increase an organization's attractiveness as a target and should be factored into the overall assessment of the magnitude of information security risk.

SUMMARY

Threats are entities, conditions, or phenomena that cause harm, damage, and/or loss. Risk is a fundamental characteristic of all threats, and is what makes a threat "threatening" to each organization. It therefore provides the context that enables prioritization of remediation efforts.

Risk has three components: impact, vulnerability, and likelihood. Impact refers to the importance of a threat incident, vulnerability is the magnitude of potential loss or the exposure as a result of a threat incident, and likelihood is the probability of a future threat incident occurrence. Successfully evaluating the three components of risk enables the prioritization of risk mitigation efforts.

Importantly, risk factors are features that enhance one or more components of risk with respect to a specific threat. Effective risk assessments must focus on identifying the spectrum of risk factors and identifying mitigation measures that address each of them with limits dictated by the assessed risk and available resources.

Varied conditions and the lack of controlled experiments make predictions of future information security threat incidents difficult. A risk-based and therefore contextual information security policy with accompanying IT standards should provide the basis for rigorous security risk assessments.

References

[1] Young C. The science and technology of counterterrorism; measuring physical and electronic security risk. Waltham, MA: Butterworth-Heinemann; 2014.

[2] Cost of developing a new drug. Tufts Center for the Study of Drug Development, Tufts School of Medicine, November 18, 2014. <http://csdd.tufts.edu/files/uploads/Tufts_CSDD_briefing_on_RD_cost_study_-_Nov_18,_2014.pdf>.

[3] Young C. Metrics and methods for security risk management. Boston: Syngress; 2010. p. 45–75.

[4] NIST framework for improving critical infrastructure cybersecurity, version 1.0; February 12, 2014.

[5] Jorion P. Value at risk: the new benchmark for managing financial risk. 3rd ed. New York: McGraw-Hill; 2006.

[6] Jobst A. The sting is still in the tail, but the poison depends on the dose. IMF working paper. <https://www.imf.org/external/pubs/ft/wp/2007/wp07239.pdf>.

[7] Jaisingh J, Rees J. Value-at-risk: a methodology for information security risk assessment. West Lafayette, IN: Purdue University. <http://citeseerx.ist.psu.edu/viewdoc/download?doi=10.1.1.108.5140&rep=rep1&type=pdf>.

Modeling Information Security Risk

INTRODUCTION

Information security strategies tend to focus on network security issues to the exclusion of other attacks. This focus is due to the reliance on the Internet, the history of successful network attacks against organizations of every variety, and the impact of many of these attacks resulting in significant information compromise.

The Internet uses protocols such as IP/TCP and UDP to send electronic signals in the form of packets, which are transmitted via wire or fiber-optic cable, or radiated to/from antennae. However, signals presumed to be confined to wires and cables do leak, and thereby propagate through the air and building materials with the potential for detection by unauthorized parties. Wireless systems intentionally broadcast signals for wide reception, and sometimes rely on encryption to make the data contained therein unintelligible except to authorized users.

For example, Wi-Fi systems facilitate wireless connectivity to the Internet. A signal is intentionally broadcast over the air to anyone in physical proximity and in possession of appropriate log-in credentials. The problem is that there may be individuals who are not authorized to connect to that network who also detect this Wi-Fi signal. By subterfuge and/or technical prowess they manage to connect to this network and thereby access confidential information. A well-known hacking technique is to gain unauthorized access to a corporate wireless network and pivot to that organization's internal network.

One might be inclined to believe that the radiated signal is too weak to be detected by an attacker covertly ensconced in some remote hideout (eg, a car parked on a nearby street). This assumption might lead to assuming physical separation is effective for risk mitigation. Confirming such an assumption would be especially prudent if it represented the basis for a defensive strategy.

To that end, a physical *model* of signal intensity is required. Such a model will enable general estimates of the signal-to-noise ratio as a function of distance from the radiating source and/or other relevant parameters. As will become clear in Chapter 6, the signal-to-noise ratio is *the* key metric for determining vulnerability to unauthorized signal detection.

Let us explore the notion of a model in more detail. Why are models so important to information security? Briefly, a model enables generalizations about the vulnerability to information loss for a spectrum of scenarios. More specifically, a model in the context of security defines a key security parameter for a given threat in terms of risk factors.

Furthermore, it specifies the sensitivity of that parameter to these risk factors, and thereby yields estimates of vulnerability for any relevant scenario. Such estimates can be used to assess the effectiveness of a specific security control or defensive strategy more broadly. It quickly becomes obvious why the risk factors are so important in developing an information security strategy.

For example, if the intensity of a radiating signal can be specified in terms of the distance from the source, and intensity is central to the signal-to-noise ratio security metric, then distance is a risk factor for information compromise. Based on the model for signal intensity plus knowledge of the ambient noise power, the minimum signal-to-noise ratio required for signal detection can be estimated. From this estimate the vulnerability to unauthorized signal detection can be determined for all locations.

The purpose of this chapter is to introduce concepts that are helpful in the construction and analysis of these types of simple risk models. Individual sections focus on the mathematical machinery that is relevant to a wide variety of information security risk scenarios.

BASIC FUNCTIONS AND UNITS OF MEASUREMENT

Functions and Risk Factor Dependence

A quantitative analysis of risk often entails determining the magnitude of some threat parameter, Y, that affects the vulnerability component of risk. Y could be the intensity of electromagnetic energy radiating through space that is encoded with information, acoustic energy propagating within building structural elements that also carries information, etc.

Moreover, in assessing the vulnerability component of risk with respect to Y, one seeks to identify and understand the dependence on another quantity X, a risk factor for this threat parameter. For example, X might be the distance from the source of radiating energy to the point of detection. The value of Y is therefore dependent on the value of X. The objective is to define a quantitative relationship between the dependent variable Y and the independent variable X.

In other words, how does Y "behave" with changes in the value of X? The dependence of Y on X establishes X as a risk factor for a given threat, and one often wants to know how Y "scales" or changes with changing values of X.

The simplest expression for this dependence can be written as follows where the letter a is some constant of proportionality:

$$Y = aX \tag{2.1}$$

A graph of (2.1) where $a = 2$ and X has integer values from 0 to 5 is shown in Fig. 2.1.

The line in Fig. 2.1 is certainly very straight, and this straightness could have significant implications to the vulnerability component of risk.

But note that Y might have a very different dependence on the risk factor X. For example, Y could be a function of X times X. X times X is written more compactly as X^2. So the expression in this case might read as follows:

$$Y = aX^2 \tag{2.2}$$

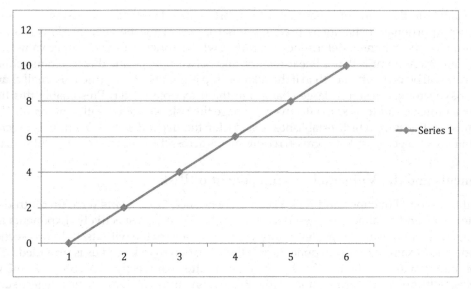

FIGURE 2.1 $Y = 2X$.

The "2" directly above the X is known as an exponent, a concept that is discussed in more detail in the next section. A graph of (2.2) with X ranging from 0 to 5 and $a = 1$ is shown in Fig. 2.2.

Since the line in Fig. 2.2 is anything but straight, it might be appropriately described as "nonlinear." Importantly, a change in the risk factor X yields disproportionate changes in the security parameter Y. For example, if X equals 2, the value of Y is 4. But doubling the value of X to 4 results in a quadrupling of the value of Y to 16.

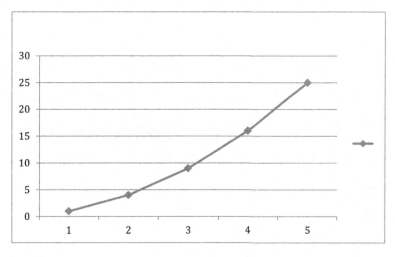

FIGURE 2.2 $Y = aX^2$.

I. THREATS, RISK AND RISK ASSESSMENTS

The jumps in the value of Y become disproportionately larger for increasing values of X. This disproportionate behavior is precisely what is meant by the term nonlinear, and the magnitude of the exponent determines the rate at which Y increases with larger values of X.

The important point is that a linear relationship between a specific threat parameter and a risk factor will be very different than if the relationship is nonlinear. In particular, small changes in the risk factor can result in large changes in the threat parameter. Presumably this threat parameter must be addressed to effectively manage the risk associated with that threat. Therefore, this relationship, which establishes a *model* for the dependence of Y on X, is crucial to determining the specific risk mitigation requirements across the spectrum of relevant scenarios.

Exponents and the Vulnerability Component of Risk

In the section "Functions and Risk Factor Dependence," exponents were first introduced via the linear and nonlinear expressions $Y = aX$ and $Y = aX^2$, respectively. Exponents are a compact way of indicating repeated multiplications of a variable with itself. In this section a more detailed examination of exponents and their relation to risk models is provided.

Continuing with this theme, $X \times X \times X$ can be written compactly as X^3. So for X^3 the variable X is "self-multiplied" three times. Note that exponents do not have to be integers such as 1, 2, and 3. A variable could just as easily be multiplied with itself in fractional amounts. For example, a function could assume the form $Y = X^{1.2}$, $Y = X^{2.7}$, etc.

Small differences in an exponent can have profound effects on the value of the dependent variable. Consequently, the value of an exponent can also have profound implications to information security risk models where a given security parameter is a function of a risk factor(s) that scales according to a so-called power law.

Let us examine $Y = X^2$ and $Y = X^3$. One might mistakenly conclude that because the difference between 2 and 3 is relative small, there would not be a significant difference between the values of Y. To illustrate the fallacy of such a conclusion, a graph of these two equations is shown in Fig. 2.3.

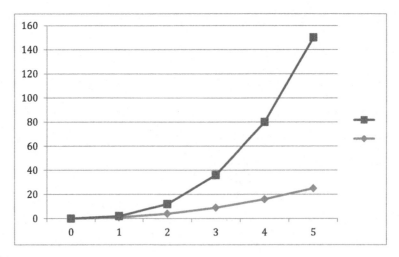

FIGURE 2.3 $Y = X^2$ (diamonds) and $Y = X^3$ (squares).

Observe that for $X = 0$, 1, and 2, the corresponding values of Y for these two functions are identical or are relatively close. However, for $X = 3$, 4, and 5 the values of Y begin to diverge. This pattern would continue for all values of X greater than 5 but is simply not shown in this graph. This depiction captures the essence of exponential growth; the value of the exponent drives the divergence of X and Y.

The incremental security benefit of increasing password length exemplifies the exponential effects of nonlinear models. Consider a password source consisting of the numerals 0–9, and the 26 letters of the English alphabet to include upper and lower cases or 62 symbols in total.

Suppose the password policy of organization A mandates that passwords use this source alphabet and be a minimum of eight characters in length. The policy of organization B specified the same source of characters but requires a minimum of 10 characters. Assume neither organization salts their passwords in the interest of simplicity. (*Note*: This situation is precisely the case for Windows account passwords.)

The number of possible passwords for organization A is 62^8 or 2.18×10^{14}. This figure may seem quite large, but now calculate the total number of possible passwords for organization B. That number is 62^{10} or 8.39×10^{17}. Although the difference between the exponents 14 and 17 is only 3 integers, the difference between 2.18×10^{14} and 8.39×10^{17} is huge: 218 trillion versus 839,000 trillion! Such is the dramatic effect of exponential growth.

So in this case an additional two characters in password length results in a huge difference in the number of passwords an attacker must try in a brute force attack. Such attacks involve attempting to decrypt every possible combination of symbols.[1] This additional resilience is due to the exponentially accruing benefits of longer password lengths in combination with a diverse source of symbols.

Another example of the effect of exponents in security relates to the Enigma machine used by the Germans in World War II. This electromechanical device was used to encrypt messages sent to the German naval surface ships and U-boats. The naval version of the device used a series of three or four rotors, where each rotor could assume a large number of possible settings corresponding to the number of possible keys used to encrypt the message.

The 4-rotor configuration allowed for 10^{22} possible settings. The setting was changed every 24 h so deciphering efforts were forced to begin anew each day. Alan Turing famously led the effort to develop a machine that could try all possible settings and determine the one in use and thereby decrypt the daily traffic in time to invoke military action.

Note that the relationship between a threat parameter Y and a risk factor X could actually *decrease* as the value of X increases. Such an expression might be written as $Y = 1/X$ or equivalently $Y = X^{-1}$. Similarly, $Y = 1/X^2$ can be written as $Y = X^{-2}$.

As one might expect, the *rate* of decrease of an exponential function, that is, the steepness of the decline, is also greater for larger exponents. For example, the rate of decrease of $Y = X^{-3}$ is greater than it is for $Y = X^{-2}$. Fig. 2.4 shows a plot of $Y = X^{-3}$ and $Y = X^{-2}$. For increasing values of X the value of Y for both functions asymptotically approach zero.[2]

---

[1] Brute force attacks can be made less computationally intensive through the use of dictionaries, compendiums of common phrases, and the ineluctable tendency of human beings to do predictable things.

[2] A function that asymptotically approaches a limiting value gets closer and closer to that value but never actually reaches it.

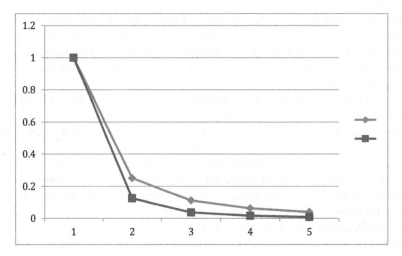

FIGURE 2.4 $Y = X^{-3}$ (squares) and $Y = X^{-2}$ (diamonds).

The Exponential, e, and the Functions e^x and e^{-x}

The exponential "e" is known as "Euler's Number." It is defined as 2.7183.[3] From the discussion on exponents it is apparent that $e^1 = 2.7183$, $e^2 = 7.389$, $e^3 = 20.086$, etc. The exponential function should not be confused with exponents which were discussed earlier in this chapter.

Many processes can be modeled using the exponential function since it is the solution to a number of differential equations. The simplest of these are $dx/dt = ax$ and $dx/dt = -ax$.[4] The solutions to these equations are $x_0\, e^{at}$ and $x_0\, e^{-at}$, respectively, where x_0 is the value of x at time $t = 0$. Graphs of these two functions are presented in Figs. 2.5 and 2.6. Specific examples of the applicability of exponentials to security scenarios will be provided as they arise in the text.

The Logarithm and Natural Logarithm

As noted previously, an exponent indicates how many times a variable is multiplied with itself. As one might expect, there is a function that "undoes" exponentiation. This function is known as the logarithm. Although they sometimes cause anxiety in high school students, the logarithm merely specifies the number of self-multiplications. For example, 10 multiplied with itself 3 times equals 1000. Therefore the logarithm of 1000 is 3 or equivalently $\log(10^3) = 3$.

---

[3]Named after Leonhard Euler (1707–83), a preeminent German mathematician who contributed significantly to many areas of mathematics and physics.
[4]For those unfamiliar with differential calculus, dx/dt is referred to as the first derivative. The first derivative specifies the rate of change of the variable being differentiated relative to another variable. In this case it is the variable, x, with respect to the variable, t. In an information security risk problem, x might be some physical parameter and t might be time.

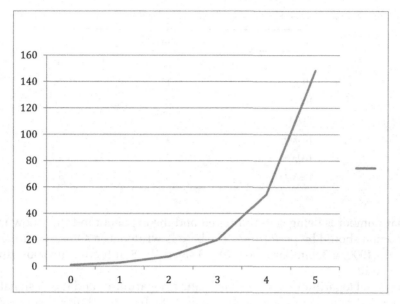

FIGURE 2.5 $f(x) = e^x$.

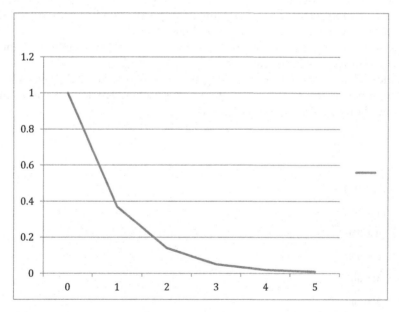

FIGURE 2.6 $f(x) = e^{-x}$.

Of course, this exact relation is true only for the number 10. For example, the number 2 multiplied by itself 3 times or 2^3 equals 8. Therefore, when identifying the logarithm of a number, the so-called base of the self-multiplication process must be identified. The base

TABLE 2.1   A Set of Numbers N and Their Corresponding Logarithm

N	$\log(N)$
1	0
10	1
100	2
1,000	3
10,000	4
100,000	5
1,000,000	6

specifies what number is being self-multiplied and the exponent indicates how many times this multiplication should be performed. The base is written as a subscript of the logarithm as follows: $\log_{10}(1000) = 3$. Similarly, $\log_2(8) = 3$ since $2^3 = 8$. If there is no subscript, the base is assumed to be 10.

There is a special logarithm known as the "natural logarithm," and it is designated as "ln." The natural logarithm is merely a logarithm where the base is e, Euler's Number. Since e is defined as 2.7183, $\ln(e^1 = 2.7183) = 1$, $\ln(e^2 = 7.389) = 2$, and $\ln(e^3 = 20.086) = 3$.

Why are logarithms important? It is because logarithms appear frequently in scientific contexts, and in information security risk assessments in particular. The slide rule, the precursor to portable electronic calculators, was based on logarithms.

It is easy to see why logarithms are useful. Consider the set of numbers N and their corresponding logarithms as listed in Table 2.1.

Now consider what happens when plotting these numbers. Fig. 2.7 shows a linear plot of N versus the number of zeros in the corresponding number. The lowest values of N appear compressed and therefore are indistinguishable.

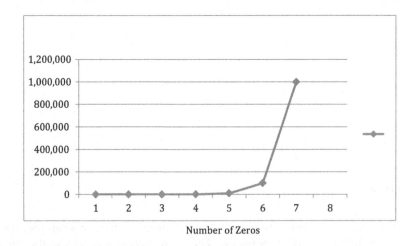

FIGURE 2.7   A linear plot of numbers, N, versus the number of zeros in N.

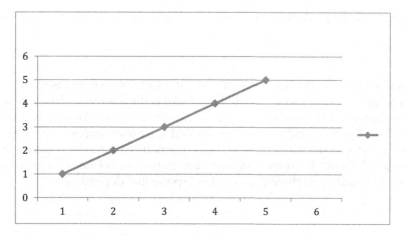

FIGURE 2.8   log(N) versus the number of zeros in N.

If better resolution is sought for these lower values using a linear scale, the vertical access might run into the next page and beyond. Providing a well-behaved scale is the principal motivation for displaying numbers logarithmically. Fig. 2.8 is a plot of log(N) versus the number of zeros in N and demonstrates how the vertical axis is now expanded.

In summary, representing N in terms of logarithms has the effect of expanding the scale to accommodate a wider range of values. This presentation can be convenient in many information security scenarios. In fact, units of measurement have been created that are defined exclusively in terms of logarithms. Almost everyone has heard of the Richter scale, which categorizes the intensity of earthquakes in terms of logarithms. A magnitude 4 earthquake is actually 10 times the energy of a magnitude 3 and so on. Another such unit is the decibel, which will be described in the next section.

The discussion on logarithms highlights the fact that it is imperative to observe the scale being used in any graphical representation of data. If the horizontal and/or vertical axes are logarithmic, each increment corresponds to a difference of a power of 10. Therefore, unit changes in the value of the number on the axis actually correspond to a 10-fold difference.

One additional property of logarithms is worth noting. The astute reader will realize that Fig. 2.8 is actually a log–log plot. In other words, both the Y- and X-axes are specified in terms of logarithms. The number of zeros in a number N is equivalent to log(N).

It turns out that an important feature of log–log scales is that they convert exponential functions into linear plots. Furthermore, the slope of the log–log plot corresponds to the exponent of the function being plotted, and can be seen from the following simple derivation.

Let $y = ax^k$.

According to the property of logarithms,

$$\log(y) = k\log(x) + \log(a)$$

Now let $X = \log(x)$ and $Y = \log(y)$.

Substituting these values into the equation for log(y) yields an equation of the following form:

$$Y = sX + b$$

This expression is the canonical equation for a straight line, where s is the slope of Y and corresponds to the exponent k in $y = ax^k$ and $b = \log(a)$ is the intercept of the function.

Information security risk models can sometimes be characterized as a power law, which is an equation where the independent variable is raised to a power (an exponent). The exponent is critical to estimates of risk since these indicate the nature of the dependence of a security parameter on a risk factor. Therefore, log–log plots transform nonlinear expressions into linear representations and immediately reveal this exponential dependence.

The Decibel

The decibel is another logarithmic unit of measurement. Specifically, the decibel is a ratio of two numbers expressed as a logarithm, usually in base 10. In other words, dB = $10 \log(A/B)$, where A and B represent the magnitudes of two quantities of interest.

Note that any two quantities are comparable in this way. For example, if the intensity of Carl's appetite for vanilla ice cream is 100 times his intensity for chocolate ice cream, the ratio of intensities is 100:1. Therefore, the magnitude of Carl's preference for vanilla ice cream is 20 dB greater than it is for chocolate. The simple calculation is as follows:

$$20\,dB = 10\log\left(\frac{100}{1}\right)$$

Because a decibel is always expressed as a ratio, it is meaningless to speak of decibels without some reference. For example, it would make no sense to say, "The intensity of radiation is 30 dB." One's response to such a statement should be, "30 dB *relative to what?*"

That said, sometimes the reference is incorporated in the particular form of decibel, but it might not be obvious from the way it is written. For example, a dBm is often used to specify units of power. 0 dBm is defined to be 1 mW. The term dBm actually means, "decibel referenced to a milliwatt."

Since dBm is defined as $10 \log(P/1\,mW)$, where P is the power expressed in milliwatt, 30 dBm is equivalent to 1 W. Memorizing that 0 dBm is equivalent to 1 mW could prove useful.

Another frequently used example is the value of sound pressure. Sound pressure is sometimes expressed relative to the minimum threshold of human hearing or $10^{-12}\,W/m^2$. The relevant unit of reference in this context is sound pressure level (SPL).

The definition of decibel earlier applies to relative measurements of power and intensity. However, sometimes it is useful to compare amplitudes. How might a comparison of amplitudes change the form of the decibel?

Signal power and intensity, that is, the power/unit area, are proportional to the square of the signal amplitude. Measurements related to electricity provide a simple example. Power = i^2R or equivalently v^2/R. Here the current i and voltage v are amplitudes, and R and $1/R$ are the respective constants of proportionality.

TABLE 2.2   Linear and Decibel Representations

Linear	Decibels
2	3
3	5
4	6
5	7
6	8
7	8.4
8	9.0
9	9.5
10	10
20	100
30	1,000
40	10,000
50	100,000
60	1,000,000
70	10,000,000
80	100,000,000
90	1,000,000,000

For two intensities I_1 and I_2, the decibel representation of their ratio is $10 \log(I_1/I_2)$. Since the ratio of intensities is proportional to the ratio of amplitudes squared (A_1^2/A_2^2), the following derivation expresses logarithms in terms of amplitudes:

$$10 \log\left(\frac{A_1^2}{A_2^2}\right) = 10 \log\left[\left(\frac{A_1}{A_2}\right)^2\right] = 2 \times 10 \log\left(\frac{A_1}{A_2}\right) = 20 \log\left(\frac{A_1}{A_2}\right)$$

Therefore, the coefficient 20 is used in the expression for decibels when comparing amplitudes.

Table 2.2 specifies decibels and the equivalent linear representation. Notice the striking similarity to Table 2.1.

Table 2.3 illustrates various sound intensities using a decibel scale, and these values are weighted according to how humans perceive sound, that is, "A-weighted". In this case the reference unit is 20 µPa (20×10^{-6} Pa), where the pascal (PA) is a unit of pressure.[5]

Finally, another useful property of logarithms is that they can be directly added. Suppose it is important to know the vulnerability to speech detection by an attacker who is located in a room distant from the speaker. This very scenario will be examined in more detail in Chapter 10.

[5]https://www.osha.gov/dts/osta/otm/noise/health_effects/soundpressure_aweighted.html.

TABLE 2.3   A-Weighted Sound Pressure Levels (Decibel Relative to 20 μPa, the Threshold of Human Hearing)

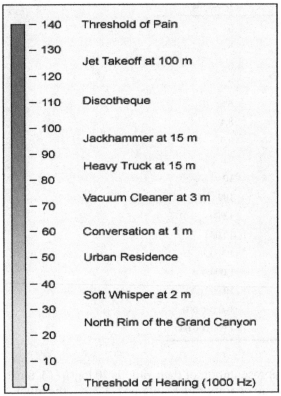

— 140	Threshold of Pain
— 130	
	Jet Takeoff at 100 m
— 120	
— 110	Discotheque
— 100	
	Jackhammer at 15 m
— 90	
	Heavy Truck at 15 m
— 80	
	Vacuum Cleaner at 3 m
— 70	
— 60	Conversation at 1 m
— 50	Urban Residence
— 40	
	Soft Whisper at 2 m
— 30	
	North Rim of the Grand Canyon
— 20	
— 10	
— 0	Threshold of Hearing (1000 Hz)

Assume there is only one pathway for the signal energy to travel between the source and the attacker. Suppose further there are three walls separating the source from the attacker and these walls attenuated the audible signal by 20, 30, and 40 dB, respectively. Using decibels it is a trivial exercise to calculate the total attenuation of the audible signal due to the presence of the three walls.

Namely, the total attenuation equals the sum of the individual contributions to the attenuation by each wall: 20 + 30 + 40 = 90 dB. Converting this logarithmic expression to a linear representation reveals that the signal intensity has been reduced by a factor of 10^9 or 1 billion.

LINEARITY AND NONLINEARITY

Linearity Revisited

As its name implies, the straight line graphically represents the concept of linearity. Recall the concepts of linearity and nonlinearity were introduced in the discussion of exponents. Consider Fig. 2.9, which is a plot of the function $Y = 2X$.

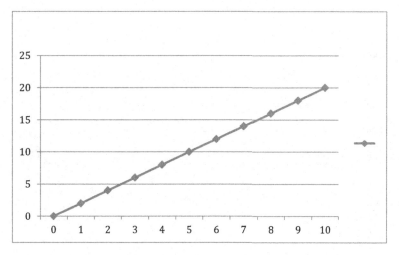

FIGURE 2.9 Y = 2X.

The line in Fig. 2.9 is clearly straight, and the mathematical implication of this straightness is that increases in the value of the independent variable X will yield proportionate increases in the value of the dependent variable Y.

In other words, doubling X will double the value of Y, tripling the value of X will triple the value of Y, etc. In addition, the slope of the line in Fig. 2.9 is constant. This condition is what characterizes a straight line. So the ratio of any point Y with respect to the corresponding value of X or Y/X always equals 2 for every ordered pair (x, y). Why are these properties important?

As discussed previously, understanding the dependence of a security parameter on a risk factor is a key objective in building a model of security risk. For example, suppose understanding the dependence of radiated intensity of energy from a Wi-Fi access point as a function of distance is the objective. The intensity of radiated signal energy is the threat parameter and the distance from the access point is a risk factor for signal detection by an attacker.

Moreover, if exceeding some critical intensity I_c produces a sufficient signal-to-noise ratio to facilitate signal detection, either increasing the standoff distance or decreasing signal intensity would be justified pursuant to developing a risk mitigation strategy.

Now suppose that the relationship between a threat parameter and a particular risk factor is linear. One such scenario might be the effect of increasing the minimum distance between a telescope operated by an attacker and a target computer screen. The proportionate effect of increasing this physical separation is due to the linear but inverse dependence of the lens resolving power on distance, where lens resolution affects the vulnerability of the visible image to compromise.

A linear relationship between a threat parameter and a risk factor implies that changes in the risk factor will cause proportionate changes in the threat parameter. The implication is that a risk mitigation strategy that is based on reducing the effect of a threat parameter must be modified in proportion to estimated changes in the relevant risk factor.

In this example, each doubling of the distance between the telescope and the computer monitor would halve the resolution of the image and thereby reduce the vulnerability to information compromise accordingly.

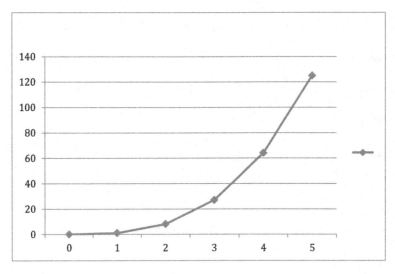

FIGURE 2.10 $Y = X^3$.

Nonlinearity Revisited

What if the relationship between two variables is nonlinear? Fig. 2.10 is a plot of one such nonlinear function.

Notice the dramatic increase in Y as the values of X becomes larger. Recall this same phenomenon occurred in Fig. 2.3. In other words, the increase in the value of Y becomes *disproportionately* larger for larger values of X. Table 2.4 indicates the increasingly significant differences in the values of Y with unit increases of X for the function $Y = X^3$.

A nonlinear relationship between a threat parameter and a risk factor for a given threat can have a profound effect on a risk mitigation strategy. This is because an increase in a relevant risk factor can have disproportionately larger effect on that threat parameter. Therefore significant changes to the risk management strategy might be required as a result.

For example, if a model for signal intensity scales inversely with the square of distance from a radiating source, halving the separation distance between the source and an attacker's detection equipment will result in a quadrupling of the signal intensity. Conversely, reducing

TABLE 2.4 $\Delta X = 1$ and Corresponding Values of ΔY for $Y = X^3$

$\Delta X = 1$	ΔY
$1 - 0 = 1$	$1 - 0 = 1$
$2 - 1 = 1$	$8 - 1 = 7$
$3 - 2 = 1$	$27 - 8 = 19$
$4 - 3 = 1$	$64 - 27 = 37$
$5 - 4 = 1$	$125 - 64 = 61$

the attacker separation distance by one fourth results in a factor of 16 increase in signal intensity, etc.

Note that if the exponent of the risk factor is less than unity, the effect of changes to the risk factor will nonlinearly *decrease*. The operational implications are that the effect of the risk factor on the threat model will accrue less rapidly than for linear or nonlinearly increasing dependencies. The preceding discussion underscores the benefits of a security model and the importance of the precise relationship between a threat parameter and risk factors.

LINEAR, AREAL, AND VOLUMETRIC DENSITY

Quantities relating to density occur frequently in information security scenarios. Sensors such as antennas and photodetectors are designed to detect intensity, which by definition is the power *density*. A sensor only captures a fraction of the total radiated energy, and it is the total energy captured per unit area per unit time that matters with respect to signal detection.

The density of a quantity is by definition a ratio. It specifies a quantity of "something per unit amount of something else." If this definition seems fantastically vague, it is because a density can be specified between almost any two quantities.

Densities appear quite frequently in everyday life. Pressure or force per unit area is one such quantity. For example, most readers have likely heard weather forecasts describing the trend in atmospheric pressure, an important indicator of future weather conditions. Atmospheric pressure is typically specified in pounds per square inch and a normal reading is $14.7 \text{ lb}/(\text{in.})^2$.

In theory there is no restriction on the variety of density measurements as exemplified by the following examples:

- the density of a fluid, gas, or solid, for example, grams per cubic centimeter;
- the density of bagels on a kitchen counter, for example, number per square meter;
- the density of cars on a road, for example, number per linear mile;
- the price density of kitchen countertops, for example, dollars per linear foot;
- the magnetic field intensity/strength, for example, amperes per meter or oersted;
- the density of vulnerabilities in computers/end points, for example, average number of vulnerabilities per end point;
- the density of guns among the general population, for example, number of guns per number of people;
- the density of signal power (intensity), for example, watts per square centimeter.

Notice that density can be expressed in terms of linear, areal, or volumetric units. In other words, a density measurement relates to one, two, or three dimensions. In information security scenarios the denominator in the density ratio is often a unit of distance, area, or volume.

Densities are useful because they specify a rate of occurrence. Armed with that rate, one can determine the total number of that item by a simple multiplication. For example, if the areal density of bagels on a kitchen counter is known, one merely multiplies the density figure by the area of the counter to obtain the total number of bagels on the countertop.

So if the density is 5 $\text{bagels}/(\text{ft.})^2$ and the area of a countertop is 2 $(\text{ft.})^2$, multiplying the density by 2 $(\text{ft.})^2$ yields the total number of bagels on the countertop.

In theory one could also specify the density of bagels in terms of a unit volume or the number of bagels per cubic foot. If such a calculation makes any sense it would only do so if the bagels were not confined to the surface. In exact analogy with the surface calculation, multiplying by the number of cubic feet yields the total number of bagels enclosed within a given volume.

Bagels are no doubt of great importance, but let us consider a potentially more relevant example. Suppose the radiated power from an omnidirectional antenna is known. Multiplying the intensity by the surface area of an imaginary sphere with a radius corresponding to the distance from the antenna will yield the total radiated power.

It is easy to show that the *total* radiated power is independent of the distance from the antenna. The important point is that knowledge of the density of a given parameter and the value of the denominator enables a calculation of the numerator. Importantly, in information security scenarios, the density of a security parameter is often specified in terms of risk factors for a specific threat. This statement provides a natural segue to the next section.

GEOMETRY AND PARAMETRIC SCALING

Information security scenarios that obey physical models often display a spatial dependence. This dependence occurs because both and noise power often vary with location, and are measured relative to some source of radiating energy containing information, i.e., a signal. It is therefore useful to investigate geometric features that enable analyses of the signal and noise intensities as a function of distance or direction. These analyses can lead to estimates of the vulnerability to signal detection.

To begin it is worth defining terminology that will be useful in characterizing various information security risk scenarios. Such scenarios are often most conveniently analyzed using spherical coordinates, which uses a standard nomenclature for angles and axes. Spherical coordinates come in handy because many signals can be modeled as point sources, which radiate energy into an ever-expanding sphere of signal intensity.

Two geometric parameters that recur in this context are azimuth and altitude. These are depicted in Fig. 2.11.[6]

Azimuth is the angle between any two points about the vertical axis on the surface of a sphere (the zenith). Altitude measures the angle between the zenith and a given point on the surface of the sphere. Altitude and azimuth are represented as angles θ and ϕ, respectively, in a spherical coordinate system. In the context of information security, the separation between a signal source and the point of measurement is often represented by a distance r. The spherical coordinate system is illustrated in Fig. 2.12.[7]

The geometry of a scenario will affect the magnitude of those information security parameters that have spatial and/or directional dependence. For example, the magnitude of signal intensity can be highly direction-dependent depending on the relative orientations of the transmitting and receiving antennae. Therefore, directionality has important implications to the vulnerability to signal detection.

[6]https://en.wikipedia.org/?title=Azimuth.

[7]https://en.wikipedia.org/wiki/Spherical_coordinate_system.

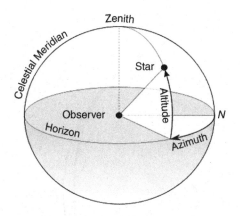

FIGURE 2.11 Azimuth and altitude.

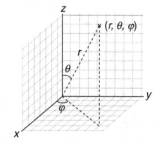

FIGURE 2.12 Radial distance (r), altitude (θ), and azimuth (ϕ) as depicted in spherical coordinates.

Moreover, specifying a range of values for the risk factors enables estimates of vulnerability for a spectrum of scenarios. In creating security models, the objective is to determine how such parameters "scale" or change as a function of the risk factors.

What if the vulnerability to signal detection by an attacker was determined by the magnitude of the signal-to-noise ratio at the point of closest approach to the signal source? In addition, what if various locations of that attacker with respect to that source were known? If the signal intensity I scales as the inverse of the distance r squared, and has an initial intensity I_o, the intensity can be succinctly expressed as follows:

$$I = I_o r^{-2} \tag{2.3}$$

Here the risk factor is distance between the location of the source and the point of detection, and the security parameter is the signal intensity. This model was introduced earlier in the chapter, and will recur throughout this book.

Because of this inverse relationship between intensity and distance, the effect on signal intensity and hence vulnerability to signal detection decreases *disproportionately* as the distance from the radiating source increases. Data that are indicative of signal intensity from a so-called point source such as omnidirectional antennae are presented in Table 2.5.

The implications of this model are unambiguous: if one knows the initial intensity of the radiated signal and the ambient noise, one can immediately estimate the vulnerability to signal

TABLE 2.5 Signal Intensity as a Function of Distance From an Omnidirectional Source of Radiated Energy

Distance from a radiating source (m)	Signal intensity (W)
2	$1 = I_o$
4	$0.25 = I_o/(2)^2 = (1/4)I_o$
8	$0.06 = I_o/(4)^2 = (1/16)I_o$
16	$0.02 = I_o/(8)^2 = (1/64)I_o$
32	$0.004 = I_o/(16)^2 = (1/256)I_o$

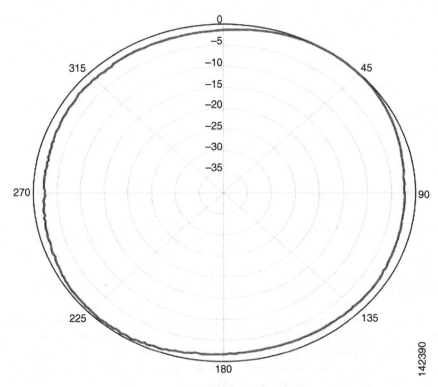

FIGURE 2.13   **Radiation pattern from an omnidirectional antenna as measured along the azimuth.**

detection at any attacker location.[8] It is crucial to appreciate that the radiated intensity characterized by Eq. (2.3) scales *nonlinearly* and *inversely* with distance from the radiating source.

If the radiated signal intensity at a given distance from the antenna is roughly the same in all directions, the radiation pattern measured circumferentially, that is, along the azimuth, is an omnidirectional pattern and will resemble Fig. 2.13.[9]

Note the nearly uniform circumferential pattern of radiation intensity where the antenna is oriented out of the page and toward the reader. Omnidirectional patterns of radiation are useful when the position of the receiver cannot be predicted or where there may be many receivers in disparate locations.

The omnidirectional radiation pattern has been emphasized because it is encountered frequently in information security scenarios due to the prevalence of point sources of radiation. However, it is certainly not the only model for radiated signal energy, and signal patterns from various antennae that provide directionality, also known as gain, significantly depart from this model.

What if the relationship between intensity and distance scaled according to the inverse distance to the *fourth* power $(1/r^4)$? This power law applies to the signal intensity of passive

[8]It is important to note that this analysis is limited to signal *detection*. The transmitted signal could be encrypted, which might reduce the vulnerability to signal reconstruction. However, and as noted in the text, signal interception is always a precursor to reconstruction.

[9]http://www.cisco.com/c/en/us/td/docs/wireless/antenna/installation/guide/ant5175v.html.

I. THREATS, RISK AND RISK ASSESSMENTS

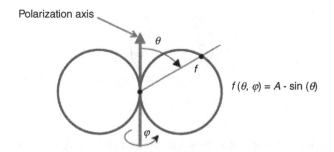

Polarization axis

θ

f

φ

$f(\theta, \varphi) = A \cdot \sin(\theta)$

FIGURE 2.14 Time-averaged radiation intensity from a short dipole antenna.

radio-frequency IDs as a function of distance from the irradiating source. The implications to information security and the associated risk management strategy can be very different depending on how signal intensity varies with distance.

In general, the geometry of the scenario greatly influences estimates of signal intensity and the associated vulnerability to detection. For example, if a short dipole antenna is the source of signal radiation, the intensity varies with altitude angle θ and specifically is proportional to the square of the sine of θ in the familiar figure-eight pattern.[10] Therefore, a receiver antenna located in the figure-eight pattern will detect the source intensity and antennae not located therein will not. Fig. 2.14 illustrates this scenario.

Antennas are designed to produce specific patterns of radiation intensity when either transmitting or receiving energy. The pattern is chosen based on scenario-specific conditions. Sometimes a uniformly distributed intensity pattern is sacrificed in favor of enhanced directionality. The concept of antenna "gain" applies here and will be discussed in Chapter 3.

For a point source of radiated energy, the intensity or equivalently, the power density is the same in all directions, and can be modeled as the surface of an expanding sphere. Therefore, the intensity becomes more dilute with increasing distance from the source.

Because of this spherical pattern of radiated energy, it is sometimes useful to parameterize problems relating to signal detection in terms of spherical coordinates. Recall the spherical coordinate system was introduced in the discussion of azimuth and altitude. In addition, quantities relating to radiating energy such as luminous intensity, luminance, radiant intensity, and radiance are all defined in terms of solid angles, a quantity that has uses in many physical contexts.

A solid angle (Ω) is the two-dimensional angle in three-dimensional space that an object subtends when viewed from a point. It is a measure of how large the object appears to an observer looking from that vantage. In the International System of Units (SI), a solid angle is expressed in a dimensionless unit called a steradian (sr).

One steradian is an area on a sphere that corresponds to the square of the sphere's radius, when observed from its center. Quantitatively, the solid angle subtended by a given area A on the surface of a sphere of radius R is A/R^2.

So if a circular area of radius r on the surface of a sphere has an area πr^2 and the sphere itself has radius R, this geometry corresponds to a solid angle of $\pi(r^2/R^2)$ sr.

Now suppose the circular area on the surface of a sphere of radius R is $4\pi R^2$. In other words, the area on the surface area corresponds to the entire surface of the sphere. In this case

[10]https://en.wikipedia.org/wiki/EMF_measurement.

FIGURE 2.15   The solid angle.

the solid angle becomes $4\pi R^2 / R^2 = 4\pi$. This tells us that the number of steradians in a sphere is always 4π. Fig. 2.15 illustrates the concept of a solid angle.[11]

It might be interesting to know that living objects as well as other entities in our universe radiate thermal energy in the electromagnetic spectrum and the geometry of energy detection is identical to those in information security scenarios. Moreover, the wavelength of that energy is proportional to temperature.[12] Objects such as humans maintain a temperature of 37°C and radiate energy at wavelengths of around 10 μm, which is in the infrared portion of the electromagnetic spectrum. Other objects such as stars radiate thermal energy at wavelengths that are also proportional to their temperature. The theory of blackbody radiation explains this phenomenon.

As noted above, the geometry of measuring thermal energy from a distant star is identical to the one faced by an attacker attempting to detect radiated energy that contains information, albeit the latter scenario involves a much closer source. Fig. 2.16 is illustrative of the geometry of solid angles relative to signal detection.[13]

Specifically, an attacker would use an antenna or lens to capture the signal energy over the solid angle of radiation subtended by his/her detector and over the signal frequency

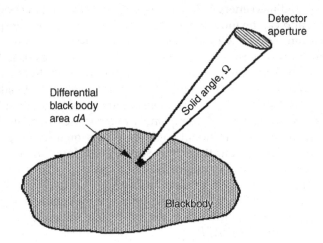

FIGURE 2.16   The geometry of solid angles and radiated electromagnetic energy.

[11]https://en.wikipedia.org/?title=Solid_angle.
[12]The Stefan–Boltzmann law states that the radiated power of a blackbody is given by $P = A\sigma T^4$, where A is the area of the object, σ is the Stefan–Boltzmann constant = 5.68×10^{-8} W/(m^2 K^4), and T is the absolute temperature.
[13]http://goes.gsfc.nasa.gov/text/MITRE-GOES_MP93W62/a-a/a-a.html.

spectrum. In other words, the attacker is interested in detecting the intensity of a signal entering a given solid angle over a specific bandwidth. The intensity is the total signal power divided by the area of illumination. In this case the attacker is measuring the "specific intensity," which has units of watts per square meter per hertz per steradian.

The total signal intensity or equivalently the power density or flux density is achieved by integrating the specific intensity with respect to frequency. This expression is equivalent to the power of the emitted radiation per unit area or intensity, which has units of watts per square meter.

If the solid angle into which a source is radiating is known, the surface of illumination S for any sphere of radius R can be determined since $S = R^2\Omega$ and Ω is the solid angle. For example, suppose a single-frequency source of electromagnetic energy is radiating energy that is confined to a solid angle of 2π steradian. Therefore, the illuminated area A at a distance of 100 m is $100^2(2\pi) \sim 6.3 \times 10^4$ m^2. If the source power P is known, the intensity, $I = P/A$, can be calculated trivially.

However, if the incoming radiated energy is at some angle θ with respect to the face of an attacker's detector aperture, the component of the intensity incident on the detector is proportional to cos θ. Therefore, maximum energy is detected when the source and the detector face each other, that is, the angle θ equals 0 degrees. The geometry will be explained in more detail in the discussion on vectors, flux, and Maxwell's equations in Chapter 4. The geometry of signal detection is illustrated in Fig. 2.17.[14]

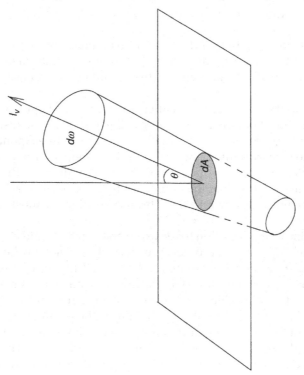

FIGURE 2.17 **Geometry of signal detection.**

[14]http://www.starlink.rl.ac.uk/docs/sc6.htx/sc6se5.html.

EXPONENTIAL AND LOGISTIC GROWTH

Recall the exponential function was introduced previously in this chapter. The relatively brief description belies the importance of this function in characterizing the behavior of various physical processes. In particular, exponentials are solutions to equations describing processes where the rate of growth or decay of a quantity x is proportional to the amount of x remaining.

Equations for exponential growth and decay, respectively, might take the form of the following expressions:

$$\frac{dx}{dt} = ax \tag{2.4}$$

$$\frac{dx}{dt} = -ax \tag{2.5}$$

The symbol dx/dt is familiar to anyone who has studied calculus, and is the derivative of x with respect to time t, or equivalently the rate of change of x with respect to the change in t. In Eqs. (2.4) and (2.5), the symbol "a" is a constant of proportionality.

The solutions to (2.4) and (2.5) are $x = e^{at}$ and $x = e^{-at}$, respectively. These solutions can be verified by direct substitution noting that the derivative of $f(t) = e^{at}$ with respect to t is $a\,e^{at}$ and is $-a\,e^{-at}$ for $f(t) = a\,e^{-at}$.

Although a model for growth and decay of a given quantity that is proportional to the remaining amount of that quantity may seem trivial, it can be applied to many scenarios. Radioactive decay and bacterial growth are two well-known examples of processes that behave in this manner.

Another example in the world of information security is the behavior of radiated energy encountering an absorbing boundary. For example, the intensity of acoustic energy decreases exponentially with the thickness of the shielding material. This exponential behavior has direct applicability to scenarios involving audible information security.

In another example, one might propose a naïve model for the growth of computer viruses based on the simple assumption that the number of future infected machines is proportional to the number of machines already infected. This model might be most applicable in the initial phase of infection.

Yet a seemingly simple modification to the exponential growth and decay model produces very different results. Suppose a computer virus initially spreads unchecked through a network by infecting nearest neighbor machines. An exponential rate of infection might be a reasonable model for growth, but ultimately the number of infections might decline because of either a lack of uninfected machines or the effect of antivirus efforts.

A model that includes the effect of remediation or the eventual lack of targets would introduce a constraint that accounts for this slowdown in infections. This constraint would ultimately produce drastic changes in the number of infections. There is a name for a model that characterizes such behavior and it is referred to as logistic growth or the Verhulst model. It is instructive to point out the differences between exponential and logistic growth.

Let us assume the rate of infection of a population of infected computers is designated by P, and is proportional to the number of computers. The constant of proportionality that governs the rate of growth is r. In this case the model for exponential growth applies:

$$\frac{dP}{dt} = rP \tag{2.6}$$

The solution to (2.6) is as follows:

$$P = P_o\, e^{rt}$$

where P_o is the initial number of infected computers.

Now assume there is some limiting value to P, and call this limit K. The equation that describes this model for growth is given by the following:

$$\frac{dP}{dt} = rP\left(1 - \frac{P}{K}\right) \tag{2.7}$$

Eq. (2.7) shows that if P is much less than K, the equation reduces to Eq. (2.6), that is, unconstrained growth. However, if P equals K, P/K becomes unity and the infections stop, that is, $dP/dt = 0$.

Hence, there are two limiting values for P in Eq. (2.7): 0 and K. Fig. 2.18 compares the graphs of unconstrained or exponential growth versus constrained or logistic growth using Eqs. (2.6) and (2.7).[15] In this depiction, the exponential growth is unbounded, whereas the logistic growth asymptotically approaches the value, K.

Understanding network features that affect the value of K might prove useful in developing a security model to assess, and ultimately reduce, the risk of wide-scale infection. Determining those features and applying them to scenarios of interest transforms a seemingly academic exercise into a practical risk prevention strategy.

A very different model for the growth of network infections is presented in Chapter 13. In that model, the scaling that affects infection rise and decay is more complex. Risk-relevant

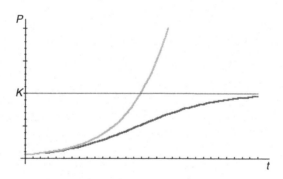

FIGURE 2.18   Exponential versus logistical growth.

[15]https://www.math.duke.edu/education/ccp/materials/diffeq/logistic/logi1.html.

parameters that affect the vulnerability to network infection are specified as well as a prescription for prioritizing the application of security controls to manage infection growth.

SUMMARY

A model for information security risk specifies the dependence of a security parameter on one or more risk factors. Models are useful in making generalizations regarding the behavior of security/threat parameters as a function of risk factors, which can enable estimates of vulnerability.

Specific mathematical functions and concepts are useful in developing simple information security models. Logarithmic functions, exponents and exponential growth, logistic growth, and elementary solid geometry facilitate quantitative risk models, and in particular an understanding of risk factor dependencies. Decibels are expressed as logarithms, and are useful in presenting data that span many orders of magnitude.

Linearity and nonlinearity are essential to the concept of scaling, which compactly expresses the quantitative relationship between security/threat parameters and risk factors as specified in a model. The concept of density has direct application to estimates of vulnerability. In particular, signal intensity or power per unit area is a density measurement that occurs frequently in information security risk assessments.

P A R T II

SCIENTIFIC
FUNDAMENTALS

3

Physics and Information Security

INTRODUCTION

The importance of physics to information security is not always fully appreciated. But consider for a moment that all electronic machines that process information radiate energy and all energy obeys the laws of physics. Similarly, the behavior of acoustic energy in the form of speech is also described by well-understood physical principles.

An attacker intent on obtaining confidential information by covertly detecting radiated energy must focus on optimizing one critical parameter: the signal-to-noise ratio. The ability to enhance the signal-to-noise ratio at the point of detection will determine success or failure.

The physics of energy propagation plays a critical role in understanding the limits on the signal-to-noise ratio, and therefore the vulnerability to information compromise. Since all energy obeys the laws of physics, and a signal is merely energy encoded with information, one must understand the principles that govern energy propagation in order to estimate the vulnerability of signals to detection for a given scenario.

From an operational perspective, the remote detection of radiated energy leaves no signature or sign of an attacker's presence. There is simply no way to detect an attack of this kind unless a sensor is discovered or observed. This is one reason such an attack is so pernicious.

This chapter provides background material that is useful for analyzing various signal detection scenarios. These scenarios involve both electromagnetic and mechanical energy, which comprise *all* signals. Moreover, signal behavior in materials, which affects the vulnerability to detection, is dictated by the physics of wave propagation.

WAVES

Information encoded in signals is conveyed via electromagnetic or mechanical vibrations. The interaction of electromagnetic energy with materials in which it propagates depends greatly on the interaction of the electric and magnetic fields with the electrons in the material. This interaction is embodied in the relative permittivity or dielectric constant, discussed later in this chapter. By contrast, vibrating mechanical energy consists of the very material in which it is propagating, where that material expands and contracts as the energy wave affects nearest neighbor molecules.

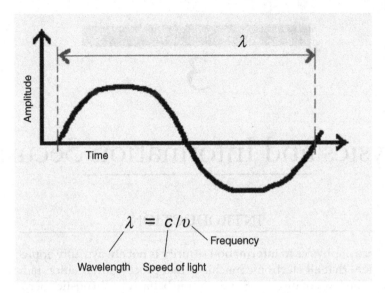

FIGURE 3.1   Amplitude, wavelength, and frequency of waves.

A wave is a convenient model for the physical motion of propagating energy. As noted earlier, signals are forms of energy that exhibit wave-like motion and are encoded with information. Conveying information is the raison d'être of a signal. In this way wave motion and signal propagation are inexorably linked.

A mathematical description of wave motion is a function whose amplitude is changing with time. The change in amplitude repeats itself at a rate characterized by its frequency or, equivalently, the wavelength, which is the inverse of frequency. The repetitive nature of wave motion is characterized by periodicity.

Fig. 3.1 illustrates a simple wave pattern and the parameters of wavelength, amplitude, and frequency.[1] Frequency and wavelength are inversely related through the wave velocity, which for electromagnetic waves is the speed of light, c. Angular and linear representations of waves are related by a factor of 2π as follows:

$$\omega = 2\pi\upsilon = ck = c\left(\frac{2\pi}{\lambda}\right) \tag{3.1}$$

In this expression, $k = \lambda/2\pi$ is known as the wave number. From (3.1) it is clear that the following relation holds:

$$\upsilon\lambda = c \tag{3.2}$$

How is wavelength affected by wave velocity, and how would wavelength differ for a wave traveling at the speed of sound versus the speed of light?

[1]https://heasarc.gsfc.nasa.gov/docs/xte/learning_center/universe/energetic.html.

Let the wavelengths of sound and light be λ_S and λ_L, respectively, and similarly c_S and c_L are the velocities of sound and light, respectively. For a given frequency v it is clear from (3.2) that the following expressions are true:

$$\lambda_S = \frac{c_S}{v} \quad \text{and} \quad \lambda_L = \frac{c_L}{v} \tag{3.3}$$

Therefore,

$$\frac{\lambda_S}{\lambda_L} = \frac{c_S}{c_L}$$

Or equivalently,

$$\lambda_S = \lambda_L \left(\frac{c_S}{c_L} \right) \tag{3.4}$$

Thus the ratio of the wavelengths of two waves is proportional to the ratio of their respective wave velocities.

The ratio of the speed of sound to speed of light, c_S/c_L, is roughly 0.11×10^{-5}. The wavelength of light at 1 kHz is 299,792.458 m. From (3.4) the wavelength of sound is found to be 0.3 m or about 1 ft. at 1 kHz.

Fig. 3.1 shows the wave amplitude changing as a function of time in a sinusoidal pattern. This type of wave action is characteristic of electromagnetic waves in particular, and such waves are generally known as "transverse" waves. Mechanical wave motion is demonstrably different and the differences are discussed later in this chapter.

The change in amplitude occurs at some frequency that is often measured in units of cycles per second or hertz. The inverse relationship between frequency and wavelength is worth reiterating. In other words, frequency is the reciprocal of wavelength; a longer wavelength implies a lower frequency and shorter wavelengths correspond to higher frequencies.

The inverse relationship between frequency and wavelength is directly observable when listening to musical instruments. The wavelength of sounds produced by string instruments roughly corresponds to the length of the instrument. This effect is in evidence when one hears the lower registers emanating from a bass versus the more diminutive violin, viola, and cello. The pitch varies inversely with the length of the strings.

In Fig. 3.1 the wave speed is shown as the speed of light, c (3×10^8 m/s in a vacuum), but waves can certainly travel at other speeds. The difference in time between an observed flash of lightning and the accompanying sound of thunder dramatically illustrates the difference in the speed of light versus sound.

The frequency, wavelength, and amplitudes of different types of waves can also vary and can affect its propagation depending on the media in which it is propagating. Fig. 3.2 shows wave motion of different amplitudes and frequencies.[2]

Figs. 3.1 and 3.2 show the wave amplitude changing as a function of time. However, an equally valid perspective is in the so-called frequency domain. In this view the wave

[2]http://www.cdc.gov/niosh/mining/content/emergencymanagementandresponse/commtracking/commtrackingtutorial1.html.

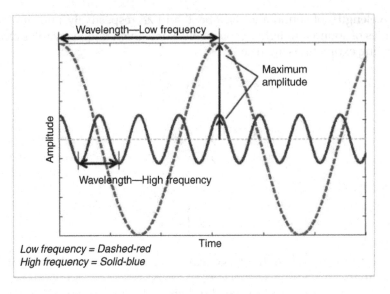

FIGURE 3.2   Two waves of different frequencies and amplitude.

amplitude is shown as a function of frequency. For a single sine wave a frequency representation would consist of a single vertical line centered on a single frequency, typically specified in cycles-per-second or hertz.

Representing a wave in both the time and frequency domains can be helpful in assessing the vulnerability to signal compromise. Each can reveal useful structural features of the signal in question. As such, both representations will be used throughout this text, and both will be particularly relevant in the discussion on Fourier analysis of log data in Chapter 13. In that discussion data derived from network intrusion detection devices are analyzed in the frequency domain and yield insights that otherwise might go unappreciated.

Time and frequency domain representations convey different perspectives of the same signal. These representations are merely inverses of each other, but the simplicity of this relationship belies the benefits of viewing a signal from both vantages. As its name implies, the time domain shows how the signal amplitude is changing as a function of time.

Signals are encoded with information as a result of a process known as modulation. This creates additional frequencies that complicate the spectrum thereby making time domain representations challenging to interpret on a sufficiently granular level. Fig. 3.3 shows a signal represented in the time and frequency domains.[3]

Fig. 3.3 might not immediately convey the virtues of viewing this time–frequency duality. As mentioned previously, signals are modulated sources of energy and their spectra can consist of many frequencies. Fig. 3.4 depicts time–frequency representations for a series of signals of varying complexity, where each contains energy at multiples of some fundamental frequency.

[3]http://www.ni.com/tutorial/13042/en/.

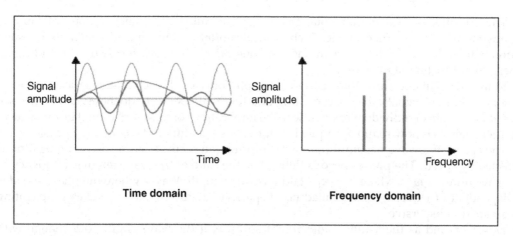

FIGURE 3.3 Time and frequency domain representations of signals.

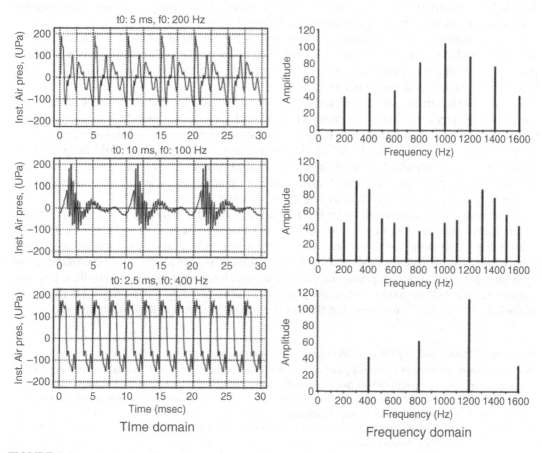

FIGURE 3.4 More time and frequency representations of signals.

These multiples of a fundamental frequency are called harmonics, a concept familiar to anyone who has studied music. Such examples offer a glimpse of the insights revealed through time–frequency transformations since one can readily view the distribution of signal energy as a function of frequency.[4]

In the late 17th and early 18th centuries, Joseph Fourier, a French mathematician, showed that band-limited signals, that is, consisting of a finite number of frequencies, can be decomposed into a sum of individual frequencies. The implications of this work cannot be overstated. Fourier analysis is now routinely applied to numerous scientific and engineering problems.

The speed of a wave has implications to information security since wave propagation is affected by speed. The phase speed is defined as the ratio of the wave angular frequency to its wave number ω/k, where $k = 2\pi/\lambda$ and λ is wavelength. Waves where the phase speed is independent of wavelength are called nondispersive.[5] Radio-frequency waves propagating in air are nondispersive.

However, and as the astute reader might surmise, if the wavelength does change with phase speed, such waves are called dispersive. In dispersive waves, the carrier wave propagates at the phase speed but the modulation envelope propagates at the group velocity, $d\omega/dk$. For nondispersive waves, $\omega = ck$ with constant phase speed c. So for nondispersive waves the group velocity c_g equals the phase velocity.

Since the group velocity of dispersive waves differs from the phase speed, the wave crests in a wave packet will move at a different speed than the envelope. This causes the packet to change shape.[6] If $c > c_g$, new wave crests appear at the rear of the wave packet, move forward through the packet, and disappear at its leading edge.

Of critical importance to discussions on phase and group velocity is that even though the phase velocity can exceed the group velocity, and there is no theoretical upper bound to the phase velocity, the *information* is encoded in the signal envelope. Moreover, the envelope propagates at the group velocity. If this situation was not the case, one would be able to see an image before it actually appeared since the information could travel at a speed greater than the speed of light! So, the theoretical upper limit of velocity for the information in signals is the velocity of light. Thankfully, causality is not violated.

An appropriate analogy might be the following. Consider a family traveling on a train, where each family member is analogous to a constituent frequency in a complex wave. The train is the wave envelope. Each family member might get up and walk around inside the train while en route to their destination. One or more of the kids might even be moving faster than the train during certain phases of the journey much to the consternation of their parents. However, despite the speed one or more kids might achieve while a passenger, it is the speed of the train alone that determines the time of the family's arrival at their destination.

---

[4]University of Western Michigan, http://homepages.wmich.edu/~hillenbr/206/ac.pdf.

[5]A simple derivation for the phase velocity ω/k is presented. The number of amplitude oscillations in a specified time is given by the rate of oscillation or frequency, ω, times the duration of the time period, t. However, during that time the wave also travels a distance, x. That distance can be expressed as a multiple of the wavelength or x times $k = 2\pi x/\lambda$. Now ωt must equal xk since the distance traveled per wavelength during a given time interval must equal the number of oscillations that occur in that same time interval for any given frequency. This implies that $\omega/k = x/t$, where x/t is distance per time or velocity.

[6]http://www-eaps.mit.edu/~rap/courses/12333_notes/dispersion.pdf.

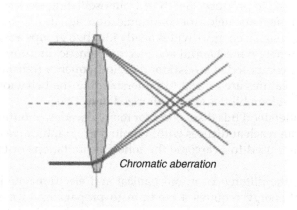
Chromatic aberration

FIGURE 3.5 **Dispersion causing chromatic aberration.**

Familiar examples of wave dispersion are the spectrum of colors resulting from a prism as well as the distortion produced by some lenses. The latter is a phenomenon known as chromatic aberration. In prisms, different wavelengths that comprise visible light travel at different speeds, which produce the familiar rainbow of colors. Chromatic aberration is a manifestation of the same phenomenon, but in that case it results in the defocusing of the image on a focal plane. Fig. 3.5 illustrates the effect of chromatic aberration.[7]

WAVE ENERGY AND POWER

Up to this point there have been mentions of the term energy, but no formal definition has been provided. Although the term energy is often used in casual conversations, and sometimes in very imprecise ways (eg, "The energy of the human spirit …"), it actually has a specific scientific meaning. The following definition is fit-for-purpose in this context[8]:

Energy, in physics, is the capacity for doing work. It may exist in potential, kinetic, thermal, electrical, chemical, nuclear, or other various forms. There are, moreover, heat and work – i.e., energy in the process of transfer from one body to another. After it has been transferred, energy is always designated according to its nature. Hence, heat transferred may become thermal energy, while work done may manifest itself in the form of mechanical energy.

All forms of energy are associated with motion. For example, any given body has kinetic energy if it is in motion. A tensioned device such as a bow or spring, though at rest, has the potential for creating motion; it contains potential energy because of its configuration. Similarly, nuclear energy is potential energy because it results from the configuration of subatomic particles in the nucleus of an atom.

The key point in the definition is that energy involves motion, either realized or potential. Humans use energy to convey signals among other things. This energy can result from the

[7]https://en.wikipedia.org/wiki/Achromatic_len.
[8]http://www.britannica.com/science/energy.

vibration of vocal chords to produce speech or from oscillating electrons in electric devices that yield electric and magnetic fields for communication signals.

As noted previously, signal energy divides neatly into two groups according to the process used to generate that energy: mechanical and electromagnetic. In information security these groups are principally composed of acoustic and radio-frequency transmissions, respectively. Their distinguishing features are critical to understanding the behavior of each signal and consequently to their vulnerabilities to unauthorized detection.

Engineers have understood this distinction for many decades. Shouting or even electrically amplified speech can reach audiences within limited geographic areas. Therefore AM/FM radio transmissions are used to overcome the inherent limitations of transmitting acoustic energy in air.

What are some of the differences in mechanical and electromagnetic energy? First and foremost, mechanical energy requires a medium to propagate. As mentioned briefly, the propagation of mechanical energy results from sequential vibrations of molecules "excited" by neighboring molecules. Absent molecules that can be so stimulated, acoustic energy will not propagate. The sounds caused by a variety of sources during the day are the result of air molecules vibrating in response to a multitude of stimuli.

In contrast, electromagnetic energy requires no such molecular support system. Consider radios that communicate with vehicles in deep space over distances of hundreds of thousands of miles. This does not mean that electromagnetic energy is not affected by the medium in which it propagates, but merely that such energy is transmitted perfectly well in a vacuum.

In fact, the effect of intervening media on both electromagnetic and mechanical signal propagation can be profound. And the effect can be quite different for the two types of signal energy or even different frequencies of the same energy type. The magnitude of reflection, transmission, and absorption for optical, radio-frequency, and acoustic signals in various scenarios is a central element of Part III of this book.

There are other significant differences between electromagnetic and mechanical energy. For example, the wave motion for each is often not the same. As noted previously, electromagnetic waves are known as transverse waves because the direction of propagation is perpendicular to the plane of oscillation.

In contrast, mechanical waves that characterize acoustic energy propagate parallel to the direction of oscillation. This phenomenon is known as longitudinal wave motion. Maybe you remember playing with a slinky as a child or perhaps even more recently in a less inhibited moment. This toy provides an intuitive feel for longitudinal wave motion, and, in particular, the accordion-like motion of molecules that constitute an acoustic wave. Specifically, the sequential excitation of neighboring molecules caused by changes in pressure affects the transfer of energy through a given material.

Fig. 3.6 illustrates longitudinal wave motion showing regions of compression and rarefaction, that is, expansion, plus regions of peaks and troughs in amplitude. Longitudinal wave motion should be compared with transverse motion, which was depicted in Fig. 3.1.[9]

What physical characteristics of signal energy are important in estimating the vulnerability to signal detection? Recall that energy is the capacity to do work. Work is defined as the distance over which a force is applied. The signal energy is therefore the work it exerts on

[9]http://mierochaj.wikispaces.com/Types+of+waves.

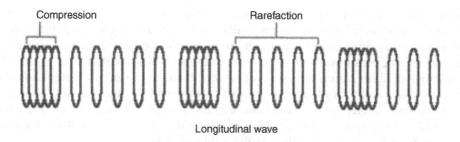

Longitudinal wave

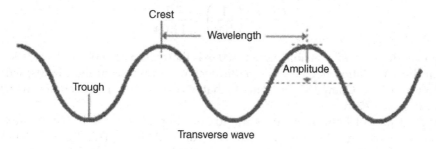

Transverse wave

FIGURE 3.6 **Longitudinal versus transverse wave motion.**

electrons (to generate a voltage) and a mass (to generate displacement) for electromagnetic and mechanical energy, respectively.[10]

All signals require a sensor to facilitate detection. A sensor is designed to respond to the energy of a particular signal. In the case of an electromagnetic signal that sensor is an antenna or lens. With respect to antennae, an electric field exerts a force on electrons in the metal. A voltage is created that is detected, processed, and amplified to reconstruct the original signal. Specifically, the instantaneous *rate* of signal energy incident on the antenna must be sufficient to generate a voltage, which can then be amplified and demodulated by a receiver.

Signal energy per unit time is defined as the signal *power*. It is the signal power that is important in information security scenarios rather than the total energy radiated by an information source. The difference between energy and power can best be understood in terms of a practical example.

Suppose this book proves so compelling that reading it at night as well as during the day has reached obsessive proportions. Satisfying this desire will require an artificial light source. There is a choice of light bulbs, where one is rated at 1 watt (W) of power that can remain illuminated for 100 h and the other is rated at 100 W that can be illuminated for only 1 h.

In each case the energy is the same: 100 W-h. However, one might strain to read this or any book with only 1 W of available power. On the other hand, 100 W of power should provide ample energy to read the text at reasonable distances even if the experience only lasts an hour.

---

[10]As its name implies, an electromagnetic signal is composed of an electric and a magnetic field. The electric field, E, does work on charges. The force is given by the magnitude of the charge, q, multiplied by E. Although changing magnetic fields do not exert a force on static charges, they produce electric fields (see Chapter 5 and Maxwell's equation number 3 or Faraday's Law), and these electric fields exert a force on charges and therefore do work.

But power alone does not convey the entire story regarding sensors such as the human eye, cameras, and antennae. Imagine if the transmitted power was somehow diluted, where the detector moved away from the energy source. How can this power dilution be quantified?

For example, suppose one now attempted to read this book at 100 m using the 100-W light bulb as a source of illumination versus doing so at a distance of 1 m. If the light bulb can be considered a point source, it radiates equal amounts of power in all directions.

So the radiation spreads out over the surface of an imaginary sphere of increasing radius. The surface area of any sphere of radius r is $4\pi r^2$. Therefore, the intensity will decrease as one moves farther from the source according to the following ratio:

$$\left(\frac{r}{R}\right)^2 = \left(\frac{1}{100}\right)^2 = \frac{1}{10,000}$$

The power density of the visible light at 100 m is therefore $1/10,000 \times 1$ W or 0.0001 W/m^2. Note that this calculation neglects the inefficiency of incandescent light bulbs, which is between 1.5% and 2.5%. Compare this figure to that of compact fluorescent bulbs, which vary in efficiency between 7% and 10%.[11]

A standard unit of light intensity is the lux or alternatively the luminous flux per unit area. A comfortable light level for reading is around 500 lux.[12] This figure is equivalent to 334×10^3 W/m^2 or 95 dB above the intensity of a 100-W incandescent light bulb at a distance of 100 m.

Note that the total power radiated by the bulb is the same at 100 m as at 1 m, but the distance from the source effectively dilutes the *intensity* to a level below what is useful to human optical sensors, that is, the eye.

CONSTRUCTIVE AND DESTRUCTIVE INTERFERENCE

If two waves arrive at a point in space at precisely the same time and in phase, their respective amplitudes would reinforce each other and the intensity increases. This phenomenon is known as constructive interference and is illustrated in Fig. 3.7.[13]

However, if the two waves arrive 1/2 wavelength apart, or 180 degrees out of phase, their amplitudes would cancel each other and result in no sound. This particular phenomenon is known as destructive interference, and is illustrated in Fig. 3.8.[13]

Both constructive and destructive interference are relevant to a number of information security scenarios. Interference is clearly linked to the phase relationships between waves. What does that mean and how does it apply to security scenarios?

---

[11]The luminous efficacy or light output relative to electrical power consumption of compact fluorescent bulbs is 50–70 lumen/W. Incandescent bulbs are 10–17 lumen/W. A theoretical, 100% efficient bulb would have a luminous efficacy of 680 lumen/W. Therefore, the efficiency of compact fluorescent bulbs is calculated to be between 50/680 (0.07) and 70/680 (0.10%), and that of incandescent bulbs is calculated to be between 10/680 (0.015) and 17/680 (0.025).

[12]http://www.e2energysolutions.com/Resources/Light%20levels%20in%20schools%20all%20interior%20and%20 exterior%20-%20USE.pdf.

[13]http://www.nasa.gov/missions/science/f_interference.html.

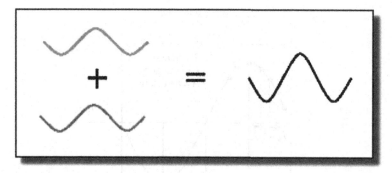

FIGURE 3.7   Constructive interference.

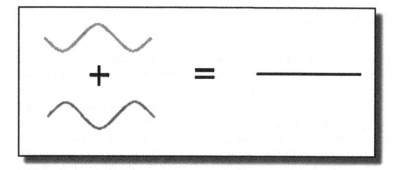

FIGURE 3.8   Destructive interference.

Earlier in the chapter the oscillatory nature of wave motion was introduced. Multiple waves can exist along the path of signal propagation due to reflections, multiple signal sources, multiple frequencies, etc. Engineers sometimes attempt to exploit the phase relationship between waves to minimize or maximize the resultant signal through destructive or constructive interference, respectively.

Consider wave motion where the amplitude is represented as a sine wave. This representation is a typical depiction. The amplitude can be in any units of one's choosing: volts, amperes, dollars, watts per square meter, etc. The point is that the magnitude of some quantity is oscillating up and down over time. This oscillation can be thought of as repeated laps around a circle. Every lap corresponds to 360 degrees, and a cycle consists of one complete lap.

In exact analogy, the amplitude of wave motion repeats each cycle, one cycle consists of the 360 degrees in a circle, and 360 degrees is equivalent to 2π radian. This time progression can be depicted in terms of a phase angle measured in either radians or degrees. Fig. 3.9 illustrates periodic wave motion where the amplitude of the wave is plotted relative to phase angle in degrees and radians, and the amplitude is measured in volts.[14]

Let us assume two waves are propagating independently and each has a constant frequency. Furthermore, one wave is advanced in time relative to the other by a half-wavelength. In

[14]http://www.nist.gov/pml/div688/grp40/enc-p.cfm.

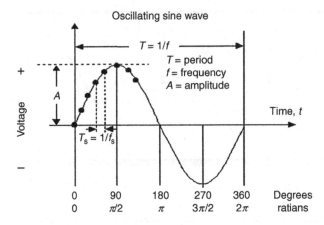

FIGURE 3.9   Sine wave depicting wave motion.

other words, one wave is experiencing a maximum while the other is experiencing a minimum. If two such waves intersect at a given point in space, their phase relationship will cause destructive interference as depicted in Fig. 3.8.

Anyone who has listened to a ground-based radio transmission in a car has experienced the effect of multipath firsthand. AM and FM radio transmissions can take multiple paths to reach a particular destination. One path might be a direct transmission from the broadcasting antenna. Another path might result from a reflection off a big object such as a building or a truck.

Let us assume the car is located a distance D from the building, and the direct and reflected signals add, that is, arrive simultaneously at the same point and in phase. Recall a wavelength corresponds to 2π radian so one-half wavelength is equivalent to π radian. If the car moves one-half wavelength closer or farther from the building, the radio signal will disappear.

In a similar vein, if the phase relationship between the two waves could be shifted, that is, one wave is advanced or retarded by π radian, the two waves will constructively interfere and their maximum amplitudes will coincide as depicted in Fig. 3.7. Objects that transmit energy can be shaped to exploit the phase relationship between waves as will become evident in discussing parabolic reflectors in Chapter 10.

RESONANCE

A concept that is of exceptional importance to analyzing physical phenomena is resonance. When waves interact with materials, certain physical characteristics profoundly affect the response of that material. These conditions relate to the properties of both the material and the incident wave.

Resonance is the condition where maximum energy is absorbed by a material or structure. It is exhibited at a preferred frequency or set of frequencies. The response to a force over a spectrum of frequencies is critical to understanding how a system will react under various operational conditions.

The simple harmonic oscillator is central to explanations of resonance. A harmonic oscillator system can be modeled as a mass on a spring, and is used to model situations where a

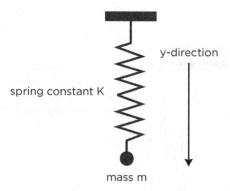

y-direction

spring constant K

mass m

FIGURE 3.10   Simple mass and spring harmonic oscillator.

driving force is acting on such a mass. Fig. 3.10 illustrates a mass and spring system where the displacement is in the vertical or y direction.[15]

The force required for restoring a mass to the equilibrium position after being displaced is proportional to the displacement of the mass. This condition is expressed as $F = -ky$, where F is referred to as the restoring force, k is the constant of proportionality or Young's modulus, and y is the magnitude of the displacement.[16] This equation is known as Hooke's Law.[17] Note that if the spring is at the resting position, the mass will not accelerate, which is an excellent segue to the following discussion.

In order to displace the mass, an external force (eg, gravity) must be applied. According to Isaac Newton's Second Law of Motion, the external force equals the mass times its acceleration. But in keeping with Hooke's Law, the restoring force exerted by the spring is proportional to the displacement caused by an external force.

Equating the two forces yields the displacement of the mass as follows:

$$F = -ky = ma \tag{3.5}$$

Recall that m is mass and a is acceleration. Since acceleration is just the change in the change of the displacement y with time t, that is, the second derivative of the displacement with respect to time, (3.5) can be written as a differential equation:

$$-ky = \frac{m\, d^2 y}{dt^2} \tag{3.6}$$

Importantly, the solution to (3.6) reveals that the mass oscillates in time. The sinusoidal pattern implies that the response of a structure to this forcing function is oscillatory motion.

---

[15]Florida State University, http://www.math.fsu.edu/~fusaro/EngMath/Ch2/MFO.html.

[16]The minus sign in front of ky exists because the restoring force applied by the spring is in opposition to the external force displacing the mass.

[17]Named after Robert Hooke, an English scientist (1635–1703).

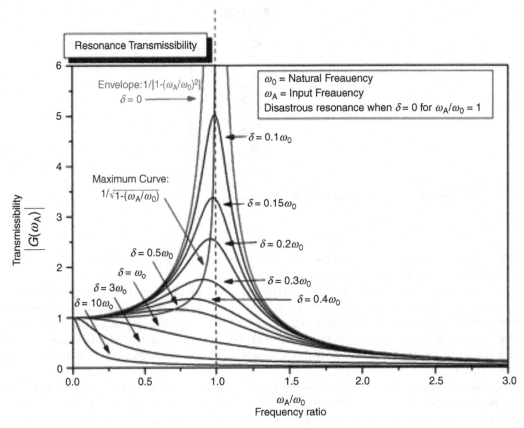

FIGURE 3.11 Response of a simple damped harmonic oscillator to decreases in damping as the frequency approaches resonance. δ, damping coefficient.

However, all oscillating structures experience some loss in energy in each cycle of oscillation, and this loss is referred to as damping. When the damping effect is small, the resonant frequency is approximately equal to the natural frequency of vibration of the system. Some systems have multiple resonant frequencies.

Anyone who has ever used a swing has experienced the natural frequency of oscillation for that system. Maximum height is achieved when one applies energy, that is, kicks one's feet at the resonant frequency of the system, which is the swing's natural frequency.

Readers interested in a more dramatic testament to the effect of resonance need only witness the video of the destruction of the Tacoma Narrows Bridge in Washington State. In that case the wind supplied significant energy at a resonant frequency of the bridge, which caused large-amplitude oscillations and ultimately catastrophic failure of the structure.

A more quantitative representation of the effect of resonance for a damped system is shown in Fig. 3.11. Here the increase in amplitude as damping decreases and the frequency approaches the resonant frequency is shown for a driven and damped simple harmonic oscillator.[18]

[18]https://en.wikipedia.org/wiki/Resonance.

Technically, true resonance occurs only if all of the following conditions are satisfied[19]:

- There is no damping.
- A periodic forcing function is present.
- The frequency of the forcing function exactly matches the natural frequency of the system.

However, a large-amplitude oscillation occurs when damping is present but insignificant, and/or when the frequency of the forcing function is very close to the natural frequency of the system.

The phenomenon of resonance is exhibited in both mechanical and electromagnetic systems. Resonance has implications to information security scenarios since signals are transmitted via wave motion. Electromagnetic and mechanical signals interact with structures that can exhibit resonance and thereby enhance or absorb signal energy, potentially affecting the vulnerability to compromise.

DIFFRACTION AND LENSES

Diffraction is perhaps the most important physical process associated with wave motion relating to information security scenarios. An entire section is dedicated to explaining diffraction because it imposes a fundamental limit on the resolution of images. Diffraction results from interference where energy interacts with an obstacle whose physical dimension is comparable to the wavelength of the incident energy. The result is a spreading of the wave front.

Diffraction occurs with all waves including sound waves, water waves, and electromagnetic waves, for example, visible light, X-rays, and radio waves. Fig. 3.12 graphically illustrates the effect of diffraction.[20]

A discussion of the effect of diffraction with respect to optical lenses is illustrative since it provides useful background for the optical attack scenarios discussed in Chapter 9. Specifically, diffraction governs the limit to which focusing can increase image resolution.

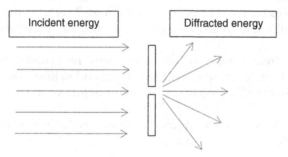

FIGURE 3.12   The effect of diffraction.

[19]http://www.math.psu.edu/tseng/class/Math251/Notes-MechV.pdf.
[20]http://missionscience.nasa.gov/ems/03_behaviors.html.

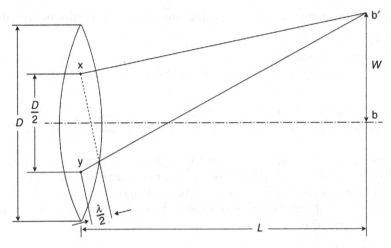

FIGURE 3.13   Geometry illustrating diffraction for a lens. *Figure provided by Kate McManus based on the image in Pierce JR. Electrons, waves, and messages. Garden City, NY: Hanover House; 1956. p. 92–3.*

Imagine an attacker is attempting to resolve the text on a computer monitor from an adjacent building. Diffraction dictates the minimum lens size of the letters that can be distinguished for a given lens size.[21]

A graphical depiction of diffraction is provided next [1]. Consider electromagnetic waves in the form of visible light incident on a lens.

Fig. 3.13 shows a lens of width D that focuses waves on a point b at a distance L from the lens. λ is the wavelength of light.

The lens has been divided into two halves; the centers of each half and points x and y are a distance $D/2$ apart. Suppose that one moves up a distance W from b to b'. The distance W is such that the distance from b' to the center of the lower half of the lens is $\lambda/2$ greater than the distance from b' to the center of the upper half of the lens.

At b' troughs of the waves from the lower half of the lens will arrive simultaneously with peaks of the waves from the upper part of the lens. Therefore there will be no wave at b' since the waves will undergo destructive interference and their amplitudes will exactly cancel.

Since L is much greater than W or λ, the lens resolution limit, $W/L \sim (\lambda/2)/(D/2) = \lambda/D$ radian. Therefore waves will fall above and below b but at approximately W above and below b there will be no wave. A great fraction of the waves will fall between $b \pm W/2$.

For circular lenses/apertures, the angular resolution is defined by the Rayleigh Criterion and is given by the following expression:

$$\alpha = 1.22 \frac{\lambda}{D} \tag{3.7}$$

[21]Other scenario features affect the vulnerability to compromise such as the intensity of visible background light. These will be discussed in Chapter 6.

(3.7) specifies the so-called diffraction limit, and this limit has profound implications to optics, acoustics, antennae theory, and wave phenomena in general. To illustrate a simple application of the principle, consider the rather unlikely scenario of needing to determine at what distance it is possible to distinguish two headlights of an oncoming car.

Let us assume the headlights of the car are a distance $d = 1.5$ m apart. The diameter of the circular pupil of the human eye $D = 3$ mm, and an average wavelength of light $\lambda = 5000$ Å.[22]

The angular resolving power of a circular lens α is given by (3.7). Therefore one can calculate the angular divergence of optical energy entering the pupil:

$$\alpha = \frac{1.22(5 \times 10^{-7})}{3 \times 10^{-3}} = 2.03 \times 10^{-4} \text{ radian}$$

Two sources separated by a distance d at a distance R will appear separate if $\alpha = d/R$. In other words, the spot size d required to resolve the two lights corresponds to $R\alpha$.

So solving for R yields the following:

$$R = \frac{d}{\alpha} = \frac{1.5}{2.03 \times 10^{-4}} = 7.38 \text{ km} = 4.6 \text{ miles}$$

ANTENNAE AND GAIN

Diffraction also applies to antennae that focus electromagnetic energy at radio-frequency wavelengths. Just as with optical lenses, diffraction sets the limit on the focusing power of transmitting and receiving antennae. Let us work out an example that will lead to a formula with crucial implications to information security [1].

Antennae are capable of exhibiting directionality, and thereby concentrate signal energy. That is, they exhibit signal gain and thereby concentrate signal energy within narrow solid angles. But this effect occurs at the expense of other solid angles since the total radiated or received energy must be conserved. In other words, spatial diversity is sacrificed in favor of selected areas of enhanced intensity.

Suppose one is concerned about an attacker detecting a microwave signal at some distance L from a transmitting antenna of diameter D. The transmitting antenna broadcasts a beam of microwave energy of wavelength λ to a receiving antenna located at a distance R from the transmitter.

Using a modified version of (3.7), the expression for the angular divergence of a circular lens due to diffraction, the beam width W at the receiving antenna is $W \sim \lambda R/D$. If the beam is assumed to be circular, the area A of the spread in energy due to beam divergence is approximately equal to the area of a circle of diameter W. That is,

$$A = \left(\frac{\pi}{4}\right)W^2 = \frac{\pi\lambda^2 R^2}{4D^2}$$

[22]One angstrom equals 10^{-10} m.

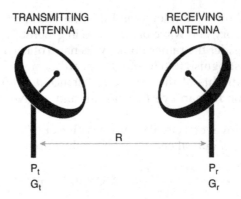

FIGURE 3.14   Transmit/receive antennae configuration relevant to Friis formula.

If A_r is the area of the receiving antenna, the ratio of the power P_r that is detected by the receiving antenna to the total transmitted power P_t is given by the following expression:

$$\frac{P_r}{P_t} = \frac{A_r}{A} = \frac{4A_rD^2}{\pi\lambda^2R^2} \qquad (3.8)$$

If the transmit antenna is circular, its area is $A_t = \pi D^2/4$ or $D^2 = 4/\pi A_t$. Therefore, the ratio of received power to transmitted power is as follows:

$$\frac{P_r}{P_t} = \frac{(4/\pi)(2A_rA_t)}{\lambda^2R^2}$$

Performing a bit of algebra, the basic relationship becomes:

$$\frac{P_r}{P_t} \sim \frac{A_rA_t}{\lambda^2R^2} \qquad (3.9)$$

Eqs. (3.8) and (3.9) are formulations of Friis formula.[23] Simply put this formula specifies that in order to increase the ratio of the received to transmitted power for a given distance, an increase in the area of the receiving and/or transmitting antenna and/or a decrease in the wavelength of the signal is required.

Fig. 3.14 depicts the scenario described by Friis formula.[24] In this case G_t and G_r represent the gains of transmitting and receiving antennae, respectively, where Friis formula can also be written as follows:

$$P_r = \frac{P_tG_tG_r\lambda^2}{(4\pi R)^2} \qquad (3.10)$$

The Friis formula is often used in performing calculations to determine the vulnerability of a signal to detection. Typically one knows the distance between a signal transmitter and

[23]Harald T. Friis (1893–1976) was a Danish-American engineer who made important contributions to radio-frequency propagation and radio astronomy.
[24]http://www.everythingrf.com/rf-calculators/friis-transmission-calculator.

a presumed detection site. This is used to calculate the signal-to-noise ratio at that site. Alternatively, one hopes to determine at what distance is P_r at the threshold of detection relative to the ambient noise, where the signal power-to-noise ratio is assumed to be a minimum of 10.

Note that in this formulation A_r and A_t represent the physical areas of the antennae. An ideal antenna transmits a wave of equal strength across its entire area. Similarly, an ideal receiving antenna focuses a wave of equal strength across its entire area. Actual antennas are not ideal, and one must use the so-called effective area. For example, the effective area of a dipole antenna is $\lambda^2/4\pi$, a fact that will be used in several calculations in future chapters.

POINT SOURCES OF RADIATING ENERGY

One physical model of information compromise stands out in terms of its general applicability and therefore deserves special attention. This model was first mentioned in Chapter 3 and is applicable when the radiating source is considered to be a "point source." Two criteria are used to determine if a source qualifies as a point source:

- The physical dimension of the source is small compared to the distance between the source and the detector.
- The wavelength of the radiated energy is large compared to the physical dimension of the source.

The intensity of a point source of radiating energy exhibits unique behavior as a function of distance from the source. This behavior is what makes it useful to analyze certain information security scenarios.

The intensity of a point source is by now familiar to the reader. Namely, the intensity I from a source with power S decreases as the inverse squared of the distance r between source and detection sites. This relationship is as follows:

$$I = \frac{S}{4\pi r^2} \tag{3.11}$$

One can imagine a source radiating energy at the center of an imaginary sphere. At increasing distances from the source the intensity is diluted as the surface area over which it is distributed increases. However, the total power remains the same at any given sphere radius. Since intensity scales inversely with the square of distance, the intensity is I at an initial radius r, is $I/4$ at $2r$, is $I/9$ at $3r$, etc. Fig. 3.15 illustrates a point source of radiating energy in action.[25]

The intensity can also be expressed in terms of decibels. Consider a robust point source of sound energy. The intensity is measured to be 90 dB sound pressure level (SPL) at 1 m from the source. Recall sound energy is often implicitly referenced to the minimum threshold of hearing or SPL.

Doubling the distance to 2 m from the source, the intensity is reduced by a factor of 4 or 84 dB SPL. At 4 m from the source, the point source model predicts that the intensity will

[25]http://imagine.gsfc.nasa.gov/science/activities/try_l2/supernovae.html.

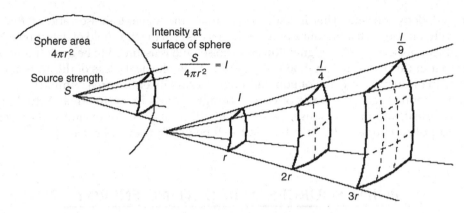

FIGURE 3.15 A point source of radiating energy.

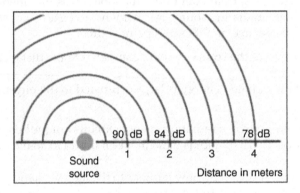

FIGURE 3.16 The intensity of a point source of sound energy.

decrease by another 6 dB, that is, an intensity of 78 dB SPL. Fig. 3.16 shows the intensity of a point source of sound energy as a function of distance in terms of decibels.[26]

Point sources of radiating energy are common to information security scenarios since one of the two qualifying conditions often applies to scenarios of interest. The model enables estimates of intensity as a function of the separation between source and detector, where this distance is a key risk factor for the threat of information compromise.

SUMMARY

All electronic devices radiate energy, and all forms of energy obey the laws of physics. Therefore, familiarity with basic physical concepts that govern energy propagation, reflection, absorption, and transmission through various media contributes to an understanding of information security risk. Moreover, this understanding can enable estimates of the

[26]https://www.osha.gov/dts/osta/otm/new_noise/.

vulnerability to information compromise in electromagnetic, acoustic, and optical attack scenarios.

Energy is transmitted via waves, and wave motion is described by the wave amplitude, frequency, and phase. Although both electromagnetic energy and mechanical energy are transmitted via wave motion, the type of motion in each case differs. In the former, the electric and magnetic fields oscillate in mutually perpendicular planes that are themselves perpendicular to the direction of motion. In the case of mechanical energy that characterizes acoustic waves, the wave motion exhibits longitudinal behavior, where the direction of propagation is parallel to the wave motion.

Different types of sensors are used to detect and/or resolve electromagnetic and mechanical forms of energy. Electromagnetic energy at optical frequencies requires lenses to produce a focused image. Below infrared frequencies, electromagnetic energy requires antennae to detect propagating energy. Microphones are used to detect airborne acoustic energy, and accelerometers detect structure-borne energy. Power is defined as energy per unit time, and intensity is power per unit area. Sensors used to detect signal energy are respond to intensity.

Friis formula can be used to calculate the link margin, that is, the transmitted power as measured at the receiver between transmitting and receiving antennae. It can also be used to determine the vulnerability of a signal to detection. Typically one knows the distance between a signal transmitter and a potential detection site in order to calculate the signal-to-noise ratio at that site. Alternatively, one hopes to determine at what distance is P_r at the threshold of detection relative to the ambient noise.

When the source of energy is a point source, the intensity of the energy decreases with distance from the source at a rate corresponding to the inverse of the separation distance squared. A point source is a useful model for estimating the vulnerability to signal detection since many information security scenarios involve an energy source that qualifies as a point source.

All energy detection requires a sensor, and the resolution of all sensors that focus energy is limited by diffraction. Diffraction is an interference phenomenon that occurs when the wavelength of incident energy is comparable to the dimension of the sensor. The effect of diffraction is to cause incident energy to spread out. Diffraction occurs with all waves including sound waves, water waves, and electromagnetic waves such as visible light, X-rays, and radio waves.

Reference

[1] Pierce JR. Electrons, waves, and messages. Garden City, NY: Hanover House; 1956. p. 92–3.

4

Electromagnetic Waves

INTRODUCTION

Electromagnetic energy is all around us and is always present. Energy can be natural or man-made and originate from terrestrial or extraterrestrial sources. Energy encoded with information is radiated from electronic devices and constitutes the emanations targeted by an attacker. Such emanations are electromagnetic waves, and these waves obey the fundamental physical principles explained in this chapter. Therefore these principles govern the behavior of signals that require protection from compromise. The contention is that understanding these principles is helpful in developing effective information security strategies.

Many books and papers have been written on electromagnetic theory since 1864 when James Clerk Maxwell (1831–79), a British physicist, first formulated the fundamental equations of electromagnetism. Maxwell's equations were followed by experiments that proved the existence of electromagnetic waves by Heinrich Hertz (1857–94), a German physicist.[1] The details regarding the interaction of electromagnetic energy with materials are now well understood, and, furthermore, are crucial to a deeper understanding of the vulnerability to signal detection and ultimately information compromise.

The presentation in this book is admittedly very basic. Fundamental scientific concepts with relevant examples are provided that leverage the quantitative machinery discussed in previous chapters. The objective is to convey a high-level understanding of electromagnetic theory and other physical phenomena to facilitate a deeper understanding of the risk factors

---

[1]There is no shortage of textbooks on electromagnetic theory. Three very different versions are noted here to accommodate diverse tastes and backgrounds. Of these, the most accessible and directly relevant to information security is *Electrons, Waves and Messages* by John R. Pierce (Garden City, NY: Hanover House; 1956). Unfortunately this exceptionally well-written book is out of print, although there are copies available online as of this writing. A brilliant if significantly more technical treatment is *Electricity and Magnetism*, by Edward M. Purcell (Berkeley physics course, vol. 2. New York: McGraw Hill; 1965). Finally, the standard graduate text is *Classical Electrodynamics* by John D. Jackson (New York: John Wiley & Sons; 1975), and remains a classic in the field.

for information security threats. There is a huge volume of potentially relevant material that has been omitted from this discussion, and hopefully readers will forgive this concession to brevity.

ELECTROMAGNETIC FIELDS AND FLUX

Electromagnetic Fields

It was noted in Chapter 3 that electromagnetic waves were transverse waves. In other words, the direction of propagation is perpendicular to the mutually perpendicular planes of oscillation of the electric and magnetic fields. These fields represent the components of an electromagnetic wave of energy. Fig. 4.1 illustrates an electromagnetic wave in action.[2]

Electric and magnetic fields are defined in terms of the forces they exert on static and moving test charges, respectively. Electric and magnetic fields are vector quantities so each of them possesses a magnitude and direction. Examples of vector forces abound, and lines corresponding to the force they exert are a convenient way of visually representing them. A higher density of lines translates to a bigger force. These forces affect signal transmission, absorption, and reflection and hence information security.

Electric fields exert forces on charged particles, and so vectors are handy to characterize the field direction and magnitude. Magnetic fields do not directly exert forces on charged particles except if the particle is moving perpendicular to the field.[3] However, changing magnetic fields generate electric fields, which in turn exert such forces. This is one of the key results of Maxwell's equations discussed later in this chapter.

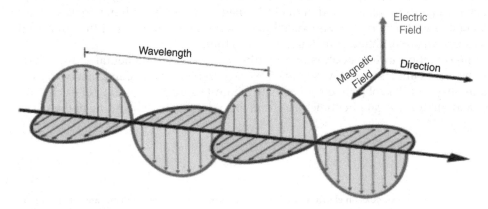

FIGURE 4.1   An electromagnetic wave.

[2]http://www.srh.noaa.gov/jetstream/remote/remote_intro.htm.
[3]This is an example of a so-called "apparent force" because it acts only in response to motion. Another and perhaps more familiar example is centrifugal force, which acts on bodies that are moving in a circle.

An electric field is associated with both static and moving charges, whereas magnetic fields result *only* from moving charges, that is, currents. The notion of movement is more nuanced than one might expect since motion depends on the reference frame of the observer. This statement is worth additional commentary.

Consider an observer who is stationary and a car passes this person at 60 miles/h. Clearly there is motion by the vehicle. If physical evidence is required, if the stationary individual were holding a well-calibrated speed gun aimed at the vehicle, the gun would measure the car's speed to be 60 miles/h to within the precision of the instrument.

Now consider the case when the observer is traveling at 60 miles/h in the same direction as the moving vehicle. The observer aims his or her gun at the vehicle. This time the vehicle will appear to be motionless *relative to the observer*. Believe it or not this discussion has profound relevance to electromagnetic theory. Electric and magnetic fields are actually equivalent constructs viewed from different reference frames. This is a rather flippant statement whose brevity is disproportionate to the magnitude of its implications.

As a simple extension of the moving automobile example, consider an individual in reference frame F who observes a charge moving in reference frame F'. He or she will observe both an electric and a magnetic field since the charge will be moving and thereby produce a current. Now consider the same observer in the reference frame of the moving charge. In reference frame F' the charge appears stationary so only an electric field is present and therefore no magnetic field will be observed.

Special relativity is needed to fully explain the relationship between electric and magnetic fields. In this book, electric and magnetic fields will be treated as separate entities, noting their interrelationship is explicitly defined through Maxwell's equations. In fact, the very designation of an electric or magnetic field is dependent on the frame of reference.

This section concludes with a list of physical quantities and their respective symbols that are used throughout the remainder of the book and will be explained as they are introduced:

D, electric flux density = $\varepsilon_0 E$
E, electric field in volts per meter
B, magnetic flux density = $\mu_0 H$
H, magnetic field in amperes per meter
ε_0, free space permittivity = 8.85×10^{-12} F/m
μ_0, free space permeability = $4\pi \times 10^{-7}$ H/m

Electric and Magnetic Flux

As noted earlier, the strength of an electric or magnetic field is proportional to the density of their respective lines of force in a region of space. These lines of force correspond to electric and magnetic flux, a physical quantity that is central to electromagnetic phenomena as described by Maxwell's equations.

A definition of flux is introduced right away since it is the time rate of change of electric and magnetic flux that results in the generation of magnetic and electric fields, respectively. There is some justification for this economical treatment since it is an efficient way of enabling simple calculations relating to information security.

The electric flux ψ across a surface of area A that is perpendicular to the direction of the electric field E is defined as follows:

$$\psi = \varepsilon EA \tag{4.1}$$

where ε is the relative electric permittivity or dielectric constant. In words electric flux is the total number of electric field lines crossing a surface of area A.

In exact analogy, the magnetic flux ϕ across a surface of area A that is perpendicular to the magnetic field B is defined as follows:

$$\phi = \mu BA \tag{4.2}$$

where μ is the permittivity of free space. Magnetic flux is the total number of magnetic field lines crossing a surface of area A.

The concept of flux is crucial to understanding electromagnetic phenomena and is therefore important to understanding the fundamentals of information security. An analogy with a more intuitive physical quantity may be helpful.[4]

Consider an imaginary rectangular loop or surface of area A. Water is flowing across the plane of this loop with velocity v. For simplicity let us assume the water is flowing perpendicular to the plane of A, although recognize this is a special case since the water could be flowing at an angle to the loop. For this particular geometry, the flux of water across the imaginary surface is the volume of water per unit time v that passes across the cross-sectional area A. So the flux of water $\Phi_w = vA$.

Importantly, what is being characterized by flux is the number of "things," for example, water, particles, bananas, automobiles electric fields, and magnetic fields, that cross an arbitrary boundary per unit time.

Now suppose the plane of the loop or surface is oriented at an angle parallel to the direction of the flow of water. In that case no water is flowing across the plane of the loop. Therefore, the flux as defined earlier is zero. Perpendicular and parallel orientations of the loop relative to the direction of flow are the two simplest geometries that pertain to flux.

In general, the scenario is not so convenient. In fact, the purpose of the discussion on vectors and surface integrals is to address more complicated geometries that arise in information security scenarios.

The more general problem is to calculate the flux when the plane of the loop is oriented at some arbitrary angle with respect to the direction of "stuff" flowing across a surface. In scenarios pertaining to information security, the flux is typically the lines of force of a magnetic or electric field. Moreover, the magnitude of the force exerted by these fields is proportional to the density of the electric or magnetic field lines that "flow" across a surface.

Fig. 4.2 is helpful in visualizing the two extreme cases of flux. Two surfaces are depicted that are perpendicular and parallel to the direction of the incident flux.[5] In the former the flux is maximum and in the latter the flux is zero.

It is probably becoming apparent that the flux of electric and magnetic fields is somehow relevant to electromagnetic signal detection. However, several concepts are still lacking.

[4] http://kestrel.nmt.edu/~raymond/books/radphys/book2/book2.html?sa=X&ved=0CC4Q9QEwDDgUahUKEw japbbuzv7GAhVllR4KHXfDAPY.
[5] http://betterexplained.com/articles/flux/.

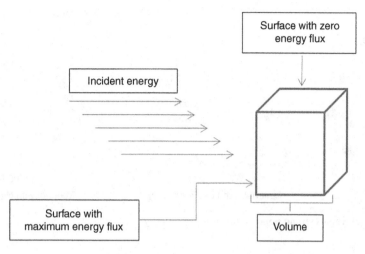

FIGURE 4.2   Maximum and minimum flux of a vector field across a surface.

Specifically, the concept of a vector is introduced followed closely by a discussion of surface integrals. These enable general calculations of the time rate of change of electric and magnetic flux, which help explain the limits of signal detection.

When any medium that consists of electric charges is placed in an electric field, the charges therein align according to the orientation and strength of the applied field. In general, the charges become polarized or slightly separated in accordance with the orientation of the applied field.

Note that the applied electric field is typically oscillating at some specified frequency and therefore the polarization or charge separation will change in response. But not all materials and the charges therein will respond in the same way to the force exerted by the applied electric field. The permittivity of a medium indicates the magnitude of polarization that exists within a material as a result of an applied electric field.[6]

In Fig. 4.3, an electric field resulted in the polarization of the positive and negative charges.[7] The same-magnitude electric field causes the charges in one material to polarize more than the other as evidenced by the difference in the separation of positive and negative charges. The more polarized material is said to have a higher permittivity.

An equally valid interpretation of the same effect is illustrated in Fig. 4.4. The low electric flux density in the material on the left causes the same polarization as the material on the right which has a high electric flux density. Therefore, the material on the left has high permittivity since the same polarization was achieved with a lower flux density.

The *relative* permittivity of a material is known as the dielectric constant and this term may be more familiar to readers. Relative permittivity is the permittivity relative to a vacuum. The dielectric constant of a vacuum is defined to be unity, and for air it is $1.00058986 \pm 0.00000050$. So the relative permittivity of air is roughly equivalent to that of a vacuum.

---

[6]The term "relative" here means relative to the permittivity of a vacuum, ε_0.
[7]http://www.sharetechnote.com/html/RF_Handbook_Permittivity.html.

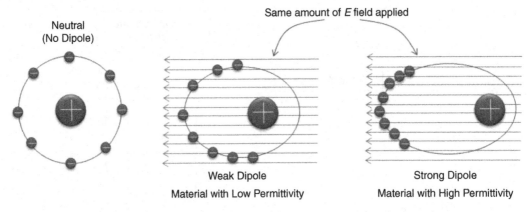

FIGURE 4.3   Weak versus strong polarization and permittivity.

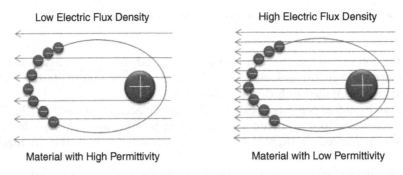

FIGURE 4.4   Low and high electric flux density per unit charge versus permittivity.

VECTORS

Vector Basics

Armed with a basic understanding of flux, a slight digression on vectors is warranted that will prove helpful later. Simple vector geometry will enable calculations of the normal component of electric and magnetic flux across surfaces of arbitrary orientation.

Let us digress even further and review the basics of trigonometry, which is used to resolve forces into its vector components.

Consider a right triangle, which is defined as a triangle where one of the angles is 90 degrees. The cosine of an angle θ is defined as the ratio of the length of the side of the triangle adjacent to θ relative to the length of the hypotenuse. The sine of the angle is defined as the ratio of the length of the side opposite to θ relative to the length of the hypotenuse.

Refer to Fig. 4.5, where A is the side adjacent to the angle θ, B is the side opposite to θ, and C is the hypotenuse. The 90-degree angle is between sides A and B and is indicated by two perpendicular lines.

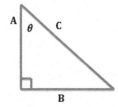

FIGURE 4.5 A right triangle.

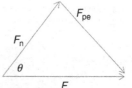

FIGURE 4.6 Components of forces using vectors.

The cosine and sine of θ are A/C and B/C, respectively. For the interested reader, the tangent of θ is defined as sin θ/cos θ = (B/C)/(A/C) = B/A and the cotangent is its inverse A/B.

Fortunately, vectors are relatively simple constructs that are used to represent the magnitude and direction of fields/forces and their vector components. A vector is any quantity that has both magnitude and direction. In contrast, a scalar quantity has only magnitude. Speed is a scalar quantity since it specifies only how fast an object is moving. By contrast, velocity is a vector quantity since it specifies how fast an object is moving as well as its direction of movement.

An arrow is often used to represent a vector where the arrowhead is pointing in the direction of the applied force. When attempting to diagram fields or equivalently lines of force pursuant to calculations of flux across a surface, it is useful to apply the following prescription.

Let F be a vector oriented at some arbitrary angle θ with respect to a surface, which represents the lines of force across that surface. The goal is to determine the component of F that is normal to that surface, and to express that component in terms of F and θ.

- Specify a vector that is perpendicular (i.e., normal) to a given surface, F_n.
- Draw a vector perpendicular to F_n called F_{pe}. F_{pe} originates from the arrowhead of F_n.
- Draw a resultant vector F, which is the vector sum of F_n and F_{pe}.
- The normal component of F is F_n and is used to calculate flux across the surface and can be expressed in terms of F and θ as follows:

$$F_n = F\cos\theta$$

Therefore, the goal of expressing F_n in terms of F and θ has been accomplished. As an aside, note that the F_{pe} equals F sin θ. Fig. 4.6 shows a vector F oriented in some arbitrary direction relative to an imaginary surface, and F_n is pointing in a direction normal to that surface. F is resolved into components F_n and F_{pe}.

To reiterate, the flux of "stuff" flowing across a surface is only the component of the flow that is perpendicular to the surface. As a preview of what is to come, in this case the stuff of interest is the electric and magnetic field lines of force.

It is now possible to address the scenario where the direction of the flow of stuff is not perpendicular to a given surface, but is oriented at some arbitrary angle with respect to the surface. The goal is to determine the perpendicular component of the flow, which will lead to a calculation of flux. Fig. 4.7 illustrates this scenario.[5]

Let us apply this prescription once again in order to find the total flux of an electric field across a surface, where the flux density E is at an arbitrary angle θ with respect to E_n,

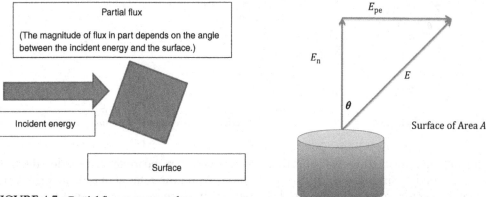

FIGURE 4.7   **Partial flux across a surface.**

FIGURE 4.8   **The component of the electric field E normal to a surface of area A.**

the normal to a surface of area A. Obviously things would be simpler if the angle between E and E_n was zero degrees. But life is not always so cooperative, hence this interlude on vector geometry.

Refer to Fig. 4.8. Let the vector E specify the magnitude and direction of an incident electric field. Since by definition the flux across a surface consists only of the component of the field that is normal to that surface, the first objective is to resolve E into its relevant components. The sought-after expression appears after applying the prescription and then merely turning the crank as follows.

First draw a vector that is normal to the surface E_n. Next draw a vector perpendicular to E_n, which is E_{pe} in Fig. 4.8. This configuration forms a right triangle. Simple trigonometry can now be used to express E_n in terms of E as follows:

$$E_n = E \cos\theta \qquad (4.3)$$

Again, E_n is the component of the vector field that is normal to the surface. Therefore the flux of E across a surface of area A as defined by (4.1) equals $A\varepsilon E_n$ or equivalently $A\varepsilon E \cos\theta$.

The previous discussion partially prepares the reader for calculations involving electric and magnetic flux. Two more concepts must be presented in order to leverage Maxwell's equations, which in turn will facilitate estimates of the vulnerability to electromagnetic signal compromises.

The Surface Integral

The previous discussion assumed that the magnitude of the flux of stuff across a surface was constant. This might not always be the case. Therefore, what is required is a means of addressing situations when the direction of the field is not perpendicular to the plane of the surface and/or the magnitude of the electric or magnetic field is not constant. In fact, the normal component of the incident electric or magnetic field could be changing if the surface is not flat.

With respect to incident fields that are not perpendicular to a surface of interest a convenient pattern has emerged. One can always write an arbitrary vector in terms of its component that is normal to the surface. Such an expression is presented in (4.3). This representation leads to a general expression for the flux of a field E across an arbitrarily oriented surface of area A, or $AE_n \cos \theta$.

To deal with nonconstant surfaces, a trick is employed that is fundamental to the calculus. The surface is divided into infinitesimally small mini-surfaces over which the electric field is assumed to be locally constant. Each of these mini-surfaces is represented by a mini-area dA.

One adds up all the mini-areas to yield the total flux across the entire surface. Since the orientation of the mini-areas might not be constant, the addition is accomplished by integrating with respect to dA over the surface. Hence, the name "surface integral" or sometimes "area integral" is used.

The sole purpose of the surface integral in this context is to calculate the flux of the electric or magnetic field lines of force across a surface. Note that *how* one divides the surface into constituent pieces is important in the calculation of flux. Fig. 4.9 depicts a surface integral.[8]

In general, the prescription for calculating electric or magnetic flux across an arbitrary surface is as follows[9]:

1. Divide the surface into mini-areas.
2. Check if the flux through any of the surface is zero.
3. Find an expression for $E \cdot \hat{n}$, where $\hat{n}$ is a unit vector that points in a direction perpendicular to the area in question and $E \cdot \hat{n}$ is the dot product of the vectors E and $\hat{n}$.[10] Note that the method to calculate flux for magnetic fields is identical to the one for electric fields.
4. Check that $E \cdot \hat{n}$ is not constant. If it is constant, it can be pulled out of the integral.
5. Find dA for each portion of the surface.
6. Set the correct limits on the integral.
7. Solve the integral.

Some simple examples are illustrative of the technique.[10] The first is to calculate the flux of an electric field from within a cube. The magnitude of the electric field E is constant and perpendicular to each side of the cube. This condition implies there is a unit vector normal to each side of the cube $\hat{n}$. Each side of the cube is of length L as illustrated in Fig. 4.10.[10]

Specifically, the electric field E is pointing in the plus and minus x direction, plus and minus y direction, and the plus and minus z direction. In other words, the E field for the x, y, and z directions is $\pm E\hat{x}$, $\pm E\hat{y}$, and $\pm E\hat{z}$.

Therefore the flux is parallel to the unit normal vector for each of the six sides (refer to Fig. 4.7). Hence, $E \cdot \hat{n}$ is constant for each face since $\hat{n}$ in the x, y, and z directions is parallel to E in each direction, the magnitude of a unit vector is unity, and the cosine of 0 degrees is unity.

---

[8]http://hyperphysics.phy-astr.gsu.edu/hbase/intare.html.
[9]http://web.mit.edu/8.02T/www/materials/StudyGuide/Flux.pdf.
[10]The dot product of two vectors A and B by definition equals the magnitude of A times the magnitude of B times the cosine of the angle between them. The dot product of two vector quantities yields a scalar quantity and hence has only magnitude and not direction.

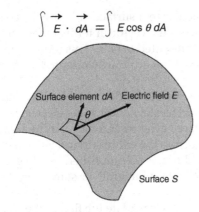

$$\int \vec{E} \cdot \vec{dA} = \int E \cos \theta \, dA$$

FIGURE 4.9   **Surface integral.**

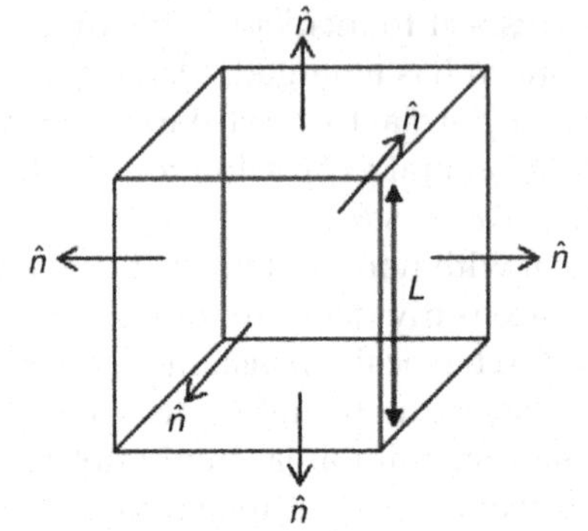

FIGURE 4.10   **Unit vectors that are normal to each face of a cube.**

Therefore, the dot product of E and the unit vector $\hat{n}$ equals E for each face of the cube, and the flux through each face is E times the area of each face L^2. Since there are six sides to a cube, the total flux across the surface of the cube is given by the following:

$$\text{Total Flux of the Electric Field } E \text{ Across a Cube} = 6L^2E$$

Now suppose the total flux of an electric field E from within a sphere is required. This scenario is depicted in Fig. 4.11 where a quadrant of the sphere is shown. Here the field is everywhere pointing radially outward.[9]

The radius of the sphere is R. Therefore, the normal vector for each infinitesimally small mini-tile of area dA, that is, the shaded area in the figure, also points radially outward.

In this case the magnitude of the field is given by $1/r^2$. So $E = (1/r^2)\hat{r}$. In other words, E is pointing radially outwards and has a magnitude of $1/r^2$. Also, in the case of a sphere $\hat{n} = \hat{r}$. Therefore $E \cdot \hat{n} = 1/r^2$.

The problem is actually easier than it appears. $E \cdot \hat{n}$ for a given mini-tile is constant since it is measured only at the surface and equals $1/R^2$. But we must add up the contribution of the flux from all the mini-tiles over the entire surface by integrating over the surface. As noted earlier, each mini-tile contributes $1/R^2$ to the magnitude of the flux and the total surface area of the sphere is $4\pi R^2$. Therefore, the flux across the surface is as follows:

$$\text{Total Flux of } E \text{ Across a Sphere} = \frac{1}{R^2}(4\pi R^2)E = 4\pi E$$

One additional example illustrates the benefits of exploiting symmetry in calculating flux. In this case the flux of an E field of magnitude $E\hat{r}$ across the surface of a cylinder of length L and radius r is examined. The magnitude of the field is changing with direction but its direction is always pointing radially outward from the line through the center of the cylinder that runs along its length. Fig. 4.12 illustrates the scenario.[9]

In this problem the results of the previous two examples are used for the calculation. Although the magnitude of the field is in general changing, the flux is calculated only at the surface. So the magnitude of the flux is the same at every point on the cylinder surface.

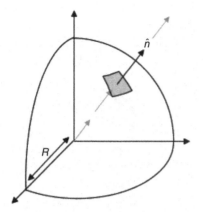

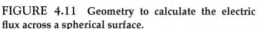

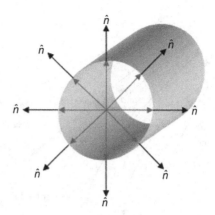

FIGURE 4.11 Geometry to calculate the electric flux across a spherical surface.

FIGURE 4.12 Geometry for calculating the flux across the curved surface of a cylinder.

Therefore, the magnitude of $E \cdot \hat{n}$ is just E since the unit vector $\hat{n}$, which is everywhere normal to the surface (except the ends), is constant and parallel to the unit vector $\hat{r}$, and the cosine of 0 degrees in the dot product is 1. In other words, $E\hat{r}$ is parallel to $\hat{n}$.

The flux through the ends of the cylinder is zero. Therefore the total flux of the electric field across the curved surface of a cylinder equals E times the surface area of the cylinder minus the ends as follows:

Total Flux of E Across the Curved Surface of a Cylinder $= 2\pi rLE$

It is important to note that these examples were chosen for their symmetry which enabled simple analyses. If the magnitude of the vector field indeed changed as a function of position on the surface, that is, it has changed with respect to the angle θ, an actual integration would be required rather than a straightforward multiplication. Integration was invented to address these types of scenarios.

The Line Integral

Calculating the flux of vector fields is essential to understand Maxwell's equations. This is because Maxwell's equations specify that the time rate of change in electric/magnetic flux across a surface equals the line integral of the magnetic/electric field around the boundary of that surface. Therefore, it is also helpful to recognize a line integral and understand its purpose. Fig. 4.13 depicts a line integral along a designated path A–B in a vector field E.[8]

The line integral measures the total effect of a vector or scalar field along a specific path where the magnitude and/or direction of the vector can change. Because it involves a dot product, the result of this vector operation is a scalar quantity.

A simple example illustrates the concept. Consider a current flowing in a straight wire. The reader will soon see that Maxwell's fourth equation specifies that the magnitude of a magnetic field along a given path in space equals the currents that are enclosed within that path. The left-hand side of the equation, which yields the magnitude of the magnetic field, is the

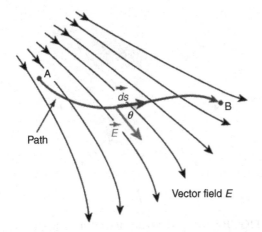

FIGURE 4.13 **Line integral along a path in a vector field.**

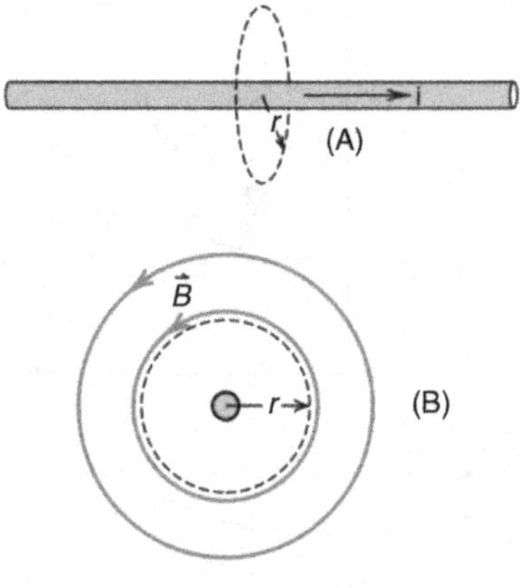

FIGURE 4.14 (A) Current-carrying wire; (B) magnetic field surrounding a current-carrying wire (current is flowing out of the page).

line integral of B evaluated along a closed path, where dl represents an infinitesimal length element of that path.

In other words, the line integral adds the component of B that is tangential to each infinitesimal length of the closed path along the entire length of the path:

$$\oint \vec{B} \cdot d\vec{\ell} = \mu_0 i_{\text{enclosed}}$$

The clever reader will realize that the key to this method is that B is being calculated incrementally; infinitesimally small pieces of the total length l are added piecewise to produce the final result, thereby allowing for a calculation along any path irrespective of its shape.

The right-hand side of the equation specifies i_{enclosed} (also written as i_{enc}), which is the current encircled by the path used to evaluate the line integral, and μ_0 is the magnetic permeability of free space.

Fig. 4.14A depicts the current in the wire flowing to the right, and Fig. 4.14B shows the magnetic field surrounding the wire with the current flowing out of the page.[11]

To apply Ampere's Law, draw a closed circular path of radius r around the wire as shown in Fig. 4.14A and B. The path is centered on the wire such that each infinitesimal section of the path dl is parallel to B. Therefore the dot product of the vectors B and dl produces a scalar quantity. B is constant along the circular path and so the integral of B with respect to dl is just the circumference of the circular path or $2\pi r$.

Therefore, by evaluating this simple line integral one arrives at the magnitude of the magnetic field as follows:

$$B = \frac{\mu_0 i}{2\pi r}$$

[11]http://www.physics2000.com/PDF/Text/Ch_32_MAXWELLs_EQUATIONS.pdf.

Note that the situation would be different if B varied along the path of integration. In that case a more complex integration would be required.

Understanding the physical implications of this expression is the point of this exercise. Ampere's Law specifies that the magnetic field scales directly with the electric current and inversely with the distance from a current source.

Imagine if a long wire was conducting an electric current encoded with confidential information and radiating the fields associated with that current into the surrounding space. Ampere's Law could be used to calculate the field generated by that current source and that result in conjunction with other data could be used to determine the minimum distance required for signal detection.

MAXWELL'S EQUATIONS

Introduction

In this section it will hopefully become clear why so much attention has been paid to the concept of flux. The end game is to demonstrate the linkage between Maxwell's equations and information security.

As mentioned earlier, all electromagnetic phenomena can be described by Maxwell's four equations. It seems remarkable that four compact expressions describe all electromagnetic phenomena but it is true.

Fig. 4.15 shows the spectrum of electromagnetic radiation that extends from "DC to Daylight" as the saying goes. It also shows the relationship between temperature and wavelength, a relationship that is important to thermal noise, which was introduced in the previous chapter.[12]

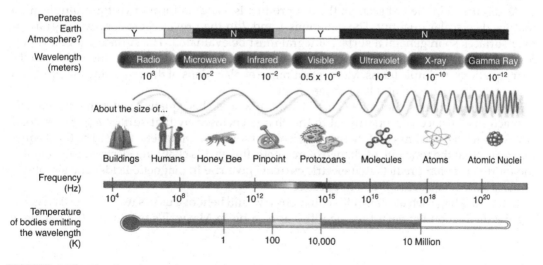

FIGURE 4.15 The electromagnetic spectrum.

[12]http://mynasadata.larc.nasa.gov/science-processes/electromagnetic-diagram/?sa=X&ved=0CBgQ9QEwAWoV ChMI2OyJupL3xgIVCnQ-Ch39RgYc.

Maxwell's equations can be written in differential or integral form, but they have equivalent meaning. The differential representation requires an understanding of the divergence (div) and curl operators, which somehow seem less intuitive than an integral. Therefore, the integral form of Maxwell's equations is used in this book. However, a short discussion on the divergence and curl operators is included in Appendix A for the interested reader as are Maxwell's equations in differential form.

Maxwell's four equations in integral form can be written as follows:

1. $\oint E \cdot dA = \dfrac{q_{enc}}{\varepsilon_0}$

2. $\oint B \cdot dA = 0$

3. $\oint E \cdot ds = -\dfrac{d\Phi_B}{dt}$

4. $\oint B \cdot ds = \mu_0 \varepsilon_0 \dfrac{d\Phi_E}{dt} + \mu_0 i_{enc}$

These equations may appear daunting, but they can be explained using the definitions and concepts provided above. Their inclusion in a discussion on information security arises from the fact that they explain the behavior of all electromagnetic phenomena, which includes the fields associated with signals targeted by attackers.

With respect to terminology and symbols, dA is a vector representing an infinitesimally small sub-area of a surface that encloses a given volume. As before, the big dot between dA and the electric and magnetic flux densities denotes the dot product of two vectors.

As discussed in the last section, the dot product is a special form of vector multiplication that yields a scalar quantity. The equations 1 and 2 in the previous list specify integrations over surfaces so in general a surface integral must be evaluated. The surface integral is performed with respect to dA. The first order of business is to state the meaning of Maxwell's four equations in simple terms. More quantitative explanations of their meaning are provided separately for each equation later in the chapter.

The first equation is known as Gauss' Law.[13] In words, this equation states that the electric flux across a surface is proportional to the charge enclosed by that surface q_{enc}. The second equation in brief specifies that there are no isolated sources of magnetic fields. The third equation states that the time rate of change of magnetic flux yields changing electric fields. Finally, the fourth equation predicts that electric currents give rise to magnetic fields. The simplicity of these statements belies their significance.

Before tackling each of Maxwell's equations it would behoove us to say a few words regarding the distinction between the quantities appearing in Maxwell's equations: the magnetic

---

[13]Karl Friedrich Gauss (1777–1855) was a German physicist and mathematician who made some of the most significant contributions to science. His research resulted in seminal contributions to mathematics, optics, physics, differential geometry, mechanics, astronomy, and geophysics.

flux density B, the magnetic field H, the electric displacement vector D, and the electric flux density E. These are four quantities that are sometimes used rather casually in speaking of electromagnetic phenomena but it is worth explaining their meaning in brief.

These terms have historically been a source of confusion as documented in at least one academic paper [1]. Some books merely define flux in terms of E and H, assume the fields exist in a vacuum, and do not bother to explain the distinctions between these quantities. However, a more pedagogical approach is taken here.

The electric field E arises from a distribution of electric charges. Consider the case when there are charges in a vacuum followed by the case of an electric field incident on a material with charges, typically referred to as a dielectric. The point is to describe the resulting electric field in each case.

If charges exist in a vacuum, then there is clearly no contribution to the electric field from the material itself since it has no electric charges. On the other hand, if there is an incident electric field E interacting with a dielectric, E will exert a force on the charges in the material and cause them to move slightly. The charges become polarized in response to E, and the resulting charge configuration has its own electric field.

The polarization can be described by a vector quantity P, the polarization density, which describes the average magnitude and direction of this configuration of charges. The dielectric constant ε is proportional to P. Moreover, the electric displacement vector D is proportionate to E, where the constant of proportionality is the dielectric constant ε. To summarize, $D = \varepsilon E$, and E is a function of P.

D represents the total electric field inside and outside a material and its magnitude derives from two sources: the configuration of so-called bound charges that become polarized by E plus the presence of any free charges. In free space, that is, in the absence of matter, $\varepsilon = 1$ so $D = E$.

The situation for the magnetic quantities B and H is analogous but not equivalent. Magnetic fields arise from moving charges, that is, currents. Bound and free currents are real quantities, where each give rise to magnetic fields. Bound currents are those that result from the motion of orbiting electrons or the inherent "spin" of nuclei in materials.

Such phenomena are what cause certain materials to have magnetic properties and thereby explain properties of certain materials such as ferromagnetism. Free currents are moving charges of the kind that move through wires, which also result in magnetic fields. Fields so generated are the targets of attackers since they can be encoded with information.

The total magnetic field that exists inside and outside materials must account for the field resulting from both free and bound currents. In analogy with electric fields, H can be defined in terms of the field B and a vector quantity resulting from bound currents M. M is known as the magnetization or magnetic moment per unit volume. Therefore H relates to the presence of free current and B relates to the total current, bound plus free. However, the average macroscopic magnetic field inside materials is B and not H.

B is in fact proportional to H, where the constant of proportionality is given by the magnetic permeability μ, which is directly related to M. In free space $B = H$ since $\mu = 1$.

In common parlance, the *electric and magnetic field intensities or strengths* are designated as E and H, respectively. The electric and magnetic field intensities correspond to the density of field lines. The total flux is therefore the number of field lines crossing a surface of some area and which are normal, that is, perpendicular, to the surface.

II. SCIENTIFIC FUNDAMENTALS

Using common terminology the *electric and magnetic flux densities* are designated as D and B, respectively. As noted earlier, $D = \varepsilon E$ and $B = \mu H$, where ε is the electric permittivity and μ is the magnetic permeability of a material. The *total electric or magnetic flux* crossing a surface of area A is a key parameter in Maxwell's equations. These quantities are obtained by multiplying the flux densities by the area of the surface they cross.

Therefore the *total electric and magnetic flux are given by εEA and μHA, respectively.* Electric flux is specified in units of volt meters, and magnetic flux is specified in units of weber or in derived units, volt seconds. Flux density units are specified as weber per square meter, gauss, or tesla. Appendix B provides units of electromagnetism.

Maxwell's First Equation

Some effort has been expended thus far to explain the concept of flux, and this effort will not be in vain. Electric and magnetic flux are central to Maxwell's equations and an appreciation of their relevance yields insights into a broad class of information security scenarios.

Suppose a surface consists of vector elements dA. Each element represents an infinitesimally small area and collectively they comprise the entire surface.

Let's simplify the scenario such that E is constant across a surface of area A and is everywhere perpendicular to the surface. In that case the total electric flux ψ across the surface equals εEA. Fig. 4.16 illustrates the flux of E across two surfaces (it can be shown that the flux across each surface is identical).[14]

Maxwell's first equation, also known as Gauss' Law, states that the total electric flux across a surface equals the total charge Q that exists inside the volume enclosed by that surface. Therefore $\varepsilon EA = Q$.

The implication of Gauss' Law is there can be no electric field in the absence of electric charges. If no charges are present within the surface that encloses a volume, the flux of E across the surface must be zero. Fig. 4.17 illustrates the geometry of Gauss' Law.[15]

Maxwell's first equation can be summarized as follows: *The source of electric flux across a surface derives from charges within the volume enclosed by that surface.*

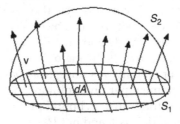

FIGURE 4.16   Flux of a vector field across two surfaces S_1 and S_2.

[14]http://pwg.gsfc.nasa.gov/Electric/-E24-Flux.htm?sa=X&ved=0CDIQ9QEwDmoVChMI0sqg5vr-xgIVS2g-Ch2SAwfp.

[15]http://hyperphysics.phy-astr.gsu.edu/hbase/electric/gaulaw.html?sa=X&ved=0CBgQ9QEwAWoVChMI_tmN29_-xgIVARseCh1QKQHw.

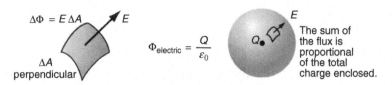

$$\Delta\Phi = E\,\Delta A \qquad E$$

$$\Delta A$$
perpendicular

$$\Phi_{electric} = \frac{Q}{\varepsilon_0}$$

$$Q \qquad E$$

The sum of the flux is proportional of the total charge enclosed.

FIGURE 4.17 Maxwell's first equation, Gauss' Law.

Maxwell's Second Equation

Maxwell's second equation is similar in form to the first but its result is profoundly different. Because of its symmetry with Gauss' Law it is also referred to as the magnetic equivalent of Gauss' Law. The same vector geometry and surface integration apply here, which are invoked as required based on the geometry of the scenario.

Maxwell's second equation states that the surface integral of the magnetic field over a closed surface is zero. In other words, the flux of the magnetic field across any surface that encloses a volume is always zero. Recall the identical geometry existed in Maxwell's first equation. But in that case the flux of the electric field across a surface enclosing a volume was proportional to the charges inside that volume.

If the flux of electric and magnetic fields across the surfaces of enclosed volumes were identical, one would expect the source of the flux in Maxwell's second equation to be a magnetic charge. However, no such charges exist, and therefore the flux of the magnetic field is zero. In other words, magnetic charge cannot accumulate at any point in space.

Moreover, for each volume element in space there are an identical number of magnetic field lines entering and exiting that volume since magnetic lines of force cannot originate from within a closed volume.

Fig. 4.18 shows the magnetic flux across a closed surface, that is, a surface that completely encloses a volume with no holes. There is no flux across the surface from within the volume enclosed by that surface, and every field line that enters the closed surface must also exit the closed surface.[4] If the flux lines were not thus, a source of magnetic fields could exist as a stand-alone entity.

For example, the south pole of a magnet is exactly as strong as the north pole. Moreover, free-floating south poles without accompanying north poles, that is, magnetic monopoles, do not exist according to Maxwell's second equation.[16]

Therefore it is not possible to break a magnet into two pieces and isolate its north and south poles. The same is *not* true for electric or gravitational fields, where the total electric charge or mass can accumulate in a volume of space.[17]

---

[16]In 1975 it was announced that a magnetic monopole had been identified. I recall my physics professor, Francis Low, remarking to our class of undergraduates taking quantum mechanics, "Don't believe it!" (Price PB, Shirk EK, Osborne WZ, Pinsky LS. Phys Rev Lett 35:487.)

[17]https://en.wikipedia.org/wiki/Gauss%27s_law_for_magnetism.

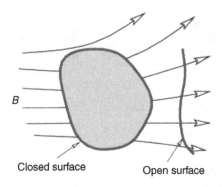

FIGURE 4.18   Maxwell's second equation and flux across closed and open surfaces.

The magnetic field of the earth at the surface is about 0.5 G or 10^{-4} T. Like any magnetic field, the flux lines terminate in the earth's north and south poles. These magnetic lines of force are what cause a compass needle to deflect in the direction of magnetic north. Fig. 4.19 illustrates the magnetic flux lines of the earth.[18]

Maxwell's second equation can be summarized as follows: *There are no sources of magnetic charges.*

Maxwell's Third Equation

Maxwell's third equation describes the generation of electric fields from the time rate of change of magnetic flux. This equation describes magnetic induction, where an electromotive force (EMF) or electric potential difference is generated by changing magnetic flux.

Induction is crucially important to information security since it explains the workings of antennae, the sensor used to transmit and receive electromagnetic signals, as well as certain noise coupling mechanisms. Hence, this equation has relevance to the analysis of risk for a number of information security scenarios as well as many other phenomena in science and engineering.

In words, Maxwell's third equation states that the time rate of change of the magnetic flux across the surface defined by a boundary produces a varying electric field whose magnitude equals the line integral around that boundary.

Specifically, consider a surface of area A that is oriented at 90 degrees to the magnetic field H. The total magnetic flux across the surface equals μHA. Magnetic flux is often designated as the Greek lower case letter phi (ϕ) and electric flux is represented by the Greek lower case letter psi (ψ).

According to Maxwell's third equation, also known as Faraday's Law, for a surface of area A and circumference S,[19,20]

$$\int E \cdot ds = \mu A \left(\frac{dH}{dt} \right) = -\frac{d\phi}{dt} \tag{4.4}$$

[18]https://www.fhwa.dot.gov/publications/research/operations/its/06108/02a.cfm.

[19]Named after the British physicist, Michael Faraday (1791–1867).

[20]The minus sign reflects the fact that if an induced current flows, its direction is always such that it will oppose the change that produced it. This is a statement of Lenz's Law, which is really a manifestation of the conservation of energy.

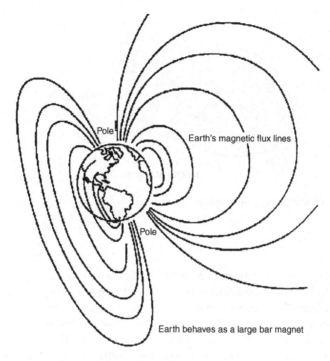

FIGURE 4.19 **The magnetic flux lines of the earth.**

It should be made clear that the boundary is not necessarily a physical boundary but can be any closed loop in space.

As noted earlier, Maxwell's third equation has significant implications to many disciplines including information security. For example, the changing magnetic flux associated with an electromagnetic signal incident on an antenna induces an oscillating electric field and corresponding voltage distribution along the antenna. This voltage is rectified, amplified, and demodulated to reconstruct the incident signal.

Fig. 4.20 illustrates Faraday's Law, which in a nutshell describes the generation of electric fields and resulting flow of currents due to the time rate of change of magnetic flux.[4]

Maxwell's third equation can be summarized as follows: *The time rate of change in magnetic flux produces changing electric fields.*

Maxwell's Fourth Equation

Maxwell's fourth equation, also known as Ampere's Law, describes the magnetic fields that result from currents in the form of time-varying electric flux plus moving charges.[21]

[21]Named after Andre-Marie Ampere (1775–1836), a French mathematician and physicist.

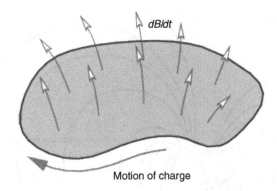

FIGURE 4.20   Maxwell's third equation, Faraday's Law.

It turns out there are two separate contributions to the magnetic field, which historically have been designated as the "conduction current" and "displacement current." The conduction current results from the presence of moving charges $i_{enclosed}$ that are enclosed by the surface. The displacement current is the time rate of change of electric flux. In other words, both moving charges and changing electric flux give rise to magnetic fields.

Imagine the same surface of area A and boundary circumference S introduced in the discussion of Maxwell's third equation. The electric field is assumed to be oriented at 90 degrees to the surface. Furthermore, the line integral of the field around the boundary of the surface is also calculated as before. However, in this case it is the *magnetic* field component that is being integrated around the boundary.

The total electric flux ψ across the surface equals $A\mu E$. The time rate of change of the electric flux is therefore expressed as follows:

$$A\left(\frac{dE}{dt}\right) = \frac{d\psi}{dt} \tag{4.5}$$

Maxwell's fourth equation in part states that the time rate of change of the total electric flux across a surface equals the line integral of the magnetic field around the boundary of that surface. Therefore the following is a partial expression of Maxwell's fourth equation:

$$\int B \cdot ds = \varepsilon A\left(\frac{dE}{dt}\right) = \frac{d\psi}{dt} \tag{4.6}$$

Recall moving charges or equivalently the current enclosed by the surface $i_{enclosed}$ contributes to the magnitude of the magnetic field. Therefore the complete expression for Maxwell's fourth equation accounts for the presence of moving charges enclosed by the surface as well as changing electric flux across the surface:

$$\int B \cdot ds = \frac{d\psi}{dt} + i_{enclosed} \tag{4.7}$$

FIGURE 4.21   Maxwell's fourth equation, Ampere's Law.

Maxwell's fourth equation can be summarized as follows: *Electric currents and the time rate of change in electric flux give rise to changing magnetic fields.*

A calculation of the magnetic field resulting from current flowing in a long wire is illustrative of scenarios encountered in information security. Fig. 4.21 shows the magnetic field due to the presence of a current-carrying wire, which is identical to the scenario depicted in Fig. 4.14A and B.[22]

A simple calculation of the magnetic field at the center of a circular loop of current-carrying wire follows. The displacement current $d\psi/dt$ is assumed to be zero since there are no changing electric fields hence, it does not contribute to the magnetic field intensity. The radius of the loop is a, and the current in the wire is I amperes. From Ampere's Law, the infinitesimal magnetic field dB (not to be confused with decibels!) at the center of the loop arising from an infinitesimal portion of the wire dl is as follows:

$$dB = 10^{-7}\left(\frac{I}{a^2}\right)dl$$

The magnetic field at the center of the loop arises from the contribution of the individual elements of the loop, which is determined by integrating dB from 0 to $2\pi a$:

$$B = 10^{-7}\left(\frac{I}{a^2}\right)\int dl = 2\pi \times 10^{-7}\frac{I}{a}\,\mathrm{Wb/m^2}$$

The field is perpendicular to the page and directed outward.

---

[22]https://en.wikipedia.org/wiki/Electric_current?sa=X&ved=0CBoQ9QEwAmoVChMIp6uw3pn_xgIVARseCh1QKQHw.

Calculation Using Maxwell's Equations

Simple calculations of the electric and magnetic fields using Maxwell's equations are illustrative of their utility and point to a seminal discovery by Maxwell.[23]

Consider a plane electromagnetic wave propagating in free space from left to right with a velocity v. A plane wave is one whose physical dimensions remain constant as it propagates from the source. Electromagnetic waves in the far field of a source are plane waves. In contrast, electromagnetic waves in proximity to a point source, that is, in the near field, are not plane waves since the leading edge or "wave front" is curved near the source.

So at significant distances from the source relative to the wavelength (refer to Fig. 5.5) the radiation spreads out and can be assumed to be a plane wave. Since electromagnetic waves are transverse, the mutually perpendicular electric and magnetic fields are each perpendicular to the direction of propagation. Here the magnetic flux density in free space H is pointing into the page and the electric field E is in the plane of the page pointing toward the top.

Now imagine a stationary square loop in the path of the wave, where the length of each side of the loop is L. Consider two conditions in time: just after the plane wave intersects with the first vertical leg of the loop and just after it reaches the last vertical leg. No currents are assumed to be flowing through the loop. Fig. 4.22 illustrates the scenario.

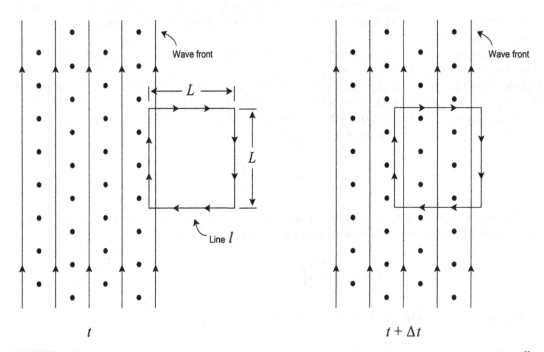

FIGURE 4.22 **Plane wave moving across a stationary loop.** *Figure provided by Kate McManus based on J. Pierce.*[23]

[23]The calculation closely follows the one provided in Pierce JR. Electrons, waves and messages, the art and science of modern electronics. Garden City, NY: Hanover House; 1956.

The area of the loop is $A = L^2$. At the left edge of the loop, the flux of H through the loop is zero. The magnetic flux when the wave arrives at the far end of the loop is $-\mu HL^2$. The sign is negative because the field is directed into the page and away from the reader and is therefore opposite to the convention for positively directed flux.

The change in the flux with time is therefore given by $-\mu L^2 H/\Delta t$. Since distance equals velocity multiplied by time, $\Delta t = L/v$. Therefore, the change in magnetic flux with respect to time is given by $-v\mu L^2 H/L$ or $-\mu HLv$.

Recall Maxwell's third equation equates the negative of the changing magnetic flux density through the loop to the line integral of the electric field around the loop. In other words, a changing magnetic flux density produces an electric field.

In this case only one leg of the loop contributes to the line integral so $\int E \cdot dl = EL$. Applying Maxwell's third equation yields the following expression for the electric field E:

$$EL = -v\mu LH$$

Therefore E can be written as follows:

$$E = \mu vH$$

Now let us change the scenario. The orientation of the propagating plane wave is such that the H is now in the plane of the page pointing up and the E field points into the page. The same calculation using Maxwell's fourth equation can now be performed.

Now the line integral $\int H \cdot dl$ is equated with the time rate of change of the flux of E, that is, the displacement current, across the loop as follows:

$$HL = v\varepsilon EL$$

This expression reduces to the following:

$$H = v\varepsilon E$$

The foregoing analysis led to expressions for E in terms of H and vice versa. Multiplying the expressions for E and H together yields the following equation:

$$EH = v^2 \varepsilon\mu EH \quad \textbf{or} \quad v = \frac{1}{(\varepsilon\mu)^{1/2}}$$

Plugging in the known values of the relative permittivity, that is, dielectric constant ε and the permeability of free space μ, yields the velocity $v = 3 \times 10^8$ m/s. This particular value of velocity corresponds to the velocity of light in a vacuum.

When Maxwell first deduced the existence of electromagnetic waves from his equations, it was this fact that led him to (correctly) posit that light is actually an electromagnetic wave. The fact that all radio-frequency energy is a form of light and therefore conforms to the same physical principles has important implications to estimates of information security risk as discussed in Chapters 7–9.

II. SCIENTIFIC FUNDAMENTALS

MAXWELL'S EQUATIONS AND INFORMATION SECURITY

The relevance of Maxwell's equations to information security can now be more easily appreciated. Suppose a computer processing confidential information was not appropriately shielded. Mechanisms that are described in Chapter 5 result in the generation of voltages and currents within the device.

Currents flowing through electronic components and wiring would be radiating electric and magnetic fields according to Maxwell's equations and therefore subject to remote detection.

Suppose further that an attacker was covertly perched near a device that was radiating electromagnetic energy. Faraday's Law would explain how the attacker would be capable of detecting the magnetic field energy using a pickup coil, that is, a magnetic core with many windings, a low-noise amplifier, signal processing instrumentation, and recording gear. A representative if overly simplified setup might look like the one shown in Fig. 4.23.[24] Note that Chapter 7 will explain why the use of a simple integrator is likely to be inadequate for the job.

The signal could potentially be demodulated and reconstructed thereby affording an attacker access to the confidential information encoded therein. Understanding Maxwell's equations would enable a defender to estimate the intensity of signal leakage as a function of distance, estimate noise amplitudes, determine the vulnerability to information compromise based on the signal-to-noise ratio, and thereby develop a mitigation strategy. Such a strategy might include shielding, eliminating the source of compromising signals, and/or moving to a new location.

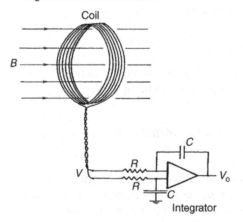

FIGURE 4.23   Simple magnetic flux detector.

[24]http://wsx.lanl.gov/tpx/steady.html.

Moreover, other features of an attack via signal detection can be gleaned from Faraday's Law. Since the EMF is proportional to the time rate of change of magnetic flux through the loop, the larger the area of the loop, the greater the EMF.[25]

Of course, the area of the pickup coil is constrained by covertness requirements. Faraday's Law facilitates an estimate of the required combination of coil area and number of windings to simultaneously maximize EMF and maintain covertness.

In addition, Faraday's Law dictates the orientation of the coil relative to the direction of the flux. Namely, the face of the coil should be perpendicular to the direction of the magnetic flux to maximize EMF. Understanding the geometric factors influencing the magnitude of induced EMF is relevant to estimating the vulnerability of a signal to detection.

For example, if the angle between the face of the coil and the direction of the magnetic flux is zero, no EMF is generated. The maximum flux and hence the largest EMF is developed when the face of the coil is perpendicular to the magnetic flux.

A particularly paranoid colleague once speculated that an attacker was using a window frame as a magnetic pickup coil to detect emanations. This theory generated some concern until a more careful analysis of the postulated attack revealed a highly unfavorable geometry according to Faraday's Law. A little physics is one of the best antidotes to "Security Theater."

SUMMARY

A linear set of equations published in 1864 by the physicist James Clerk Maxwell characterized all electromagnetic phenomena. Although a detailed understanding of Maxwell's equation is not necessary to make information security risk management decisions, a familiarity with these equations helps to understand the vulnerability to information compromise for a broad class of attack scenarios.

Electromagnetic radiation consists of electric and magnetic fields. The time rate of change in magnetic flux will produce an electric field per Faraday's Law (Maxwell's third equation). A time rate of change in electric flux, that is, the displacement current, and/or the presence of moving charges, that is, the conduction current, generates a magnetic field per Ampere's Law, Maxwell's fourth equation. The symmetry of Maxwell's equations is evident and embodied in the following summary: time-varying magnetic flux produces an electric field and time-varying electric flux produces a magnetic field.

The transformations between electric and magnetic fields form the basis of electromagnetic waves and time-varying electromagnetic phenomena per Maxwell's equations. Wave propagation occurs when both forms of energy are present and a change in one leads to a change in the other. Energy is exchanged between electric and magnetic fields as the wave propagates through media.

The transmission of modulated electromagnetic energy, is a basic method of conveying information over significant distances. Wi-Fi systems are but one example of the use of electromagnetic energy to convey information. As noted in this chapter, emanations generated by

---

[25]The induced voltage is also proportional to the number of windings in a pickup coil so an attacker could reduce the area to enhance covertness. The magnitude of the changing flux and hence the induced voltage scales linearly with the number of coil windings.

radiative and conductive coupling mechanisms in electronic devices are subject to detection by an attacker, and these emanations are explained by Maxwell's equations.

The equations that govern signal behavior and facilitate calculations of the signal-to-noise ratio offer quantitative insights into information security risk. These equations also explain the phenomenon of electromagnetic shielding, the most common countermeasure to unauthorized signal detection.

Appendix B provides commonly used units of electricity and magnetism to facilitate estimates of information security risk.

Reference

[1] Tanel Z, Erol M. Student difficulties in understanding the concepts of magnetic field strength, magnetic flux density and magnetization. Izmir, Turkey: Buca Education Faculty, Department of Physics Education, Dokuz Eylul University; 2008. <http://www.lajpe.org/sep08/04_Zafer_Tanel.pdf>.

Noise, Interference, and Emanations

INTRODUCTION

All forms of energy obey the Laws of Nature. Although energy encoded with information has distinct artifacts, the principles of physics govern the behavior of both modulated and unmodulated energy as it encounters various materials. In addition, the presence of extraneous energy from various natural and man-made sources will affect the limit on signal detection. Therefore, to understand the vulnerability of signal energy to unauthorized detection it is crucial to understand real life conditions.

The first step in that journey is to investigate the nature of the signals themselves. To that end, Chapter 4 explained Maxwell's equations, the Laws of Nature that explain all electromagnetic phenomena. The next step is to understand the mechanisms that cause emanations and contribute to noise since the signal-to-noise ratio is the single most important security metric in assessing the vulnerability to remote attacks.

Of particular relevance is the fact that an attacker must use a sensor to detect a signal, and the fact that antennae and lenses are the sensors used for electromagnetic emanations and optical energy, respectively. Typically such signals are weak relative to the noise especially in widely used frequency bands. Even sensors specially designed to detect a specific signal type within a narrow bandwidth must contend with extraneous forms of energy as well as internally generated noise within the detection equipment.

Moreover, the sensor usually cannot necessarily discriminate between desired and undesired energy. External sources of interference, such as FM radio stations, radiating cell phone towers, and power lines, all compete with the signal transmitted by the device under attack. This makes life more difficult for the attacker. Imperfections in electronic circuits and components can generate interference via conductive, capacitive, inductive, and radiative coupling, which makes life more difficult for the attacker and defender. The random motion of electrons in the detection equipment is the basis for thermal noise, and sets the detection limit for attackers and defenders alike.

However, the energy generated by electronic devices and circuit components also offers opportunities for an attacker. Virtually all circuits radiate energy to some extent. In addition, most devices also detect ambient electromagnetic fields or conduct currents that constitute sources of noise. Interference generated by targeted devices can couple to signals of interest and are potentially vulnerable to interception via so-called indirect emanations.

Indirect emanations must be distinguished from direct emanations, where the latter result from the leakage of currents that are not a result of an internal coupling mechanism. The computer video display interface attack scenario discussed in Chapter 7 is an example of a direct emanation. Both direct and indirect emanations will be discussed later in this chapter since these represent the two scenarios that are most relevant to attackers.

Of course, emanations from electronic devices are invisible to the human eye. For that reason people are completely unaware of radiating energy that engulfs them at all times of the day and night. In fact, humans are largely oblivious to much of the energy generated by many of the artificial and natural sources that exist in the environment.

For example, mobile devices, power lines, and household electronics generate electromagnetic fields that are continuously interacting with body tissues. Although it may seem somewhat devoid of empathy, physicists have been known to model human beings as a dielectric in the presence of these fields, and the penetrating field amplitudes can be calculated inside various tissues just like any other dielectric.[1] Dielectrics will be discussed in more detail in Chapter 9 in connection with attacks on visual images.

As noted earlier, natural forms of electromagnetic energy of all types are bombarding every human on the planet at this very moment. Artificial energy sources such as refrigerators, lamps, and other electronic appliances are drawing current through electrical wiring, and these wires are radiating 60 Hz (1 Hz = 1 cycle/s) electromagnetic fields in addition to other emanations.

Humans are even irradiating themselves with radioactive particles due to the presence of isotopes within their bodies. These result from the consumption and absorption of radioactive materials. In fact, about one-tenth of the annual equivalent dose of radioactivity absorbed by a 70-kg adult male is the result of self-radiation, that is, about 0.3 mSv.[2] For example, consuming a banana involves ingesting minute amounts of Potassium-40 resulting in 0.1 μSv equivalent dose of radioactive energy.

All this action occurs while radiation is striking us in the form of visible light from the sun as well as high-energy particles such as cosmic rays. In other words, there is a veritable cacophony of signal energy bombarding the earth at all times, and much of this energy is not particularly informative or helpful. Unhelpful energies within a bandwidth of interest are subsumed under the general heading of noise.

The term "noise" may seem disparaging in light of the colloquial use of the term, but here noise has a specific technical meaning. In this context, the intended receiver determines what are signals and what constitutes noise, no matter how interesting or mundane the interfering energy might seem to anyone else. A clinical approach is adopted here by necessity, where radiation and the effects of interference and noise on the vulnerability to signal detection are examined from a strictly functional perspective.

---

[1]There has been much public debate over the deleterious effects of electromagnetic energy generated by transmission lines, mobile phones, and electromagnetic fields in general. However, to date there is little confirmed evidence that levels of exposure that comport with established government standards (eg, ANSI) represent a health hazard.

[2]http://hps.org/publicinformation/ate/faqs/faqradbods.html.

THERMAL NOISE

The thermal motion of atoms within the electronic components of any electronic device or sensor sets the limit on sensitivity and therefore determines the minimum signal power that is detectable by a sensor. For example, a resistor in an electronic device will produce a noise voltage and is therefore a source of noise power. Thermal noise in electronic components is also known as Johnson noise.

The magnitude of the thermal noise power N in any electronic component is given by the following expression:

$$N = kTW \tag{5.1}$$

Here k is Boltzmann's constant, which is equal to 1.37×10^{-23} J/degree, and T is the temperature of the resistor in kelvin, which is the number of degrees Celsius (Centigrade) above absolute zero.[3] W is the bandwidth of the noise power.

The implication of expression (5.1) is straightforward: the wider the bandwidth or the greater the absolute temperature, the more noise power is generated. The simplicity of this statement belies the profound consequences to information transmission and signal detection.

Electronic receivers are rated according to the total noise the receiver adds to the signals it amplifies relative to thermal noise. The relevant rating is known as the equivalent noise temperature and it is a measure of the inherent noisiness of the receiver. Another measure of receiver noisiness that is based on the equivalent noise temperature is the Noise Figure (NF). NF is defined as the ratio of the total output noise, which consists of the thermal noise at 293 K (room temperature) at the input plus the noise produced by the receiver, relative to the thermal noise.

The important points are that a radio receiver always adds noise to signals, and it simultaneously amplifies both the unwanted noise and the desired signal across the signal bandwidth. However, thermal noise represents the *minimum* noise power in electronic devices, although other sources often dominate.

Noise is always present, and depending on the scenario, a particular source of noise will determine the limit on the minimum detectable signal power. In other words, the signal power to be measured is always referenced to noise power. Signal and noise are forever in competition, and the winner will vary depending on scenario-specific conditions. In fact, the signal-to-noise ratio is *the* critical metric in estimating the vulnerability to signal compromise.

Fig. 5.1 illustrates the magnitude of signal power relative to the noise floor at the signal demodulator and the thermal noise power.[4] It is clear from the graphic that the noise floor as seen by a demodulator exceeds the thermal noise power, kTB, which represents the lower limit in any signal detection scenario.

---

[3]The units for the absolute temperature scale are specified as "kelvin." This nomenclature differs from the relative temperature scales Fahrenheit and Celsius, where units are denoted as "degrees Fahrenheit" and "degrees Celsius," respectively. To recount a piece of history, the 13th CGPM (1967) adopted the name kelvin (symbol K) instead of "degree Kelvin" (symbol °K) and defined the unit of thermodynamic temperature as the unit of thermodynamic temperature, where k is 1/273.16 of the thermodynamic temperature of the triple point of water. http://physics.nist.gov/cuu/Units/kelvin.html.

[4]http://www.highfrequencyelectronics.com/index.php?option=com_content&view=article&id=553:receiver-sensitivity-and-equivalent-noise-bandwidth&catid=94:2014-06-june-articles&Itemid=189.

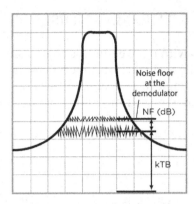

FIGURE 5.1   **Signal power relative to the noise floor and the thermal noise floor (kTB).**

Note that the thermal noise power equals kT multiplied by the signal bandwidth, B.

The distribution of thermal noise measurements has the familiar shape of a normal (Gaussian) probability distribution. Recall normal distributions were discussed in Chapter 1. Thermal noise is Gaussian, and therefore the distribution of amplitudes resembles Fig. 5.2.[5]

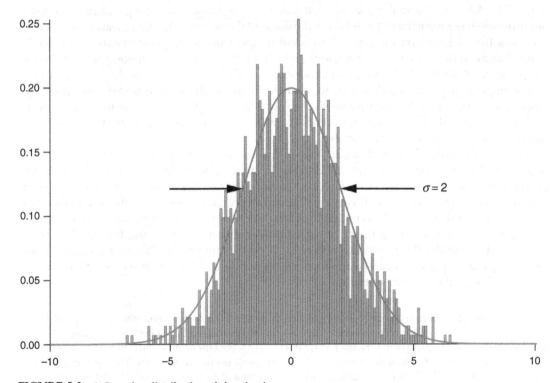

FIGURE 5.2   **A Gaussian distribution of signal noise.**

[5]http://www.ctcms.nist.gov/fipy/_images/gauss-histogram.png.

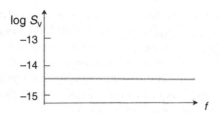

FIGURE 5.3   White noise power spectrum.

Gaussian noise plays an important role in information theory. It turns out that the channel capacity C in message transmissions is determined by so-called Additive White Gaussian noise. Channel capacity and other parameters relevant to information theory vis-à-vis information security will be discussed in Chapter 6.

The distribution of amplitudes as a function of frequency in Gaussian noise is constant. Therefore, Gaussian noise is white noise. Moreover, thermal noise is considered Additive White Gaussian noise because the signal and the noise are added together, the spectrum is white, and the noise amplitudes assume a Gaussian distribution. Again, it bears repeating that thermal noise exists in every electronic component and establishes the lower limit on signal detection. Fig. 5.3 shows the power spectrum of white noise.[6]

SHOT NOISE

The detection of electromagnetic energy ultimately depends on the arrival of individual photons at a detector, although another characterization of the energy incident on a detector is possible. Signal energy is often characterized as a wave, and this is a perfectly valid representation of physical reality. However, a statistical view of the same energy is also possible since the detection process involves the arrival of individual particles. Physicists refer to this dichotomous perspective as the "wave–particle duality."

It turns out the arrival of individual photons at a detector is a Poisson process [1]. Recall the Poisson process was introduced in Chapter 1. For a random variable N, which describes the arrival of photons at a detector, the expected number of photons received per pixel is the variance of $N = E(N)$. The standard deviation is the number of photons per pixel arriving at the detector as prescribed by Poisson process, and equals the square root of $E(N)$. Why is this characterization of noise important?

The inherent variation in the expected number of photons $E(N)$ as measured by its standard deviation represents another source of noise that results from the discrete nature of photons. This source of interference is known as shot noise.

The magnitude of shot noise increases as the square root of the expected number of measured events, which might be an electric current, the intensity of light, etc. But since the strength of the signal itself increases more rapidly than the noise, the relative proportion of

[6]https://www.tcd.ie/Physics/Magnetism/Lectures/py5021/MagneticSensors3.pdf.

shot noise decreases as the signal-to-noise ratio increases. Thus shot noise is most frequently observed with small currents or low light intensities that have been amplified.

For large numbers, the Poisson distribution approaches a normal distribution about the mean, and the individual detection events are no longer individually observed. This affects actual observations, where shot noise is indistinguishable from true Gaussian noise. Since the standard deviation of shot noise is equal to the square root of the average number of measured events N, the signal-to-noise ratio is given by $N/\sqrt{N} = \sqrt{N}$.

Therefore when N is very large, the signal-to-noise ratio is also very large, and any fluctuations in N that are due to other sources are more likely to dominate over shot noise. However, when the magnitude of other noise sources is fixed, such as the thermal noise, or grows more slowly than $\sqrt{N}$, increasing N [the direct current (DC) current or light level, etc.] can lead to shot noise dominating the signal.

Because of the discrete nature of photons, any light detector is subject to shot noise, and as noted earlier this type of noise tends to dominate with small currents or low light intensities that require amplification.

Specifically, the statistical fluctuations in the current due to shot noise, ΔI, are given by the following expression:

$$\Delta I = \sqrt{(2qIW)} \qquad (5.2)$$

Here q is the charge of an electron, I is the current, and W is the signal bandwidth.

Note that an attacker targeting visible information by counting photons might have to contend with shot noise in his or her photodetector. This is especially true when dealing with low signal intensities. Such an attack is discussed in Chapter 9.

EMANATIONS AND ELECTROMAGNETIC INTERFERENCE

Modes of Radiation Coupling

What is the origin of the unintentional emanations that are vulnerable to detection by an attacker? In general, radiation produced by a circuit occurs as a result of circuit elements at different potentials that cause currents to flow, which produce electromagnetic fields. Moreover, these fields couple to circuit elements that act like antennae and can efficiently radiate electromagnetic energy.

However, it is not necessary to physically connect an antenna to a circuit to cause it to radiate and thereby enhance the vulnerability to unwanted detection. High-frequency circuits can act as their own antennae or couple to nearby objects that act as efficient antennae.

The result is radiated electromagnetic fields that the attacker attempts to detect and demodulate in the presence of noise using methods described in Chapter 7. It is prudent to understand the underlying mechanisms associated with radiated energy that contribute to the vulnerability to signal detection.

Electronic devices such as computers contain circuits that send currents between internal components and develop voltages that generate currents across these same elements. Although such currents are confined to the wires contained in the device, the electromagnetic

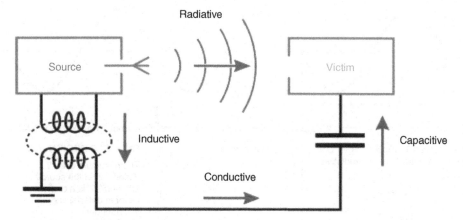

FIGURE 5.4 **Emanations and electromagnetic coupling mechanisms.**

fields generated by these currents are not so constrained. Four coupling mechanisms are responsible for interference and/or emanations vulnerable to detection by an attacker:

- conductive – electric currents in transmission lines;
- radiative – electromagnetic fields;
- capacitive – electric fields from current-carrying components and fixed charges;
- inductive – magnetic fields between current-carrying components.

A convenient and generally adopted coupling model subdivides the scenario into a source, coupling path/mechanism, and "victim."[7,8] Fig. 5.4 illustrates these coupling mechanisms with respect to this high-level characterization.[9]

Emanations from circuit elements will vary significantly depending on whether they are measured in the near or far fields of the source. In general, attack scenarios involve far-field emanations. Fig. 5.5 shows the near- and far-field zones for an electrically short antenna.[10] Note the relationship between the wavelength of transmitted radiation λ and the physical demarcation of each zone.

Electromagnetic interference (EMI) affecting circuits and emanations generated by circuits are now briefly described at the electronic component level.[11] Descriptions at the circuit level are provided in later discussions in this chapter with calculations of the resulting electric field amplitudes included for completeness.

Radiated energy from a corrupting source may enter a circuit wherever there is an electrical impedance mismatch or discontinuity in a system. In general, this mismatch occurs at the interface where cables carrying sensitive analog signals are connected to PC boards as well as through power supply leads. Improperly connected cables or poor power supply filtering schemes are often conduits for interference.

[7]http://www.ursi.org/proceedings/procGA11/ursi/ET-1.pdf.
[8]http://www.radioing.com/eengineer/intro.html.
[9]https://commons.wikimedia.org/wiki/File:EMI_coupling_modes.svg.
[10]https://en.wikipedia.org/wiki/Near_and_far_field.
[11]http://www.analog.com/media/en/training-seminars/tutorials/MT-095.pdf.

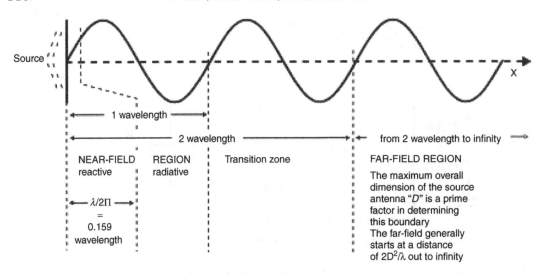

FIGURE 5.5   The near and far fields of electrically short antennae.

Conducted noise is coupled between components through interconnecting wires such as power supplies and ground wires. Conducted noise may also be encountered when two or more currents share a common path impedance. This common path is often a high-impedance "ground" connection. If two circuits share this path, noise currents from one will produce noise voltages in the other.

Inductive and capacitive coupling are near-field effects and therefore play a role only when source and victim are in close proximity. Electric field coupling (capacitive) is caused by a voltage difference between conductors, and the coupling mechanism may be modeled as a capacitor. Magnetic field coupling (inductive) is caused by current flow in conductors, and this coupling can be modeled as a transformer. These near-field coupling mechanisms are described in Appendix C for the interested reader.

Of particular relevance is radiative coupling because electromagnetic emanations so generated can be detected in the far field. The far field is often defined as greater than or equal to a wavelength from the radiation source. Energy in the far field generated via radiative coupling is potentially vulnerable to detection by an attacker depending on the magnitude of the signal-to-noise ratio at the point of detection. In the far field electromagnetic coupling involves plane wave coupling where the wave impedance E/H is 377 Ω.[12]

Radiative coupling exists as distinct cases for electric and magnetic fields, and can be further delineated in the near and far fields. In the near field, E and H field coupling are treated separately since their respective impedances differ. Fig. 5.6 illustrates radiated and conducted emissions, where the former exists as emanations in the far field and is a source of EMI in both the near and far fields.[8]

---

[12]A more complete discussion of the near and far fields in connection with electromagnetic shielding is provided in Chapter 8.

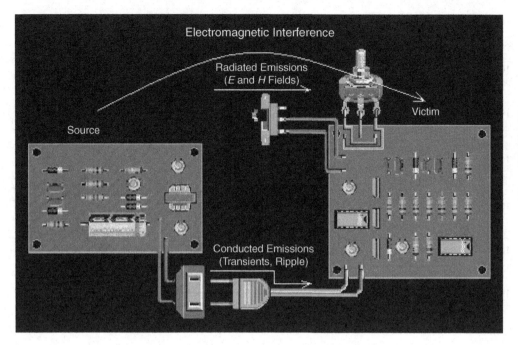

FIGURE 5.6   Near-field radiative coupling.

Although thermal noise sets the lower limit on signal detection as noted earlier, typical security scenarios are subject to internal and external noise power that exceeds the thermal limit.[13] In particular, external sources of noise such as TV stations, radio broadcasts, and other electronic devices can be continuous, transient, and impulsive, and therefore require signal averaging as described in Chapter 6.

External Sources of EMI

External sources of EMI are ubiquitous and include the following examples:

- AM, FM, and TV broadcasts
- mobile telephones
- Wi-Fi access points
- power transmission lines
- web-enabled portable devices, for example, smart phones and tablets
- household devices, for example, microwave ovens
- terrestrial energy, for example, lightning
- muons (~10,000 m^{-2} min^{-1})

---

[13]See Shannon C, Weaver W. The mathematical theory of communication. Urbana, IL: University of Illinois Press; 1963, a seminal treatise on information theory.

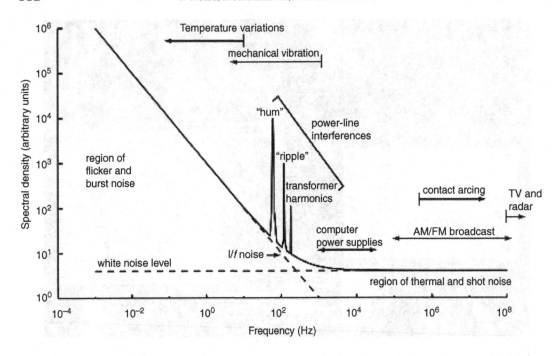

FIGURE 5.7   Sources of far-field EMI.

Indeed, the electromagnetic spectrum is becoming increasingly crowded as more devices become Internet-enabled and transmit wireless signals. The "Internet of Things" portends an even more crowded spectrum. Fig. 5.7 specifies external sources of EMI in terms of frequency versus spectral density.[14]

To quantitatively analyze the effect of far-field EMI on the vulnerability to signal detection by an attacker, mean noise levels from sources of EMI have been tabulated in the form of an external noise factor f_a [2]:

$$f_a = \frac{P_{n,B}}{kT_o W} \tag{5.3}$$

The external noise factor specified in (5.3) compares the noise energy within a bandwidth, W, to the thermal noise energy generated by a resistor at room temperature, T_o, where k is Boltzmann's constant. Again, thermal noise power represents the lower limit of noise for any detection scenario.

Noise factors have been converted to equivalent electric field strengths for electromagnetically quiet and busy sites, for example, rural and urban areas, respectively, for a 1-MHz signal bandwidth. The data are shown in Fig. 7.8. External sources of interference play a significant role in the vulnerability of emanations to detection. Electric field amplitudes of

[14]http://www.owlnet.rice.edu/~dodds/Files331/noise_notes.pdf.

interference are compared to emanation amplitudes and other factors to determine the limits to signal detection.

RADIATING CIRCUITS

Currents and Electromagnetic Fields in Electronic Circuits

Interference can be caused by natural and artificial sources that are both internal and external to a circuit. External sources of interference can negatively affect the attacker forcing him or her to resort to signal averaging, etc., to improve the signal-to-noise ratio. However, the emanations generated by a target device can also be an unintended source of information to an attacker if a signal of interest modulates such emanations. Let's explore the genesis of interference in a circuit.

A simple and ideal circuit consists of a signal generator source and load. Energy is transferred to the load without the corrupting influence of interference. Now consider the scenario where the current return path between the signal generator and the load is not ideal and noise voltages appear in the return path. These noise voltages could produce a voltage difference between the generator and the load, and therefore appear in series with the signal generator. The net result is noise currents in the load.

Practical circuits consist of multiple source–load combinations that are interconnected. Implementing individual return paths for every source–load pair is not practical so a common ground is established with the goal of providing a zero-impedance path for all signals for which it is providing a reference. This condition will allow multiple signal currents within individual networks to return to their respective sources without coupling to other circuits. However, the reality is that circuits are not ideal and there is finite, frequency-dependent impedance associated with grounding elements due to the physical nature of circuit elements (eg, capacitance, inductance) and the impedance results in currents with associated electromagnetic fields [3].

Every circuit that draws current radiates RF energy to some extent. Ampere's Law, Maxwell's fourth equation, explains this phenomenon. If the circuit dimensions are small relative to the wavelength of the radiated energy, the radiation intensity will be low. However, as these relative dimensions change, either by increasing the conductor length or by increasing the frequency and thereby decreasing the wavelength, the radiation efficiency increases.

This unintentional improvement in radiation efficiency increases the vulnerability to signal interception since the circuit is now behaving like a proper antenna.[15] This phenomenon is well known from antenna theory, where the goal in many operational contexts is to optimize radiation efficiency rather than attenuate it.

Electromagnetic fields generated by electric circuits have been categorized and derive from five possible sources: differential-mode radiation, coupling to input–output (I/O) radiation, voltage-driven common-mode radiation, current-driven common-mode radiation, and power bus radiation.[16] These sources are described briefly in the following discussion.

---

[15]http://www.emc-zone.com/2012/07/unwanted-conductive-and-radiative.html.
[16]http://www.clemson.edu/ces/cvel/Presentation_Slides/PCB_Expert_System07.pdf.

Signals that couple to I/O conductors carry high-frequency power signals away from the circuit board. Such signals would likely not be of significant interest to an attacker.

In voltage-driven radiation, a signal or electronic component voltage is established between two elements that function as antennae. Therefore there is capacitive coupling between the two circuit elements. This voltage can produce significant electric fields. For example, a 1-V potential difference at a 500-MHz frequency has been calculated to produce an electric field of 360 mV/m at a distance of 3 m. However, this mode of coupling would likely not be available to an attacker due to its relatively short range.[16]

In current-driven common-mode radiation, a signal current loop generates a voltage between two circuit elements that function as efficient antennae, for example, a cable and the circuit board. Current-driven voltages tend to be 3 or 4 orders of magnitude smaller than voltage-driven voltages. However, antenna efficiencies can be 5 or 6 orders of magnitude higher thereby radiating into the far field for possible detection by an attacker.[16]

For radiation emanating from power buses, the resulting electric fields are proportional to the current, the dimensions of the power plane, and the Quality factor (Q) of the resonant circuit, which is a function of frequency.

Currents generated by circuits and targeted by attackers can be divided into two categories: differential- and common-mode currents. Differential-mode currents are equal in magnitude but are oppositely directed currents that exist on parallel conductors. Common-mode currents are equal in magnitude and have the same direction on parallel conductors.[17]

The implication of differential- and common-mode currents to the vulnerability to signal detection derives from the magnitude of the electric fields associated with those currents since this is what an attacker detects using his or her receiver antenna. A vector analysis of these fields shows that the radiated electric field components due to differential-mode currents subtract, thereby producing a small net radiated electric field.

However, the radiated electric field components resulting from common-mode currents add, thereby producing a larger net electric field.

It can be shown by geometric arguments that at distances much greater than the conductor separation, the total electric field due to the differential-mode currents is negligible, whereas the total electric field due to the common-mode currents is more substantial.[17] Fig. 5.8 illustrates the electric fields generated by both differential- and common-mode currents.[17]

Differential-mode currents and resulting emanations are generated by loops formed by circuit components, printed circuit traces, ribbon cables, etc. In general, a ground loop is created by interference coupling such that the ground plane or return is involved as described earlier. These loops act as small circular antennas, which generally emit low-amplitude radiation.

The following is a more detailed description of the genesis of ground loop emanations. Consider a conducting loop that exists among other circuits on a printed circuit board. In this case an electrical potential might develop between the circuits, and currents will return to the source via an alternate ground reference due to radiation coupling or unbalanced circuits. Moreover, in-phase currents will flow in the same direction on multiple conductors. External cables that are part of the ground loop act as antennae, which radiate as a result of these internal voltages.

[17]http://www.egr.msu.edu/em/research/goali/notes/module9_radiated_emissions.pdf.

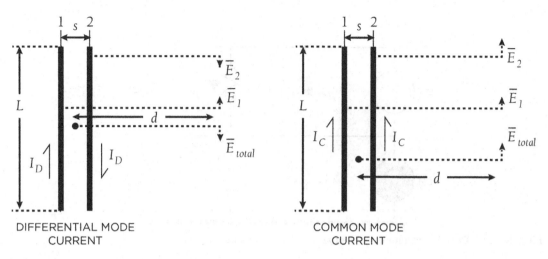

FIGURE 5.8   Electric fields generated by differential- and common-mode currents.

But the radiative process is inefficient, and emanations would be minimal until the dimensions of the circuit approach resonant lengths at the radiation frequencies. Even though the magnitude of common-mode currents is generally smaller in magnitude than the differential mode, the loop area of the source is much larger than sources of differential-mode currents resulting in improved radiation efficiency. Therefore, common-mode currents typically dominate differential-mode currents.

Common-mode emanations can be more insidious than differential-mode currents since they are generally more difficult to detect and control. Fig. 5.9 is a depiction of common- and differential-mode currents. Note the larger loop corresponding to a source of common-mode currents.[18]

Direct and Indirect Emanations

The various circuit configurations and resulting currents that lead to emanations have been described in the previous section. However, from an attacker's perspective there are two signals of interest: direct and indirect emanations.[19]

In digital devices such as computers, data is encoded with logic states, generally described by narrow (in time) square waves, that is, pulses with sharp rising and falling edges. During the transition time between two logic states, electromagnetic energy is emitted at a maximum frequency that is related to the duration of the rise/fall time of the pulse. Because this radiation emanates directly from the wire transmitting the data, it is known as direct emanation.

---

[18]http://www.emc-zone.com/2012/08/what-is-differential-and-common-mode.html.
[19]http://infoscience.epfl.ch/record/171931/files/texfile.pdf.

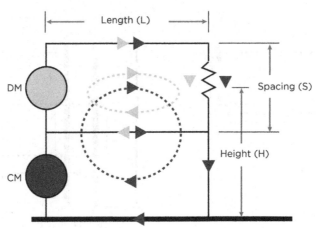

FIGURE 5.9   Circuits generating differential- and common-mode currents.

Indirect emanations result from interference mechanisms that couple to sensitive data signals. EMI may interact with active electronic components, which induce new forms of radiation. The radiated signal is modulated by the signal with sensitive information, which is potentially detectable by an attacker.

Recall Faraday's Law described the generation of electric fields (and resulting voltages) induced by changing magnetic flux. Near- and far-field sources of interference manifest themselves as modulations and intermodulations of signals or as carrier signals (eg, a clock frequency) plus additional frequencies called harmonics.

Moreover, nonlinear coupling between these carrier signals and sensitive data signals, crosstalk, ground pollution, and/or power supply DC pollution may generate indirect emanations that are targeted by an attacker. Indirect emanations may actually propagate better than direct emanations, and therefore may be susceptible to interception by an attacker at longer ranges. Moreover, they are difficult to predict, which adds to the complexity of implementing consistent and effective countermeasures.

Emanations Caused by Ground Loops

Grounding issues in electrical circuits can be a significant source of common- or differential-mode currents and therefore should be understood in some detail.[20] A ground loop is a condition where extraneous current flows in a circuit or through connections between components because of unintended differences in voltage. Fig. 5.10 shows the high-level anatomy of a ground loop, which can be caused by a number of circuit design issues.[21]

Ground-related interference often involves one of two mechanisms. The first mechanism is when a common signal ground is used for multiple circuits or electronic equipment. This

[20]http://m.eet.com/media/1114898/duff_ch_5.pdf.
[21]http://www.wici.com/blogs/2012/08/how-to-wiring-for-trouble-free-signal-conditioning/1euro/.

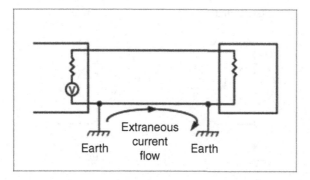

FIGURE 5.10   Ground loop.

mechanism is called common-ground impedance coupling. Any shared impedance within a circuit or system can facilitate interference of this kind.

As noted previously, ideally a grounding system should provide a zero-impedance path for all signals for which it serves as a reference. If such paths exist, signal currents from various circuits or equipment that are connected to the ground could return to their respective sources without creating unwanted coupling between these elements.[21]

Although the ground may indeed represent a low-impedance path, it will always exhibit some capacitance, resistance, and/or inductance. The result is a nonzero impedance with respect to ground thereby producing currents and associated emanations as discussed previously in this section. Recall impedance is frequency-dependent, so what constitutes a good ground at a low or high frequency will change depending on whether capacitive or inductive reactance dominates.

The second grounding-related interference mechanism involves a system ground as a radiative source where the ground loop acts as a receiving or transmitting antenna. A ground is defined as any reference conductor that is used as a common return. The return can be a low-voltage side of a wire pair or the outer jacket of a coaxial cable or conductor that provides a path for the intended current to return to the source.[21]

It is important to appreciate that ground loop interference problems can exist without a physical connection to ground. At radio frequencies, distributed capacitance to ground can create a ground loop condition even though interconnected circuits or equipment are floating, that is, not physically connected, with respect to ground. Fig. 5.11 depicts a physically grounded circuit versus a floating circuit.[22]

Reducing the coupling of EMI with respect to the ground loop or suppressing the source of common-mode EMI is effective in reducing the vulnerability to signal compromise.[22] Grounding as a countermeasure to emanations will be discussed in Chapter 8.

Like all electromagnetic phenomena, ground loops are ultimately explained by Maxwell's equations. In this case, Maxwell's third equation applies. Time-varying magnetic flux generated by currents in circuit elements induces a voltage relative to the various grounds in the circuit that in turn create currents circulating within and between circuit elements. Reducing the

[22]http://www.ni.com/white-paper/3394/en/.

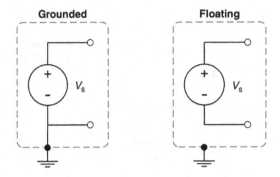

FIGURE 5.11   Grounded versus floating circuits.

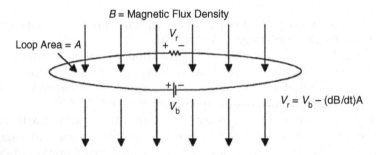

FIGURE 5.12   Faraday's Law and the genesis of ground loops.

magnitude of the magnetic flux, decreasing the rate of change of magnetic flux, and/or decreasing the area of the ground loop will minimize the emanations produced by a ground loop.

Fig. 5.12 is intended to refresh the reader's recollection of the essence of Faraday's Law, where the illustration depicts the voltage generated by the change in the total magnetic flux, $A\,dB/dt$, across a conductive loop of area A.[23] It is the voltage so generated that is responsible for ground loop currents.

Finally, Fig. 5.13 depicts common-mode radiation from a ground loop.[20]

CIRCUIT ELEMENT MODELS AND ELECTRIC FIELDS

The previous sections described coupling mechanisms and resulting EMI and emanations. This section discusses several basic models of radiating circuit elements. These models enable estimates of electric field amplitudes in the far field. They also facilitate calculations of signal power relative to noise power and therefore can be used to characterize the vulnerability to signal detection and ultimately information compromise.

[23]http://incompliancemag.com/article/a-dash-of-maxwells-a-maxwells-equations-primer-part-2-why-things-radiate.

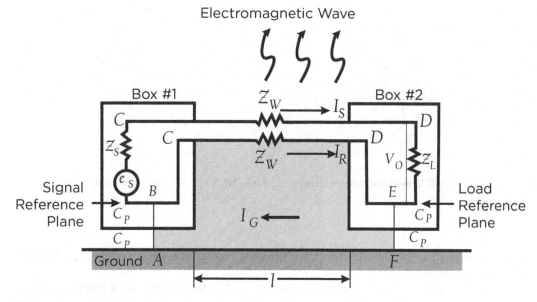

FIGURE 5.13   Electromagnetic emanations caused by a ground loop.

There are two basic physical models that can be used to describe the electric fields derived from currents flowing in circuits as discussed earlier: time-varying current filaments and small current loops. This section will describe these models and estimate the electromagnetic fields that exist in the far field.

A time-varying current filament is depicted in Fig. 5.14.[24]

It is important to appreciate that this depiction is just a model and should not be subject to a literal interpretation. No such circuit could exist in real life since any functional circuit containing electric current requires a closed path. However, realistic current distributions can be modeled using superposition, that is, a linear combination of current filaments such as the one shown in Fig. 5.13.

Maxwell's equations describe the electric and magnetic fields associated with charges, currents, and electrical potentials in circuits. The operational implication of the fields so generated is that they are vulnerable to detection at some distance from the radiating device depending on scenario-specific conditions. Specifically, the concern is that a remotely located attacker could use an antenna and signal-processing equipment as described in Chapter 7 to detect these fields and reconstruct the original signal. The maximum distance for the attacker is highly dependent on scenario-specific conditions.

Returning to the time-varying current filament, the derivation of the near and far fields resulting from this model is a bit detailed and beyond the scope of this book. However, the

[24]http://learnemc.com/electromagnetic-radiation.

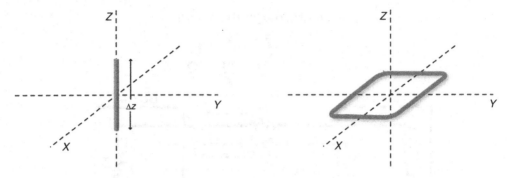

FIGURE 5.14   A small, time-varying current filament.   FIGURE 5.15   A small current loop.

significant results can be merely stated and thereby convey the points relevant to far-field radiation from circuit elements.

Namely, both electric and magnetic fields will exist in the far field as a result of a short filament containing a time-varying current. The respective oscillations are in phase and they oscillate in mutually perpendicular planes, both of which are perpendicular to the direction of propagation.

Next consider a small current loop. This might be modeled as four current filaments attached to form a square. Fig. 5.15 illustrates such a loop.[24]

In this case it can be shown from Maxwell's equations that the amplitude of the electric and magnetic fields is proportional to the inverse of the distance between the loop and the point of detection, and to the loop area.

As was the case with a single time-varying filament, the electric and magnetic field oscillations are in phase, and the planes of oscillation are mutually perpendicular. Again, the direction of propagation of these fields is perpendicular to both the electric and magnetic field planes of oscillation.

The results of these models can be used to estimate the radiation emanation from small circuits. But a brief digression on the concept of impedance is required in advance of such estimates.

A fundamental law for circuits is Ohm's Law. This states that the circuit voltage V equals the current flowing through the circuit i times the resistance of the circuit elements R. It is written as $V = iR$. This expression is true for all circuits, but must be modified for those with alternating current (AC) voltage sources, that is, where the voltage amplitude changes with time. In these circuits, the resistance of components such as inductors and capacitors will vary with the frequency of oscillation.

The resistance in AC circuits is known as impedance, and it has two components: a resistive term and a reactive term. The resistance is a DC term and therefore does not vary. The reactive term applies to inductors and capacitors where the resistance does vary with frequency. Specifically, the reactance of inductive elements increases with increasing frequency and the reactance of capacitive elements decreases with increasing frequency.

Returning to the radiating fields of small circuits, calculated electric fields using time-varying filaments and small current loop models divide into high-impedance and low-impedance results. The impedance of an electromagnetic wave is the ratio of E/H, where E/H is 377 Ω in the far field as noted previously. The results are merely stated here with the goal of highlighting the differences in the two maximal electric field strengths and providing expressions that are applicable to any small circuit element[24]:

$$E_{max}(\text{low impedance})\left[\eta_o < \frac{E}{H} = \text{impedance of free space}\right] = \left[\frac{V\,\Delta S\beta^2}{4\pi r}\right]\left(\frac{\eta_o}{Z_{loop}}\right) \quad (5.4)$$

$$E_{max}(\text{high impedance})\left[\eta_o > \frac{E}{H} = \text{impedance of free space}\right] = \left[\frac{V\,\Delta S\beta^2}{4\pi r}\right] \quad (5.5)$$

Here V is the voltage of the circuit, ΔS is the area of the loop, Z_{loop} is the impedance of the loop, and β is the wave number or $2\pi/\lambda$, where λ is the radiation wavelength.

The only difference between the two expressions is that the low-impedance circuit expression has an additional η_o/Z_{loop} term. These expressions are potentially quite useful since they have applicability to estimating the field strength resulting from currents flowing within electronic devices targeted by attackers. Note that such calculations would be valid only if the circuit is indeed small, that is, small compared to the wavelength, at the radiated frequency.

An example is illustrative for a circuit impedance of 500 Ω.[24] This is greater than the impedance of free space (377 Ω) so the high-impedance expression for the electric field applies:

$$E_{max}(\text{high impedance}) = \left[\frac{V\,\Delta S\beta^2}{4\pi r}\right]$$

If the frequency is assumed to be 80 MHz, the voltage is 1.8 V, the area of the circuit is 10 cm^2, and the distance of the detector from the circuit is 3 m. The wavelength in free space of the radiated energy at 80 MHz is 3.75 m. The electric field is therefore calculated to be 134 μV/m or 42.5 dB (microvolt per meter).

A similar calculation for the maximum electric field can be performed for any distance r using this model, and thereby estimate the vulnerability to detection by an attacker at arbitrary locations. Note that the intensity of the radiation, the critical security parameter when combined with the noise power, is proportional to E_{max}^2.

SUMMARY

Currents and voltages generated between circuit elements in electronic devices result in electromagnetic waves that couple to other circuit components. Coupling mechanisms can produce common mode and differential currents that produce direct and indirect emanations that are targeted for detection by an attacker.

The presence of noise is a ubiquitous feature in Nature and can profoundly affect signal detection for intended recipients and adversaries alike. Electronic noise can be caused by radio-frequency interference that couples to transmission lines or other electronic components. External sources of radio-frequency interference derive from natural, artificial, cosmic, terrestrial, and primordial sources and affect both attackers and defenders.

Thermal noise is due to the random motion of atoms in receiver electronics. It represents the minimum possible noise in an electronic component, and therefore defines the lower limit on signal detection. It too affects attackers and defenders alike. Shot noise results from the discrete nature of particles such as photons, and can be an issue in optical scenarios where low–light level conditions prevail.

Determining the principal sources of noise and their magnitude for a given attack scenario pursuant to estimating the signal-to-noise ratio is perhaps the most important factor in estimating the vulnerability to information compromise.

References

[1] Jenkins TE. Optical sensing techniques and signal processing. Englewood Cliffs, NJ: Prentice Hall International; 1987.
[2] Kuhn M. Security limits for compromising emanations. In: Rao, J.R., Sunar, B., editors. CHES 2005, LNCS 3659. Heidelberg: Springer Verlag; 2005. p. 265–79.
[3] Denny H. Grounding for the control of EMI. 1st ed. Gainesville, VA: Don White Consultants, Interference Control Technologies, Inc; 1983.

PART III

THE COMPROMISE
OF SIGNALS

Signals and Information Security

INTRODUCTION

In this chapter some of the key concepts discussed in previous chapters are used to estimate the vulnerability of electromagnetic signals to compromise. Various factors contribute to the signal-to-noise ratio, which determines the vulnerability to signal detection by an attacker. Each of these must be identified and evaluated. The key point is that the physical limits on signal detection derive from well-understood scientific and engineering principles.

Modulation is essential to conveying information. It is modulation that transforms a mere wave of energy into a signal encoded with information. In the process, additional frequencies are created, which produces a complex waveform that affects the detection effort since a wider bandwidth must be detected.

The limits on information transmission will vary for a given communication channel. In all cases the signal-to-noise ratio and bandwidth affect channel capacity where varying combinations of each are allowed for a given data rate. The statistical properties of coherent versus incoherent signals can be leveraged to lift signals out of the noise.

Quantitative estimates on the vulnerability to signal detection are possible because signals behave according to the principles discussed in Chapter 4. Moreover, weak signals are successfully detected using equipment that is specifically engineered for this purpose. The limits on detection ultimately derive from a combination of physical proximity to the source and available resources.

MODULATION

Modulation changes some feature of a wave in order to convey information. Specifically, the amplitude, frequency, or phase of a wave must be changed in order to encode the information of interest. A pure sine wave consisting of a single frequency does not convey any information. The modulation process is what transforms wave energy into a proper signal. Therefore, it is useful to investigate the modulation process in some detail since the waveform is strongly affected by the modulation details.

As a result of modulating a carrier frequency additional frequencies are generated resulting in a more complex spectrum. Fig. 6.1 shows the results of modulation with a single

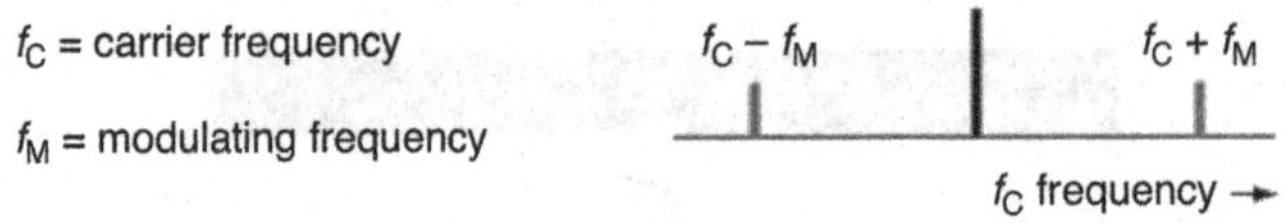

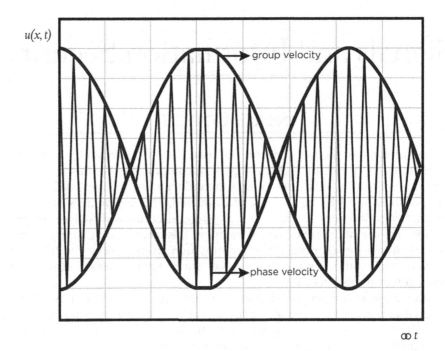

f_C = carrier frequency

f_M = modulating frequency

$f_C - f_M$

$f_C + f_M$

f_C frequency →

FIGURE 6.1   The effect of modulation as represented in the frequency domain.

$u(x, t)$

group velocity

phase velocity

∞ t

FIGURE 6.2   The effect of modulation as represented in the time domain showing the phase and group velocities.

frequency as represented in the frequency domain. The result is the creation of sum and difference frequencies or sidebands that are offset from the carrier by the modulation frequency.[1]

Modulation can produce a superposition of frequencies with more complex spectra than the one shown in Fig. 6.1. Fig. 6.2 shows a time domain representation of this superposition. Note the group and phase velocities associated with the envelope and constituent frequencies, respectively, concepts that were introduced in Chapter 3.[2]

When the amplitude of a carrier frequency is modulated, it is rather unimaginatively referred to as amplitude modulation. In a similar burst of creativity, if the frequency of a carrier is changed, it is referred to as frequency modulation. Modulating the phase of a signal is a third modulation technique and it is closely related to frequency modulation. In phase modulation the phase of the signal is compared to that of a carrier or to itself. Differences between

[1]http://hyperphysics.phy-astr.gsu.edu/hbase/audible/sumdif.html.
[2]http://physics.gmu.edu/~dmaria/590%20Web%20Page/public_html/qm_topics/phase_vel/phase.html?sa=X& ved=0CBgQ9QEwAWoVChMI4rqY0dj2xgIVTD0-Ch3dBguw.

III. THE COMPROMISE OF SIGNALS

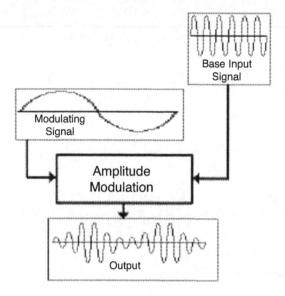

FIGURE 6.3   Amplitude modulation.

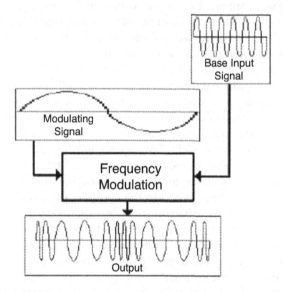

FIGURE 6.4   Frequency modulation.

the phase of the signal and the reference are used to encode information. Figs. 6.3–6.5 show the amplitude, frequency, and phase modulation processes, respectively.[3,4]

As noted previously, modulating a carrier frequency creates additional frequencies in the signal spectrum. Although the type of modulation can vary, the existence of frequencies that are by-products of modulation will be present in any radiated energy that conveys information. This is important because the signal bandwidth, that is, the width of the frequency spectrum of the signal, affects the detection of weak signals.

[3]http://www.danalee.ca/ttt/index.htm.
[4]http://ironbark.xtelco.com.au/subjects/DC/lectures/7/.

III. THE COMPROMISE OF SIGNALS

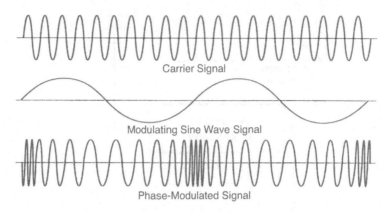

Carrier Signal

Modulating Sine Wave Signal

Phase-Modulated Signal

FIGURE 6.5   Phase modulation.

The previous examples depicted amplitude, frequency, and phase modulation for analog signals. Analog signals contain continuous values of amplitude, whereas digital signals transmit only discrete values. These days many signals are digital. In digital transmissions, the analog carrier must be first converted to a digital signal through a process called analog-to-digital conversion before being modulated and transmitted.

Let us return to first principles so as to not lose track of why a discussion on modulation relates to attacks on information. An attacker is fundamentally interested in the information encoded in an electromagnetic wave of energy. This encoding is accomplished via modulation where one or more parameters of the wave are changed. What characteristics of a wave are amenable to encoding such that digital symbols can be used to characterize these changes and thereby reconstruct the wave/signal following demodulation?

An electromagnetic wave consists of electric and magnetic fields as discussed in Chapter 3 and examined more extensively in Chapter 4. The electric field of a modulated light wave is as a vector quantity that can be represented in the complex plane using an I–Q diagram. I is the in-phase or real part and Q is the quadrature or imaginary part. A symbol corresponds to a point on a constellation diagram shown later, and is defined by I and Q in Cartesian coordinates or by the electric field amplitude E and phase ϕ in polar coordinates.

The constellation points correspond to the symbol clock times.[5] Fig. 6.6 shows the I–Q representation of a signal at an instant in time.[6]

Furthermore, electromagnetic waves are transverse. As discussed in Chapter 3, this means the planes of oscillation of the magnetic and electric fields are perpendicular to the direction of propagation. If the electric field is oscillating in the x–y plane, that is, the z-component is zero, a vector representation of the electric field has two components, x and y. The field is therefore polarized in the x–y plane and encoding can be based on changes in polarization. The reader may be familiar with sunglasses that use polarized lenses. These lenses work by filtering the electric field except for a single plane of oscillation and thereby reduce glare.

[5]http://www.lightwaveonline.com/articles/2013/07/complex-coding-concepts-for-increased-optical-bit-transfer-efficiency.html.
[6]http://whiteboard.ping.se/SDR/IQ.

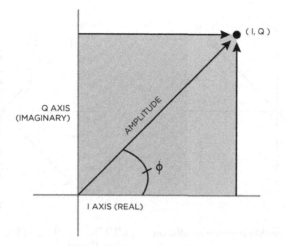

FIGURE 6.6 *I–Q* representation of signal amplitude and phase relative to *I–Q* vector components.

Light is a transversal electromagnetic wave

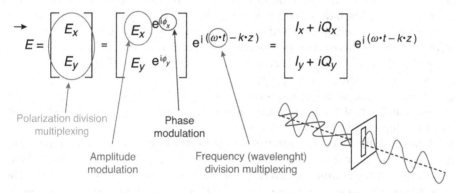

FIGURE 6.7 Mathematical description of the electric field of a Signal and Possible Quantities for Modulation.

The electric field amplitude of the wave corresponding to the signal is fluctuating in the *x–y* plane as depicted in the mathematical representation shown in Fig. 6.7. The wave frequency and its phase are also fluctuating. These parameters can be changed in a defined way and thereby encode information. Fig. 6.7 is a mathematical representation of the electric field vector in terms of the *I* and *Q* components.[5] Note that the frequency component $e^{i\omega t}$ and the phase component $e^{i\phi t}$ can be written as cos ωt + i sin ωt and cos ϕt + i sin ϕt, respectively, and therefore are oscillatory components of the electric field.[7]

Phase shift keying is one technique that allows for efficient encoding and the transmission of high-bandwidth signals such as those used in wireless local area networks (LANs). In all digital signals, an analog signal is sampled at a minimum rate dictated by the Nyquist

[7]These relations are based on de Moivre's Theorem.

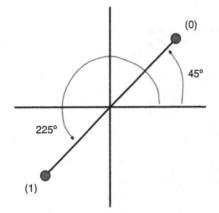

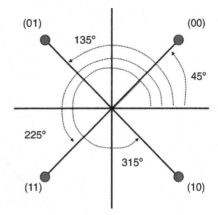

FIGURE 6.8   Binary phase shift keying constellation.   FIGURE   6.9   Quadrature   phase   shift   keying constellation.

sampling theorem, which is defined later in the chapter. The analog signal is then encoded with digital values via modulation. One specific digital modulation method is described next.

As noted earlier, constellation diagrams using the *I–Q* representation relate discrete digital values to changes in amplitude and/or phase of the analog carrier. In a simple binary phase shift key (BPSK) scheme, two phase shifts of 45 and 135 degrees are used to represent a 0 and 1, respectively. Fig. 6.8 depicts a constellation diagram for a BPSK scheme.[8]

More complex phase shift key modulation schemes are used to encode more bits. For example, Quadrature Phase Shift Keying is used to encode 2 bits with one symbol thereby doubling the data rate. Each of the four phase shifts is assigned one of four possible 2-bit codes. This situation is depicted in Fig. 6.9.[8]

A more detailed depiction of Quadrature Phase Shift Keying encoding of an analog signal is shown in Fig. 6.10. One can observe the phase shift associated with elements of the constellation as indicated in the counterclockwise increase in the phase of the sine wave. The mapping of specific combinations of bits, for example, 11 and 00 are mapped to symbols A and B, respectively, is also illustrated.[5]

Higher-order PSK schemes are theoretically possible but Eight Phase Shift Keying (8-PSK) is typically the maximum implemented. A constellation diagram for 8-PSK is shown in Fig. 6.11.[9]

The baud rate, or the number of modulation symbols transmitted per second, is relevant to digital signals. Signal transmission systems attempt to maximize the number of bits per symbol through efficient modulation schemes. When 1 bit/symbol is being transmitted, the baud rate is the same as the bit rate.

Encoding of information is a principal focus of communication engineers. As discussed in a later section signal encoding relates to information security through the parameters that ultimately limit channel capacity, that is, signal bandwidth and noise. From an information

[8]http://www.hill2dot0.com/wiki/index.php?title=PSK.
[9]https://documentation.meraki.com/MR/WiFi_Basics_and_Best_Practices/Wireless_Fundamentals%3A_Modulation.

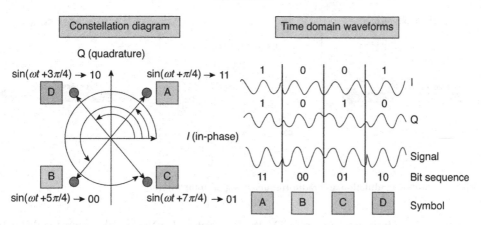

FIGURE 6.10 Detailed depiction of quadrature phase shift keying. In this figure, we have constructed four vectors. One vector position in the complex plane codes 2 bits.

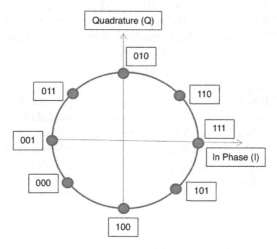

FIGURE 6.11 An 8-PSK constellation.

theory perspective, the engineer is hoping to maximize the signal information entropy while transmitting the minimum number of bits. Therefore increasing the number of bits per symbol is a principal goal of modulation. What modulation techniques are most successful at encoding to achieve this outcome?

Basic binary transmissions use 1 bit/symbol but others can generate higher rates. For example, the creation of symbols that are some combination of amplitude and phase can increase the number of bits transmitted per symbol. A digital modulation scheme that incorporates both phase and amplitude modulation is Quadrature Amplitude Modulation (QAM). 8-QAM uses four carrier phases plus two amplitude levels to transmit 3 bits/symbol. Other popular variations are 16-QAM, 64-QAM, and 256-QAM, which transmit 4, 6, and 8 bits/symbol, respectively.

QAM represents an efficient use of the spectrum, but it is more difficult to demodulate in the presence of noise, which consists of random amplitude variations. Because of its spectral

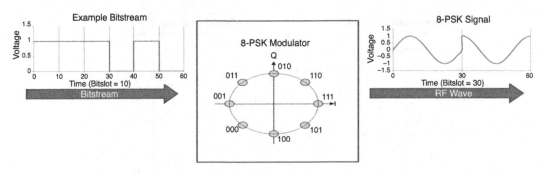

FIGURE 6.12   8-PSK modulation and radio-frequency signal transmissions.

efficiency, QAM is often used in cable TV, Wi-Fi wireless LANs, satellites, and cellular telephone systems to produce a maximum data rate in limited bandwidths.

Fig. 6.12 depicts the end-to-end 8-PSK modulation scheme to include the transition to a digital radio-frequency signal, for example, the 802.11 protocol for Wi-Fi.[9] The bit stream enters the modulator and the 8-PSK modulator simultaneously specifies 3 bits to generate the PSK-modulated signal. The PSK modulator relates these 3 bits to its constellation diagram and generates a PSK waveform. The waveform is shown here in the time domain representation. Because it clocks 3 bits to every state change, the RF signal is one-third the rate of the bit stream, that is, 3 bits/symbol.

As noted earlier, additional frequencies are created as a result of modulation. Fig. 6.1 showed a carrier frequency and resulting sidebands from modulation by a single analog frequency. The same principle applies to digital modulation schemes, where the transmitted energy is shared between the carrier frequency and the sidebands. Fig. 6.13 illustrates the frequency spectrum of a modulated digital signal. Note that the energy is concentrated in the sidebands in this particular representation.[9]

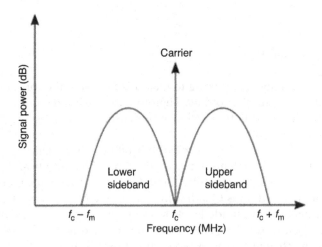

FIGURE 6.13   Modulated digital signal in the frequency domain.

SIGNAL AVERAGING

The technical objective of an attacker in compromising a radiated signal is to increase the signal-to-noise ratio. The attacker has a number of options. He or she might attempt to increase the signal footprint or in other words capture more signal. But the attacker is ultimately constrained by covertness requirements since using a large antenna to achieve more gain might draw unwanted attention.

A more sensitive receiver might be deployed to detect weaker signals. Of course, a more sensitive receiver will also detect more noise. Finally, an attacker might attempt to increase the signal relative to noise using statistical methods, which will only cost him or her additional time by virtue of additional measurements. How much time? To answer this question a brief interlude on statistics is required.

A canonical attack scenario involves intercepting a weak signal in a noisy environment. All signals in real world are affected by noise, which by definition consists of random fluctuations in signal amplitude. That is, noise introduces uncertainty in a signal measurement, and this uncertainty can be quantified.

For two random variables, x and y, the expectation value, that is, the variance, of their sum equals the sum of their expectation values. By definition, the variance of a signal voltage is the average power assuming the mean value is zero and therefore there is no DC component.

If two sources with a random phase relationship, that is, noise, are summed, the average power of their sum equals the average power of each signal added separately. So adding two independent recordings of noise will increase the RMS voltage by $\sqrt{2}$ and therefore double the noise power. The noise power is given by $(\sqrt{2})^2 = 2$.[10]

However, if two signal sources with a constant phase relationship are added together, the signal voltages double. Therefore the power *quadruples* since the power is proportional to voltage squared.

So if N measurements of the signal plus noise are performed, the signal will be enhanced relative to the noise by a factor of $\sqrt{N}$.[11]

The details of the calculation are instructive. Let S_i equal individual measurements of signal plus noise power. If n such measurements are summed to produce a signal S_n, the result increases with each individual measurement S_i. Recall that the signal power is equal to its variance.

The total signal S_n is the sum of all S_i from $i = 1$ to n:

$$S_n = \sum_{i=1}^{n} S_i = nS_i$$

[10]RMS is a statistical average of quantities that fluctuate and, as its name implies, involves taking the square root of the mean value of the square of the quantity. For example, the RMS value of a sine wave is 0.707 of the peak value.
[11]Alternatively, the standard deviation about the mean of a distribution of N signal measurements will be reduced by $\sqrt{N}$ relative to the standard deviation about the mean of N noise signal measurements. The standard deviation indicates the spread in the likelihood that a randomly chosen value in that distribution is proximal to the mean. Of particular note is that if N represents a normally distributed random variable, the standard deviation of that distribution is $\sqrt{N}$.

The variance of the noise is also additive. Therefore summing n measurements of the variance, which is the standard deviation (σ) squared and equal to the signal power, is equivalent to n independent measurements of the variance/signal power:

$$\sigma_n^2 = \sum_{i=1}^{n} \sigma_i^2 = n\sigma_i^2$$

The standard deviation σ_n of a distribution of n such measurements is the total RMS noise. The standard deviation of n measurements of a random variable equals $\sqrt{n}$ (see footnote 11). Therefore after n measurements the total noise equals N_n and is given by the following:

$$N_n = \sigma_n = (\sqrt{n})\sigma_i = \sqrt{n}N_i$$

Stating the result in words, the signal power of n signals is n times an individual signal power measurement. However, the power of n individual noise signals equals the square root of n times a single noise power measurement. The ratio of the signal-to-noise ratio after n measurements is as follows:

$$\text{Signal-to-noise ratio} = \left(\frac{S}{N}\right)_n = \frac{nS_i}{(\sqrt{n})N_i} = \sqrt{n}\left(\frac{S_i}{N_i}\right) \tag{6.1}$$

Eq. (6.1) is the basis for the statement that averaging N signal samples improves the signal-to-noise ratio by $\sqrt{N}$. The implication is that computing the average of the signal plus noise over many samples will enhance the signal relative to the noise. For example, averaging 100 repetitions of the signal plus noise will improve the signal-to-noise ratio by $\sqrt{100} = 10$. Fig. 6.14 graphically illustrates the effect of signal averaging as a function of the number of averages.[12]

Signal averaging can be effective in increasing the signal-to-noise ratio of periodic signals such as those that are likely to be targeted for compromise by an attacker. One such compromise targeted the signal generated by the image-refresh circuitry of video displays with the intent of reading the information displayed on the computer monitor [1]. This attack will be described in Chapter 7 but a key attack feature is mentioned now.

Flat-panel video interfaces continuously refresh the entire image content between 60 and 85 times/s. This continuous refresh ensures that signals on the video interface are periodic. The spectral lines of a periodic signal are spaced according to the signal repetition frequency. The periodicity associated with the refresh process plays a critical role in the vulnerability to information compromise as processing gain can be achieved for periodic signals relative to the noise.

Sampling a signal is required in order to determine its information content. It is common to sample the targeted signal input with an analog-to-digital converter at regular intervals. However, the sampling process could introduce aliasing, a form of signal distortion resulting from infrequent sampling. The Nyquist sampling theorem specifies the minimum sampling rate that is required to faithfully reconstruct an analog signal.[13]

---

[12]http://web.khu.ac.kr/~tskim/DSP%2018-2%20Signal%20Averaging.pdf.

[13]Harry Nyquist (1889–1976) was a Swedish-born American engineer who made seminal contributions to communication and information theory.

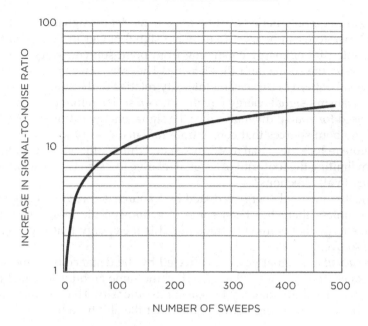

FIGURE 6.14   The effect of signal averaging on signal-to-noise ratio.

That minimum sampling rate is twice the highest frequency component of the original signal. Later in the chapter we will see that Nyquist sampling condition affects the requirement for signal filtering, which is an essential step in an attacker's quest to enhance the signal-to-noise ratio.

If noise is the attacker's enemy, averaging a periodic signal is his or her best friend. However, several factors limit the degree of signal-to-noise ratio enhancement attainable by time averaging. One cannot average indefinitely and expect to see improvements in the signal-to-noise ratio. For example, digital systems measure inputs to a specified accuracy and perform arithmetic to a similar level of precision. This constraint limits the inherent accuracy of the computed average.

In addition, there may be time- or voltage-dependent drifts in the instrument. These have the effect of adding variations to the true signal. The signal can also change with time, perhaps due to internal changes in the system or a slow variation in external conditions.

RISK FACTORS FOR SIGNAL COMPROMISE

The Signal Footprint

It may seem a bit gratuitous, but the mere presence of signal energy is a risk factor for detection. Moreover, and as has been stated several times, the critical feature that determines the vulnerability to detection by an attacker is the signal-to-noise ratio at the detection location.

Put succinctly, if the signal power relative to the ambient noise power at the point of detection exceeds a certain value, the signal is vulnerable to detection and potential reconstruction. The one caveat is that the use of encryption could clearly affect the vulnerability component of risk but this important security control is not considered here. Moreover, compromising emanations can exist *before* a signal is encrypted.

Point sources of electromagnetic radiation are one model for signal intensity as a function of distance, and therefore can be used to estimate signal power in the signal-to-noise ratio. To reiterate, the intensity of energy emanating from point sources scales as $1/r^2$, where r is the distance between the source and the detector. The intensity can be viewed as an ever-expanding spherical pattern of decreasing intensity relative to the source.

Point sources transmit signal energy equally into 4π sr. Therefore intensity at a particular location is sacrificed for spatial diversity since the signal energy is transmitted over a greater solid angle. What about sources that concentrate radiated energy in a particular volume of space and therefore reduce the signal footprint? Stated differently, what benefits in covertness are derived from limiting the footprint of a signal relative to a signal source radiating an equal amount of energy in all directions?

It is axiomatic that the total energy radiated by a source is constant at any given distance from the source unless there has been some direction-specific loss mechanism. In other words, the total energy that is initially transmitted is the energy that is detected at a given radius from the source.

However, the *density* of signal power is affected by the distance from the source and/or if the signal is concentrated in a solid angle. Thus the same amount of signal power can be focused into a smaller volume thereby increasing its intensity. The intensity can be concentrated through the use of focusing but recognize that the ability to focus is limited. What is that limit?

Recall the physical limit to focusing electromagnetic energy is dictated by diffraction. The minimum angular divergence (AD) for circular apertures was given by (3.7) in Chapter 3. This limit is given by $1.22\lambda/D$, where λ is the energy wavelength and D is the diameter of the lens or antenna.

Therefore the limit on focusing increases when either the wavelength is made smaller relative to the antenna or the aperture size is increased for a fixed wavelength. In other words, the bigger the lens or antenna, the more focused is the beam for a given wavelength.

The concept of antenna gain was introduced in Chapter 2. Antenna gain is a measure of antenna focusing power. It is often expressed in units of decibels, i.e., the logarithm of the ratio of the signal intensity relative to a lossless isotropic antenna. An isotropic antenna detects or radiates an equal amount of energy in any given direction and therefore exhibits no gain.

Parabolic reflectors are a common sight due to the proliferation of satellite TV systems. Their general appearance is familiar to most people, and therefore they are useful in illustrating the implications of antenna gain. Parabolic reflectors have sprouted all over the urban landscape, and point in unison toward geospatial satellites hovering high overhead.

The operation of a parabolic reflector in conjunction with a microphone is identical to devices used to collect electromagnetic signals from a satellite. The former is used to compromise audible information, and the latter is used to enhance electromagnetic signals received from satellites. Parabolic reflectors used in conjunction with microphones will be analyzed in Chapter 10 when audible information compromises are discussed.

For parabolic reflectors, the width of the antenna can correspond to hundreds of signal wavelengths and is therefore capable of achieving tremendous gain. The magnitude of gain can be deduced from the formula specified below. In scenarios involving television reception, considerable signal enhancement is required since TV satellites are in geosynchronous orbit above the earth. The physics of orbiting bodies demands that these satellites remain 22,000 miles overhead. How much gain would be expected from a satellite dish in order to achieve sufficient signal-to-noise ratio?

The gain G of a parabolic reflector is given by the following expression:

$$G = k\left(\frac{\pi D}{\lambda}\right)^2 \tag{6.2}$$

Here k is an efficiency factor (about 0.55), D is the diameter of the dish, and λ is wavelength.[14] So if the antenna is receiving or transmitting microwave energy with a wavelength of 0.01 m, and has a diameter of 1 m, the gain is roughly 41 dB or a factor of about 10,000.

For a fixed antenna diameter, increasing the wavelength of the signal energy decreases the gain, and this decrease scales as the inverse of the square of wavelength. In other words, the antenna will experience nonlinear reductions in gain for increasing wavelengths. Eq. 6.2 reveals that quadratic *increases* in gain will be achieved with increases in dish diameter for a given wavelength.

But this tremendous gain comes at a price. Since energy cannot be created out of thin air, the increase in signal intensity in one slice of space must result from a decrease elsewhere. Therefore, an antenna exhibiting high gain is by definition highly directional. This fact has significant implications to the vulnerability to signal interception and therefore to information compromise since higher gain results in a smaller signal footprint. Let's be precise about the security benefits that accrue from a smaller signal footprint.

Although the parabolic reflector concentrates energy in a small solid angle relative to an antenna that broadcasts equally in all directions, the transmitted energy does diverge or spread out from the point of transmission. To be sure, the magnitude of this divergence is less for higher-gain antennae, but the signal will diverge nonetheless. The limit on this divergence is again dictated by diffraction.

The angular divergence (AD) of a signal exiting a transmitting parabolic antenna is as follows[14]:

$$AD = 70\frac{\lambda}{D} \tag{6.3}$$

Note the similarity of (6.3) to Eq. (3.7) in Chapter 3 where the latter specified the AD for circular lenses. If λ is assumed to be 0.01 m (i.e., a microwave signal) and D is 1 m, the AD is 0.7 radian.

So (6.3) is an expression for the AD of the signal exiting the parabolic reflector. The beam diameter can be determined by multiplying AD by the distance between the antenna and the detector. The beam diameter scales linearly with the AD of the beam and distance.

At a separation distance of 100 m, the microwave beam width or diameter is calculated as follows:

$$\text{Microwave Beam Width} = 0.7\,\text{radian} \times 100\,\text{m} = 70\,\text{m}$$

[14]http://www.radio-electronics.com/info/antennas/parabolic/parabolic-reflector-antenna-gain.php.

III. THE COMPROMISE OF SIGNALS

Since the radius (r) of the microwave beam width equals half the diameter or 35 m, the microwave signal footprint or area of the beam at the detector can be simply calculated as follows:

$$\text{Microwave Signal Footprint at the Detector} = \pi r^2 = 3848 \text{ m}^2$$

If the power radiated by the parabolic antenna is 1 W, the signal intensity at the detector is now easily computed:

$$\text{Intensity of the Microwave Signal at the Detector} = \frac{\text{Signal Power}}{\text{Signal Footprint}} = \frac{1 \text{ W}}{3848 \text{ m}^2} = 0.0003 \text{ W/m}^2$$

If the antenna used by an attacker is also a parabolic dish with a diameter of 1 m, the attacker's antenna intercepts some fraction of the total transmitted power. This fractional power corresponds to the beam intensity times the area of the dish assuming the signal occupies the entire face of the attacker's dish:

$$\text{Intercepted Microwave Signal Power} = 0.0003 \text{ W/m}^2 \times 0.79 \text{ m}^2 = 0.2 \times 10^{-3} \text{ W}$$

A 0.2-mW signal should be readily detectable assuming usual noise conditions prevail. Therefore, the incremental security that could be achieved with an antenna radiating a microwave signal at this distance is not significant. To be more covert, the signal transmitter must either transmit a higher frequency, that is, a shorter wavelength, or use a larger dish. The latter might be problematic depending on the location and associated requirements for covertness.

The earlier example is an excellent illustration of how the limits of an information security attack scenario are dictated by physical parameters that are known or can be calculated. Although tremendous gain can be achieved with a parabolic dish, it might not be the antenna of choice for an attacker depending on scenario-specific operational constraints.

The clever reader might be thinking, "What about using devices that radiate signals with even shorter wavelengths? How would the use of such devices affect the vulnerability to signal detection?" In fact, transmitting a shorter-wavelength signal is an option. What about using optical wavelengths?

Optical signals would work well except that visible energy might give away the presence of a signal to an attacker. However, an infrared laser might be an ideal candidate for signal transmission. Infrared wavelengths are roughly 10,000 times shorter than microwaves, that is, 10^{-2} m versus 10^{-6} m. As an added bonus infrared energy is usually invisible to the human eye.

Of course, one significant operational consequence of focusing is that the transmitter and the receiver must be appropriately aligned since the signal exists only in certain regions of space. Mother Nature does not give something for nothing. The trade-off for a smaller signal footprint is an increase in required precision with respect to detection geometry.

In other words, the more gain exhibited an antenna, the greater is the alignment criterion since the transmitted signal is confined to a narrower slice of space. Eq. (6.3) explicitly states that a larger antenna aperture can produce a smaller beam divergence or more tightly focused beam. Note that this problem also exists for an attacker hoping to detect the same signal.

III. THE COMPROMISE OF SIGNALS

The geometry of signal transmission and detection argues for using sources that have a smaller footprint if covertness is the principal objective. Optics and specifically diffraction dictates the areal limit on such footprints. Lasers are excellent candidates since the laser beam does not diverge much even at substantial distances from the source. For this reason a laser beam is said to be highly collimated.

The explanation for this collimation is that light emitted from a laser is formed in an optical cavity between two parallel mirrors. The mirrors constrain the light to a path perpendicular to the surfaces of the mirrors. The divergence of high-quality laser beams is commonly less than 1 mradian (0.001 radian), and can be much less for large-diameter beams. As noted earlier, an infrared laser would be an attractive device to use for covert communications because the beam is not visible to the naked eye.[15] Another important operational consideration in using a device that operates at optical wavelengths is that line-of-sight between transmitter and detector would be required.

Let us assume such a device is being considered as a means of discreetly communicating to a neighboring building. What is the vulnerability to fortuitous detection by an attacker? In other words, how lucky would an attacker have to be in order to "randomly" intercept a signal from an infrared laser?

The AD of the laser is assumed to be 0.3 mradian.[16] Therefore, the beam width or diameter of the laser beam at a distance of 100 m will be the AD times the distance between the transmitter and the detector:

$$\text{Diameter of an infrared laser at 100 m} = 0.3 \times 10^{-3} \times 100\,\text{m} = 0.03\,\text{m}$$

Recall the beam width of a microwave signal at the same distance was 70 m or over 2300 times greater in diameter. This diameter translates to a difference of 6 billion times in area or equivalently its footprint! In general, the beam radius at a distance D between laser and detector is given by the following expression for small divergence angles ϕ[17]:

$$\text{Laser beam radius at the detector} = D\tan\left(\frac{\phi}{2}\right) \sim \frac{D\phi}{2} \tag{6.4}$$

An exaggerated depiction of the laser beam divergence is shown in Fig. 6.15.[18]

Let P equal the power of the laser. Using (6.4) the intensity at the detector is given by P divided by the signal footprint neglecting atmospheric attenuation[18]:

$$\text{Laser Intensity at the Detector} = \frac{4P}{\pi D^2 \phi^2}$$

[15]Detection equipment that operates in the infrared portion of the electromagnetic spectrum is available and is commonly referred to as "night vision gear."

[16]A radian is a unit of angular measurement. There are 2π radian in a circle of 360 degrees. A measurement in radians is numerically equal to the length of a corresponding arc of a unit circle. One radian is equal to just under 57.3 degrees when the arc length is equal to the radius.

[17]Diffraction as discussed in Chapter 3 sets the limit on the minimum beam divergence. Recall for circular apertures the diffraction limit is given by $1.22\lambda/D$, where λ is the wavelength of the signal energy and D is the diameter of the aperture.

[18]http://www.robkalmeijer.nl/techniek/electronica/radiotechniek/hambladen/hr/1990/05/page18/.

III. THE COMPROMISE OF SIGNALS

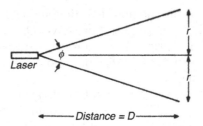

FIGURE 6.15   Angular divergence of a laser beam (highly exaggerated).

The maximum distance yielding a signal-to-noise ratio of 10 for a radio-frequency transmitter will be calculated later in this chapter for comparison. That calculation is used to estimate the maximum distance of vulnerability to compromise by an attacker who knows roughly where to look for the signal.

The same calculation could be performed using a figure for the laser intensity. The calculation would assume the attacker is in possession of a lens with a given focal length, and a background intensity of infrared energy would compete with the signal of interest.

However, here the problem of estimating the risk of detection is approached differently. Rather than estimate the vulnerability to detection by calculating the signal-to-noise ratio, the *probability* of detecting the laser signal is calculated.

Assume such an attacker is located in a nearby building, and is using a 300-mm telescope lens at a fixed but randomly selected location. The attacker could be in any building that is 100 m from the building with the laser source, and there is direct line-of-sight between the laser and the attacker's detector. Furthermore, the attacker does not know where to look for the beam.

To reiterate, this calculation leverages simple probability and optics, and is not a vulnerability assessment. This is an important distinction. Both calculations yield potentially useful information relative to formulating a security strategy albeit from two entirely different perspectives. Obtaining both perspectives yields additional insight on risk and each component should complement the other.

Said differently, the probability of detection measures a different component of risk than does the vulnerability to detection. One defensive strategy might be to reduce that probability below a specific threshold based on the organizational tolerance for risk. However, the strategy should incorporate the results of the likelihood *and* vulnerability measurements. An understanding of both components yields a more textured view of the risk associated with this attack vector and therefore better informs a risk management strategy.

The probability calculation does *not* specify the likelihood of an attacker actually mounting an attack and therefore searches for the signal. Rather, it indicates the probability of an attacker stumbling upon the signal by fortuitously being in the right place at the right time with the appropriate detection gear. This is an important distinction. Classically the likelihood component of risk refers to the probability that a threat incident will occur and not the likelihood that it will be successful if it does occur.

It is initially assumed that the laser and the detector are aligned in the vertical direction. Therefore, the calculation is reduced to a one-dimensional problem. A calculation in the vertical dimension will follow, and the product of the two dimensions will yield the sought-after probability.

Recall in this case the beam diameter is 0.03 m and the lens diameter is 0.3 m. So the lens is 10 times the diameter of the beam. If the beam were larger than the lens, the calculation would differ from the one shown below.

The laser beam diameter is assumed to be anywhere along the circumference of a circle since the attacker could be at any location surrounding the laser. In other words, the attacker could set up his or her telescope lens anywhere on the circumference of a circle that surrounds the laser transmitter.

Let the circumference of the circle equal C, the diameter of the lens equals Y, and the diameter of the laser beam at 100 m equals X. Recall possible locations in the vertical plane are ignored for now so it is assumed that the attacker is vertically aligned with the laser.

The probability that the lens falls entirely within the laser beam equals the probability that the attacker is in the proper segment of the circle, where a segment would be roughly defined by a building width, times the probability that the beam is in that segment. Assume the space between buildings is negligible. The probability is given by the following simple expression:

$$\frac{Y}{C} \times \frac{X}{Y} = \frac{X}{C} \qquad (6.5)$$

The laser beam diameter at 100 m is 0.03 m and the circumference of a circle of radius 100 m is $2\pi \times 100$ m = 628.3 m.

The probability of detection X/C is therefore equal to the following:

$$\frac{X}{C} = \frac{0.03}{628.3} \sim 4.8 \times 10^{-5}$$

This expression is the probability of fortuitously detecting an infrared laser signal using a telescope lens of the specified diameter at a distance of 100 m from the laser source assuming the location of the signal in the vertical direction is known. If no information is known about the signal location, a similar calculation is performed in the vertical direction, and is multiplied by the result in the horizontal dimension. That calculation will be performed next.

Let Y be the diameter of the lens and L is the vertical length of a single story of the building. For a 30-story building and assuming 3 m/story, the probability of detection is the probability the detector lens is placed at the correct location within a given story times the probability that the attacker's lens happens to be at the correct story, that is, 1/30 if a particular story is selected at random. So the probability of vertical detection is given by the following:

$$\text{Probability of Vertical Detection} = \frac{Y}{L} \times \frac{1}{30} = \frac{0.3 \text{ m}}{3 \text{ m}} \times \frac{1}{30} = 0.3 \times 10^{-2}$$

The probability of an attacker fortuitously detecting the infrared laser signal anywhere in a building located 100 m from the source is the probability of detection in the horizontal direction times the probability of detection in the vertical direction. This figure is now easily calculated to be 1.6×10^{-7} or about 1 in 5 million. The use of a laser for covert signal transmission appears to be quite effective assuming the scenario provides flexibility in the alignment of the laser transmitter and receiver.

III. THE COMPROMISE OF SIGNALS

Physical Proximity

One risk factor for unauthorized signal detection is the proximity of an attacker to the signal source. Previous calculations estimated the probability of fortuitous detection of a laser signal by an attacker. The limited angular diversion of the laser beam and the fact that it is highly collimated greatly reduce the risk of detection by an attacker.

But lasers are not practical for a number of communication scenarios, precisely because of the lack of spatial diversity and the requirement for line-of-sight between transmitter and detector. Therefore, the vulnerability to signal detection will now be estimated for a different mode of communication.

Consider the following scenario: An attacker accessed a conference room prior to its use by corporate executives. Moreover, there is concern that the attacker concealed a microphone/recorder and radiofrequency transmitter in the room in order to eavesdrop on conversations that occurred during the meeting.

What is the vulnerability to detecting the covert signal assuming the attacker broadcasts the signal in real time and a countermeasures team deploys their equipment in the conference room?

Our newfound understanding of electromagnetic fields is used to calculate the covertness of a radio-frequency signal as a function of distance from the transmitter. Note that this somewhat contrived scenario favors the defender. The high-risk area has been identified and the countermeasures team knows approximately where to look for a concealed device.

It is assumed that the technology used by the attacker is relatively crude. Therefore methods of covert transmission such as spread spectrum are not considered, although the incremental covertness it would afford might not be sufficient given the close proximity between the signal transmitter and the countermeasures team's detection gear.

In fact, our hapless attacker is using straightforward surveillance technology purchased from "The Spy Shop." Moreover, he or she does not bother to turn the transmitter off once it is installed. The continuously radiated peak power of the transmitter is assumed to be 10 mW.

But the attacker leverages one asset that is potentially more useful than sophisticated surveillance technology: a company employee who has unlimited physical access to the conference room. The attacker puts that individual to good use by instructing him or her on how to cleverly conceal the surveillance device.

As noted above, commercial technical surveillance countermeasures (TSCM) inspection team has been hired to conduct a "sweep," and is armed with a spectrum analyzer. This spectrum analyzer has a "video bandwidth" of 100 MHz, which implies a detector rise time of 3.5×10^{-9} s, and therefore is capable of following the fluctuating amplitude of the signal envelope.[19]

While moving the analyzer antenna around the room, the countermeasures team fortuitously positions the antenna approximately 1 m from the radiating transmitter antenna. What is the power as detected by the analyzer assuming isotropic radiation by the device antenna and unity antenna gain of the detection system?

---

[19]"Video bandwidth" is a term used for the frequency range of the power envelope fluctuations or, alternatively, the AM component of the modulation only. A rule of thumb is the detector rise time = 0.35/(Video Bandwidth).

The total energy density in the electromagnetic wave broadcast by the transmitter is the sum of the electric and magnetic energy densities specified as follows:

$$\text{Total Electromagnetic Energy Density} = \frac{1}{2}\varepsilon_o E^2 + \left(\frac{1}{2}\right)\left(\frac{1}{\mu}\right)B^2 \qquad (6.6)$$

where ε_o is the electric permittivity of free space or 8.85×10^{-12} F/m in SI units. μ_0 is the magnetic permeability of free space or 1.3×10^{-6} Wb/(A m) in SI units.

From Maxwell's equations it is known that the B and E fields are related by the speed of light, c. Specifically, $B = E/c$ and $c = (1/\varepsilon_o\mu_0)^{1/2}$. Therefore, the following relation can be established:

$$\frac{1}{2}\left(\frac{1}{\mu_0}\right)B^2 = \frac{1}{2}\left(\frac{1}{\mu c^2}\right)\varepsilon_o E^2 = \frac{\varepsilon_o\mu_0 E^2}{2\mu} = \frac{1}{2}\varepsilon_o E^2 \qquad (6.7)$$

Half of the radiated energy is derived from the electric field and the other half from the magnetic field.

The radiated intensity I has units of watts per meter squared. For a plane wave, $I = c\varepsilon_o E^2$. The transmitter frequency is assumed to be 1 GHz, and therefore the wavelength is 0.3 m so the detection antenna is approximately three wavelengths from the source. This distance is in the far field of the radiating source, and therefore the transmitted signal is a plane wave.

The radiated signal is idealized to be passing through an imaginary sphere at some distance from the source. Its intensity equals the signal power divided by the surface area of the sphere at the prescribed radius, that is, at the point of detection by the countermeasures team. Therefore, the intensity at a distance of 1 m is calculated as before:

$$I = \frac{P}{4\pi r^2} = 0.8 \times 10^{-3} \text{ W/m}^2$$

Plugging I into (6.7) yields the following:

$$\frac{1}{2}I = \frac{1}{2}c\varepsilon_o E^2 = \left(\frac{1}{2}\right)(0.8 \times 10^{-3} \text{ W/m}^2)$$

This leads to the magnitude of the electric field at a distance of 1 m from the covert transmitter:

$$E = \left(\frac{0.8 \times 10^{-3}}{\varepsilon_o c}\right)^{1/2} = 0.55 \text{ V/m}$$

Note that TV and FM radio broadcast signal electric fields are typically millivolts per meter or microvolts per meter. So the electric field of the hidden transmitter as measured at 1 m is approximately 1000 to 1,000,000 times greater in amplitude.

Assuming the receiver antenna is 0.5 m in length, the electric field as calculated earlier yields an EMF of roughly 0.3 V. If one assumes 50 Ω for the spectrum analyzer input impedance R and noting that Power = V^2/R, the detected signal power at that distance is 1.8 mW.

III. THE COMPROMISE OF SIGNALS

This signal power should be easily detectable by even an unsophisticated countermeasures team.

Compare this figure with a similar measurement at 25 m while neglecting any attenuation by intervening structures. The signal power measured at 25 m is roughly 2.8 μW $(2.8 \times 10^{-6}$ W).[20]

Although this signal is still quite detectable assuming excessive noise is not present in the signal bandwidth, the power is reduced by a factor of 625 relative to the same signal strength at 1 m. The thermal noise in a 100-MHz bandwidth is roughly -95 dBm or 0.05×10^{-12} W so external sources of interference will likely dominate.

One can confidently conclude that the TSCM team should have no trouble detecting this signal, but neither would an attacker located 25 m from the conference room assuming ambient noise and signal attenuation due to walls, barriers, etc., were not significant. A more complete discussion of factors that affect the vulnerability to electromagnetic signal compromise will be provided in Chapter 7.

Electromagnetic Noise and Interference

It is intuitively understood that a greater distance from the signal source reduces the signal intensity as measured by a would-be attacker. It was shown in Chapter 3 that point sources experience a signal intensity reduction that scales as the inverse of distance squared from the source.

For systems exhibiting more gain the falloff in intensity would be less, but the signal footprint would be concentrated within a narrower slice of space. A more realistic scenario is now examined, where the effect of noise on the vulnerability to signal detection is considered.

A would-be attacker requires a minimum signal-to-noise ratio in order to intercept a signal of interest. Often this ratio is quoted as 10, and is the nominal figure used throughout this book. Note that this figure will vary depending on the modulation scheme.[21]

One should also appreciate that a minimum signal-to-noise ratio exists for both attackers and legitimate signal consumers. Presumably the latter are located closer to the signal source. Therefore, the signal power as seen by the attacker is decreased, and hence contending with the signal-to-noise ratio is often more challenging for him or her as well.

Wireless LAN systems are ubiquitous these days. They facilitate Internet access for users, and they obviate the need to establish a physical network connection. But as with all security–convenience trade-offs, a wireless LAN increases the vulnerability to unauthorized access to private network resources.

A number of successful attacks on wireless LANs have been documented. These can be found in texts devoted to this issue or to network vulnerabilities more generally. At a high level, the use of weak encryption, for example, Wireless Encryption Protocol (WEP), providing connectivity between a "Guest" wireless network and the internal "Corporate" network,

---

[20]Note that if we assume the transmitter is a point source, it will exhibit the characteristic $1/r^2$ falloff in intensity. Therefore at 25 m the signal intensity will be reduced from 1 m by a factor of $(1/25)^2$ or 625.

[21]The required signal-to-noise ratio will vary depending on the modulation scheme. For an analog FM land mobile radio system using 25-kHz channels, the receiver must have approximately 4 dB more signal power than noise power. This represents a carrier-to-noise ratio of 4 dB.

and/or users simultaneously connecting to a Guest and the Corporate network, all represent potential avenues for compromising the Corporate network via network attacks.

However, if part of the defensive strategy assumes that the wireless signal is not detectable outside a facility perimeter, it would be wise to perform a basic calculation to support that assumption. If the signal-to-noise ratio of a wireless LAN is roughly 10 or greater at a remote location not under the control of the LAN sponsor, this scenario is equivalent to extending a long wire and connector to that point for the attacker's convenience. With the benefit of a stable and sufficient signal-to-noise ratio, the attacker is free to begin scanning for available resources and open network ports and thereby exploit existing network vulnerabilities.[22]

Of course, implementing various security controls can make an attacker's life more difficult. It is assumed that one of those controls is the enforcement of a minimum distance between an unauthorized listener and the radiating access point. Estimating the vulnerability to unauthorized signal detection as a function of distance is the objective of the following calculation.

First, a particular wireless LAN model is selected, and system-specific technical specifications are used. The scenario under consideration is a wireless LAN access point positioned near the perimeter of a facility. Therefore, building elements do not contribute significantly to signal attenuation. For this exercise the Aruba (HP) 320 series access point has been chosen.[23]

It is assumed the system is running the 802.11n wireless protocol, is transmitting at 2.45 GHz with a transmit power of 250 mW, and is using an antenna with a gain of 3 dBi.[24] It is also assumed that the noise floor is determined by thermal noise across the signal bandwidth. Later we will perform the same calculation with more realistic conditions to show the profound effect noise has on the system link margin.

Wireless LANs operate by dividing segments of the signal bandwidth into channels to accommodate simultaneous users, and each channel determines the available bandwidth for a given user during a session. A 20-MHz channel width is assumed in this particular analysis. (*Note*: Both 20- and 40-MHz channel bandwidths are options with this system.)

The Aruba system can actively search across available channels for sources of radio-frequency interference in order to maintain adequate channel capacity, which affects the ability to transmit and receive data to/from the access point.

The thermal noise power limit at 293 K (room temperature) relative to a milliwatt (dBm) in decibels is given by the following expression, where Δf is the noise bandwidth:

$$P_{dBm} = -174 + \log_{10}(\Delta f) \tag{6.8}$$

The lower limit of noise in an electronic device at room temperature in a 1-Hz bandwidth is −174 dBm, which explains the figure of −174 in (6.8). For the 802.11 wireless LAN channel,

---

[22]Numerous attacks on wireless networks have been documented to include Access Control Attacks, Confidentiality Attacks, Integrity Attacks, Authentication Attacks, and Availability Attacks as specified in http://www.google.com/search?client=safari&rls=en&q=description+of+a+wireless+attack+against+a+network&ie=UTF-8&oe=UTF-8.

[23]http://www.arubanetworks.com/assets/ds/DS_AP320Series.pdf.

[24]The dBi unit specifies decibels relative to an isotropic antenna.

the thermal noise floor is calculated to be −101 dBm or slightly less than 10^{-13} W. This figure represents the lower limit of noise power in a 20-MHz bandwidth at room temperature.[25]

What is the maximum distance at which an attacker could detect the Aruba wireless LAN signal assuming thermal noise represents the noise floor?

Friis formula was specified in (3.10) of Chapter 3. It can now be applied to a security scenario, where the effective cross-section of the dipole receiver antenna is given by $\lambda^2/4\pi$:

$$P_r = \left(\frac{P_t}{4\pi r^2} \right) \times \left(\frac{\lambda^2}{4\pi} \right) \times G_t \qquad (6.9)$$

P_t, the access point transmitted power, is 250 mW, the signal wavelength λ at 2.45 MHz in air is 0.12 m, the gain of the access point antenna is a factor of 2 relative to an isotropic antenna (3 dBi), and the criterion for detection is that the minimum ratio of the received signal power P_r to the noise floor is 10.

The thermal noise power in a 20-MHz bandwidth at room temperature is −101 dBm or 7.9×10^{-14} W. So the power of the received signal must be at least 10 dB greater or 7.9×10^{-13} W.

Rearranging (6.9) and solving for the maximum distance yields an expression for r:

$$r = \left[\frac{P_t \lambda^2 G_t}{P_r 16\pi^2} \right]^{1/2} \qquad (6.10)$$

Plugging the Aruba system specifications into (6.10), r is calculated to be an astounding 7597.0 m or 4.7 miles! This number defies both experience and intuition but also illustrates the potential effect of an ultralow noise environment on the vulnerability to detection. Similar effects will be observed for acoustic scenarios in Chapter 10.

In real life, intended signal recipients would be swamped by a virtually unlimited number of competing devices if wireless LAN signals could be detected at this distance. Of course, an attacker would experience similar difficulties. But it does not pay to debate who would be worse off than whom since the situation differs so much from reality. What is actually wrong with this scenario?

The noise floor at this frequency in urban areas is assumed to be −80 dBm based on anecdotal reporting.[26] This power level is 21 dB above the thermal noise floor. The principal sources of noise at this frequency are solar radiation and radio-frequency and television transmission interference.

Recalculating the distance while assuming the same criterion for signal detection requires P_r to equal −70 dBm, r is now a more realistic but still seemingly excessive 675 m.

However, other measurements of noise in this frequency range have been reported to be significantly higher. For example, one urban measurement at 2420 MHz (2.42 GHz), an

---

[25]A calculation of the thermal noise power is as follows: The thermal energy of atoms, KT_0, at room temperature = 1/40 eV (where K is the Boltzmann's constant and T_0 is the absolute temperature in kelvin). The thermal noise power is given by $KT_0 B$, where B is the signal bandwidth = 20 MHz. So, $KT_0 B$ = (1/40 eV) × (20 MHz) = (1/40 eV) × (1.6×10^{-19} J/eV) × (20 MHz) = (0.04×10^{-19} W s) × (20×10^6 s^{-1}) = 0.8×10^{-12} W. Recall 0 dBm is 1 mW. To convert dBm to watts use the following formula: watts = $10^{P(dBm)/10}/1000$.

[26]http://www.quora.com/How-high-is-the-ambient-RF-noise-floor-in-the-2-4-GHz-spectrum-in-downtown-San-Francisco.

allotted 802.11 frequency, was measured to be -70 dBm/MHz or 2.42×10^{-7} W.[27] Using the same criterion for the signal-to-noise ratio and plugging the resulting figure for P_r into (6.4) yields a much diminished $r = 4.3$ m.

Ignoring the veracity of either measurement for the moment, the takeaway is that a difference of 44 dB in ambient noise power translates into a link margin decrease from 675 to 4.3 m!

The variation in calculated link margins should be sobering. It might give pause to those who assume proximity to the source and ambient noise offers an effective defensive strategy. Organizations might consider placing access points closer to internal areas within a facility to minimize the vulnerability to unauthorized signal detection.

Even if these theoretical calculations overestimate the maximum system link margin by a factor of 10, the resulting distances could be tens of meters. In an urban area, a circle of that radius could include a significant number of buildings or vehicles that could serve as listening posts.

For example, in one ethical hacking exercise, my company alighted in the client's parking lot to intercept their public Wi-Fi broadcast. The most significant obstacle to success was the fact that the link margin was often less than satisfactory. Once our team managed to obtain a stable connection using a high-gain antenna they were able to exploit existing IT vulnerabilities.

Of course, a low-intensity signal should not be used as a compensating control to offset weak application or network security. But it does highlight the importance of good "signal governance," and the fact that signal detection is *the* gateway to all other efforts at signal compromise.

Wireless LAN systems are not meant to be covert. One quarter watt of radiated power is not insignificant. These systems are designed to allow the remote user population to establish robust and spatially diverse connections. But the same calculation applies to adversaries intending to detect such signals or to covertly send a signal to a listening post. Everyone is obliged to obey the laws of physics.

In the latter case an attacker would likely employ various measures to reduce the vulnerability to detection. These might include lowering P_t to much less than 0.25 W, utilizing spread spectrum techniques to drop the peak signal intensity in favor of a wider signal bandwidth, and reducing the time the device is actually transmitting.

INTRODUCTION TO INFORMATION THEORY

The noise power associated with signal transmissions is not just a theoretical consideration. In addition to setting the limit on detection, it also is one of two parameters that determine the maximum rate at which information can be sent over a communication channel, that is, the channel capacity. The great achievements of information theory are in describing the limits on information transmission and formalizing the statistical nature of information itself. A brief discussion of information, information theory, and the implications to information security are discussed in the remainder of this chapter.

It is immediately worth noting that the word "information" in this context differs from the colloquial use of the term. It is important to think of information not as data conveying

---

[27]http://ntrs.nasa.gov/archive/nasa/casi.ntrs.nasa.gov/20050041714.pdf.

meaning, but as a source of symbols that can be characterized in terms of its statistical diversity. This diversity is a measure of uncertainty. The concept of "information entropy" has been established to facilitate this statistical characterization.

Entropy in information theory is a measure of unpredictability associated with a source of symbols. Specifically, the entropy associated with an information source H is defined as follows:

$$H = -\sum_i \{p_i(x)\log_2[p(x)]\} \tag{6.11}$$

The units of entropy are in bits per symbol, bits per second, or simply "bits."[28]

Let's analyze the entropy associated with a simple binary process. Consider the process of coin flipping where the probability of flipping a heads or tails is either 0 or 1. Note that any coin where the probability of flipping a head is not equal to the probability of flipping a tail would imply a distinctly nonkosher coin, but such coins are mathematically instructive if not exactly fair.

The two states of the coin, heads and tails, constitute a data source. Moreover, it is an example of a Bernoulli process, which is defined as a statistical process where only two outcomes are possible. The maximum entropy occurs when the probability of a head and the probability of a tail are equal, that is, a fair coin. In other words, a fair coin yields equally probable outcomes. The fairness condition also implies maximum uncertainty in the outcome of an individual flip:

Probability of a heads [p(heads)] = Probability of a tails [p(tails)] = 0.5

Therefore, applying (6.11) to this process it is apparent that the entropy of this information source is as follows:

$$-\left[\frac{1}{2}\log_2\left(\frac{1}{2}\right) + \frac{1}{2}\log_2\left(\frac{1}{2}\right)\right] = -\left[\frac{1}{2}(-1) + \frac{1}{2}(-1)\right] = 1\,\text{bit/symbol}$$

Therefore 1 information bit is required to generate the source of outcomes produced by the entire coin flipping process. Fig. 6.16 illustrates the entropy of an information source generated by a binary process such as coin flipping.[29] Note that the maximum information entropy occurs when the probability of a 1 or 0 is 0.5.

Let us say an information source now consists of three characters, and each character could again assume a value of 0 or 1. There are 2^3 or 8 possible outcomes that characterize the entire information source: 100, 110, 111, 001, 010, 011, 101, and 000.

The probability of any single three-digit outcome x is $p(x) = 1/8 = 0.125$.

Again applying Eq. (6.11) and noting there are eight equally likely symbols with a probability of 1/8 yields the entropy of this information source:

$$H = -8\left[\left(\frac{1}{8}\right)\log_2\left(\frac{1}{8}\right)\right] = -8\left[\left(\frac{1}{8}\right)(-3)\right] = 3\,\text{bits/symbol}$$

[28]So-called "information bits" should not be confused with binary digits. This distinction will be explained in the text but is mentioned here to avoid confusion at the earliest opportunity.
[29]http://tekmarathon.com/.

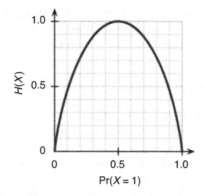

FIGURE 6.16 **Entropy of a binary process.**

Therefore 3 bits are required to represent a given symbol and thereby delineate the entire information source. Continuing in this manner, suppose an information source consisted of four elements and each element could again be either a 0 or a 1. Therefore there are $2^4 = 16$ possible outcomes or symbols for this information source as follows: 0000, 0001, 0011, 0111, 1111, 1110, 1100, 1000, 1001, 0110, 0010, 0100, 0101, 1010, 1101, and 1011.

The probability of a given symbol is $1/16$ and $p(x) = 1/16$. Therefore, the entropy, H, of this information source according to (6.11) is equal to $-16(1/16)\log_2(1/16) = 4$ bits/symbol.

In general, if each element in an N-element information source can assume two values, there are 2^N possible symbols in the information source. If each symbol appears with equal probability, that is, $p(x) = 1/2^N$, the entropy of the information source is $-\log_2(1/2^N) = N$. In other words, it will require N bits/symbol to represent the entire information source if each symbol occurs with equal probability.

Pulses of energy used to transmit digital signals often represent binary digits in electronic information systems. These pulses can have a constant amplitude that is often measured in fractions of a volt and a constant width measured in fractions of a second. As discussed earlier in the chapter, the pulse train is modulated to convey information, where various combinations of pulses comprise the source alphabet. Therefore the entropy of the information source will be quite different than if each pulse representing a symbol occurs with equal probability.

Importantly, binary digits (contracted to form the word "bit") used to transmit data and entropy bits used to transmit information are not necessarily equivalent. For example, one might envision an information source where the probability of transmitting a 0 is $1/4$ and the probability of transmitting a 1 is $3/4$. In that case, applying (6.11) reveals the entropy of the information source is 0.811 information bit per binary digit or 0.811 information bit/symbol.

A transmitter broadcasting a signal data for a source of symbols with this entropy at a rate of 100 binary digits/s is indeed transmitting 100 symbols, characters, pulses of energy, binary digits, etc., per second. However, the information rate of the source is only 0.811 information bit per binary digit. Therefore only 0.811 information bit/symbol × 100 symbols/s = 81.1 information bits are required to transmit 100 binary digits of the signal.

In another example of the nonequivalence of information bits and data bits, consider a transmitter broadcasting at a rate of 10,000 pulses/s. It clearly has a channel capacity of

10,000 binary digits/s since data is being transmitted at this rate. Yet what if the pulse train consists of a repetitive string of 1's? In that case there is no uncertainty in the data stream and according to (6.11) the entropy is zero. Hence no *information* is transmitted in the information theoretical sense:

$$H = -p(1)\log_2 p(1) = 1\log_2(1) = 0$$

Note that $p(1) = 1$ and $2^0 = 1$; therefore $\log_2(1) = 0$.

Said another way, the transmitter is actually broadcasting zero information bits per second. The information rate must therefore be distinguished from the *data* rate where the latter is the number of binary digits being transmitted regardless of the underlying alphabet or information source.

The information rate can also be a stream of 1's and 0's, but the data reflects the uncertainty (or conversely the redundancy) of the underlying data source. The lower the redundancy (or the greater the uncertainty) of the source, the more information is being transmitted. The implication is that more diverse sources of information will require more symbols to fully represent the source, which will affect the information rate for a given signal bandwidth.

Information theory prescribes limits on the rate of information transfer over a communication channel based on the inherent uncertainty of the message source plus specific physical parameters associated with the communication channel. Again, information in this context refers to the diversity of the message source. The specifics associated with those limits are defined next.

The entropy of a data source equals the average number of bits per symbol needed to encode it. Is there a relationship between the entropy of an information source and the rate at which information can be transmitted? The answer is "yes" and the theorem specifying that relationship is one of the central tenets of information theory.

A theorem formulated by Claude Shannon[30] states that if there is an information source with entropy H and a channel capacity C, then the limit on the average information transmission rate is given by the following:

$$\text{Average information transmission rate} \leq \frac{C}{H} \tag{6.12}$$

The implication of (6.12) is that no amount of fancy encoding can facilitate the transmission of information at an average rate greater than C/H. Stated even more bluntly, only the entropy H of an information source is less than the channel capacity C, can a message can be successfully transmitted over a communication channel.

Note that when transmitting messages, the number of binary digits being transmitted is known but the entropy of the information source is likely not known. If the entropy of the information source were known to be less than the number of binary digits used per second, presumably fewer binary digits per second would be required to transmit a given message.

---

[30]Claude Shannon (1916–2001) is considered "the father of information theory" and published a seminal paper in 1948, *A Mathematical Theory of Communication*.

III. THE COMPROMISE OF SIGNALS

Recall the example of a binary information source where the probability of the first state is not the same as that of the second state. In that case it was shown that a single binary digit could be represented by less than 1 information bit.

What has been missing from the discussion thus far is to specify the channel capacity C and to determine the parameters that limit C. In other words, what are the specific features of the communication channel that limit the rate at which a source of symbols can be transmitted? Once this rate is known, it will be possible to relate the limit on encoding as specified earlier to specific communication channel features.

Transmitting a signal requires sampling that signal. Nyquist established the fact that sampling a signal at a minimum rate of twice the bandwidth is required to avoid distortion of the signal being sampled. In 1928 Ralph Hartley specified a limit on the number of binary digits that can be transmitted per second as a function of the signal sample [2] [31]:

$$\text{Binary digits per second} = n \log m \tag{6.13}$$

Here m is the average number of different symbols per signal sample and n is the number of signal samples per second. What factors limit m and n in transmitting messages over a communication channel, and, more specifically, can one relate m and n to specific features of the signal?

The Shannon–Hartley law establishes such a relation. It expresses the limit on channel capacity (bits per second) as a function of signal bandwidth and the signal-to-noise ratio assuming the source of noise is Additive White Gaussian noise (AWGN) [3] [32]:

$$C \text{ (bits per second or bits per symbol)} = W \log_2 \left[1 + \left(\frac{S}{N} \right) \right] \tag{6.14}$$

Eq. (6.14) states that the channel capacity C is proportional to bandwidth and to the logarithm of the signal-to-noise ratio. Moreover, it relates C to the average number of different symbols per sample (m) and the number of samples per second (n) as characterized by Hartley in (6.13). Recall m and n are the parameters that determine the theoretical rate at which binary digits can be transmitted over a communication channel.

The theoretical limit of C can be achieved only if an ideal form of encoding is used in which many characters representing many bits of information are encoded into long stretches of signal. Actual communications do not approach the limit on C as specified in (6.14).

Various modulation schemes use encoding to increase data transmission efficiency. (6.14) implies the channel capacity can be increased linearly by either (1) increasing bandwidth given a fixed signal-to-noise ratio or (2) using a fixed bandwidth and increasing the modulation rate but this requires a higher signal-to-noise ratio.

As the modulation rate increases, the spectral efficiency improves, but at the cost of an increase in the signal-to-noise ratio. For example, there is an exponential increase in the

---

[31]Ralph Vinton Leon Hartley (1888–1970) was a pioneer in information theory who conducted foundational research at Bell Laboratories.

[32]As noted previously, AWGN is wideband or white noise with a constant spectral density (expressed as watts per hertz of bandwidth) and a Gaussian distribution of amplitudes.

III. THE COMPROMISE OF SIGNALS

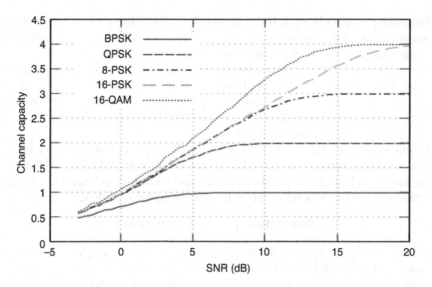

FIGURE 6.17   Channel capacity versus signal-to-noise for various modulation schemes.

signal-to-noise ratio requirement for a 16-QAM versus 64-QAM modulation scheme. Again, the trade-off is that the spectral efficiency improves for higher modulation rates. Fig. 6.17 specifies the channel capacity (bits/symbol) as a function of signal-to-noise ratio for various phase shift keying modulation schemes, which are used in systems where spectral efficiency is required, for example, Wi-Fi.[33]

INFORMATION THEORY AND INFORMATION SECURITY

The channel capacity as expressed in (6.14) yields the theoretical limit on the number of information bits that can be successfully transmitted over any communication channel. Technical details associated with an 802.11 protocol wireless LAN access point will be used to illustrate the application of information theory to information security.

The thermal noise power at a temperature T (kelvin) is inherent to all devices, and represents the lower limit on noise power and therefore signal detection. Thermal noise is AWGN, and therefore (6.14) applies.[34] The following are representative wireless LAN access point parameter values:

- Signal bandwidth = W = 40 MHz.
- Thermal noise (40 MHz bandwidth) = N.
- Signal power = $P \sim$ 250 mW = 24 dBm = 0.25 W (250 mW).

[33]http://www.wikiwand.com/en/Phase-shift_keying.
[34]Thermal noise at room temperature is −174 dBm/Hz. Since the channel bandwidth is 20 MHz, the thermal noise floor for the system is calculated as follows: −174 dBm + 73 dB = −101 dBm.

The theoretical limit of the channel capacity, C, is determined using (6.14) and noting thermal noise is given by kTW, where k is Boltzmann's constant:

$$C = W\left[1 + \log_2\left(\frac{P}{N}\right)\right] = 40 \times 10^6/\text{sec}\,[1 + \log_2(0.25/(1.6 \times 10^{-13}))] = 1.6 \times 10^9 \text{ information bits/s}$$

The Aruba wireless access point advertises a maximum binary digit transmission rate of 800 Mbits/s (800 × 10⁶ bits/s). However, this specification more likely means it is transmitting at 200 Mbits/s *per channel* because four data streams are being transmitted simultaneously.[35]

(6.14) dictates that the number of information bits per second cannot exceed 1.6×10^9 for this signal bandwidth, signal power, and noise power irrespective of the encoding scheme.

The primary takeaway of (6.14) is that both bandwidth and signal-to-noise ratio affect channel capacity. It would not be unreasonable to think one might want to encode information such that the minimum number of bits is transmitted. That is less difficult if sufficient signal bandwidth is available.

However, and as prescribed by (6.14), a narrow-bandwidth signal requires a compensatory increase in the signal-to-noise ratio for successful transmission at a specified channel capacity. In other words, there is a trade-off between signal bandwidth and signal-to-noise ratio to achieve a given channel capacity. Table 6.1 specifies the minimum signal-to-noise ratio required to transmit 1 bit/s as a function of signal bandwidth [4].

Note the precipitous rise in the signal-to-noise ratio required to maintain a 1-bit/s channel capacity for a decreasing signal bandwidth. However, many possible combinations of bandwidth and signal-to-noise ratio are possible at a given channel capacity. Therefore (6.14) can be interpreted more broadly as stipulating that reducing the signal-to-noise ratio will require an increase in the bandwidth W for a given channel capacity, C, and vice versa.

TABLE 6.1 Minimum Signal-to-Noise Ratio Required to Transmit 1 bit/s

Bandwidth (Hz)	Minimum signal-to-noise ratio
0.01	1.3×10^{30}
0.1	1024
1	2
10	1.07
10^2	1.07
10^3	1
10^6	1
10^9	1

---

[35]http://www.arubanetworks.com/assets/ds/DS_AP320Series.pdf. Aruba access points utilize Multiple-Input/Multiple-Output (MIMO) technology. This is a technique for sending and receiving more than one data signal on the same radio channel at the same time via multipath propagation. The advertised channel capacity is quite close to the theoretical limit calculated using (6.10), but it appears that four separate signals are being transmitted simultaneously.

III. THE COMPROMISE OF SIGNALS

TABLE 6.2   Possible Variations in Bandwidth and Signal-to-Noise Ratio to Achieve a 4-Mbit/s Channel Capacity

Bandwidth	Signal-to-noise ratio
2×10^6	1,000,000
4×10^6	1,000
8×10^6	30.6

The two degrees of freedom presented by combinations of bandwidth and signal-to-noise ratio have implications to information security via enhancing signal covertness. The most obvious implication is that increasing signal bandwidth will relax the requirement on signal power making life more difficult for a would-be attacker. Another is that reducing the overall rate of transmission would allow for both reduced bandwidth and signal-to-noise ratio.

Table 6.2 specifies some of the possible combinations of bandwidth and signal-to-noise ratio to establish a channel capacity of 4 Mbits/s [4].

The security implication of Table 6.2 is that an attacker wanting to covertly transmit a signal to his or her redoubt using limited signal power might attempt to send data over a broad frequency spectrum rather than transmitting a more powerful signal.

Conversely, this technique could be used to subvert a potential attacker. In fact, it is one motivation for the use of spread spectrum technology. Specifically, so-called direct sequence spread spectrum is available with the explicit purpose of enhancing covertness and/or reducing the vulnerability to interference by widening the broadcast bandwidth.[36]

Some simple examples illustrate the types of calculations that yield the bandwidth and signal-to-noise ratio requirements for a given channel capacity[37]:

- If $S/N = 0$ dB, that is, the signal power equals the noise power, the Capacity C (bits per second) is equal to the bandwidth (hertz or cycles per second). It is possible to transmit signals that are below the background noise level but the error rate will grow very quickly.
- If the signal-to-noise ratio is 20 dB (a linear factor of 100) and the available bandwidth is 4 kHz, which corresponds to telephone communication links, the following is calculated for the channel capacity using (6.14):

$$C = (4000 \text{ bits/s}) \log_2 (1 + 100) = (4000 \text{ bits/s}) \log_2 (101) = 26.63 \text{ kbits/s}$$

- If C is required to be 50 kbits/s and a signal bandwidth $W = 10$ kHz is available, the minimum S/N required is calculated as follows using (6.14):

$$50,000 \text{ bits/s} = (10,000 \text{ bits/s}) \log_2 \left(1 + \frac{S}{N} \right)$$

Therefore, $C/W = 5$, which implies $S/N = 2^5 - 1 = 31$. This figure corresponds to a signal-to-noise ratio of 14.91 dB.

[36]http://www.spektrumrc.com/Technology/DirectSeqSpread.aspx.
[37]https://en.wikipedia.org/wiki/Shannon–Hartley_theorem.

The salient points of the previous discussion are as follows:

1. The total noise power affects the rate of signal transmission.
2. Thermal noise is an inherent source of noise in all devices used to detect signals and applies equally to intended signal recipients and adversaries alike.
3. Thermal noise imposes a theoretical limit on the rate of signal transmission, that is, channel capacity in the parlance of information theory.
4. One can attempt to decrease signal power to decrease the vulnerability to interception, but this action requires increasing the signal bandwidth to achieve a specific data rate with attendant complications.
5. Both the channel capacity and the physical limit on signal detection are limited by noise. In fact, information security and information theory are themselves related by noise. An attacker can estimate the minimum system power required to satisfy channel capacity requirements in light of noise assuming the noise source is Additive White Gaussian. Conversely, defenders can use estimates of channel capacity to determine the signal-to-noise ratio for a given signal bandwidth and thereby estimate the vulnerability to information compromise assuming the noise source is Additive White Gaussian.

It was shown in Chapter 5 that the thermal noise inherent to electronic devices dictates the fundamental limit on signal detection. It also can be used to specify the minimum energy required to transmit a single bit of information. This limit only reinforces the profundity of Eq. (6.14), and is also another example of the connection between information theory and physics.

Let us substitute the expression for thermal noise as specified by Eq. (4.5) of Chapter 4 into (6.14) to determine the minimum energy required to send a single bit of information. Eq. (6.14) now becomes the following [4]:

$$C = W \log_2 \left[1 + \left(\frac{P}{kTW} \right) \right] \tag{6.15}$$

(6.15) can be rewritten as follows:

$$C = \frac{1.44\, P}{kT} \quad \text{if} \quad \frac{P}{kTW} \ll 1 \tag{6.16}$$

(6.16) can rewritten as $P = 0.693\, kTC$, which sets the minimum threshold for the required energy of transmission for a single information bit per second (or symbol per second), and is independent of bandwidth. Therefore, the following statement can be made:

> Even if a wide bandwidth is used, 0.693 joules per second of signal power is required to transmit one bit of information-per-second. Therefore, transmitting a bit of information on average requires a minimum of 0.693kT joules of energy. [4]

Transmitting data with a sufficient link margin requires significantly more energy than $0.693\, kTJ$. That is because extra power is required for a signal consisting of short pulses each specifying a single binary digit compared to using one of many long signals consisting of many different samples of different amplitudes to represent many successive binary digits.

III. THE COMPROMISE OF SIGNALS

Approaching Shannon's minimum energy limit for a given bandwidth requires the use of long, complicated signals as elements of the code that resemble Gaussian noise [5].

Finally, the Nyquist sampling theorem is another fundamental result of information theory. It specifies that all of the spectral content is represented within half the highest frequency in any band-limited signal/waveform. This result has significance to implementing remote attacks on electromagnetic emanations as described in Chapter 7.

For example, in the attack on the video display interface of a laptop, harmonics of the pixel repetition rate are frequency shifted to an intermediate frequency. A specific harmonic with frequency f in a quiet portion of the spectrum is selected for filtering. The sampling theorem enables the narrowing of the intermediate-frequency bandwidth to within $f/2$ of the selected harmonic frequency.

The effect is to reduce the noise power relative to the signal since signal energy in a bandwidth outside $f/2$ is superfluous, and the noise therein would only vitiate efforts at signal detection. This method is generally applicable to attempts at information compromise in environments with low signal-to-noise ratios, and is a notable example of information theory applied to information security.

SUMMARY

Signal wavelength and the physical dimensions of radiating or focusing elements (eg, antennae, lenses) determine the angular divergence of a signal. Specifically, the beam diameter increases linearly with distance and the area increases quadratically with beam radius. Sensors used to detect electromagnetic and acoustic energy respond to intensity, which is the power per area or power density. Diffraction is the physical process that limits the focusing power/resolution of an antenna or lens.

Elementary electromagnetic theory and optics can be used to estimate the vulnerability to detection of signals radiating from different sources. The likelihood of "random" laser communication signal detection by an adversary is provided and leverages geometry and optics. This complements calculations of the vulnerability radiofrequency signal detection using the signal-to-noise ratio.

Noise always establishes the limit on signal detection and it is always present. The theoretical limits on detection are significantly greater than the limits achievable in the real world because of the presence of noise. Thermal noise resulting from the motion of atoms in detection equipment represents the minimum noise in any detection scenario.

Information theory specifies theoretical limits on information transmission where information relates to the diversity of a message source. The information entropy H specifies the diversity associated with a message source as follows[38]: $H = -\sum_i \{p_i(x) \log_2[p(x)]\}$.

[38]Thermodynamic entropy is defined as the number of possible states of a system. Information entropy and thermodynamic entropy are not directly related *per se*, but can be shown to have a connection. Namely, and most generally, a decrease in the uncertainty of a system state, that is, decrease in thermodynamic entropy and an associated increase in free energy, exactly offsets the energy required to communicate the information entropy bits specifying the change in state.

Units of entropy are specified in bits, bits per second, or bits per symbol. In the general case information bits differ from the more familiar data bits or "binary digit" but these are equivalent when each symbol in the information source has equal probability of occurrence.

The channel capacity C is a function of the logarithm of the signal power-to-noise power S/N and signal bandwidth W where the noise is Additive White Gaussian: $C = W[1 + \log(S/N)]$.

A signal-to-noise ratio that is greater than or equal to 10 is a rule-of-thumb threshold for the vulnerability of a signal to detection. However, this figure will vary depending on the modulation scheme. For a given channel capacity various combinations of signal-to-noise ratio and bandwidth are possible. This provides options for signal covertness via a reduction in signal power with a concomitant increase in signal bandwidth.

References

[1] Kuhn M. Security limits for compromising emanations. In: Rao, J.R., Sunar, B., editors. CHES 2005, LNCS 3659. Heidelberg: Springer Verlag; 2005. p. 265–79.
[2] Hartley RVL. Transmission of information. Bell Syst Tech J 1928;7(3):535–63.
[3] Shannon C, Weaver W. The mathematical theory of communication. Urbana, Chicago, IL: University of Illinois Press; 1963.
[4] Pierce JR. Electrons, waves and messages. Garden City, NY: Hanover House; 1956.
[5] Pierce JR. An introduction to information theory; signals, symbols and noise. Massachusetts: Dover; 1980.

The Compromise
of Electromagnetic Signals

INTRODUCTION

In previous chapters several primitive attack scenarios were described. In these scenarios attackers did little to enhance their stealthy efforts. However, these scenarios were useful in identifying some of the fundamental issues associated with data compromises. They provided a segue to estimating the vulnerability of electromagnetic signals to detection. Unfortunately they would likely fall short of the mark in actual attacks because of inadequate signal-to-noise ratios.

The fundamentals of electromagnetic theory and basic mathematics as presented in previous chapters provide the background to enable discussions of more realistic attack scenarios.[1] Such scenarios are described in this chapter as well as in Chapters 8–10. Countermeasures are also noted as appropriate.

However, pure theory alone is insufficient to make realistic estimates of vulnerability. Specifications relating to technology used in information security attacks are linked to operational conditions that are scenario-specific. In fact, these conditions drive technology performance specifications in the real world and therefore understanding the operational constraints is critical for defenders and attackers alike. From an attacker's perspective decisions regarding technology often represent a trade-off between enhancing the signal-to-noise ratio and ensuring covertness. Decisions for defenders invariably relate to convenience versus security.

---

[1]Much of the discussion of the limits on electromagnetic compromises is based on the paper by Kuhn M. Security limits for compromising emanations, <https://www.cl.cam.ac.uk/~mgk25/ches2005-limits.pdf>. This is required reading for anyone interested in information security.

A NAÏVE ATTACK[2]

An unsophisticated attacker might be tempted to conduct a remote attack targeting electromagnetic emanations from an electronic device such as a computer by merely using an antenna coupled to an amplifier and a recording device, for example, a digital storage oscilloscope. Specifically, such an attack might consist of a loop antenna of area A oriented at 90 degrees to the magnetic flux density B generated by direct or indirect emanations from a targeted electronic device. We know from Chapter 4 and Faraday's Law that the voltage induced in the loop antenna is given by $A[dB/dt]$ where t is time, and assuming A is constant and B is uniform over the loop area.

In order to measure the magnetic flux directly, a naive attacker might connect the loop antenna in series with a resistor of resistance R and a capacitor of capacitance C. Recall Figure 4.23 depicted a similar setup.

If the impedance of the capacitor to a sinusoidal magnetic field input is small compared to R at the frequencies of interest, the current is approximately $(A/R)[dB/dt]$. If the output signal is the voltage across the capacitor, the current can be integrated to yield $[A/RC]B(t)$. Therefore, the magnetic flux density could, in theory, be measured as a function of time with this type of apparatus.

If the signal-to-noise ratio was sufficient, the attack might be feasible. However, it would entail capturing the entire signal bandwidth, which would likely not be feasible due to the combination of ambient noise and weak signal. The efforts expended in the attack on the video link described later are focused on lifting a weak signal from the noise produced by radio broadcasts between 10 kHz and 10 GHz plus other noise sources across the spectrum.

The earlier discussion is not meant to imply that the electromagnetic spectrum is uniformly noisy. But noise exists across the electromagnetic spectrum to varying degrees, and technology is required to reduce such noise by shifting the signal to a more quite portion of the spectrum. This method enables an attacker to selectively amplify parts of the spectrum that provides the best signal-to-noise ratio.

But once such a portion of the spectrum has been identified, information theory is leveraged to enable signal filtering with the objective of reducing detected noise. As noted in Chapter 6, the Nyquist sampling theorem dictates that all of the spectral content is represented within half the highest frequency in any band-limited signal/waveform.

Emanations subject to attack are not modulated by another frequency. These unmodulated signals are referred to as baseband signals, and therefore are not shifted to a specific part of the spectrum.

Emanations are in fact digital signals and consist of discrete symbols such as bits and pixels that are being transmitted as a train of impulses at a specific rate. Assume symbols are transmitted at a frequency, f. If individual symbols have spectral energy concentrated at higher frequencies, possibly due to the sharp rise times of radiated pulses, that is, shorter than the duration of the symbol duration, that information will be repeated in $f/2$-wide intervals centered on higher harmonics of f.

---

[2]This discussion is based on observations noted in Kuhn M. Electromagnetic eavesdropping risks of flat-panel displays, 4th workshop on privacy-enhancing technologies, 26–28 May, Toronto, Canada; 2004.

This phenomenon is exploited in the filtering process in AM superheterodyne receivers. Superheterodyne receivers used in spectrum analyzers provide for selective tuning in order to shift the frequency of the received signal as well as apply appropriate filtering. The net result is to leverage quieter portions of the spectrum and narrow the signal bandwidth to optimize the signal-to-noise ratio. This flexibility in tuning and filtering is required because both the ambient and signal spectra will vary according to physical location and the signal of interest.

Use of a superheterodyne receiver does result in some loss of information due to signal rectification by the AM demodulator. Such information includes differentiating between rising and falling edges of the received pulses that characterize the targeted emanation. The trade-off is a lower-frequency signal that can be digitized using a sampling rate that is close to twice its bandwidth per the Nyquist sampling theorem.

Introduction to Signal Filtering

The basics of filtering and its limitations are important to understanding enhancements to the signal-to-noise ratio, which is the technical Holy Grail of an attacker. Its importance is due to the fact that filtering is essential to reducing noise, which in turn is critical to detecting weak signals.

The basic idea of band-pass filtering is to allow selected frequencies of the input signal to pass and eliminate or greatly suppress all other frequencies. The situation is illustrated in the frequency domain in Fig. 7.1.[2] The signal center frequency is f_s and the bandwidth of the input signal is B_I. The output spectrum is determined by the filter and is specified as B_O.

It turns out that the improvement in signal-to-noise ratio of the input signal relative to the filtered signal is given by the ratio of their bandwidths:

$$\frac{\text{SNR}_o}{\text{SNR}_I} = \frac{B_O}{B_I}$$

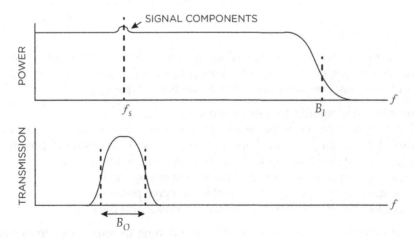

FIGURE 7.1 Band-pass filtering.

But the signal is not static, and the filter must respond to changes in signal amplitude. The response time of any linear filter is inversely proportional to its bandwidth. The implication is that narrowing the filter bandwidth means the filter will take longer to respond to changes to the input signal. So improvement in the signal-to-noise ratio implemented by narrowing the filter comes at the expense of increased measurement time. What is the exact price one pays for increasing the signal-to-noise ratio through filtering?

Recall the discussion on signal averaging in Chapter 6. There it was shown that N independent signal plus noise measurements added linearly. However, the result of N independent noise measurements will be proportional to $\sqrt{N}$. Therefore the signal-to-noise ratio improves as $N/\sqrt{N} = \sqrt{N}$.

The filter bandwidth is by definition inversely proportional to the time constant t of the filter. Since measurements and therefore measurement time increases directly with t, improvement in the signal-to-noise ratio through filtering can improve only as the square root of time.

As an example, the improvement in signal-to-noise ratio when sampling for 100 s versus 10 s is not a factor of 10 as one might expect if the improvement was linear. Rather the improvement in time occurs at a rate equal to $\sqrt{10}$ or ~3.2.

ASSUMPTIONS ON ATTACKERS AND ATTACK PARAMETERS

Attackers looking to compromise the information contained in electromagnetic signals can reasonably be expected to engage in activities and/or deploy technical enhancements pursuant to improving signal-to-noise ratio as follows:

1. Deploy high-gain antennae directed at the target device, for example, a computer.
2. Look for broadband impulses in a quiet part of the frequency spectrum.
3. Use notch filters to suppress the effect of strong, narrowband signals (eg, switching power supplies) that potentially interfere with the signal of interest emanating from the target device.
4. Use signal processing techniques to include periodic averaging, cross-correlation, digital demodulation, and maximum likelihood symbol detection to separate the desired signal from sources of interference/noise.

The aforementioned items drive the following best case (from an attacker's perspective) assumptions regarding a given attack. They help to establish the limits on required signal protection and represent the worst case from the defender's perspective:

1. Detect the minimum possible background noise.
2. Establish line-of-sight between the target and the receiving antenna or at least minimize the number of attenuating barriers between the target and the receiving antenna. Recall the magnitude of attenuation will likely be frequency-dependent.
3. Develop the maximum signal gain obtainable by a covert antenna.
4. Develop the maximum signal gain obtainable by signal processing.
5. Achieve the closest distance between the radio receiver and the target.

All of the aforementioned are driven by the overarching technical objective of improving the signal-to-noise ratio.

BROADBAND SIGNAL DETECTION

The Frequency Spectrum

Radiated signal energy from digital sources of information such as video displays of computers appears as pulses. These pulses are broadband, meaning they are of short duration, and are also transmitted at a high repetition rate. Their frequency spectrum consists of harmonics of the repetition frequency.

Fig. 7.2 shows a pulse train and associated harmonics in the time domain. T is the time between pulse repetitions, $1/T$ is the pulse repetition frequency or rate, and t is the pulse width. The pulses constitute the unmodulated, that is, baseband signal.[3]

The spectrum of rectangular pulses is shown in Fig. 7.3 in the frequency domain. The individual lines represent harmonics and therefore multiples of the fundamental frequency $1/T$. Importantly, the spacing between the harmonics is also given by $1/T$, and the envelope

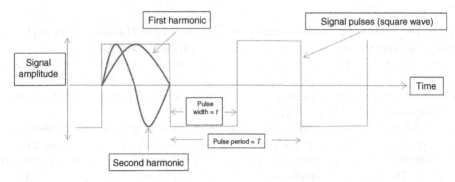

FIGURE 7.2   Signal pulses and harmonics.

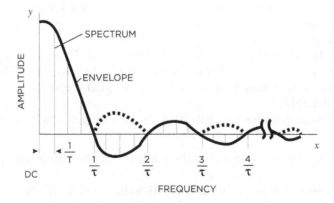

FIGURE 7.3   The frequency spectrum of a rectangular pulse.

[3]http://www.radio-electronics.com/info/t_and_m/spectrum_analyser/pulsed-signal-spectrum-analysis.php.

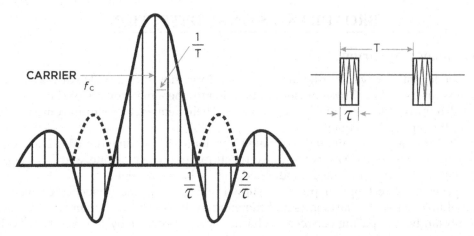

FIGURE 7.4 **The frequency spectrum of amplitude-modulated rectangular pulses.**

frequency corresponds to the inverse of the pulse width or $1/\tau$.[4] The spectrum envelope (solid line) follows the well-known $\sin x/x$ shape associated with pulsed energy.

Pulses can also be modulated to produce a more complicated spectrum. Fig. 7.4 shows a plot in the frequency domain of rectangular amplitude pulse modulation. The individual lines under the envelope represent the product of the modulation of the carrier with the pulse repetition frequency and its harmonics.[4]

Recall Fig. 6.1 showed the sidebands generated by modulating a single carrier frequency for an analog signal. The same principle applies to pulses except in this case modulation produces multiple sidebands due to the presence of multiple harmonics of the pulse repetition frequency. The sidebands manifest themselves as lines on a spectrum analyzer. Again for emphasis, these lines are spaced according to the pulse repetition rate $1/T$, and the periodicity of the envelope is determined by the inverse of the pulse width.

The pulse width and repetition rate are important to an attacker because he or she must use filtering that is adjusted according to that rate. The goal is to reject energy that vitiates the desired signal while accepting the pulse spectral content.

Specifically, the attacker will leverage the signal periodicity by signal averaging the pulse repetition rate over many cycles in order to lift the signal out of the noise. The detected pulse stream is then used to determine features relevant to signal reconstruction. The process is described in more detail later.

In general, broadband impulsive signals have the following characteristics:

- short duration;
- a frequency spectrum that is wider than the receiver intermediate frequency (IF) filter bandwidth;
- a repetition frequency that is significantly less than the receiver IF filter bandwidth;
- spectral intensity measured in terms of volt per megahertz.

[4]http://www.anritsu.com/en-GB/Media Room/Newsletters/files/GuideToSpectrumAnalyzers.pdf.

Broadband Signal Detection

Consider an attempt at remotely compromising an electromagnetic signal emanating from a computer where the ultimate goal is to resolve the display on a computer monitor. The electronic component of interest radiates electric and magnetic fields by virtue of voltage differences and currents associated with the generation of signal pulses. Let us consider the scenario where the radiating element is a computer display interface that generates direct emanations. This exact scenario is described in more detail later in the chapter.

The attacker uses an antenna that converts the radiated field into an EMF in accordance with Faraday's Law. The voltage waveform corresponding to the rise and fall of each signal pulse is of interest because every switching activity results in an electromagnetic impulse.

The pulses so generated consist of a spectrum of frequencies that collectively provide information about the pixels displayed on the computer monitor. If the pixel sequencing and mapping to the screen is known, the intercepted signal pulses corresponding to each pixel yield the information displayed on the monitor.

Moreover, these pulses are broad in frequency and hence narrow in time. The filtering used to reject unwanted frequencies must be at least as wide as the pulse repetition rate $1/T$.

The central problem for the attacker is that the signal is likely to be weak and contaminated by external sources of interference. Therefore, specific methods are used to increase signal-to-noise ratio. As noted previously, one effective method is to shift the received signal frequency to a low-noise portion of the spectrum where a band-pass filter is applied to reject narrow-band sources of interference. How is this signal enhancement/noise reduction accomplished?

An attacker might attempt to detect such pulses using the superheterodyne receiver. This technique is used by spectrum analyzers, and mixes the desired signal with a tunable internal local oscillator to produce IFs that are filtered and amplified.

The mixer is essentially a variable modulator that modulates the received signal with the local oscillator signal. It can be shown mathematically that multiplying two periodic signals produces additional frequencies corresponding to the sum and difference of the two original signals. A block diagram of a superheterodyne receiver is depicted in Fig. 7.5.[5]

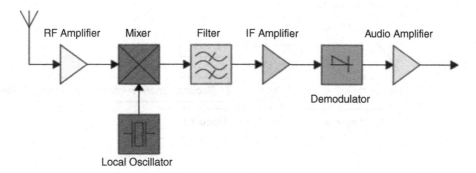

FIGURE 7.5   The superheterodyne receiver.

[5]https://en.wikipedia.org/wiki/Superheterodyne_receiver.

IF Filtering and the Impulse Bandwidth

IF filtering is critical to the heterodyne process, and, to repeat for emphasis, is invoked to improve the signal-to-noise ratio. In remote attacks on computers such as the signal produced by the computer video display interface, the vulnerable signal consists of narrow impulses that are transmitted with a specific repetition rate and consist of multiple frequencies that are multiples of this repetition rate.

These pulses are considered broadband signals, where this classification is based on the ratio of the bandwidth occupied by the signal to the bandwidth of the receiver, that is, the IF filter used to measure it.

Impulsive signals cause transient responses in receiver filters, which in turn are caused by a disturbance of a steady-state input signal. In other words, it is the rapid rise and decay times that are characteristic of pulses that cause these transients, and such transients can distort measurements of the signal.

Because of this distortion, the impulse response of the filter must be known in order to accurately measure the signal pulses. The impulse response in this context is defined as the ideal rectangular filter bandwidth that has the same voltage response as the actual instrument IF filter. The energy content of the pulse is equal to the peak (maximum) power level of the pulse multiplied by the pulse width.

In other words, the filter response is not perfect, and this imperfection will affect pulse measurements by an attacker. Therefore a measurement of impulsive signals must be normalized to the instrument's impulse bandwidth to obtain an accurate signal measurement. Fig. 7.6 illustrates the impulse bandwidth relative to an ideal rectangular filter and the spectrum analyzer's IF filter.[6]

The ratio of the IF filter bandwidth to the pulse repetition frequency is also critical to accurate measurements of signal intensity. In the attack on the computer display interface it is the pixel repetition rate relative to the IF filter bandwidth that determines the broadband criterion.

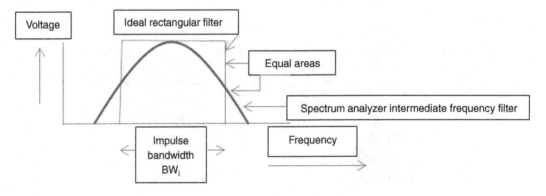

FIGURE 7.6 Impulse bandwidth (BW$_i$).

[6]http://uspas.fnal.gov/materials/11ODU/AN150-4.pdf.

That is, if the receiver IF bandwidth is smaller or larger than the pixel repetition frequency, it will result in different measurements in each case. For example, the receiver IF bandwidth might be significantly smaller than the pulse repetition frequency of a given signal, that is, the IF filter width is narrower than the signal spectral line spacing. In this case the IF filter resolution is narrow enough to resolve individual spectral lines, and only one spectral line would be in the IF filter's passband.

However, the receiver IF bandwidth might be significantly larger than the pulse repetition frequency. Such is the case with broadband signals, where many spectral components exist in the filter's passband. Importantly, the maximum RMS value of the filter's transient impulse response is proportional to the impulse bandwidth as defined earlier.

Therefore, knowledge of the impulse bandwidth is required to correctly interpret broadband measurements. Put another way, the filter's response typically deviates from the "ideal" filter response with respect to the impulse bandwidth, and therefore the measurement must be adjusted accordingly. Appendix D provides additional technical details on filtering.

Additional Techniques

Finally, because of the presence of noise, statistical methods are often leveraged for signal compromises. As noted previously, signal averaging uses the coherence of the signal to differentiate it from the incoherent noise.

In addition, cross-correlation is another statistical technique that is effective in increasing signal-to-noise ratio. Cross-correlation takes advantage of the fact that two signals, in this case the actual signal and the noise signal, are statistically independent. Correlation functions are a measure of the relationship between all products of pairs of points of two time series that are separated by a time delay. Cross-correlation can be used to detect a known signal within noise.

Specifically, the correlation coefficient can be calculated for a sample of data for two time series. Creating a preconditioned signal for a random test signal and performing a mathematical operation known as convolution with a band-pass–filtered version of the test signal, followed by the cross-correlation with the actual received signal, that is, signal plus noise, will result in the desired signal minus the noise [1].

A SECURITY LIMIT ON EMANATIONS

Introduction

The compromise of a video signal generated by a computer is the basis for ascertaining more general security limits on emanations. This discussion is limited to radio-frequency leakage of video signals where the successful compromise of a video signal has been demonstrated and documented in the literature. The redundancy offered by a repetitive signal coupled with detecting the approximate pixel clock frequency and precise line and frame frequencies facilitated such an attack [2].

Recall in previous sections it was assumed that a figure of 10 represents the minimum signal-to-noise ratio required to detect and subsequently demodulate a signal. This ratio is in general a valid security metric, but in order to estimate vulnerability in the real world it would be helpful to understand each of the features that contributes to the signal-to-noise ratio and their individual limits.

Fortunately this analysis has been done, and the precise expression for the signal-to-noise ratio is given by the following [3]:

$$\text{Signal-to-Noise ratio (S/N)} = \frac{EBG_aG_p}{a_d a_w E_{n,B} f_r} \tag{7.1}$$

where E is the maximum electric field strength emanated by a device; B is the impulse bandwidth of the attacker receiver filter; a_d is the free-space path loss corresponding to the distance d, between the attacker antenna and the target device; a_w is the building attenuation; G_a is the gain of the attacker's antenna; G_p is the processing gain achieved via signal processing by the attacker; $E_{n,B}$ is the electric field strength of natural and man-made noise at the location of the attacker's antenna within a quiet radio-frequency bandwidth; f_r is the noise factor of the attacker receiver.

The assumed noise levels and the magnitude of attenuation are random variables, which, in the absence of good data, must be modeled as a normal distribution.[7] The mean and variance would be determined by numerous measurements in a variety of environments.

For the other parameters in (7.1), reasonable estimates are required to establish a maximum electric field that would still keep the signal-to-noise ratio below the level required for signal detection. Therefore, these parameters must be estimated for each signal type of interest and for a given scenario.

Radio-Frequency Interference

An attacker intent on compromising information encoded in a signal is subject to the same constraints as those individuals authorized for detection. However, the bad news for an attacker is that he or she is not likely to have exceptional physical proximity to the signal source. Therefore, improving the signal-to-noise ratio through technical methods is essential to a successful attack.

The discussion of electromagnetic interference in Chapter 5 showed that an attacker must overcome external sources of radio-frequency interference and noise introduced by his or her own electronic gear to achieve an acceptable signal-to-noise ratio. The objective in this section is to be more specific about the effect of noise on signal detection limits. Therefore, a more precise formulation of the contribution of significant sources of noise is presented.

Ambient outdoor radio-frequency noise levels have been measured as a function of frequency.[8] At frequencies below about 10 MHz atmospheric noise and man-made noise dominate over thermal noise. All attackers must contend with this type of interference, which drives the required technical heroics in the form of frequency translation, filtering, etc. Fig. 7.7 illustrates the noise spectrum as measured in the United Kingdom as a function of frequency and relative to thermal noise power, kT_oB.[9]

[7]Refer to Chapter 13 for a discussion of the Probability of Protection method.
[8]https://www.itu.int/dms_pubrec/itu-r/rec/p/R-REC-P.372-7-200102-S!!PDF-E.pdf.
[9]https://en.wikipedia.org/wiki/Loop_antenna.

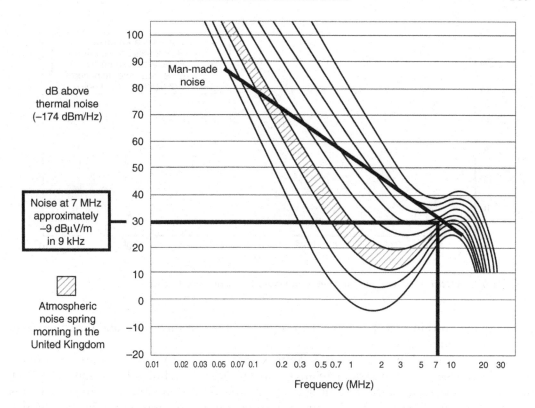

FIGURE 7.7 Noise spectrum relative to thermal noise.

In addition, mean noise levels in the radio-frequency spectrum have been specified in the form of a noise factor [3]. This factor is defined as the ratio of the noise energy detected over a bandwidth B to the thermal noise energy of a resistor at room temperature (293 K), T_o, that is, $P_{n,B}/kT_oB$. In other words, this ratio specifies the ambient radio-frequency noise power relative to the thermal noise power limit.

This noise factor has been converted to electric field levels as a function of frequency and is specified in decibels relative to microvolt per meter (dBμV/m) [3]. Mean value measurements were made in a 1-MHz bandwidth and include rural and business areas. Fig. 7.8 shows the results of these measurements and electric field conversions [3].

For example, at 1 GHz the mean electric field amplitude in a business area is 30 dBμV/m or 1 mV/m, which is roughly 8 dB above the thermal noise as measured by a half-wavelength dipole antenna at room temperature.

Radio-Frequency Signal Attenuation

There is enormous variance in the measured signal attenuation for radio-frequency signals in buildings. This situation will be discussed in more detail in Chapter 8, where quantitative models for intrabuilding and interbuilding scenarios are presented. Building materials,

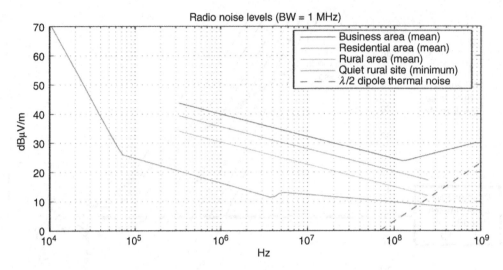

FIGURE 7.8   Electric field level measurements and radio-frequency interference.

geometry (eg, corridors vs open rooms), the number of intervening walls and floors, etc., will affect the magnitude of signal attenuation.

Although it is admittedly a gross approximation, a conservative approach from a defensive perspective is to assume relatively insignificant building attenuation a_w, in (7.1), unless a measurement of the specific scenario in question is possible and contradicts this assumption. Five decibels is used as an indicative figure in referenced publication, which roughly corresponds to the attenuation resulting from two internal walls of an unspecified composition.

Antenna Gain

The antenna used by an attacker is physically limited in size since the requirement for covertness imposes an operational constraint. Recall in the discussion on diffraction that the ratio of wavelength to the effective aperture of an antenna or lens establishes the physical limit on focusing.

Since the signal-to-noise ratio would typically be enhanced through antenna gain, part of this exercise is to engage in informed speculation regarding what type of antenna an attacker would use. It does not require a huge stretch of the imagination to assume that he or she would attempt to optimize antenna gain relative to its physical size in order to be as covert as possible.

There are a number of candidate antenna designs that could be used by an attacker. These include biconical, log-periodic, log-spiral, and double-ridged-horn designs. The gain associated with these antennae is between 2 and 6 dBi. Recall a dBi compares the measured signal amplitude to the amplitude as measured by an isotropic antenna [3].

A design that would optimize gain and also offer a measure of covertness is the Yagi–Uda antenna. The antenna dimensions are half as wide as the wavelength λ and its gain G

can be optimized to achieve the following figure, where L corresponds to the length of the antenna [3]:

$$G = 7.8\,\text{dB} \times \log_{10}\frac{L}{\lambda} + 11.3\,\text{dBi} \tag{7.2}$$

Increased gain and length of an antenna come at the expense of bandwidth, and, by definition, an increased sensitivity to direction. In the 200- to 400-MHz frequency range and for bandwidths of 50 MHz, which have been posited as good choices for compromising video signals, Yagi antennae with four elements offer an acceptable trade-off, yielding a gain of 8.6 dBi and a length $L \sim \lambda/2$.

Further gain can be achieved by connecting multiple Yagi antennae, where each doubling of their number increases the directional gain by 2.5–2.8 dB. M. Kuhn also cites specific numbers to illustrate what such a system would look like in practice: a 2×3 group of 6 Yagi antennae each with 4 elements and tuned to a center frequency of 350 MHz would have dimensions of $0.4 \times 1.3 \times 1.1$ m or about 0.6 m^3.

Importantly, a system of this size could be hidden behind a window or used within a vehicle. Regular glass would not substantively affect the received signal intensity unless it was tinted with metallic material. The antenna gain would be approximately 16 dBi. Doubling the reception frequency to 700 MHz (or equivalently halving the wavelength) would roughly quadruple the number of dipoles that could fit into the same space thereby providing 5–6 additional dB of gain. Fig. 7.9 shows a photograph of one high-gain Yagi–Uda antenna.[10]

Processing Gain

Signal averaging was discussed earlier in this chapter and in Chapter 6. To reiterate, signal averaging is used for one purpose: increase the signal-to-noise ratio. It has previously been established that periodic signals are amenable to enhancement via signal averaging. The specific attack described in this chapter is intended to illustrate the application of averaging methods, etc.

Specifically, Chapter 6 revealed that signal averaging can achieve theoretical signal enhancements on the order of $\sqrt{N}$ relative to noise, where N is the number of signal repetitions

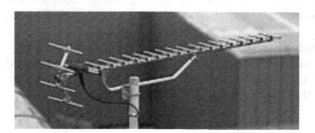

FIGURE 7.9   A Yagi–Uda antenna.

[10]https://en.wikipedia.org/wiki/Yagi-Uda_antenna.

that can be observed and added with correct phase alignment. The principle of signal averaging yields a generalized expression for processing gain G_p, as follows[11]:

$$G_p = \sqrt{N} = 3\,\text{dB} \times \log_2 N = 10\,\text{dB} \times \log_{10} N \qquad (7.3)$$

However, and with respect to the remote attack on the video displays of computers, the number of video frames that can be averaged in practice depends on whether the screen content is stable for an appropriate interval. The stability is determined by the frame rate. In addition, periodic averaging can be successful only if the frame rate can be determined with a low error rate.

Receiver Bandwidth

As noted earlier, the receiver bandwidth B will affect the measurement of the signal-to-noise ratio as measured by an attacker. In the detection of digitized video signals, the attacker would likely require B to be near the pixel frequency of the video mode in order to distinguish individual impulses generated by each pixel, and thereby reconstruct the full video bandwidth.

In general, wider receiver bandwidth will produce a better signal-to-noise ratio for these types of attacks. Digital waveforms under attack are switching impulses that are inherently wideband signals. As noted earlier, averaging correlated signals yields a $\sqrt{N}$ theoretical advantage over uncorrelated signals, that is, noise.

Recall the pulse repetition rate was cited as a critical signal feature with respect to its detection and compromise of signals generated by computers. One reason is that the frequency components of an impulse are harmonics of the pulse repetition rate. Therefore, the harmonics are correlated since they are multiples of the fundamental frequency, and signal averaging can be employed to pick these out of the noise.

The discussion on signal averaging in Chapter 6 applies here assuming the detection equipment has a sufficient impulse bandwidth. Specifically, detected impulse voltages will grow linearly with B. By contrast, measurement of thermal noise and narrowband background signals will increase only as $\sqrt{B}$ since the spectrum is Additive White Gaussian noise with uncertainty about the mean, that is, the noise is equal to $\sqrt{B}$.

Therefore, signal averaging to improve the signal-to-noise ratio will yield a processing gain proportionate to $B/\sqrt{B} = \sqrt{B}$. However, this situation is idealized since some of the background interference such as emanations from other computers also consists of broadband impulses.

There is also a reason to actually limit the receiver bandwidth as opposed to increasing it to enhance signal averaging. Limiting bandwidth will have the effect of reducing the interference caused by powerful narrowband radio and television transmitters. A receiver bandwidth of 50 MHz has been suggested as a compromise to resolve these competing requirements [3].

---

[11]Kuhn M, Security limits for compromising emanations. op cit. We note that cited reference includes a discussion on the factors influencing the number of frames of a video signal that can be stored. Much of that author's work in the area of compromising emanations is related to reconstructing signals from computer monitor displays and other electronic devices that process information.

Physical Proximity

The assumption is an attacker will not get closer than 30 m to the signal source. This assumption is more realistic in a rural setting, noting that ambient radio-frequency noise levels are on average 10 dB higher in urban scenarios. If the threat model includes attackers within the same facility and in nearby rooms, for example, a separation distance of about 3 m, the resulting test limits are lowered by 10 dB.

Emanation Security Limits

It is generally recognized that a minimum signal-to-noise ratio of 10 is required to detect signals and compromise the encoded information. For attacks against video signals generated by liquid crystal displays (LCD) of computers, it has been suggested that this figure might be reduced by a few decibels depending on the font.

Therefore 0 dB signal-to-noise ratio, that is, signal power = noise power, as measured at the attack location should probably be considered the maximum value to ensure immunity from compromise.

Cited reference established a security limit on the magnitude of the electric field resulting from emanations. This limit was based on estimates of the parameters specified in (7.1) and the attacker's presumed capabilities.[12] Assuming those values, the emanation limit, that is, the maximum electric field amplitude that ensures the signal-to-noise ratio is below 10, was calculated to be 41 dBμV/m (41 dB relative to an electric field amplitude of 1 μV/m ~ 0.01 V/m).

This measurement assumes the detection equipment is capable of operating at a sufficiently high bandwidth, which highlights the importance of adequate filtering in low signal-to-noise ratio environments. Consistent with the previous discussion on signal averaging, the goal is to leverage the fact that the impulse voltage increases in proportion to B, but the noise voltage grows only in proportion to $\sqrt{B}$, and thereby exploit the processing gain offered by signal averaging.

If narrower impulse bandwidths of 5 and 1 MHz are used, the electric field emanation limits are reduced to 21 and 7 dBμV/m, respectively.

ANATOMY OF A REMOTE ATTACK 1: THE COMPUTER VIDEO DISPLAY INTERFACE

Considerable attention has been paid to the contribution of noise to the vulnerability to signal detection [4]. There is good reason for this level of attention. Overcoming a poor signal-to-noise ratio is likely to be *the* technical obstacle for an attacker because signal strengths associated with electromagnetic emanations will likely be weak and in competition with powerful radio and television broadcasting signals.

---

[12]Assumptions used to calculate an emanation security limit were as follows: (1) the attacker will have difficulty aligning the Yagi antenna array, (2) the attacker will experience problems tuning to a suitable center frequency and synchronizing to the exact frame rate if there is no visibly usable signal after averaging $N = 32$ frames, (3) the processing gain is limited to 15 dB, and (4) the attacker will experience minimal attenuation from intervening material, that is, 5 dB.

The number one priority of an attacker aside from getting as close as possible to the signal source, also pursuant to improving the signal-to-noise ratio, would be to identify a relatively quiet part of the frequency spectrum. So the three most important operational considerations of an attacker would likely be as follows[13]:

1. Minimize the distance between the receiver and the source.
2. Shift the signal to a quiet part of the electromagnetic spectrum.
3. Optimize signal bandwidth, gain, and sensitivity by using the best detection equipment available.

Item number one is often out of the control of the attacker. Clearly a defender should attempt to control as extensive a perimeter as possible but this is often not feasible especially in urban areas.

There have been numerous articles in the open literature documenting successful TEMPEST attacks against computers, and considerable work is available in the public domain.[14] An excellent reference that describes various passive and active attacks as well as the history of electronic compromises can be found in the open literature [5].

A paper by Wim van Eck in 1985 stimulated public interest in TEMPEST attacks [6]. In that paper the author documented the successful reconstruction of a video signal from a word processor at significant distances. The source of the radiated signal was broadband harmonics of the video signal, which were amplified from transistor-to-transistor (TTL) logic levels, that is, several volts, to several hundred volts prior to being fed into a cathode ray tube (CRT).

In recent years CRT technology has given way to LCD and plasma tube technology for use in flat panels. A common misperception is that LCD technology is more secure than CRTs relative to electromagnetic emanations derived from internal signals.

It has been demonstrated that emanations from video display interfaces can be used to reconstruct the signal appearing on a flat-panel monitor [4]. The attack was accomplished by exploiting the periodic signal generated by the video interface due to image refreshment, and by suppressing other spectral content through signal averaging at the pulse repetition frequency.

As discussed above, an attacker would likely crave signal periodicity to facilitate signal averaging and thereby increase the signal-to-noise ratio by $\sqrt{N}$, where N is the number of averages. Aside from getting as close to the device of interest as possible, locating and syncing to the pulse repetition frequency would likely be the first order of business in a remote attack on computer emanations.

This process will be discussed in more detail later. The key takeaway from the discussion here is to appreciate how technical vulnerabilities could be exploited to enhance the signal-to-noise ratio and thereby compromise the confidential information encoded in electromagnetic signals. The attack on video displays in computer video interfaces is illustrative of the challenges associated with this attack, but also proves that such vulnerabilities could be exploited under the right conditions.

---

[13]Recall the most important technical parameters affecting security were discussed in the previous section.
[14]TEMPEST, Transmitted Electro-Magnetic Pulse/Energy Standards and Testing.

To that end, a high-level review of video displays is now presented for background.[15] Video interfaces are used to transfer the information from computer memory to the monitor for visualization. Various connector designs and associated pin configurations are currently in use that comport with commercial video interface standards. These designs include VGA, DVI, HDMI, and DisplayPort.

The video interface consists of three video signals corresponding to the colors red, green, and blue (RGB) plus two synchronization signals, horizontal synchronization (H-sync) and vertical synchronization (V-sync). In order to represent the video signal on a computer monitor, the signal must be sampled, and thereby assign to each pixel on the display surface its updated color and position in two dimensions. Ultimately pixel placement must be mapped to the proper column and row on the monitor.

The video screen is merely a visual representation of the information stored in computer memory. The information is reconstructed on the screen by sampling the analog video signal and instructing individual pixels of various colors to be turned on and off according to its assigned position on the horizontal and vertical axes with prescribed timing.

Rows of video signal are stored in buffers, and all pixels in a given row are driven concurrently to maximize visual contrast. The rate of drawing pixels on the video monitor is controlled by the pixel clock, which produces pulses of specified width and at a specified transmission rate. Pixel rates have increased over the years, where high-end displays operate at hundreds of megahertz as of this writing.

Flat-panel displays store video lines in digital memory and therefore encode color information and position data as a sequence of discrete pixel values. Although flat-panel displays digitally buffer only a few pixel rows, the entire frame image is stored in the frame buffer of the video controller. Flat-panel video interfaces must refresh the entire image at some periodic rate.

This periodic signal has a frequency spectrum, and, importantly, contains the encoded instructions regarding discrete pixel position, sequence, and color across the display panel.

This is the signal that is radiated into the atmosphere and is the target in the attack described later. Moreover, the video cable connecting the display panel with the graphics controller was identified as the source of the emanation.

The frequency spectrum of periodic signals has lines that are separated by the repetition frequency. At a high level, the success of the attack is predicated on increasing signal-to-noise ratio by attenuating all other frequencies through periodic averaging *at the repetition frequency*. The attacker would also attempt to shift the signal to a quiet part of the spectrum and apply filtering to maximize signal content relative to detected bandwidth.

How would an attacker actually mount an attack to detect and reconstruct the video display signal? An understanding of the process requires delving deeper into the video signal reconstruction process from the perspective of the attacker [7].

Most raster-display technologies periodically refresh each pixel at a fixed frequency. If the displayed information changes slowly compared to the refresh rate, the high redundancy of the refresh signal helps in separating it from unwanted background noise through periodic averaging.

---

[15]https://www.ntt-review.jp/archive/ntttechnical.php?contents=ntr200810sf2.pdf&mode=show_pdf.

III. THE COMPROMISE OF SIGNALS

Since the information on each pixel is processed sequentially, that is, one pixel at a time, successive samples from a detected signal can be attributed to individual pixels and thereby reconstructed as a raster image. In computer video displays, the standardized video interfaces (VGA, DVI, etc.) use a simple timing scheme.

In order to reconstruct the entire video signal, the attacker must determine the relationship between the pixel, line, and frame rates. This relationship was determined in the attack recounted here using trial and error with the help of known industry specifications. An attacker must also adjust and track the pixel clock frequency to deal with fluctuations.

A savvy attacker will also leverage information theory to enhance the signal-to-noise ratio. Specifically, the Nyquist sampling theorem can be leveraged to limit the noise detected by the receiver. Symbols transmitted in digital devices have spectral energies that exceed the transmitted frequency f, and so the information in the signal will be repeated within $f/2$-wide bands at harmonic multiples of the pulse repetition rate f. Recall this critical theorem of information theory was introduced in Chapter 6 where its relevance to information security was also highlighted.

Therefore an attacker could in principle choose one such harmonic as the center frequency in the middle of a relatively quiet frequency band. He or she would then use a filter bandwidth corresponding to half the pixel transmission rate $f/2$ as dictated by the Nyquist sampling theorem.

But producing high-quality adjustable filters that operate over a wide frequency range is nontrivial. Therefore direct filtering of the baseband signal is not practical. A likely method would be to use a superheterodyne receiver as depicted in Fig. 7.5 and described previously.

However, the IF filter on the receiver must also be able to resolve short pulses, that is, short in the time domain and therefore wide in the frequency domain. The duration of the shortest pulse that can be resolved by the receiver equals $1/B$, the inverse of the IF filter bandwidth.

For an attack on digital video displays, the filter bandwidth must be comparable to the pixel clock frequency, which dictates the arrival of pulses that result in pixels on the monitor. Therefore a balance must be achieved between a narrow bandwidth to reduce the contribution of noise and a wide bandwidth to resolve pulses of short time duration.

The attacker can average voltage samples observed at the output of the receiver at consecutive times at the required rate. The results would be displayed as a grayscale value of a pixel in the reconstructed raster image.[16] As noted above, the IF resolution bandwidth of the receiver should be close to the pixel frequency in order to limit interpixel interference. What is the nature of the data targeted by the attacker that is used to reconstruct the video display that appears on the monitor?

The display information that is targeted by an attacker is based on emanations from the low-voltage differential signaling standard (LVDS). Recall the video cable connecting the display panel with the graphics controller is the source of the emanations. The cable consists of twisted pairs of wires to reduce the vulnerability to interference as well as radiated energy, and is part of an LVDS circuit.

---

[16]Grayscale means the pixel carries intensity information and is composed of shades of gray corresponding to that intensity.

LDP-Link was the first large-scale application of LVDS. It was introduced in order to reduce cable size and electromagnetic signal radiation in connecting the output of a graphics processing unit to the display panel's graphics controller.

The LVDS receiver detects differences in voltage that exist between the twisted pair wires. However, the noise affects each wire equally, and therefore the receiver is oblivious to the interfering noise since the *difference* in the noise-induced voltage is zero. This type of noise was first identified in Chapter 5 and is called common-mode noise. The method of noise reduction in this case is called common-mode rejection.

LVDS in its basic form serializes and distributes incoming data among four differential wire pairs, along with a clock signal transmitted on a similar pair. Fig. 7.10 shows the LVDS configuration in its basic form.[17]

In addition to reducing interference, the equal and opposite currents flowing in the twisted pair of wires produce electromagnetic fields that tend to cancel, thereby reducing the radiated energy. However, although the radiation is attenuated, it is not eliminated, and this radiation is the technical focus of the attacker's attention. Fig. 7.11 illustrates an LVDS circuit in a laptop or computer that uses a flat-panel display.[18]

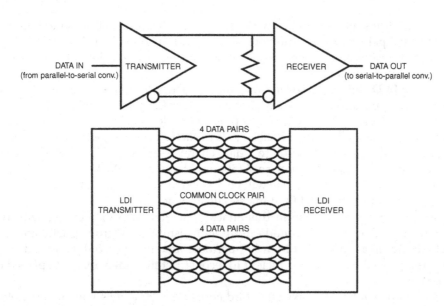

FIGURE 7.10 The basic LVDS configuration.

[17]http://what-when-how.com/display-interfaces/digital-display-interface-standards-part-1/.
[18]Wikipedia.

III. THE COMPROMISE OF SIGNALS

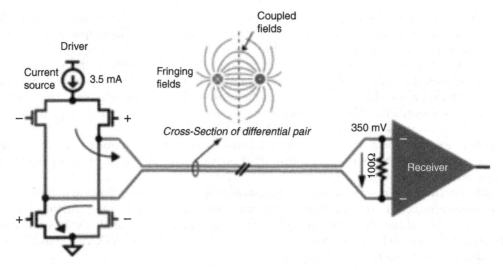

FIGURE 7.11   LVDS circuit in the flat panel display of a laptop or desktop computer.

The FPD-Link transmits the 18-bit RGB data using LVDS to send the video information over three twisted pairs of wires. Another twisted pair transmits the LVDS clock signal. The FPD-Link data transmission scheme serializes seven single-ended data bits per clock cycle into each of the LVDS channels.

Therefore the LVDS bit rate is seven times the frequency of the clock signal. For example, in the 18-bit RGB application there are 6 sub-bits each for R, G, and B color and an additional 3 bits for horizontal and vertical sync pulses plus an enable signal.

The net result is there are 21 total data signals in each clock cycle, which means the 7-to-1 serialization reduces this transmission to 3 data channels. If the clock signal is 50 MHz, the LVDS streaming video data rate will be 7 bits per channel × 50 MHz = 350 Mbits/s per channel, and the total data transfer rate will be 3 × 350 Mbits/s = 1.05 Gbits/s over the three channels. Fig. 7.12 illustrates the FPD-Link serializer in action.[18]

Although the targeted machine in this attack contained an LVDS circuit with twisted pairs of wires to reduce common-mode noise and resulting electromagnetic emanations, the signal amplitude as measured by a log-periodic antenna was 100 μV at a distance of 3 m. This setup proved more than sufficient to reconstruct the video image displayed on the laptop monitor.

The induced voltage (recall Maxwell's third equation = Faraday's Law again) yielded an electric field strength of 57 dBμV/m in a 50-MHz bandwidth. This electric field corresponds to an equivalent isotropic radiated power of approximately 150 nW. The power was sufficient to reconstruct the laptop video signal across several rooms.

In another experiment the same laptop signal was compromised using the identical receiver and antenna from a distance of 10 m, a more operationally realistic scenario.[18] In this case the laptop and receiver equipment were located in different offices with two offices in between, and were separated by three, 105-mm-thick plasterboard walls.

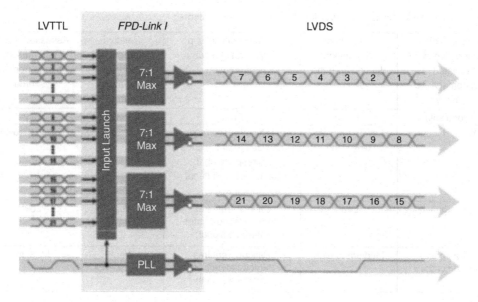

FIGURE 7.12   **FPD-link serializer.**

Twelve consecutive frames were acquired using a sampling rate of 50 MHz in one recording of 160-ms duration, which corresponds to 8 million samples. The required frame rate was determined by cross-correlation of the first and last recorded frames.

This particular attempt at signal compromise produced readable text. The measured signal was 12 μV, which corresponded to an electric field amplitude of 39 dBμV/m using the same log-periodic antenna. This result is consistent with the expected free-space loss resulting from trebling the distance between the laptop and the receive antenna from 3 to 30 m.

Other video interface technologies will differ in their vulnerability to signal compromise. The encoding scheme and bit arrangement used in digital video links can reduce the vulnerability. In particular, it was reported that randomizing the less significant bits of the transmitted RBG pixel values would represent an effective jamming signal that is immune to signal averaging. This immunity derives from the fact the jamming signal has the same periodicity as the desired text signal thereby affecting signal averaging efforts [4].

Similar efforts at video interface compromises have been successful pursuant to developing jamming technologies to thwart similar attacks.[19] An effective jamming signal was developed using video interface technology by synchronizing its basic frequency with the original pixel clock. That said, the measured electric field amplitudes at 3 m ranged from 20 dBμV/m to nearly 40 dBμV/m.

These electric field amplitudes are significantly reduced from the compromised video signal data presented earlier, but the simulated attack was successful nonetheless.

---

[19]https://www.ntt-review.jp/archive/ntttechnical.php?contents=ntr200810sf2.html.

TABLE 7.1   Attacks Against Information Technology Components

Source of information via radiated electromagnetic energy	Quantity of information derived from the source	Relative difficulty in Regenarating source information	Relative strength of source radiated energy	Assessed risk of information leakage from the source
Monitor displays	High	Easy	Strong	High
Keyboard input	Low to medium (text only)	Difficult (assuming knowledge of the code corresponding to keyboard keys is not known)	Weak	Low to medium
Print signals	Low	Difficult (requires demodulating printer interface signal)	Weak	Low
Intermachine communications	Medium to high	Difficult (requires demodulating LAN interface signal)	Weak	Medium

Finally, attacks against various categories of information are shown in Table 7.1 along with their relative ease of execution.[19]

ANATOMY OF A REMOTE ATTACK 2: KEYBOARD EMANATIONS

In the world of computer compromises, so-called side-channel attacks are often cited as a possible approach. Side-channel attacks refer to ancillary methods of obtaining information that is used to facilitate the compromise of the information of interest. In this case, keyboard emanations revealing user passwords are compromised via remote signal collection, which can then be applied to traditional network compromises.

Most users begin a session by authenticating their identity using a keyboard and entering their username and password. Anyone in possession of that information inherits all the access rights and privileges of that user's account irrespective of the actual user. For this reason, the first objective in a phishing or spear phishing attack is to trick the victim to divulge his or her username and password.[20]

Therefore, keyboards likely represent a focus of attention for attackers. This contention is substantiated by the varied attacks that have been devised to compromise information typed into keyboards. Other modes of compromise against keyboards include optical attacks that will be analyzed in Chapter 9, as well as an acoustic attack discussed in Chapter 10. The use of keystroke loggers is a well-known attack vector against keyboards.

---

[20]The reader should note for future reference that two-factor authentication is one of the best antidotes to social engineering attacks.

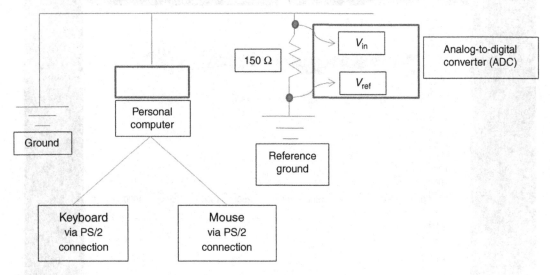

FIGURE 7.13 Keyboard ground wire attack setup.

A specific keyboard attack focused on compromising electromagnetic emanations that occurred during keystrokes from a PS/2 model keyboard.[21] Some details regarding the origin of keyboard emanations are provided first. There are four active wires that connect to this type of keyboard: data, ground, +5VDC, and clock. In this device, the wires were physically close together and poorly shielded. Energy was found to leak from the data wire to the ground wire and/or cable shield. The ground wire is routed to the main power/adapter cable ground, which is then connected to the power socket that is wired to the power grid.

The attack consisted of a differential measurement that examined the voltage drop between the power line and a reference ground using an oscilloscope. Fig. 7.13 illustrates this setup.[21]

Information about individual keystrokes could be detected on the power plug. The clock frequency of the PS/2 was 10–16.7 kHz, which was lower than any other frequency leaked by the PC. Therefore, filtering can be used to remove the noise from the signal as described later.

The keyboard-derived data signal is sent 1 bit at a time. Each data byte is sent in a frame consisting of 11–12 bits. As would be expected from an AC power line, the simulated attack encountered significant noise. The challenge is to detect the 10- to 16.7-kHz signal buried in this noisy spectrum.

To overcome this challenge, the attackers used the Finite Impulse Response as a band-pass filter where frequencies between 1 and 20 kHz were selected. The results of the attack are illustrated in Figs. 7.14 and 7.15 where individual letters have been reconstructed.[21]

In another simulated attack, 12 different keyboard models using PS/2, USB connectors, and wireless communication links in different setups were tested in a semianechoic chamber, a small office, an adjacent office, and within an apartment in a building [8].

---

[21]Inverse Path Ltd., https://www.blackhat.com/presentations/bh-usa-09/BARISANI/BHUSA09-Barisani-Keystrokes-SLIDES.pdf.

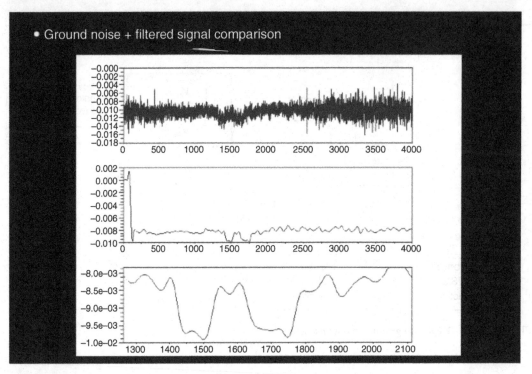

FIGURE 7.14 Ground noise compared to filtered signal.

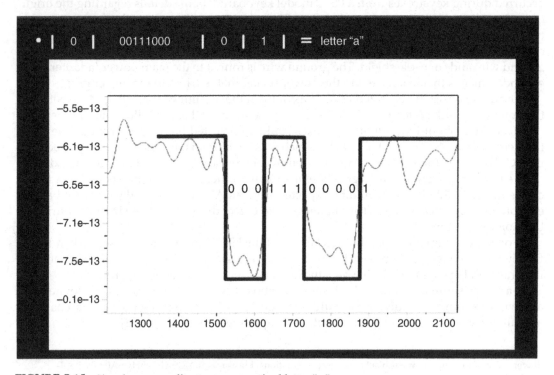

FIGURE 7.15 Signal corresponding to a compromised letter "a."

In that attack the raw signal was collected directly from the antenna instead of using a filtered and demodulated signal with limited bandwidth. The Short-Time Fourier Transform (STFT) was then computed, which yields a signal in time, frequency, and amplitude.

An analog-to-digital converter (ADC) can provide high sampling rates (eg, 10^9 samples/s). An ADC was connected directly to a wideband antenna, and the raw sampled signal was imported to a computer where software radio libraries were used to instantly highlight potentially compromising emanations. The STFT computation of the raw signal reveals even short-duration carriers and peaks.

Four keystroke recovery techniques were invoked. Specifically, the electromagnetic radiation emitted when a key was pressed was measured. The following direct and indirect electromagnetic emanations were found to leak information on keystroke initiation:

- the falling edges, that is, the transition from a high logic state to a low logic state, from the bidirectional serial cable used in the PS/2 protocol (these signals yielded keystroke information with 1 bit of uncertainty per keystroke);
- the rising and falling edges of the signal from the same source as earlier to recover keystrokes with 0 bit of uncertainty per keystroke;
- the harmonics emitted by the keyboard to recover the keystrokes with 0 bit of uncertainty per keystroke;
- the emanations emitted from the matrix scan routine (used by PS/2, USB, and wireless keyboards), yielding about 2.5 bits of uncertainty per keystroke.

These keyboards were all vulnerable to at least one of the four keystroke recovery techniques noted earlier. The best attack successfully recovered 95% of the keystrokes at a distance up to 20 m including distances traversing walls. Because each keyboard has a specific fingerprint based on clock frequency inconsistencies, the source keyboard of a compromising emanation could be determined even if multiple keyboards from the same model were used simultaneously.

SUMMARY

Electromagnetic emanations from electronic devices that process, store, and/or transmit data represent a potentially rich source of confidential information for would-be attackers. These emanations consist of time-varying electric and magnetic fields, whose behavior is described by Maxwell's equations.

The remote detection of emanations to compromise information encoded in signals is a quest to enhance the signal-to-noise ratio. To that end, an attacker hopes to gain close physical proximity to the signal source, but would most likely be required to invoke filtering, signal averaging, cross-correlation, knowledge of the signal, and trial and error to achieve success.

Parameters that contribute to the measured signal-to-noise ratio include the electric field strength, interference at the point of detection, signal bandwidth, signal attenuation by barriers interposed between the signal source and the detector, the antenna gain, the processing gain, and the IF filter impulse bandwidth of the receiver.

A number of technical methods have been developed to detect weak signals in noisy backgrounds. Broadband signals that are characteristic of pulsed communication systems inherent to computers must be differentiated from interfering sources such as TV and radio broadcasts.

A method known as AM superheterodyne detection is particularly suited for this application. This device modulates the targeted signal with a variable oscillator to shift the incoming signal to a quieter portion of the spectrum. The resultant signal is filtered to remove as much noise as possible. Filter characteristics relative to the targeted signal bandwidth are critical to a successful attack.

Signal averaging is another key method used to improve signal-to-noise ratio by an attacker. It exploits the fact that the result of N signal measurements, that is, N measurements of signal plus noise, will be proportional to N, and N exclusively noise measurements will be proportional to $\sqrt{N}$. Therefore N averages of the signal-to-noise ratio will yield a signal-to-noise ratio improvement of $N/\sqrt{N} = \sqrt{N}$. In words, the periodicity of the pulse repetition rate is exploited by averaging the total signal relative to interfering sources of noise.

The technical details of an attack against computers are described in detail. In this case the signal emanating from a flat-panel video interface circuit is the signal source. A successful compromise of a laptop display was achieved at a distance of 10 m.

Keyboards represent a source of risk-relevant information since usernames and passwords that provide account access are entered via these devices. Several successful simulated keyboard attacks have been described herein, where one exploited the presence of compromising signals on the AC power line and the other detected radiated emanations.

References

[1] Kuhn M. Compromising emanations: eavesdropping risks of computer displays. Technical report UCAM-CL-TR-577. University of Cambridge; 2003.
[2] Kuhn M. Electromagnetic eavesdropping risks of flat-panel displays. In: 4th workshop on privacy technologies, May 26-28, Toronto, Canada; 2004.
[3] Kuhn M. Security limits for compromising emanations. Cambridge: University of Cambridge; 2005. <https://www.cl.cam.ac.uk/~mgk25/ches2005-limits.pdf>.
[4] Kuhn M. Electromagnetic eavesdropping risks of flat-panel displays. op. cit.
[5] Ross A. Security engineering; a guide to building dependable distributed systems. 2nd ed. New York: Wiley; 2001.
[6] van Eck W. Electromagnetic radiation from video display units; an eavesdropping risk? Comput Secur 1985; 4:269–86.
[7] Kuhn M. Compromising emanations from LCD TV sets. In: IEEE symposium on electromagnetic compatibility, EMC (2011), August 14-19, Long Beach, CA; 2011.
[8] Vuagnoux M, Pasini S. Compromising electromagnetic emanations of wired and wireless keyboards, <https://www.usenix.org/legacy/event/sec09/tech/full_papers/vuagnoux.pdf>.

Countermeasures to Electromagnetic Signal Compromises

INTRODUCTION

Electromagnetic energy is ubiquitous. Every person on the planet is literally bombarded with artificial and/or natural energy sources every second of the day. In the preceding chapters the behavior of this electromagnetic energy was presented in order to facilitate estimates of the vulnerability to signal detection and resulting information compromise.

The remote detection of computer-borne electromagnetic emanations was described in Chapter 7. It is not difficult to imagine that if such an attack were implemented, it could have serious consequences depending on the specific computer in use. Therefore, it would seem prudent to reduce the risk associated with this threat by erecting barriers and thereby confine electromagnetic signals within a trusted zone.

To that end, the physical basis for electromagnetic signal confinement, otherwise known as shielding, is discussed in this chapter. In addition, practical considerations relating to the effect of specific materials on signal attenuation are investigated.

In addition, coupling mechanisms were shown to be responsible for common- and differential-mode currents within target devices, which in turn gave rise to electromagnetic emanations. Therefore methods to reduce these coupling mechanisms such as grounding might be advantageous in reducing the vulnerability to signal compromise, and are therefore reviewed in this chapter.

Finally, electromagnetic signals "naturally" attenuate as a result of absorption and reflection by materials in the propagation path. The magnitude of the effect is a function of signal frequency and the type of material. These are not always deliberate countermeasures *per se*, but they do contribute to signal attenuation and therefore are relevant to attackers and defenders alike.

ELECTROMAGNETIC SHIELDING[1]

Signals are targets for attack precisely because they are encoded with information. Therefore, it is prudent to invoke countermeasures that reduce the vulnerability to unauthorized signal detection. One way to accomplish this objective is to confine emanations to areas under the control of the signal owners. This confinement is known as shielding, and various materials are used for this purpose and are implemented in various ways. How does electromagnetic shielding actually work?

As discussed in Chapter 4, electromagnetic signals have both electric and magnetic field components. Electromagnetic shielding must attenuate both components in order to be effective, although the relative magnitude of shielding for each will vary depending on scenario-specific conditions. The dynamics of an electromagnetic wave as it propagates and encounters dissimilar materials help explain the effectiveness of shielding.

The wave or radiation impedance of an electromagnetic wave is defined as the ratio of its electric to magnetic field intensities, that is, E/H. E is measured in volts per meter and H is measured in amperes per meter. E/H is measured in ohms. The wave impedance in free space is determined by the source of the radiation. Specifically, the relevant parameters are whether the source is open ended/dipole-like or closed/current loop, and whether the measurement is made in the near or far field of the radiating source. The near and far fields are defined by the distance from the source relative to the wavelength of radiated energy.

For purposes of this discussion, circuits that cause electromagnetic fields to propagate can be divided into four categories as follows:

1. electrostatic
2. magnetostatic
3. electric and time-variant
4. magnetic and time-variant

Chapter 4 introduced physical models for the maximum electric field amplitudes generated by time-varying current elements and small current loops. These models can be applied to small electrical circuits and thereby explain the emanations they generate. Moreover, these models enable simple calculations of the magnitude of the electric and magnetic fields produced by radiating circuit elements.

The principles and calculations discussed in Chapter 4 will now be leveraged to provide more detail on circuit radiation and the resulting electromagnetic fields that are simultaneously the source of emanations and the target of attacks.

The electrostatic circuit is simply a fixed distribution of charges. Since the charges do not move, no current flows. A simple case is the charge dipole, where two equal and opposite charges are spaced some distance apart. Another example of an electrostatic circuit is a wire held at some fixed voltage.

In these scenarios, there is a constant electric field associated with the charges per Maxwell's equations. However, there is no magnetic field since moving electrical charges are required to generate magnetic fields. Since H is zero, the concept of wave impedance is not useful in electrostatics because E/H is infinite.

---

[1]http://www.rfcafe.com/references/electrical/near-far-field.htm is the principal reference used in this discussion.

For a charge dipole, the electric field in the near field decreases as the inverse of distance cubed, that is, $1/r^3$. The inverse cube law is derived from the near-cancellation of the fields by opposite charges. Each charge has an E field, which falls off as $1/r^2$, but because the charges are of opposite signs the resulting field strength decreases more rapidly with distance from the charge configuration.

Magnetostatic circuits consist of direct current (DC) current loops. This magnetic field scenario is the mirror image of the electrostatic case. There is a constant magnetic field H, which is therefore time-invariant and falls off with the cube of distance, but there is no electric field. Hence, the wave impedance E/H in this case is zero.

So for both the electrostatic and magnetostatic cases, the notion of wave impedance is meaningless because electromagnetic waves do not exist and therefore energy is not propagating.

However, if either the charge or the current distribution varies, there will be changing electromagnetic fields in the form of Fig. 4.1. Maxwell's third and fourth equations specify that a changing electric flux must produce a changing magnetic field and changing magnetic flux will produce a changing electric field. These changes yield an electromagnetic wave that propagates away at the speed of light into the surrounding medium.

In that vein, the third class of circuit mentioned earlier is a time-variant electric circuit. The following are examples of circuit configurations that will produce time-varying electric fields:

1. a charge dipole where the charge position oscillates like a sine wave;
2. a current element, where the current oscillates back and forth along a line so that charges would build up and reverse at the ends (this scenario is functionally equivalent to a dipole configuration of charges);
3. open-ended wires driven by voltage sources such as dipole antennae and leads exiting circuit boards driven by common-mode voltages;
4. an oscillating current loop.

The near fields and corresponding impedances for 1–4 are now examined. These are examples of circuits that produce propagating electromagnetic energy and therefore will be relevant to the discussion on shielding. We first examine circuits relating to 1–3 since these are functionally equivalent.

Consider a short, oscillating current element, which is also known as a Hertzian dipole. Recall this concept was introduced in Chapter 4 in modeling small circuits. In this case "short" means small relative to a wavelength at the oscillating frequency. If this condition holds, the current can be assumed to be uniform over the wire. As noted earlier, the relative field strengths E/H determine the impedance in both the near and far fields, and the near-field versus far-field designation is based on the distance from the source in terms of wavelengths.

For distances from a Hertzian dipole source that are much less than a wavelength the electric field dominates. In the far field, the wave impedance equals the intrinsic impedance of the medium. The intrinsic impedance of free space is calculated using Equation 8.2. There is also a transition region where all electromagnetic field terms are approximately of the same magnitude. Fig. 8.1 depicts E/H in the far field of a Hertzian dipole.[2]

---

[2]http://openi.nlm.nih.gov/detailedresult.php?img=3247718_sensors-10-05503f9&req=4.

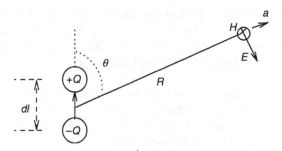

FIGURE 8.1 The wave impedance, *E/H*, in the far field of a Hertzian dipole.

The circuit category number 4 above is the magnetic analog of the Hertzian dipole. That is, a current loop is characterized by its magnetic moment, which is defined as the product of the current times the loop area. Recall from Chapter 4 that the magnetization *M* was defined in terms of the magnetic moment and current loops were introduced in Chapter 5 in connection with the source of electronic device emanations.

The electric and magnetic fields of an oscillating, infinitesimal current loop mirror the fields of a Hertzian dipole. But here the magnetic field in the near field decreases as $1/r^3$ while the electric field in the near field diminishes as $1/r^2$. Therefore, the intensity of current loop signal sources decreases more quickly in the near field than in the far field.

In the far field both *E* and *H* exhibit $1/r$ behavior and the wave impedance equals the intrinsic impedance of the surrounding medium. E/H is therefore the same value for a current loop as it is for a Hertzian dipole in the far field. Fig. 8.2 illustrates E/H in the far field of a current loop.[3]

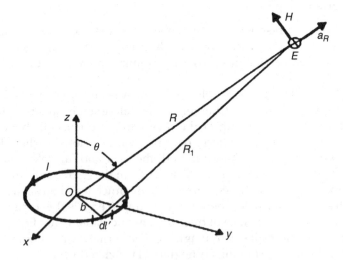

FIGURE 8.2 The wave impedance *E/H* in the far field of a current loop.

[3]http://www.dannex.se/theory/5.html.

Of operational importance to an attack scenario is the fact that in the far field both sources "look" the same with respect to detection since their impedances are identical. In other words, there is no way of knowing whether the source of the electric and magnetic fields is a dipole or a current loop in the far field.

The dividing line between near and far fields is sometimes specified as $\lambda/2\pi$, where λ is the wavelength. Different references specify other figures for the demarcation between the near and far fields, and often it is quoted as between one and two wavelengths. For high-frequency/short-wavelength signals the near field–far field transition distance would be located close to the source.

At low frequencies the situation is quite different. Consider a magnetic source such as a current loop driven at 60 kHz. Examples of such sources could be the horizontal drive of a cathode ray tube (CRT) monitor (if there are any still in use!), a switching power supply, or the field coil in a magnetic security system. The transition between near and far fields at this frequency would occur at about 800 m from the source.

Therefore, practical attempts at magnetic field detection would be performed in the near field. A loop antenna would be used for detection to maximize the change in magnetic flux per Faraday's Law. Electric field strengths would be expected to be relatively low in the near-field region if a current loop were the source of signal energy.

If either a low E-field or a high H-field is measured in the vicinity of a source, this condition implies low wave impedance. And low impedance would be indicative of an oscillating current loop as the source. To reiterate, the wave impedance measures the relative strength of the electric and magnetic fields and reflects the type of radiating source, that is, an oscillating dipole versus a current loop.

Conversely, a dipole source measured in the near field would exhibit high electric field amplitudes and low magnetic field amplitudes. This would be indicative of high wave impedance, which would imply the source is a Hertzian dipole.

For both oscillating dipole and current loop sources, as the distance from the source approaches the far field the magnitude of the wave impedance approaches that of free space or 377 Ω per Eq. (8.2). In general, the wave impedance in the far field approaches the impedance of the medium in which it propagates. Fig. 8.3 illustrates the wave impedance as a function of r/λ for both oscillating dipoles and current loops, that is, high- and low-impedance sources, respectively.[1]

Note that the wave impedance for low- and high-impedance sources converge for $r/\lambda = 1/2\pi$ and are equal for all values of r/λ thereafter.

Table 8.1 summarizes electric and magnetic field characteristics in the near and far fields for low- and high-impedance sources.

So what is the relationship between wave impedance and a given material relative to shielding effectiveness (SE)?[4] All homogeneous materials are characterized by a quantity known as intrinsic impedance Z_i, which is given by the following expression:

$$Z_i = \left[\frac{j\mu\omega}{\sigma + j\omega\varepsilon} \right]^{1/2} \tag{8.1}$$

[4]The following technical details are based on the discussion in White DR. Electromagnetic shielding, materials and performance. 2nd ed. Interference Control Technologies, Inc; 1980.

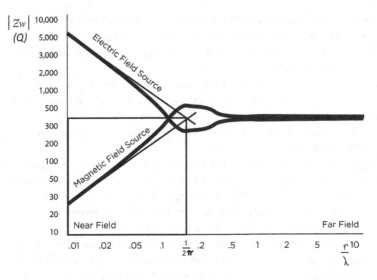

FIGURE 8.3   Wave impedance for electric and magnetic field sources as a function of r/λ.

TABLE 8.1   Near- and Far-Field Characteristics for Electric and Magnetic Field Sources

	Near-field impedance (E/H)	Far-field impedance (E/H)	Electric field strength distance dependence – near field	Magnetic field strength distance dependence – near field	Field strength distance dependence – far field
Electric Field Sources (Hertzian dipole)	High	Equal to Magnetic Field	$1/r^3$	$1/r^2$	$1/r$
Magnetic Field Sources (current loop)	Low	Equal to Electric Field	$1/r^2$	$1/r^3$	$1/r$

where j is the electrical engineering symbol denoting a complex number (mathematicians and physicists denote complex numbers with an "i"), $\omega = 2\pi f$ radian, f is the frequency in hertz, μ is the magnetic permeability of the material $= \mu_0 \mu_r$, μ_0 is the absolute permeability of air $= 4\pi \times 10^{-7}$ H/m, μ_r is the permeability of the material relative to air, σ is the conductivity of the material in mhos per meter, ε is the permittivity of the material $= \varepsilon_0 \varepsilon_r$, ε_0 is the absolute permittivity of air $= 1/(36\pi \times 10^9)$ F/m, and ε_r is the permittivity of the material relative to air.

The greater the difference between the impedance of the incident wave and the intrinsic impedance of the material it encounters, the more energy is reflected at the boundary of the two materials. As stated previously, as an electromagnetic wave propagates through a material the wave impedance approaches the intrinsic impedance of that material, Z_i.

For air, the conductivity is extremely small, that is, $\sigma \ll \omega \varepsilon$. Z_i for air is Z_a and is calculated as follows:

$$Z_a = \left(\frac{\mu}{\varepsilon}\right)^{1/2} = \left(\frac{\mu_o}{\varepsilon_o}\right)^{1/2} = [4\pi \times 36 \times 10^2]^{1/2} = 120\pi = 377\,\Omega \qquad (8.2)$$

It is the impedance mismatch between electromagnetic signals in air and materials such as metals that determines the effectiveness of shielding. Specifically, (8.2) specifies the far-field impedance of an electromagnetic wave in air to be 377 Ω. The impedance of metallic surfaces is approximately 2 Ω.

Therefore, the mismatch results in incident energy being reflected, and the field intensity is therefore substantially reduced outside the shield relative to the field intensity inside. The caveat is that SE will vary if the metal is in the near field of the source and also depends on the impedance of the source.

The incident electromagnetic wave is reflected, absorbed, and/or transmitted by the metal shield. According to Maxwell's third equation, the changing magnetic flux associated with this wave results in an electric field in the metal that exerts a force on the electric charges therein. This force causes charge movement, that is, eddy currents in the metal shield. These currents generate their own electric and magnetic flux that cancel the incident electric flux.

The incident electric flux also interacts with the shield and exerts a force on the charges in the metal shield, $F = qE$. This also causes currents to move in the shield skin, which in turn generate their own electric and magnetic fields that also act to cancel the incident energy.

The induced current density and the rate of current decay in the shield are governed by the conductivity of the metal, the magnetic permeability of the metal, and the frequency and amplitude of the field source. Both the current density and the rate of current decay are a function of the shield thickness. Fig. 8.4 depicts the interaction of an incident electromagnetic wave on a metal shield.[5]

Electromagnetic fields do penetrate the surface of metals but not to great depths, which is precisely what makes metals so effective as shields. The skin depth depicted in Fig. 8.4 is a physical characteristic of metals that specifies the surface thickness of a metal at a given frequency such that $[1 - (1/e)]$ or 63.2% of the current is flowing therein.[6]

Specifically, the skin depth of a material is given by the following expression:

$$\text{Skin depth} = \frac{1}{(\sigma f)^{1/2}} \qquad (8.3)$$

where σ is the material conductivity and f is the wave frequency.

One of the best materials for shielding is copper (refer to Fig. 8.5), and its skin depth at 1 MHz is 7.0×10^{-5} cm.

Fig. 8.4 also depicts internal reflections of signal energy. These can result in resonant effects manifest by multiple internal reflections that enhance SE via the loss mechanisms noted

[5]http://www.intechopen.com/books/new-polymers-for-special-applications/microwave-absorption-and-emi-shielding-behavior-of-nanocomposites-based-on-intrinsically-conducting-.
[6]Two skin depths = 86.5% and three skin depths = 95.0% of the total current flow. For 99% of the current flow, 4.6 skin depths are required. An accepted rule of thumb for adequate shielding is to specify that the shield thickness must exceed three skin depths.

III. THE COMPROMISE OF SIGNALS

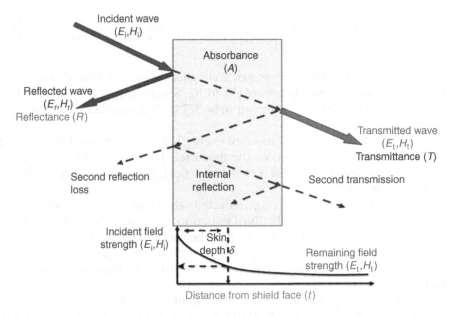

FIGURE 8.4   An electromagnetic wave incident on a shield.

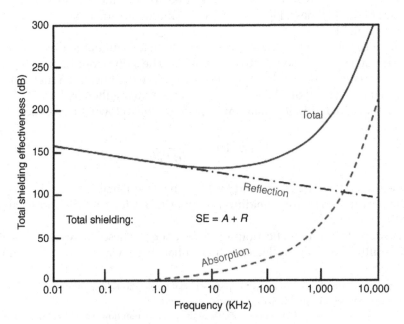

FIGURE 8.5   Shielding effectiveness of a 0.2-in. copper shield in the far field. Used with permission from Ott H. Electromagnetic compatibility engineering. New Jersey: Wiley; 2009.

earlier. Although these multiple internal reflections can contribute to SE, they contribute to attenuation less than the initial reflection.

What about the effect of absorption? Absorption is the other major contributor to attenuation by an electromagnetic shield. Absorption results in the dissipation of the energy in the form of heat as the electromagnetic wave interacts with the shielding material. The loss is related to a material's resistivity as well as its magnetic permeability μ.

The overall SE that results principally from reflection and absorption is given by the following expression[7]:

$$SE \text{ [decibels]} = 20 \log \left(\frac{Z_w}{4Z_s} \right) \qquad (8.4)$$

where Z_w is the far-field wave impedance in air = 377 Ω and Z_s is the shield impedance = 2 Ω.

Plugging these impedance values into (8.4) yields 33.5 dB, which is considered to be a sufficient shielding specification for most applications.

The reflective loss decreases with increasing frequency because impedance increases with frequency. In other words, the intrinsic impedance of the metal is closer to the plane wave value of 377 Ω at higher frequencies. Therefore the air–metal impedance mismatch is reduced and the SE decreases.

This situation seems to contradict what is predicted by (8.3) since skin depth is inversely related to frequency. However, absorption loss *increases* with frequency. Therefore, reflection and absorption complement each other such that any conductive material will typically provide significant shielding across the frequency spectrum with caveats noted regarding the source impedance.

Fig. 8.5 demonstrates the magnitude of the contributions of reflection and absorption to the total shielding effect of a 0.02-in. thick copper shield.[7] At 1 MHz the SE is a rather robust 200 dB!

Achieving effective electromagnetic shielding can in fact be challenging. Moreover, if it is done incorrectly, it can actually make matters worse. Reflections can cause the electromagnetic energy to add coherently that can result in signal enhancement or signal gain, which is the opposite of the desired effect.

MAGNETIC SHIELDING

In the previous section it was learned that magnetic fields radiating from current loops, that is, low-impedance sources, are better impedance matched to the metal shield in the near field than electric fields. Therefore, magnetic fields are more difficult to shield in the near field than electric fields especially at low frequencies. Moreover, because there are no free magnetic charges per Maxwell's second equation, it is not possible to terminate lines of magnetic flux on an electromagnetic shield as happens with electric fields. Magnetic lines of flux must terminate on an opposite magnetic pole as discussed in Chapter 4 and per Maxwell's second equation.

However, it is possible to redirect magnetic flux lines to prevent unwanted coupling. This redirection can be accomplished by the generation of electric currents in an electrically

---

[7]http://www.edn.com/design/test-and-measurement/4391240/Design-enclosures-to-meet-EMC-requirements.

conductive shield or by altering the path of magnetic flux lines using permeable ($\mu r \gg 1$) materials. The latter is especially important at kilohertz frequencies as discussed later.

There are two types of shielding for magnetic fields: active and passive.[8] "Passive" shielding utilizes ferromagnetic and/or conductive materials to concentrate magnetic lines of flux. Active shielding uses an externally energized conductor that is configured to generate magnetic fields. Fields so generated cancel the magnetic fields of the original source. However, the focus here will be on passive shielding since it is more prevalent and easier to implement.

The traditional method of passively shielding magnetic fields involves the use of ferromagnetic metals. Such metals contain iron and have a high magnetic permeability μ. Typical materials used for ferromagnetic shielding include low-carbon steel and so-called Mu-metal. The latter is an alloy of nickel, steel, and molybdenum. Since these materials have high magnetic permeability, they concentrate magnetic flux. The high-permeability material provides a path of lower reluctance for the magnetic flux relative to air. Reluctance is the magnetic analog of electric resistance.

A second passive shielding method involves the use of conductive materials such as aluminum or steel. Maxwell's third equation specifies that time-varying magnetic flux results in changing electric fields that yield potential differences (voltages) in conducting materials. As noted earlier, electric fields interacting with conductive materials, that is, the metal in the shield, cause electrical currents to flow precisely because of these induced voltages.

Specifically, for any closed-loop path on the surface of a shielding surface that is penetrated by an oscillating magnetic field, Faraday's Law specifies that an electric field must also be present on the surface. An electric field on the surface of a conductor will cause currents to flow. These currents will generate their own magnetic flux that opposes the incident magnetic flux. The latter effect is known as Lenz's Law.

Faraday's Law specifies that the fluxing field must vary in time in order to generate electric fields and resulting eddy currents. However, eddy currents caused by slowly varying magnetic flux in the conducting plate will dissipate sufficiently over a cycle of oscillation to allow the magnetic flux to penetrate the plate. For this reason, conductive materials are generally poor magnetic shields at low frequencies, that is, below a few hundred kilohertz. Conductive magnetic shields are also ineffective if they have slots or gaps that interrupt the flow of eddy currents.

For a shield that is less than a skin depth in thickness, there is a linear falloff of the magnetic field within the shield. In addition, the difference in the magnetic field on the inside of the shield and the outside is related to the total current in the shield as specified by Ampere's Law. If the attenuation is large, this condition implies that the current induced in the shield is enough to almost completely screen the incident magnetic field.

In a perfect conductor, the fields generated by those currents would perfectly cancel the incident magnetic flux. Both sides of the equation describing Faraday's Law would therefore equal zero so there would be no flux penetrating the conductor and no tangential electric field on the surface. Fig. 8.6 illustrates active and passive magnetic field shielding.[8]

In order to confine or divert a magnetic field with a conductive plate, it is important to develop sustained eddy currents. But eddy currents are driven by time-varying magnetic flux and a conductive plate cannot divert a static magnetic field.

---

[8]http://www.ehib.org/emf/ckappend.html.

Passive shielding by flux shunting

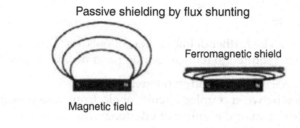

Ferromagnetic shield

Magnetic field

Shielding by eddy current cancellation

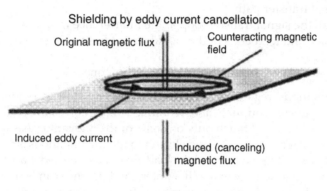

Original magnetic flux

Counteracting magnetic field

Induced eddy current

Induced (canceling) magnetic flux

FIGURE 8.6   Passive and active magnetic field shielding.

Therefore at kilohertz or lower frequencies it is generally necessary to use permeable magnetic materials ($\mu r \gg 1$) to divert magnetic fields. Since these materials have reluctance values that are much less than air, magnetic field lines can effectively be rerouted by providing an alternative path through a permeable material such as steel or Mu-metal.

GROUNDING TO REDUCE EMANATIONS

In Chapter 4 coupling mechanisms were shown to be responsible for common- and differential-mode currents that radiate electromagnetic emanations. These mechanisms can be further differentiated in terms of their effect as follows [1]:

- stray ground currents
- ground plane voltage differences
- capacitive coupling
- inductive coupling
- ground loop antenna effects
- monopole antenna effects

Moreover, in the aforementioned discussions hints were provided regarding some of the techniques that might be effective in reducing the coupling that results in electromagnetic emanations. These techniques fall into four general categories [1]:

- increased physical separation of conductive elements
- enhanced shielding

- minimization of ground-plane impedance
- breaking of ground loops

The countermeasures can be further delineated as follows. It should be noted that a combination of methods is often required to reduce coupling and resulting emanations [1]:

- Minimize the impedance of the ground or reference plane.
- Increase the separation between coupled circuits or electronic components.
- Shield the susceptible circuit or the source of interference.
- Reduce the area of the signal loop.
- Balance the signal transfer path.
- Electrically break the signal transfer loop at the interference frequency.
- Prevent the source and load ends of the signal circuit from being connected to points of different potential.
- Minimize the efficiency of ground leads acting as antennae.

More specific methods regarding these techniques are now provided. The control of unwanted electromagnetic coupling and resulting emanations is a complex subject with many facets, and this book will touch only on some of the relevant issues at a high level.

A principal means of reducing undesired electromagnetic emanations is to reduce the impedance of the ground plane. If the source and the load are interconnected via a noisy ground reference, the possibility of interference exists. If a potential difference can be reduced between the source and the load, the magnitude of electromagnetic interference can likewise be reduced.

Multiple-point grounding is one method to reduce ground plane impedance. In this method every conductive pair used for signal transfer is connected to a ground plane by the shortest path possible, and thereby reduce inductance. Recall the magnitude of the inductive reactance is proportional to the inductance of a circuit component (and proportional to frequency), which increases with the length of the component. An increase in reactance results in a larger impedance Z, which increases the voltage drop across connected circuit elements and thereby causes currents to flow with associated emanations.

In addition, the ground plane should be interconnected using the maximum number of parallel paths, and the ground plane would minimize resistivity through the use of a solid metal mass.

As noted previously, ground loops in circuits are the result of coupling mechanisms and result in emanations when loop components function as antennae. Opening these loops and thereby reducing the resulting emanations can be accomplished via the following methods [1]:

- single-point grounding
- common-mode rejection
- frequency translation
- optical coupling
- frequency-selective grounding

As its name implies, single-point grounding involves making one connection from the source or load end of the signal return side of the signal transfer loop to ground. Although this technique can be an effective method, a good ground connection can be difficult to establish and maintain.

In cases when the source and load ends of a signal circuit must be connected to a noisy ground plane, the resulting differential voltage caused by the ground plane impedance can produce common-mode currents to flow. Balancing both legs of the circuit using balanced-to-unbalanced transformers or "baluns" can be effective even over broad frequency ranges. For example, baluns can achieve up to 70 dB of common-mode rejection over several hundred kilohertz.

To address common-mode interference that is at the same frequency as the signal, the signal can be translated to a new frequency. Frequency translation can be accomplished by chopping or modulation techniques. The use of nonelectrical components such as optical isolators or fiber optics to isolate circuits can also be effective in reducing common-mode interference.

Finally, frequency-specific grounding can be used in cases where different grounding methods are required at various frequencies. For example, multipoint grounding might be useful at high frequencies and single-point grounding at low frequencies or vice versa. In the high-frequency case, a capacitor could be used to couple the circuit to ground since in this case the impedance decreases with increasing frequency. This technique effectively shorts the signal to ground. At low frequencies the circuit can be inductively coupled by inserting an RF choke to ground since inductance decreases with decreasing frequency.

SIGNAL ATTENUATION

Introduction

The reality is that intervening materials can profoundly affect electromagnetic signal energy. Sometimes such materials are intentionally introduced to reduce the vulnerability to unauthorized detection. But other times intervening materials represent a nuisance since the signal is prevented from reaching the intended audience.

The magnitude of the attenuation depends on the frequency of the signal as well as the type and thickness of material interposed between the signal source and the detection antenna. The focus of this section is to estimate the effectiveness of materials in reducing the vulnerability to signal detection and the compromise of its encoded information.

The reader is likely to already have an intuitive sense of the magnitude of radio-frequency attenuation caused by at least one material. Namely, direct experience informs us that air does little to attenuate commercial radio broadcasts or cell phone transmissions. This fact is in itself useful, but the broader objective is to estimate the magnitude of this effect for an assortment of scenarios and thereby assess the general vulnerability to signal detection.

General Electromagnetic Attenuation Due to Materials

As a rule of thumb, the higher the frequency and/or conductivity of the material, the more electromagnetic signals are attenuated. This effect is evident from (8.3), the expression for skin depth. Evidence of this effect is substantiated by direct observation: electromagnetic waves are relatively unaffected by common building materials such as wood, drywall, and glass, unless the energy is in the upper portions of the microwave spectrum.

TABLE 8.2 Signal Attenuation Due to Common Building Materials at 5.8 GHz

Building material	Attenuation (dB) (parallel polarization)	Attenuation (dB) (perpendicular polarization)
PVC	0.4	0.6
Gypsum Plate	0.8	0.7
Plywood	0.9	0.9
Gypsum Wall	1.2	3.0
Chipboard	1.3	1.0
Veneer Board	2.2	2.0
Glass Plate	3.2	2.5
6.2-cm Soundproof Door	3.4	3.6
Double Glazed Window	6.9	11.7
Concrete Block Wall	11.7	9.9

By contrast, concrete definitely affects the intensity of transmissions at cell phone and microwave frequencies. Moreover, the thickness of floor slabs in buildings can be important in determining floor-to-floor transmission losses.

Table 8.2 shows the attenuation of a 5.8-GHz electromagnetic signal propagating through a variety of building materials [2]. Results are shown for both parallel and perpendicular polarizations of the electromagnetic wave. Recall Fig. 4.1, which showed the mutually perpendicular planes of oscillation for electric and magnetic field components of an electromagnetic wave. Parallel or perpendicular polarization refers to whether the antenna is parallel or perpendicular to the incident E field that is oscillating in a plane.

An average of the listed polarizations should suffice for ballpark estimates of attenuation. Because the attenuation is specified in decibels, the total attenuation can be calculated by merely adding the contributions of individual layers of attenuation.

Notably, the attenuation will vary considerably at different frequencies. This effect has been extensively studied and numerous measurements of electromagnetic signal attenuation in buildings have been conducted in other frequency regimes [3]. Results at 5.8 GHz are specified herein to provide indicative results showing "themes" that can be generalized.

Although intrafloor transmissions vary in attenuation, the effects observed in interfloor propagation paths are more consistent. Namely, the increased attenuation is due to the presence of concrete and rebar. Intrabuilding signal margins, that is, the power available for detection at the point of interception and where transmitter and detector are in the same building, are discussed next.

Intrabuilding and Floor-to-Floor Signal Attenuation[9]

Indoor propagation of radio-frequency signals is an important factor in estimating the vulnerability to signal detection and subsequent information compromise. For example, an attacker could be a trusted insider with legitimate access to a specific floor that houses a device of interest.

An attacker might install a detection device in relatively close proximity to a source, and attempt to transmit the signal to a collection site within the same building under the attacker's control, for example, his or her office. Alternatively, there might be concern that an electromagnetic signal encoded with confidential information "leaks" from one floor to another housing a competitor, and thereby no active collection device is required near the source.

The effectiveness of each of these modes of attack is highly scenario-dependent. For this reason it is always prudent to adopt a conservative approach to estimating vulnerabilities to detection. To that end, measurements of signal attenuation in buildings have been made, and ranges of values so established can be used as an operational guide.

Measurements of propagation loss in "typical" office buildings at 914 MHz, that is, the cell phone frequency band, reveal losses of between 50 and 90 dB for 10-m separations. A factor of 1 billion may sound like a lot but radio receivers can detect very low-power signals ($\sim 10^{-12}$ W). Engineers refer to receivers that can detect weak signals as having a wide dynamic range.

As noted in Table 8.2, concrete slabs of buildings can cause significant attenuation at 5.8 GHz. This frequency is becoming increasingly popular for wireless LANs. A 10-m propagation path in the vertical direction will involve at least three concrete slabs so at that frequency and assuming 10 dB of attenuation per floor, roughly 30 dB of attenuation would be expected. That said, concrete and steel flooring would still allow for better propagation than a floor containing a steel pan into which concrete is poured.

Measurements in indoor scenarios reveal 60 dB of attenuation when the signal source and the receiver are 10 m apart. At 50 m, signal attenuation of 110 dB has been reported. So nearly the entire link budget of 120 dB is consumed at a distance of 50 m.

The situation can be expected to differ at 2.4 GHz, a traditional communication frequency for wireless LANs using the 802.11 protocol. For scenarios that include both interfloor and intrafloor communication links, the intensity of transmitted signals propagating indoors at this frequency scales as the inverse 3.5 power with distance ($1/r^{3.5}$ or equivalently $r^{-3.5}$).[9]

If this scaling relationship is accurate, the intensity of signals radiating indoors should decrease much more rapidly with distance from the source than for point source transmitters operating in open spaces. The scaling might in part explain the difference between the link margins observed in real life and the theoretical results calculated in Chapter 6 for wireless LAN signals.

In general, losses can be expected to be a factor of 4 or so higher at 2.4 GHz than the mobile phone frequency band, and will be reduced further by 3 dB per octave for each doubling of frequency. As noted earlier, wireless systems have communication link budgets of about 120 dB and the signal is significantly attenuated in the first 10 m of propagation.[9]

The general expression for the path loss associated with indoor signal propagation scenarios is given by the following[10]:

$$\text{Path Loss [decibel]} = 40 + 35 \log r \text{ [meter]} \tag{8.5}$$

[9]http://www.sss-mag.com/indoor.html.
[10]http://www.sss-mag.com/indoor.html. Note $\log_{3.5}(X) = 35 \log_{10}(X)$ according to the properties of logarithms.

III. THE COMPROMISE OF SIGNALS

According to (8.5) a 10-m indoor separation between source and receiver will yield a 75-dB path loss. Recall decibels are logarithmic. Therefore 75 dB of attenuation corresponds to a linear factor of about 31.6 million in signal power reduction. What is the signal-to-noise ratio at 10 m and therefore the vulnerability to signal detection?

The expression for path loss given earlier can be used to show that a 250-mW wireless LAN signal decreases to 8×10^{-9} W at a distance of 10 m from the access point. Recall it was previously assumed the noise floor at 2.4 GHz in an urban area was -80 dBm. This figure would imply that the peak signal-to-noise ratio at 10 m is nearly 29 dB, which is plenty of signal margin for any attacker. Even if the noise floor were 10 dB greater, the signal margin would be sufficient for detection by an attacker.

Therefore, despite the significant signal attenuation that occurs within buildings, it would be a mistake to assume an attacker with access to another floor could not detect the signal radiating from a wireless LAN access point.

According to (8.5) at a distance of 100 m the signal will be reduced by 110 dB. So if the total indoor wireless LAN link budget is assumed to be 120 dB, a system operating indoors at 2.4 GHz is at the theoretical threshold of detection at about 100 m from the access point. The caveat is that variances of about 13 dB in indoor scenarios are common.

Other research has yielded an entirely different model for indoor propagation loss of electromagnetic signals and actually incorporates building elements into this model. Specifically, the path loss for indoor propagation is given by the following expression [4]:

$$30\,\text{dB (the power loss at 1 m)} + 10n\log(d) = kF + LW \qquad (8.6)$$

Here n is a power-delay index, d is the distance between transmitter and receiver, k is the number of floors the signal traverses, F is loss/floor, L is the number of walls the signal traverses, and W is the loss/wall. Clearly the presence of floors and walls plays a role in intrabuilding electromagnetic propagation. In this study, n ranged between 1.6 and 3.3 depending on the type of facility with significant variations in model accuracy for offices and stores.

This study also found that signal strength depended on the existence of open plan offices, construction materials, density of personnel, furniture, etc. Path loss exponents varied between 2 and 6 ($1/r^2$ and $1/r^6$). This disparity in exponents translates into a significant variation in the estimate of vulnerability! Wall losses were shown to vary between 10 and 15 dB and floor losses were between 12 and 27 dB.

The lesson here is that any such calculation should be used principally to bound a vulnerability assessment within a range of reasonable values. Quantitative estimates can be used to inform a physically realistic if approximate assessment of the vulnerability to signal detection.

Interbuilding Signal Attenuation

A potentially more common attack scenario is interbuilding communications. For example, a commercial electronic device such as a wireless headset might be radiating a signal that is potentially detectable by someone located outside the company's span of control. The author analyzed this very scenario during his tenure at Goldman Sachs.

As noted earlier, the bad news for assessing vulnerability to information compromise in such scenarios is the high degree of variability in historic measurements [4]. Reported losses are a function of building materials, floor layout, building height, percentage of windows, and the transmission frequency.

However, the following observations are relevant to interbuilding radio-frequency communication scenarios, and can be useful as rules of thumb in estimating the vulnerability to signal detection:

- The received signal strength increases with increasing height within the building since the urban radio-frequency clutter/noise is reduced with increasing elevation. The effect could aid an attacker by lowering the ambient radio-frequency noise floor.
- The penetration loss decreases with increasing frequency. A possible explanation could be that shorter wavelengths are less affected by diffraction. Longer wavelength energy would be more impacted by structures with comparable dimensions, for example, windows and cracks.
- The loss through windows is typically about 6 dB or less, although this will be frequency-dependent and a function of materials used for window tinting.

For outdoor-to-indoor scenarios, the scaling relationship of signal intensity with distance has been measured to be $1/r^{4.5}$ on average. Moreover, this scaling relation has been observed to range between $1/r^3$ and $1/r^{6.2}$, which represents a huge spread in values [4]. The implications of this variability to information security are profound.

For example, if the operable scaling relation is $1/r^3$, increasing the distance between the transmitter and the receiver by a factor of 10 reduces the signal intensity by a factor of 1000. If on the other hand the scaling relation is $1/r^{6.2}$, increasing the distance by a factor of 10 will result in a 1.6 million reduction in signal intensity. So there is a 32-dB difference in attenuation depending on the assumed model.

Finally, signal attenuation by the building edifice has been measured to vary between 2 and 38 dB or nearly a factor of 4000 [4]. Such variations only reinforce the difficulty in estimating the vulnerability to information compromise for the spectrum of potential scenarios.

SUMMARY

Electromagnetic signals can be encoded with confidential information and are prevalent in business environments. Radiating circuit elements that generate electromagnetic fields associated with these signals are the sources of emanations and are the potential targets of attackers. Therefore, understanding effective countermeasures to signal detection and resulting information compromise is relevant to a comprehensive information security risk management strategy.

Electromagnetic shielding using metals is a common antidote to information loss and is explained by Maxwell's equations. The changing electric and magnetic flux causes electric fields in the skin of the metal. These fields exert a force on the charges in the metal thereby resulting in currents in the metal skin. These currents generate their own electric and magnetic fields, which cancels the fields of the original signal.

The so-called skin depth specifies the depth of penetration of incident electromagnetic energy, and is inversely related to the square root of the material conductivity and the frequency of the radiated energy. Incident energy is mostly reflected or absorbed by the metal.

The wave impedance of electromagnetic energy is given by the ratio of the electric field to the magnetic field, E/H. This impedance is different depending on the source, that is, an electric dipole or current loop, as well as the distance from the source. In the far field, the wave impedance is the same for electric and magnetic field sources.

The effectiveness of shielding for electric and magnetic field sources will depend on the impedance mismatch of the wave traveling in air relative to the shield material. The impedance mismatch depends on the type of field and the distance from the source to the shield at a given frequency.

Grounding is a method that has a number of uses to include electrical safety and reducing excess currents that cause electromagnetic emanations. In particular, ground loops are a significant source of unintentionally radiated signal energy. Implementing one or more of the following can be effective in breaking ground loops:

- single-point grounding
- common-mode rejection
- frequency translation
- optical coupling
- frequency-selective grounding

Building materials can affect the intensity of electromagnetic signals depending on the frequency and the type of material. Expressions for signal path loss are provided for indoor-to-indoor and indoor-to-outdoor scenarios, which can be used to establish link margins and thereby determine the vulnerability to unauthorized detection. Significant variability in signal intensity has been measured in both scenarios. It is prudent to assume the worst case in estimating vulnerability to signal detection pursuant to developing a robust information security risk management strategy.

References

[1] Denny HW. Grounding for the control of EMI. Gainesville, VA: Don White Consultants; 1986. [fourth printing].
[2] Hou P. Investigation of the propagation characteristics of indoor radio channels in GHz wavebands. Göttingen: Cuvillier Verlag; 1997.
[3] Hashemi H. The indoor radio propagation channel. Proc IEEE 1993;81(7):943–67.
[4] Randy K. Radio propagation. Berkeley, CA: University of California at Berkeley; 1996.

9

Visual Information Security

INTRODUCTION

Organizations often spend considerable resources protecting information that is accessible via networks. These same organizations sometimes do little to prevent anyone within line-of-sight from viewing that same information.

In addition, offices with the most window space are given to the most senior executives thereby affording their occupants a panoramic vista. The proverbial corner office is often reserved for the highest-ranking person in a department.

Although this perquisite may satisfy the egos of those in charge, it can also increase the vulnerability to information compromise. In a similar vein, conference rooms with monitors and whiteboards can be viewed by those not affiliated with the organization and/or without a "need-to-know" the information displayed therein.

In this chapter the vulnerability to information compromise via two optical methods is analyzed: the optical focusing of images using a telescope and the detection of light generated by or reflected off objects via photon counting. The risk factors associated with these scenarios are straightforward and the optical parameters are well understood.

Notably, these attacks leave no trace and are theoretically implementable at significant distances depending on scenario-specific conditions. As usual, physics imposes operational constraints on attackers that can be used to develop practical estimates of the vulnerability to information compromise.

FUNDAMENTALS OF OPTICS AND OPTICAL EQUIPMENT

Visible light is a form of energy that exists within a specific frequency band of the electromagnetic spectrum. Humans can view only that portion of the spectrum which corresponds to energy of wavelengths between 0.4×10^{-6} and 0.7×10^{-6} m. Fig. 9.1 shows the visible spectrum relative to its infrared and ultraviolet nearest neighbors.[1]

Recall the principle of diffraction was introduced in Chapter 3. This is the effect that causes energy to spread out when it interacts with objects whose dimensions are comparable to the

---

[1]http://science.hq.nasa.gov/kids/imagers/ems/visible.html.

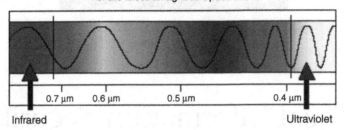

FIGURE 9.1   Visible wavelengths of electromagnetic energy.

energy wavelength. It is diffraction that dictates the limit on vulnerability to optical compromises of visible information because it imposes a limit on the focusing power of lenses.

Before restating that limit, a brief review of how lenses work is presented. Of course, the underlying behavior of all electromagnetic energy including optical phenomena is described by Maxwell's equations.

In the discussion immediately preceding Maxwell's equations the permittivity of free space, ε_o, was introduced. Recall the speed of light in materials is given by the speed of light in a vacuum divided by the relative permittivity or dielectric constant of the material in which the wave is traveling. The absolute permittivity is a measure of the effect of an applied electric field on a dielectric medium, also known as an insulator.

The relative permittivity of some common materials is shown in Table 9.1.[2]

TABLE 9.1   Relative Permittivity of Common Materials

Material	Relative permittivity
Air	1
Glass (standard)	7.6–8.0
Plexiglas	~2.8
Rubber	2–7
ABS (Plastic)	2.0–3.5
Teflon [Polytetrafluoroethylene (PTFE)]	2.1
Mica	3–6
Paper	3.85
FR4	4.7
Oxide	3.9
Diamond	5.5–10
Silicon	11.68

[2]http://www.sharetechnote.com/html/RF_Handbook_Permittivity.html.

We see from Table 9.1 that the dielectric constant of glass exceeds that of air by a factor of 8. Therefore, the high relative permittivity of glass causes an incident electric field, for example, visible light, to slow down relative to its velocity in air. This occurs because a given oscillating electric field polarizes the charges in the glass molecules more than it does air molecules. This effect was illustrated in Figs. 4.3 and 4.4. Water has a similar effect on electric fields as glass, and anyone who has seen a spoon appear to bend at the air–water interface has witnessed this effect.

Now consider a lens that consists of glass. The lens is curved and not of uniform thickness. The thicker portion is in the middle section and the lens is more tapered at the ends. Therefore, the portion of light that is incident at the center of the lens travels through more glass than does the light that is incident at the top and bottom of the lens.

Since the speed of light is determined by the relative permittivity of the medium in which it propagates, its speed and hence the time to traverse a given portion of the lens is proportional to the thickness of the particular segment of lens it encounters.

Optical lenses exist to focus visible light. To focus means that all the incident light energy exiting the lens simultaneously arrives at a point in space on the far side of the lens. That point is appropriately called the focal point, where points colinear with the focal point make up the focal plane. In the human eye the cornea and lens focus incident light and the detector is the retina. The lens focuses incident rays by changing its shape.

Longer routes to the focal plane traverse more air than glass but the light has a higher speed during the airborne portion of the route to compensate for the extra distance. Geometrically shorter routes to the focal plane are those closest to the center of the lens but the lens is thicker at the mid-point than at the top and bottom.

The lens is shaped so that the rays traveling over longer geometric routes to the focal plane traverse more air than glass, and the rays traveling along shorter routes do the opposite. Therefore, these routes trade extra distance for increased speed. This trade-off causes the energy to converge to a single point on the focal plane.

The focusing power of a lens is given in units that are likely to be familiar to those middle-aged readers who have experienced presbyopia in their dotage. These units are known as diopters. A diopter is the inverse of the focal length measured in meters.[3] Short-focal-length lenses or equivalently higher-diopter lenses have more focusing "power" as they bend the incoming parallel rays at more acute angles than lenses with longer focal lengths. Focused and defocused light caused by a lens is depicted in Fig. 9.2A and B, respectively.[4]

However, the notion of a focal point is somewhat misleading. A focal "spot" would be a more apt term because there is always a finite diameter associated with focused energy. Moreover, this spreading of energy is caused by diffraction as described in Chapter 3 and elsewhere. The circular-shaped spreading of energy is known as an Airy disk.

At the focal plane of a camera is a sensor. In the old days this sensor consisted of film. In modern digital cameras, sensors are typically charge-coupled device (CCD) arrays that

---

[3]The distance from the human cornea to the retina is about 2 cm. Therefore the total optical power of the human eye focusing system is $1/(0.02 \text{ m}) = 50 \text{ D}$, where 35 diopters result from the cornea and 15 diopters result from the lens.

[4]https://str.llnl.gov/str/Oct07/Menapace.html.

III. THE COMPROMISE OF SIGNALS

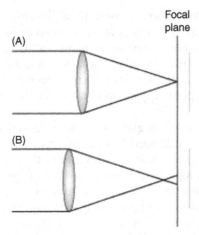

FIGURE 9.2   (A and B) Lens focusing and defocusing.

consist of photoreactive pixels. The camera lens focuses the incident light in the camera field of view onto the CCD sensor. The light causes a charge to build up on each pixel that is proportional to the light intensity.

A control circuit sends the accumulated charge to a charge amplifier, and the charge amplifier converts the charge to an analog signal. The CCD detector sends the analog signal to CMOS transistors. The signal is read at the output of one of the transistors. Other transistors buffer and reset the photodetector.

The proper light level is critical to the operation of many optical sensors. Without enough light, or, more precisely, absent illuminating electromagnetic energy at visible wavelengths, optical devices are useless. The signal intensity or power density is the physical parameter detected by sensors such as the human eye, human ear, or a CCTV camera CCD. The unit of intensity commonly used for optical sensors is the lux or lumen per square meter. For reference, 1 lux = 0.09 ft.-c, where the foot-candle is an old unit of measurement.

Unfocused light emanating from a small fixture can be considered a point source since the distance from the source to the object is typically much greater than the dimensions of the source. The wavelength of light is also usually much smaller than the dimensions of the source. Table 9.2 specifies the light intensity as a function of distance from the source. These numbers follow directly from the inverse square law for point sources.

TABLE 9.2   Light Intensity and Distance

Lux	64	16	4	1
Meters	1	2	4	8

To gain some appreciation for the relative magnitude of ambient light intensities, the following approximations are provided:

- Full Summer Sunlight ~ 50,000 lux.
- Dull Daylight ~ 10,000 lux.
- Shop/Office Environment ~ 500 lux.
- Dawn/Dusk ~ 1–10 lux.
- Main Street Lighting ~ 30 lux.
- Side Street Lighting ~ 0.5–3 lux.

It is helpful to think of the picture element or "pixel" formed on the CCD sensor as a small bucket to collect light. Let's explore image creation at the pixel level. As its name suggests, megapixel cameras use millions of pixels that are sensitive to light. Light reflects off an object and some of the reflected light is incident on the lens. The lens focuses the optical energy onto the camera CCD sensor.

The larger pixel "buckets" are capable of collecting more light than smaller pixels and are therefore able to deliver better performance in low light conditions. So more light intensity is needed for megapixel cameras than for submegapixel cameras, all other conditions being equal. Fig. 9.3 depicts a single pixel in a sensor array.[5]

There is one simple rule to remember: As the resolution of a camera increases, its sensitivity to light decreases. This effect is due to the size of the individual pixels on a sensor, which decreases with higher pixel densities. But note that higher pixel densities are required in order to achieve higher resolution.

Importantly, a camera or telescope operated by an attacker must be able to image the entire scene of interest, which is set by the lens field of view. The focal length of the camera lens, the dimensions of the optical sensor, for example, a CCD array, and the distance from the

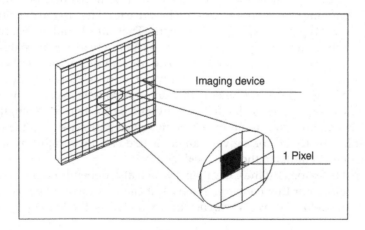

FIGURE 9.3 The pixel.

[5]http://www.securitycameraworld.com/TECHNICAL-ARTICLES/CAMERA-AND-LENSES-MADE-SIMPLE.ASP.

III. THE COMPROMISE OF SIGNALS

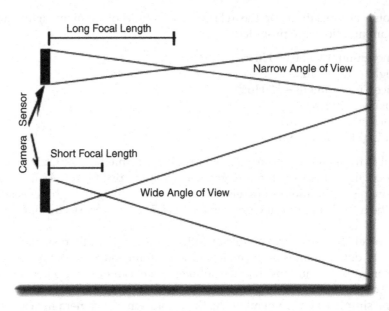

FIGURE 9.4   Focal length versus field of view.

object to the lens determine the angle of view. Focal length is a measure of the magnification of the image. Although longer focal lengths produce higher magnifications, they do so at the expense of the angle of view. Fig. 9.4 nicely illustrates this principle.[6]

The angle of view of a camera lens determines the angle of acceptance of the imaged scene across the relevant dimension of the CCD sensor, that is, horizontal or vertical. It is also important in determining the camera resolution because it relates to the density of pixels.

The angle of view is typically expressed in radians. There are 2π radian in a complete circle, which can also be characterized in terms of degrees. As the reader is probably aware, there are 360 degrees in a circle. To convert radians into degrees, multiply the number of radians by $180/\pi$. For example, an angle of 1 radian is roughly equal to $180/3.14 \sim 57$ degrees.

It can be shown by geometric arguments that an approximate expression for the angle of view equals the CCD sensor dimension (CCD_w) divided by the lens focal length f or CCD_w/f. In other words, the angle of view is a function of the relevant dimension of the sensor divided by the lens focal length. CCD_w for a given camera is fixed so the variable in determining the angle of view usually defaults to the lens focal length.

The image must be in focus at the CCD plane, which also depends on the distance between the lens and the object. For thin convergent lenses, it can be shown by geometric arguments that the width of the field of view (W) can be approximated by the following expression:

$$W \sim D \times \left(\frac{CCD_w}{f} \right) \qquad (9.1)$$

[6]http://jaspinallphotography.blogspot.com/2012/11/field-of-view-focal-length.html.

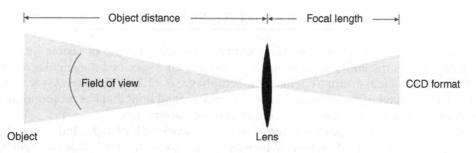

FIGURE 9.5 The camera field of view.

Here D is the distance from the lens to the object, CCD_w is the relevant dimension of the CCD sensor, and f is the focal length of the lens. In other words, the field of view equals the distance between the object and the lens times the angle of view (in radians).

The critical lessons of (9.1) are (1) increasing the focal length decreases the field of view but also increases the magnification of the object and (2) increasing the sensor width and the distance between object and lens increases the field of view. There is always a trade-off between focal length, which yields increased magnification, and the field of view.

Fig. 9.5 illustrates the field of view for a camera with a CCD sensor.[7]

The number of pixels across the field of view or pixel density determines the resolution of an image. It has been suggested that the critical parameter for specifying the resolution of security CCTV cameras is the ratio of the number of pixels to the width of the field of view or "pixels per foot" rather than the absolute number of pixels [1].

Furthermore, there is a direct relationship between the CCD sensor size and the number of pixels that are packed onto its surface. The dimensions of the CCD sensor, and hence the number of pixels, are inexorably linked to image resolution. The bottom line is that larger-area CCD sensors can provide greater pixel densities, and therefore offer greater resolution as well as wider fields of view. But as noted previously, they require more light to operate.

To reiterate, the field of view depends on the sensor size, focal length, and distance from the lens to the object. These parameters also determine the size of the object as it appears in the captured image. The size of an object in a captured image is of critical importance since this is what the attacker actually sees when peering through a lens to view displayed text.

The final size of the image in pixels depends on the pixel density, the object size, the distance to the object, and the focal length. Specifically, the size of the image for a direct line-of-sight scenario can be computed as follows [2]:

$$\text{Size}_{\text{direct}} = \frac{[\text{Sensor Resolution/Sensor Size}] \times [\text{Object Size}]}{[(\text{Target Distance/Focal Length}) - 1]} \tag{9.2}$$

[7]http://www.photogrammetry-software.com/2011/11/what-is-photogrammetric-cameras-field.html.

THE RESOLUTION LIMIT

Diffraction sets the limit on the vulnerability to the compromise of visible information since it determines the limit on resolution. (3.7) in Chapter 3 specified the angular resolution limit (α) for a circular aperture. To reiterate for emphasis, $\alpha = 1.22\lambda/D$, where λ is wavelength and D is the diameter of the aperture.[8] This is a fundamental limit that has profound implications to scenarios related to the visible compromise of information.

Fortunately an attacker has no control over the wavelength of light. But he or she can indeed limit the effect of diffraction by increasing the size of the lens. This has operational implications as larger optical devices, for example, telescopes, increase the likelihood of discovery by a defender or might not fit into their surveillance location. As always, telescopes with larger lenses enable better resolution for equivalent surveillance distances.

As with all attack scenarios, noise can be a significant factor that affects signal detection. In this case noise represents a random variation in a digital camera's pixel's intensity, causing the image to appear speckled. There can be several types of background noise in the captured image, each with a constant noise level [3].

To avoid a visual impact on the image quality by noise, the exposure time is typically chosen so that the overall amount of light overwhelms the background noise. For video capture that was used in one keyboard attack, the exposure time was limited to a single frame, which presents particular challenges for darker scenes [2].

Typically, cameras with large sensors are more resistant to noise, as individual pixels are larger and can capture more photons of the light signal. For that reason, the larger sensors provided in digital SLR cameras (as opposed to mobile phones or point-and-shoot cameras) are desirable for photography even though they produce a smaller number of pixels on the object.

OPTICAL ATTACKS

Whiteboards, Keyboards, and Computer Monitors

Of course, an attacker does not have to rely on the focusing power of the human lens alone to view written text at a distance. There are plenty of artificial lens systems at his or her disposal, but the performance of all these devices is ultimately limited by diffraction.

Recall (3.7) in Chapter 3 once again. This expression was used to calculate the maximum distance at which one could resolve the headlights of a car using the naked eye assuming the human lens is diffraction limited. The calculations that estimate the vulnerability to information compromise via optical imaging are identical to the one used for illustrative purposes in Chapter 3.

Let us say an attacker is hoping to read the font displayed on a computer monitor in a conference room that is visible from a building across the street. The attacker is stuck with using visible light so he or she cannot do much to adjust the wavelength λ. But using a lens with a wider aperture is definitely an option.

---

[8]This is the so-called Rayleigh criterion.

Unless the attacker has physical access to the room housing the computer, he or she is restricted to be at some standoff distance from the displayed information of interest. If this were not the case, the information could be observed by merely walking up to the screen or whiteboard and photographing it or copying it down. Although it is not discussed in this chapter, the latter scenario is not unrealistic, and represents a significant motivation for the physical security controls introduced in Chapter 15.

The distance between the attacker and the information of interest definitely affects the vulnerability to information compromise. The diffraction limit dictates that the minimum spot size for a lens, and therefore the smallest object that can be resolved, equals the angular resolution of the lens times the distance between the attacker's lens and the target computer monitor.

However, to further complicate the attacker's life, he or she may be at an angle with respect to the screen. If a pixel diameter is given by r, and the attacker is at an angle ϕ with respect to a perpendicular view of the monitor screen, he or she will see a viewing angle (in radians) of $(r/d)\cos\phi$ for a pixel.

So the more general expression for the spot size produced by a circular lens with an aperture diameter D at a distance d is given by the following [4]:

$$\text{Spot size} = \frac{1.22\lambda d}{Dr\cos\phi} \tag{9.3}$$

Therefore, the diameter of a circular aperture required to resolve a pixel of diameter r is equal to the following:

$$D = \frac{1.22\lambda d}{r\cos\phi} \tag{9.4}$$

Let us assume the attacker is lucky and is aligned directly in front of the targeted computer monitor at a distance of 100 m. If the wavelength of light is assumed to be 5000×10^{-10} m, and the pixel size is 0.25×10^{-3} m, the smallest-diameter lens that can achieve this resolution is the following:

$$\frac{100\,\text{m} \times (1.22 \times 5000 \times 10^{-10}\,\text{m})}{0.25 \times 10^{-3}\,\text{m}} = 0.24\,\text{m}$$

So a 0.24-m diameter lens is the smallest lens that can resolve an object the size of an individual pixel at 100 m. The size of the aperture required to resolve a given image scales linearly with the distance between the object and the lens. Therefore, a diffraction-limited lens that is one-tenth this diameter (0.024 m) could at best resolve the same pixel at a distance of only one-tenth the distance or 10 m.

However, individual characters are the building blocks of text, and text consists of multiple pixels. The objective of an optical attack is to read individual characters, and therefore resolving individual pixels is likely overkill. The so-called Y-character height of computer font is 4 mm or about 8 pixels.

Therefore at 100 m the smallest lens that is capable of resolving an individual letter on a computer monitor is 0.03 m (3 cm) assuming the lens and monitor screen were vertically and horizontally aligned.[9]

It should be emphasized that the optical quality of commercial grade telescopes does not typically approach the diffraction limit. Larger lenses would likely be required to resolve character-size objects at 100 m. However, high-grade commercial telescopes do exist and could be built or purchased by a committed attacker.

For example, a 10-in. f14.6 Maksutov-Cassegrain telescope manufactured by Astro-Physics Inc. has an advertised resolution of 0.45 arc seconds, which is equivalent to 2.0×10^{-6} radian.[10] Therefore, at 100 m this telescope is capable of resolving 0.2-mm objects.

The presence of whiteboards in conference rooms that are visible to the external environment and/or employees lacking a need-to-know represents a risk factor for information compromise. In addition, the information written on whiteboards often persists well after the conclusion of meetings where it is generated.

Therefore, although the information displayed on a whiteboard might be less dense in terms of content than information displayed on a computer monitor, its persistence in time and the size of the characters potentially enhance its attractiveness as a target for attack.

The physical parameters relevant to whiteboard attacks are identical to computer monitors; merely the scale of the imaged objects increases thereby increasing the vulnerability to compromise. As always the diffraction limit determines the optical resolution limit at a given distance between the object and the lens although creating a lens that even approaches the diffraction limit is challenging.

If the wavelength of light is again assumed to be 5000×10^{-10} m, an individual letter on the whiteboard is 3 cm or slightly larger than 1 in., and the telescope lens is 10 cm in diameter and diffraction limited, the maximum distance between the telescope and the whiteboard that can achieve this resolution is approximately 4900 m!

Reflected Images

Another potential optical attack leverages the reflection of a monitor image in nearby objects, thereby partially overcoming the operational restriction of direct line-of-sight. However, if the reflecting object is convex, for example, a pair of sunglasses or the human eyeball, the size of the observed object will be much smaller than if observed with direct line-of-sight.

Noting the expression for the size of the image through direct observation ($Size_{direct}$) as specified by (9.2), when an object is viewed via reflection, the observed size is now given by the following [2]:

$$Size_{reflection} = \frac{Size_{direct}}{(2 \text{Distance from the Reflecting Surface}) / (\text{Curvature Radius} + 1)} \quad (9.5)$$

From this expression the radius of curvature of the reflecting surface is seen to be an important factor in the observed size of the image. The more curved the reflecting surface, the more

[9]http://www.translatorscafe.com/cafe/EN/units-converter/typography/5-7/character_(X)-pixel_(X)/.
[10]http://www.astro-physics.com/index.htm?products/telescopes/10mak/10f146mak.

the reflected light will bend. For convex surfaces the bending of the light will result in a smaller observed object size. Lastly, the distance between the reflecting surface and the target object, that is, the "Distance from the Reflecting Surface" in (9.5), affects the observed object size as well.

In one documented attack using reflected images, reflections from eyeglasses, teapots, spoons, plastic bottles, and even the human eye were used [5]. The attack was successful against small font using inexpensive, off-the-shelf equipment from a distance of up to 10 m. More expensive equipment resulted in a successful compromise at distances exceeding 30 m. This result demonstrated that such attacks were feasible from across a street or from a nearby building.

The lessons regarding the vulnerability of visible information due to reflecting surfaces are relatively straightforward. The most obvious is that in order to increase the observed object size one must simply reduce the distance to the target object. However, from the attacker's perspective this is often not optimal because of the operational implications to covertness.

Therefore, all other factors being equal, using a lens with a telescope with a long focal length offers increased covertness and could produce the desired object amplification if favorable, scenario-specific conditions exist. The trade-off is a reduced field of view, but to observe objects such as text on a computer screen this is likely to be less important. Camera sensors with higher pixel density provide better resolution for a given distance from the object and focal length.

The curvature of any reflecting surface will affect the image size. For example, the human eyeball has a typical curvature of about 8 mm. Hence, when a person looks at an object that is 25 cm from their eyeball, the reflection of that object will appear about 60 times smaller than it would be if one viewed the same object using direct line-of-sight.

Finally, and as is the case with all optical scenarios, the quality of the acquired image for reflected scenarios is significantly influenced by the wave properties of light. As emphasized repeatedly, the physical limit on resolution is determined by diffraction. The maximum effective size of the observed object (Max Size) can be approximated as follows based on the Rayleigh Criterion [2]:

$$\text{Max Size} = \frac{\text{Aperture / Wavelength}}{1.22 \text{Target Distance}} \times \left(\frac{\text{Object Size}}{2 \text{Distance from Surface / Curvature Radius}} + 1 \right) \quad (9.6)$$

A more sophisticated attack against a keyboard used video surveillance that combined optical methods with analyzing fingertip motion. In addition, a process was invoked to infer the specific keys that were pressed [2].

As a supplemental postprocessing effort, the inferred keys and associated confidence values were fed into a language model in order to achieve more accurate results. The language modeling was treated as a noisy channel-decoding problem, and techniques from the speech recognition community were adapted to perform the inference in a process known as maximum likelihood decoding.

Successful attacks were performed irrespective of keyboard type, without direct line-of-sight, and at greater distances than originally anticipated. The analysis included a variety of scenarios including direct line-of-sight, single reflections, and repeated reflections as well as at distances ranging from 3 to 50 m.

III. THE COMPROMISE OF SIGNALS

Photon Counting

In addition to focusing an image onto a focal plane, other optical methods have been postulated to obtain unauthorized access to visual information. Specifically, photon counting of an optical signal in the time domain can be used to reconstruct video signals [4]. A high-level description of the process is described for an attack against light-emitting diode (LED) displays.

Note that this is indeed an optical attack since collection of optical photons is required. However, it does not involve imaging those photons. One operational implication of this distinction is that using a translucent barrier to hide the monitor might not be effective in photon counting since photons generated by the LED display could possibly still be detected despite the presence of a barrier.

LEDs are used in some modems to optically indicate the logic level of data lines. Therefore, remote monitoring of the LED luminosity could be exploited to reconstruct the transmitted data. Specifically, an estimate of the expected number of photons received from a single pulse of the LED along with the expected number of photons from the background signal is used to determine the state of the LED, that is, on or off.

With respect to the background signal, the number of photons is assumed to be a random variable and therefore is normally distributed for a sufficiently large numbers of photons. The mean of the distribution is the number of photons contributed by the noise plus signal when the LED is on plus the number of noise photons (only) when the LED is off. The standard deviation of the normal distribution of photons equals the square root of the number of noise photons detected as discussed in Chapter 6.

Assuming a transmitted bit value of 1 or 0 is equally likely, a matched filter can be used to count the photons in a bit interval. The resulting number is compared with the threshold number of photons for noise plus signal to determine if the LED is on or off. Shot noise is the source of signal uncertainty, and the normal distribution of photon counts can be used to determine the probability of a bit error.

The scenario-specific parameter values for this attack are as follows:

- a telescope aperture of 0.3 m^2;
- a distance of 500 m between the source and the detector;
- a single bit pulse time of 10^{-5} s (100 kbits/s);
- a reflection factor of unity;
- an observed area of 1 $cm^2 = 10^{-4}$ m^2;
- an ambient/background irradiance of 1 W/m^2 or roughly 10^3 lux[11];
- a green LED (wavelength of 565 nm) of radiant intensity 10^{-5} W/sr.

Using the aforementioned values, a bit error rate of 10^{-7} or 1 error in 10,000,000-bit transmissions has been reported. This may seem like a low number, and apparently was sufficient for the task at hand, but typical bit error rates are 10^{-9} for an electrical link and 10^{-12} for a fiber-optic link [6].

---

[11]Lux or lumen per meter is a unit of measurement of illuminance. For reference, direct sunlight is approximately 10^5 lux and the illuminance of an overcast night sky is 10^{-4} lux. Illuminance is a measure of how much the incident light illuminates a surface, wavelength-weighted by the luminosity function to correlate with human brightness perception.

Therefore although this attack could be successful, the attacker would experience errors at a rate that is orders of magnitude above what would be expected with standard electrical or optical communications links.

TELESCOPES

An attack aimed at accessing visual information might involve an attacker perched in a remote location and using a telescope to resolve letters on a whiteboard, computer monitor, or any physical entity displaying written information. It is therefore important to understand the basics of the telescope since this would be the facilitator of such attacks.

Fig. 9.6 illustrates the optical components and functionality of a telescope at a high level.[12]

Light rays at the target are incident on the telescope objective lens. These rays can be considered in parallel because of the distance between the object and the lens. The objective lens focuses the incoming light to a focal point, that is, the image plane. The light rays diverge from the focal point and are incident on an eyepiece lens, which "parallelizes" the light that is refocused by the human cornea and lens onto the retina.

Importantly, the eyepiece functions as a magnifier. Eyepiece lenses have different focal lengths. A shorter-focal-length eyepiece brings the focal point of the objective lens closer to the eye. Therefore, the image appears larger for shorter-focal-length eyepieces because the eye is closer to the image plane. The magnification of a telescope equals the ratio of the focal length of the objective to the focal length of the eyepiece.

The field of view is another relevant specification for a telescope used to remotely resolve images. Clearly being able to view the entire object of interest would be a priority for an attacker attempting to view data at a distance. The field of view and the magnification

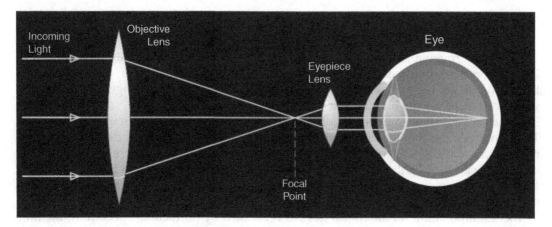

FIGURE 9.6 Telescope functionality.

[12]http://www.rocketmime.com/astronomy/Telescope/telescope_eqn.html.

TABLE 9.3   Telescope Resolution Limits (Meters)

Objective Lens (cm)	25 m	50 m	100 m
5	3.4×10^{-6}	6.7×10^{-6}	1.3×10^{-5}
10	1.7×10^{-6}	3.4×10^{-6}	6.7×10^{-6}
15	1.1×10^{-6}	2.2×10^{-6}	4.5×10^{-6}
20	8.4×10^{-7}	1.7×10^{-6}	3.4×10^{-6}
25	6.7×10^{-7}	1.3×10^{-6}	2.7×10^{-6}
30	5.6×10^{-7}	1.1×10^{-6}	2.2×10^{-6}

associated with a lens are inversely related: increasing the magnification by a factor of 10 will decrease the field of view by the same amount.

The diffraction limit for circular lenses was specified by (3.7) in Chapter 3 and subsequently referenced numerous times. The readers has now been repeatedly reminded that diffraction limit sets the theoretical limit on lens resolution for any optical device including telescopes. To review once more, key operational parameters include the wavelength of light, the diameter of the lens, and the distance between the target and the lens.

Table 9.3 specifies the resolution limit of 5-, 10-, 15-, 20-, 25-, and 30-cm diameter objective lenses at various distances for a wavelength of 550×10^{-9} m, that is, green light. Distances of 25, 50, and 100 m were used in the calculation. Computer font sizes are typically in the 3- to 5-mm (3×10^{-3} to 5×10^{-3} m) range.

From this data it appears that individual letters on a computer monitor are 3–4 orders of magnitude larger than the minimum size of an object that could be resolved by telescopes with these diameter lenses at the specified distances.

SUMMARY

Visible information can exist in multiple forms and each has potential vulnerabilities to information compromise depending on the scenario. Computer monitors, whiteboards, and keyboards are known to display confidential information that can be imaged by adversaries with direct and reflected line-of-sight to the targeted object.

Lenses are essential components of optical equipment used to compromise information. They work as a result of the difference in relative permittivity, that is, the dielectric constant, between air and the lens material, which is typically glass. The difference in permittivity causes the speed of light to decrease when traveling in glass relative to the speed of light when traveling in air. The lens is shaped such that optical energy passing through the lens converges to a spot on the focal plane.

The resolution limit for all optical devices is dictated by diffraction. Specifically, the ratio of the wavelength of light to the diameter of the lens aperture times the distance between the lens and the object determines the smallest object that can be resolved with a given lens.

Various optical attacks have been demonstrated by observing direct and reflected images. Calculations associated with various attack scenarios can be performed in order to determine their feasibility using scenario-specific parameters. An optical attack using photon counting rather than imaging has also been demonstrated. Such an attack has operational implications since images visually obfuscated by translucent barriers are potentially vulnerable to detection using this methodology.

References

[1] Young C. The science and technology of counterterrorism: measuring physical and electronic security risk. Oxford, UK: Butterworth-Heinemann; 2014.

[2] Xu Y, Heinly J, White AM, Monrose F, Frahm J-M. Seeing double: reconstructing obscured typed input from repeated compromising reflections, <http://frahm.web.unc.edu/files/2014/01/Seeing-Double-Reconstructing-Obscured-Typed-Input-from-Repeated-Compromising-Reflections.pdf>.

[3] Nakamura J. Image sensors and signal processing for digital still cameras. Boca Raton, FL: CRC Press; 2005.

[4] Kuhn M. Optical time domain eavesdropping risks of CRT displays. In: Proceedings 2002 IEEE symposium on security and privacy, May 12–15, Berkeley, CA; 2002. p. 3–18.

[5] Backes M, Durmuth M, Unruh D. IEEE symposium on security and privacy; 2008. SP 2008.

[6] Mckeown N. Error detection and correction. Stanford University computer science course CS244A, <web.stanford.edu/class/.../H13%20%20Control%202008.ppt>.

Audible Information Security

INTRODUCTION

Acoustic vibrations generally described as sound are examples of mechanical energy propagating through a material. Speech is sound that has been converted to an audible signal through modulation, and therefore conveys information. The process of speaking is an example of the generation and propagation of mechanical energy. In this section some of the material in Chapter 3 will be reviewed to refresh the reader's memory.

In Chapter 3 we had discovered that sound waves are longitudinal waves. This means that the changing amplitude of the wave is in the same direction as the wave propagation. Recall the image of a slinky toy depicted in Fig. 3.5.

Acoustic signals that are characteristic of speech do not consist of a single frequency but consist of a spectrum of frequencies ranging from a few hertz to thousands of hertz. Since human hearing has presumably evolved to accommodate human speech, it is not surprising that our ears respond to frequencies from a few hertz to about 20 kHz. The sensitivity of the human ear peaks at about 3 kHz, where the human auditory response is illustrated in Fig. 10.1.[1]

Let's now examine the acoustic waves generated by speech after the initial vibration of the vocal chords. On vibrating the initial set of air molecules, a continuum of molecular vibrations cascades in ever-increasing radii from the source. Changing the shape of the mouth while altering the vibration of the vocal chords generates intelligible sounds called speech.

Each vibrating molecule touches neighboring molecules thereby setting in motion an expanding sphere of vibrations. These create areas of compression and rarefaction or equivalently regions of contraction and expansion in the material. These movements of the material characterize the pressure fluctuations propagating in all directions outward from the source (assuming a point source) until the energy of vibration is dissipated to extinction through friction.

However, this process does not continue in perpetuity. Otherwise inhabitants of the planet would have the dubious pleasure of listening to every sound created everywhere in the world. The mouth and vocal tract can indeed be considered to be a point source, and therefore the intensity of sound decreases in proportion to the increasing surface area of an imaginary sphere.

---

[1]http://msis.jsc.nasa.gov/sections/section04.htm.

Information Security Science

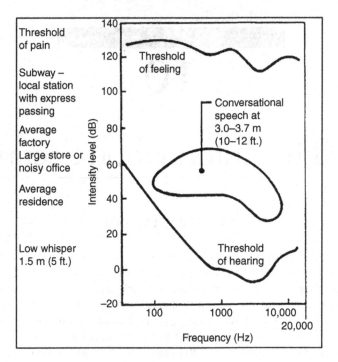

FIGURE 10.1 Human auditory response.

As noted earlier, molecular vibrations so generated eventually dissipate through friction but this dissipation can occur over long distances depending on the propagation medium. Since speech can certainly transmit confidential information, it would be useful to calculate the sound intensity as a function of distance from the sound source and thereby estimate the vulnerability to detection and potential compromise.

The total power of a radiated signal does not change with distance from the source unless some intervening structure absorbs or reflects some of the energy. However, the intensity or power per unit area of the signal most certainly does change with distance from the source. Recall the same applied to electromagnetic and optical scenarios, where the definitions of energy and power apply to all forms of energy. Specifically, the signal intensity becomes increasingly dilute with distance from the source as the energy propagates through a given medium.

Recall the discussion of the light bulb and the power required to provide sufficient light for reading noted in Chapter 3. The radiated energy was of little consequence to the reading enthusiast. It was the radiated *power* that counted in terms of leveraging the available energy for reading. This condition applies equally to acoustic, electromagnetic, and optical sensors.

When a sensor such as the human ear detects sound energy, it is the intensity or power per unit area of the acoustic pressure wave that is detected by the eardrum. So a change in intensity can result from a change in the signal power, in this case manifest by a pressure fluctuation, and/ or by a change in the physical area impacted by that energy. For a fixed signal power, the smaller the area impacted by the signal energy the greater the signal intensity. An increase in the area of the sensor would require proportionately more signal power to maintain the same intensity.

The threshold of human hearing is specified in terms of intensity. Therefore in estimating the vulnerability to audible information compromise (without electronic assistance), one must determine the intensity of speech with respect to this threshold. However, as the reader might suspect from previous chapters, the presence of noise in the bandwidth corresponding to human hearing affects the limits on the detection of speech.

A central theme in information security more generally is that noise plays an outsized role in the vulnerability of signals to detection and therefore to information compromise. In fact, the absence of noise in scenarios pertaining to electromagnetic energy yielded physically unrealistic results. The same applies to scenarios involving acoustic energy, where once again audible noise has a profound effect on acoustic signal detection.

AUDIBLE NOISE AND INTERFERENCE

Electromagnetic signals are not the only signals that contain information, and so they are not the only signals of potential interest to an attacker. So-called baseband speech, which is speech that has not been modulated for electronic recording and/or transmission, can be a rich source of information that has historically been a focus of government, industrial, and individual surveillance efforts.

An onslaught of acoustic energy affects the average urban dweller to varying degrees throughout each day. Consider the spectrum of sounds on a typical busy street. These sounds are continually affecting street inhabitants in the form of slinky-like fluctuations of air pressure. Anyone who has visited my hometown of New York City knows that signals converging on human ears are not necessarily comprehended or appreciated but the energy is detected nonetheless. Human ears involuntarily sense acoustic energy whether it is desired or not since evolution has not yet outfitted our species with the aural equivalent of eyelids.

Moreover, human hearing is extremely sensitive, presumably one of the artifacts of evolution. Recall speech is manifest as a fluctuating pressure wave incident on our human acoustic sensors, that is, the eardrum. These are capable of detecting 1 part in 10^{10} (10^{-10}) of atmospheric pressure, which is 14.7 lb/(in.)^2 at sea level or 10^5 dynes.[2] In absolute terms, the threshold of hearing occurs around 3 kHz and is approximately 0 dB relative to 20 µPa, which is equivalent to an intensity of 0.98×10^{-12} W/m^2 as shown in Fig. 10.2.[3]

Recall Table 2.3 revealed this threshold relative to other sources of sound. For example, the intensity of normal audible conversations is about 10^{-6} W/m^2 or 60 dB greater than the intensity of a source broadcasting its energy at the threshold of hearing.

Anyone who has eaten in a crowded restaurant and attempted to have a conversation has been affected by audible noise. Often many people in the room are speaking at the same time making it difficult to discern the conversation of interest. In addition, auditory conditions are greatly affected by the room architecture as well as the number of speakers. A combination of low ceilings, small rooms, hard surfaces, and lots of people is a recipe for auditory disaster. To add insult to injury, as the interference increases, customers tend to raise their voices thereby exacerbating the problem. This scenario is an example of a positive feedback loop.

[2]https://courses.physics.illinois.edu/phys406/lecture_notes/p406pom_lecture_notes/p406pom_lect5.pdf.
[3]http://www.diracdelta.co.uk/science/source/t/h/threshold%20of%20hearing/source.html#.VZbkVShhzIo.

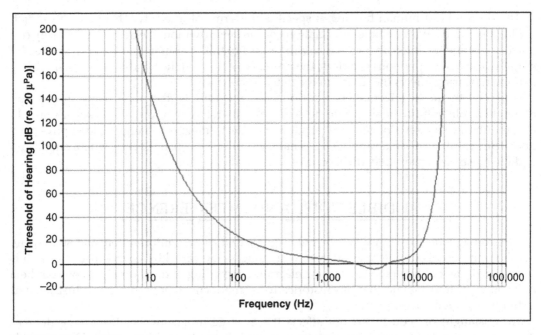

FIGURE 10.2   Threshold of human hearing as a function of frequency.

Of course, there are numerous sources of audible interference other than speech. Imagine trying to have a conversation in proximity to an active jackhammer. Table 2.3 also specified the intensity of a jackhammer at a distance of 15 m. This figure is roughly 100 dB above the threshold of human hearing or equivalently 40 dB above conversation-level speech. In fact, any acoustic energy with a frequency between about 20 and 10,000 Hz would be considered noise to people in relatively close proximity.

THE EFFECTS OF NOISE AND DISTANCE

Standard office buildings are not typically constructed with a concern for information loss. Yet sensitive information is often discussed in areas contiguous with physically uncontrolled space. Moreover, conference rooms are often quite accessible to the general employee population. In addition, business people routinely discuss sensitive information in public places, and can be oblivious to those around them. The limits of vulnerability for common security scenarios are the topics of analysis next.

The theoretical vulnerability to audible information compromise will be estimated first. Imagine two senior executives of the American Widget Corporation (AWC) are conducting a sensitive conversation in the quiet car of an Amtrak train. The intensity of the sound energy in their verbal exchange is at the subdued conversation level. A representative of the World Gadget Corporation (WGC), a fierce competitor of AWC, is sitting 3 m from the two AWC executives.

Some admittedly highly unrealistic physical conditions are now assumed but reality is somehow easily suspended while traveling on Amtrak. First, the train is acoustically isolated from the outside world so there is no external audible interference. Second, no one inside the car other than the two AWC executives is speaking.

Third, there is an unobstructed air path between the two AWC executives and the person from WGC, and no acoustic energy is absorbed or reflected by the internal furniture (eg, seats, floor, overhead rack) within the train passenger compartment.

Therefore the following conditions are in effect: (1) no external acoustic energy enters the car, (2) no acoustic energy is absorbed by structures inside the car, (3) no acoustic energy is generated inside the car except what is transmitted by the two AWC executives, (4) there is no interference in the relevant signal bandwidth, and (5) nothing but the friction of acoustic vibrations in air attenuates the audible signal.

Accepting these unusual conditions for the time being, what is the AWC executives' vulnerability to being overheard by the overly inquisitive WGC representative?

Let us assume the power P of the acoustic energy generated by the AWC executives is 10^{-6} W, that is, conversation level. From the inverse square law, at a distance r, of 3 m the intensity from this point source equals the following:

$$\text{Intensity} = \frac{P}{4\pi r^2} \tag{10.1}$$

Plugging the assumed acoustic power and distance between the AWC and WGC employees into (10.1) yields the following:

$$\frac{10^{-6}\ \text{W}}{3\,\text{m}^2} = 1.1 \times 10^{-7}\ \text{W/m}^2$$

The minimum threshold of human hearing at a frequency of 1 kHz has been experimentally determined to be 10^{-12} W/m^2. The human ear can sense pressure variations equal to 2.0×10^{-5} N/m^2. These variations are 2.0×10^{-10} less than normal atmospheric pressure, and are a testament to the incredible sensitivity of the human ear. Below this intensity the human ear is incapable of responding. Hence, there is zero vulnerability to being overheard by a third party if the intensity is less than this frequency-dependent threshold.

So the intensity of conversational sound energy that is "available" to the nosy WGC person is $1.1 \times 10^{-7}/10^{-12}$ or about 100,000 times the minimum sensitivity threshold of the human ear. The vulnerability component of risk can be expressed perfectly well in terms of this zero vulnerability condition. That condition is defined to be the distance where the signal intensity equals the minimum threshold of sound detection.

What distance of separation between source and listener would be required to achieve a zero vulnerability condition in this context? It is worth reiterating that this is a very contrived scenario, and the specific nature of that contrivance will become clear later. Yet the scenario is instructive nonetheless.

The goal is to determine the distance at which the intensity of the speech equals the minimum threshold of human hearing. This is accomplished by solving for r in (10.1) using the threshold for human hearing as the intensity:

$$\frac{10^{-6}\ \text{W}}{4\pi r^2} = 10^{-12}\ \text{W/m}^2$$

III. THE COMPROMISE OF SIGNALS

This distance is found to be an amazingly distant 282 m! For reference, an American football field is about 91 m in length. Therefore, a minimum physical separation of 282 m is necessary for the AWC executives to be invulnerable to audible information compromise by the WGC industrial spy. Invulnerability exacts a price, and in this idealized world that price is significant physical separation.

Personal experience suggests that this result is nonsense. Why? A major simplification in this analysis has been to neglect the presence of noise, which is a ubiquitous phenomenon in the real world that enters into every physically realistic detection scenario. So let us now introduce background noise into the scenario and observe how it affects the required separation to achieve a zero vulnerability condition.

The person from WGC must contend with an acoustic background in the same bandwidth as the sound emanated from the AWC executives. Let us assume the intensity of the background is 10^{-8} W/m^2. This becomes the new threshold for audibility since an acoustic signal below this intensity will be overwhelmed by the background noise.

Using this new threshold intensity and again solving for the separation distance r in (10.1), the distance required for a zero vulnerability condition is now approximately 3 m and seems physically realistic. This is a far more reasonable answer and tells us that for distances greater than about 3 m between speaker and listener there is zero vulnerability to signal detection. This is obviously a strikingly different result from that of a noiseless environment. It serves as yet another lesson on the importance of ambient noise in estimating vulnerability to signal detection.

In the interest of full disclosure the effects of ambient temperature and pressure on acoustic energy have been neglected. These effects are cumulative and can be significant over appreciable distances. However, such distances exceed those typically considered in assessing the vulnerability to audible information compromise, especially for conversational scenarios. The important takeaway is that the intensity of background noise must always be included in any assessment of the vulnerability to the compromise of audible signals.

AUDIBLE SIGNAL PROPAGATION

The effects of intervening structures on the compromise of audible signals have been neglected in the previous analyses. The effects of such objects are now considered. Recall the slinky-like induced pressure changes that result in regions of compression and rarefaction in the propagation material. This is illustrated in Fig. 10.3 where the amplitudes of the compression and rarefaction of the material supporting the sound wave are also plotted.[4]

Since sound energy is conducted by vibrating a successive chain of nearest neighbor molecules within the propagating material, dense materials actually conduct sound better than their less dense counterparts. For example, the speed of sound in wood is roughly 11.6 times that of air so sound energy conducted through wood travels a considerable distance before being attenuated. The attenuation of sound in any material is due to friction, and small

[4]https://www.osha.gov/dts/osta/otm/new_noise/.

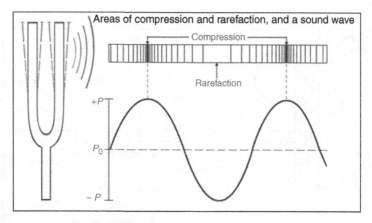

FIGURE 10.3   **Propagating sound wave effect on materials.**

quantities of heat are indeed produced by virtue of the vibration of the molecules disturbed by the acoustic energy.

The difference in the speed of sound through various materials is evident in real-life scenarios. For example, an approaching subway train can be heard well in advance of its actual appearance because of the sound energy conducted by the steel rails. The speed of sound in steel is 5000 m/s or 14.5 times the speed of sound in air (344 m/s) at standard temperature and pressure.

So if sound propagates better in materials such as wood and steel than in air, why is it more difficult to overhear conversations with a barrier interposed between speaker and listener? More to the point what is the vulnerability to audible information compromise when such a barrier is present?

As most individuals know from experience, a listener on one side of a wood barrier or a wall might strain to hear a conversation occurring on the other side of that barrier or wall. Certainly a substantial fraction of the incident acoustic energy is initially reflected at the air–wood interface. However, it would be a mistake to assume that some fraction of the incident sound energy does not cause the molecules in the wood barrier to vibrate.

That mistake would be compounded by assuming that the coupled sound energy would not propagate some distance within the structure and therefore not be detectible in other parts of the building. Fig. 10.4 illustrates the situation.[5]

The intensity of sound surely decreases from one side of a barrier to the other. Mechanical energy is definitely affected by the material in which it propagates, and, importantly, by the *difference* in densities of the materials encountered during propagation. So when vibrating air molecules meet the denser-than-air wood barrier, most of the incident energy is reflected.

But the energy that is not reflected is actually absorbed by the wood and transmitted across the barrier to the other side. Hence, conversations are overheard from one room to another.[6]

[5]http://www.gov.scot/resource/buildingstandards/2015nondomestic/chunks/ch06.html.

[6]There are frequently ducts and openings between rooms that allow acoustic energy to propagate from room to room and therefore do not experience reflection.

III. THE COMPROMISE OF SIGNALS

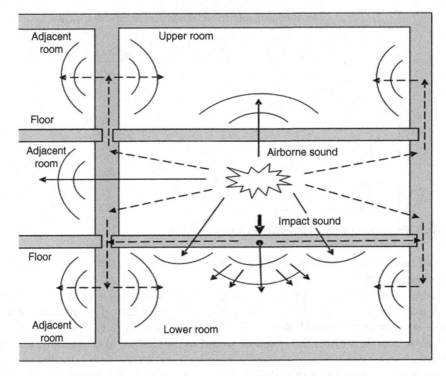

FIGURE 10.4 Propagation of sound energy from within a room in a building.

Acoustic engineers speak of the "acoustic impedance mismatch" between materials, and great attention is paid to this parameter in designing acoustic structures. The acoustic impedance of a material is defined as the density of that material times the velocity of sound in that material.

If a confidential discussion were transpiring in a conference room, it might be useful to estimate what fraction of acoustic energy that is generated inside the conference room is actually contained within that room. The fraction of energy reflected back to a source by an intervening, floor-to-ceiling barrier can be determined by examining the acoustic impedance mismatch between the air and the intervening wall.

Specifically, the ratio of the difference and sum of the acoustic impedances of two dissimilar materials yields the fraction of reflected energy. If d_1 equals the density of air, d_2 equals the density of an intervening wall, v_1 equals the velocity of sound in air, and v_2 is the velocity of sound in the wall, the fraction of reflected energy is given by R in the following expression:

$$\text{Reflection Coefficient} = R = \frac{d_1 v_1 - d_2 v_2}{d_1 v_1 + d_2 v_2} \tag{10.2}$$

The nonreflected energy initiates vibrations in the wall and is either absorbed by the barrier or transmitted across the wall to excite the air in the next room. The sum of the transmitted (T), reflected (R_e), and absorbed (A) energy constitutes all the energy in the signal. In other words, $T + R_e + A = 1$.

One must be careful with this type of analysis for rooms that are highly reverberant or "live," that is, lacking sufficient absorption. In acoustically live rooms where multiple reflections are occurring, even though the wall may transmit only 1% of the acoustic energy, 99% of the reflected energy continues to reflect off the walls.[7]

Each reflection results in small energy leaks into the adjacent room. If 1% of the energy leaks across the wall following each reflection, one-millionth of the initial energy leaks into the adjacent room after three reflections. Even a massively heavy wall will not attenuate all the transmitted energy in a highly reverberant room.

One could succinctly characterize the loss in acoustic energy that occurs across a wall separating one room from another via the transmission loss (TL) as follows:

$$TL = 10 \log \frac{I_{inc}}{I_{trans}} \tag{10.3}$$

The logarithm of the ratio of intensities is used because I_{inc}/I_{trans} is a large number and the logarithm reduces the range of values. TL is therefore specified in decibels, a concept introduced in Chapter 2.

It is important to note that even a tiny hole in the wall will allow acoustic energy to propagate to the other side and thereby significantly increase the vulnerability to detection. This is not necessarily the case with electromagnetic energy, where the aperture size relative to the wavelength of energy is the relevant parameter.

The effect of aperture size on electromagnetic energy has been experienced by anyone who has peered into a microwave while cooking a turkey burger or anything else for that matter. The mesh is made of metal, which attenuates incident electromagnetic energy. However, the openings in the mesh are spaced such that the maxima of the oscillating microwave electric field are larger than the aperture diameter so the mesh "looks" like a solid metal sheet to the incident microwave electric field. But the mesh openings are large enough to allow optical wavelengths to pass.

Sequential compressions and rarefactions of air molecules in an acoustic wave can occur perfectly well across large and small apertures. The fraction of the incident energy that is transmitted into the next room will increase as the dimension of the aperture increases up to some limit where covertness is affected.

Recall the theoretical vulnerability to detection of acoustic energy in the interior of a train car was estimated earlier in this chapter. The effect of noise was included and excluded from the estimates to illustrate its profound effect on the vulnerability to signal detection. In general, estimates of vulnerability to information loss from room to room can be a complicated technical problem, but simplified physical models can facilitate ballpark estimates of risk, as is the case with many information security scenarios.

Let us examine the speaker's effect on the wall in more detail. Although it is imperceptible to the naked eye, the wall will vibrate in reaction to the vibrations of air molecules caused by the speaker. The frequency response of the wall, that is, the amplitude of vibration as a function of frequency, will vary across the audible spectrum and will also depend on the mass of the wall.

---

[7]The room is a form of cavity that stores energy. A highly reverberant room is said to have a high Q, where Q is defined as $2\pi f_r$ (energy stored/average power dissipated), f_r being the resonant frequency of the room or, more generally, a cavity resonator.

Recall the discussion of resonance and forced oscillations in Chapter 3, and, specifically, Fig. 3.10 depicting a mass and spring harmonic oscillator. This system approximates the action of the wall (the mass) in response to a driving force (the speaker). A nonconstant force applied to a mass will result in oscillatory motion, where the frequency of oscillation depends on the ratio of the stiffness of the system to its mass. In addition, structures have natural frequencies of oscillation, and when the damping or attenuation is low, this natural frequency approximately equals the structure's resonant frequency.

At low frequencies, the wall is susceptible to resonances where it absorbs more energy and therefore vibrates preferentially at those frequencies. Resonance is an important physical phenomenon that can occur in any vibrating system. In general, resonance effects occur over a well-prescribed bandwidth and are directly related to the physical properties of the system relative to the energy of excitation.

For low-mass walls, higher frequencies might also exhibit resonance effects at the so-called coincidence frequency. In this case the wavelength of induced ripples along the wall surface matches the incident acoustic energy wavelength. In such instances resonance occurs in the 1- to 4-kHz range, and therefore results in a more efficient transfer of acoustic energy across the wall boundary. The effect of resonance from a security perspective is to increase the vulnerability to information compromise. Note that 1–4 kHz is roughly in the middle of the frequency range of human speech.

At frequencies below 100 Hz, the restoring force dominates the wall's response, and so the TL is given approximately by the following expression [1]:

$$TL = C - 20\log\left(\frac{fR^4}{Yh^3}\right)[dB] \tag{10.4}$$

where C is a constant, f is the sound frequency, R is a typical transverse dimension between wall supports, h is the thickness of the wall, and Y is the stiffness of the wall, that is, Young's modulus – no relation to the author. The important point is that the attenuating effect of wall stiffness will decrease as the sound frequency is increased.

At frequencies between 100 Hz and 1 kHz, the TL between rooms separated by a wall is given by the following expression [1]:

$$TL \leq 20\log(f\sigma) - 48[dB] \tag{10.5}$$

In this expression, f is the frequency of the acoustic wave and σ is the mass density of the wall in units of kilogram per square meter. In this frequency range, each doubling of sound frequency, that is, one octave, increases the TL by a factor of 2.[8]

It is clear from this expression that the two physical parameters that determine vulnerability to signal detection in this scenario are the density of the wall and the frequency of the incident sound energy.

Since audible energy for a human extends over many octaves, the bandwidth of speech must be considered when evaluating the TL as expressed in (10.5) since TL is a function of frequency.

---

[8]Each doubling of frequency is referred to as an octave, a term that is familiar to anyone who has studied music.

The TL for walls of various materials will yield ballpark estimates of the vulnerability to audible information loss. For example, 0.5-in. gypsum board has a mass density σ of $10\,kg/m^2$. At a frequency of 1 kHz, the TL is 32 dB [1]. The 32 dB of TL implies that the intensity of the sound in the speaker's room is 1584 times higher than the intensity in the listener's room at this frequency.

On its face this seems like a lot of attenuation, but what does this really say about the vulnerability to the compromise of audible information? Certainly one must account for the human ear's tremendous sensitivity. That is, one must estimate the signal intensity relative to the threshold of detection for human hearing recalling the scenario of the AWC executives on the train.

If the conversation-level sound intensity in a room separated from an adjacent room by a wall is $10^{-5}\,W/m^2$, the TL across the wall is $10^{-5}\,W/m^2$ less 32 dB as calculated earlier. This is equivalent to the following figure using the linear expression for 32 dB:

$$\frac{10^{-5}\,W/m^2}{1584} = 6.3 \times 10^{-9}\,W/m^2$$

If the background intensity is $10^{-8}\,W/m^2$, that is, library-level background noise, on the listener's side of the wall, the vulnerability to audible signal compromise is still a factor of 1.6 above zero vulnerability at a frequency of 1 kHz.

This is very much a ballpark approximation as site-specific conditions can vary considerably. Such conditions might include hidden airways across the wall boundary. There is also nothing to prevent the person in the next room from directly coupling one's ear to the wall or, even better, attaching a device designed to detect structure-borne acoustic energy, for example, a contact microphone.

Alternatively, this same inquisitive person might poke a small hole through the wall. In that case the acoustic energy generated by the speaker would pour through the tiny aperture. Therefore, the simple calculation of attenuation presented here goes out the window or rather through the wall.

Per (10.5), a wall consisting of low-density material such as gypsum board will attenuate lower frequencies less than higher frequencies. Therefore the spectrum of audible frequencies must be considered in evaluating the vulnerability to information compromise. Next consider what happens if denser materials were used to increase attenuation. The theory is that the increased mass of the wall would resist excitation by the acoustic energy.

For example, what is the effect on the vulnerability to signal detection if a 4-in. brick wall separates two rooms? Brick has a mass density σ of $200\,kg/m^2$, which yields a TL of 58 dB at 1 kHz [1]. The attenuation would double for every doubling of the acoustic frequency in the so-called mass-controlled region of the frequency spectrum, that is, from 100 to 1000 Hz.

There is also a doubling of the sound attenuation for each doubling of the wall mass in the 100- to 1000-Hz frequency range. However, one could imagine that this method of signal attenuation could be quite impractical if the weight of the wall is a potential concern. Table 10.1 summarizes the frequency dependence of acoustic attenuation by wall structures.

Table 10.2 shows the quantitative effect of mass on sound attenuation. These values are averages, and there could be considerable differences in response to high- and low-frequency sound energy [2].

III. THE COMPROMISE OF SIGNALS

TABLE 10.1   Audible Signal Attenuation by Wall Structures

	Wall/barrier acoustic attenuation factors
<100 Hz	Stiffness is predominant in attenuation. Resonances exist
100–1000 Hz	Doubling the mass or sound frequency doubles the attenuation
1000–4000 Hz	Resonances at coincidence angles

TABLE 10.2   Average Sound Attenuation as a Function of Wall Mass

Weight of wall [lb/(ft.)^2]	2	5	10	20	30	50	75	100	200
Weight of wall (kg/m^2)	9.8	24.4	48.8	97.6	146	244	366	488	976
Average sound attenuation (dB)	26	32	36	39	42	45	48	50	54

Unfortunately these scenarios are somewhat idealized because of reverberation. The reflected energy would continue to bounce around the speaker's room. A fraction of the energy would leak across the wall after each reflection and therefore contributes to the intensity of the transmitted signal.

This is especially true for rooms with a high Quality Factor or high "Q."[9] Anyone who has stood in a tunnel and shouted loudly has experienced a high-Q environment firsthand. In that case the vulnerability to information loss is increased. Therefore, the expression for TL as specified in (10.5) should be treated as a best case regarding attenuation when estimating the vulnerability to audible signal detection.

The previous analyses of audible vulnerability become less relevant if there is a more convenient path for the sound to travel between source and listener. More convenience for an acoustic wave means there is a pathway for which a reduced acoustic impedance mismatch exists between the two rooms. If that pathway consists of air, the impedance mismatch is zero. Such paths might include a ventilation duct or the space above a suspended ceiling.

For example, consider two adjacent rooms with a common suspended ceiling of 3/4-in. fiber tile (density $\sigma = 6$ kg/m^2) and a 60-cm utility space above the ceiling. In this scenario both rooms have the same air path above the ceiling. A ballpark estimate on the sound intensity reduction expected between rooms is between 300 and 1000.[10]

This may seem more than adequate, but if we again assume conversation-level acoustic intensity in a room corresponds to about 10^{-6} W/m^2 and the background intensity in the room next door is 10^{-9} W/m^2, even a factor of 1000 decrease in sound intensity would still yield sound levels at the limit of audibility. The caveat as usual is that this calculation should be treated as an approximation due to scenario-specific variations. Therefore a vulnerability to signal detection should be presumed unless a direct test can be performed to contradict this assumption.

---

[9]The Q of a resonator indicates the amount of oscillating energy stored divided by the energy lost per cycle of vibration. It is equal to the center frequency of the oscillatory energy divided by the bandwidth of the oscillatory energy for a particular resonator. Therefore, a highly reverberant room would be said to have a high Q.
[10]www.engineeringtoolbox.com.

AUDIBLE SIGNAL DETECTION DEVICES

Airborne Speech Detection: The Microphone

In the discussion thus far it has been assumed that the detection sensor is the human ear. Of course, this is not necessarily the case since sensors exist for the exclusive purpose of overtly and covertly detecting speech.

Everyone is likely aware of the microphone, which is a sensor used to detect audible signals. A microphone is a form of transducer. A transducer is a general term used to describe devices that convert one form of energy into another. Microphones convert mechanical into electrical energy, where the electrical signal is amplified, conditioned, and ultimately reconverted into an audible signal. Microphones produce a voltage or current in proportion to the audible signal.

There are a number of different types of microphones, but they all have one element in common: a diaphragm. This is a thin piece of material that vibrates in response to the audible energy. All microphones of this type require an unobstructed air path between the sound source and the diaphragm. In the next section we will analyze a type of microphone that does not require an air path.

Although the requirement of an air path from the audible source to the sensor might sound operationally restrictive, recall that audible signal energy propagates well through tiny apertures. So as long as the path of propagation does not contain materials of differing acoustic impedances, an audible signal will propagate quite nicely. Ultimately the friction associated with acoustically excited molecular vibrations will reduce the incident energy to zero intensity but this distance could be sufficient for a successful attack.

The operational implication is that a pinhole-sized aperture in a wall or barrier can conduct airborne acoustic energy and thereby excite the microphone diaphragm. How does a microphone diaphragm work?

We know that a voltage is induced if either a static conductor is situated within in a changing magnetic field or a conductor moves within a static magnetic field. Faraday's Law describes this phenomenon. Furthermore, a voltage applied to a resistive or reactive load will cause current to flow per Ohm's Law.

The direction of motion of the diaphragm sensor, that is, perpendicular to the lines of flux, controls the direction of current flow, where motion of the sensor results in an alternating current that is related in frequency and amplitude to this motion.

In particular, so-called dynamic microphones are frequently used for airborne speech detection. Dynamic microphones consist of a diaphragm suspended in front of a magnet to which a coil of wire is attached. The coil sits in the gap of the magnet. Vibrations of the diaphragm cause the coil to move in the gap causing an alternating current to flow.

Coils of wire are used to increase the induced voltage and current since the EMF so generated is proportional to the time rate of change of magnetic flux per Faraday's Law. The more turns of wire, the more flux is generated since the number of surfaces/loops traversed by the flux is increased. The mass of the coil–diaphragm structure impedes its rapid movement at high frequencies where there is usually a low response. A resonant peak often exists around 5 kHz. Fig. 10.5 illustrates the operating principle of a dynamic microphone.[11]

---

[11]http://www.nyu.edu/classes/bello/FMT_files/3_microphones.pdf.

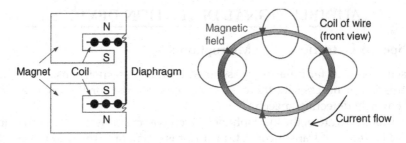

FIGURE 10.5   Operating principle of a dynamic microphone.

Microphones that respond only to pressure are omnidirectional. Some microphones are designed to exhibit gain and thereby result in a direction-sensitive response. This is operationally useful in order to preferentially amplify sources of sound that originate from one direction and thereby suppress sources in other directions.

The directionality can exist in various patterns such as cardioids. This pattern is achieved using a combination of pressure-sensitive and velocity-sensitive microphones. A particular pattern is obtained by adjusting the phase relationship of the sound wave to reinforce the amplitude in one direction and cancel it in another. The choice of pattern will depend on the operational requirements for a given scenario.

Finally, microphones based on other technologies and operating principles exist. These include capacitor microphones, also known as condenser microphones, fiber-optic microphones, laser microphones, carbon microphones, ribbon microphones, and contact microphones.

Structure-Borne Speech Detection: The Contact Microphone

What if an air path does not exist between the speaker and the acoustic sensor? Is it possible to detect speech-borne energy by direct contact with materials? We will defer answering this question for the moment in favor of a brief digression on sound propagation in solids. The physics of sound propagation directly affects the vulnerability to audible signal detection at locations remote from the sound source.

Recall it was observed that much of the vibratory energy generated by speech is reflected on initial contact with a solid surface. However, it was also learned that the surface material absorbs a fraction of that energy each time the pressure wave makes contact. The sound energy that is absorbed causes the molecules in the solid surface to vibrate and launches a wave that propagates within the material. It is noted in passing that both transverse and longitudinal waves can propagate in solid materials.[12]

What factors affect the propagation distance, which, in turn, affects the vulnerability to signal detection along the propagation path?

The velocity of sound in straight uniform bars and tubes that are thin compared to a wavelength is given by the following expression:

$$v = \sqrt{\frac{Y}{d}} \qquad (10.6)$$

[12]http://www.kayelaby.npl.co.uk/general_physics/2_4/2_4_1.html.

where Y represents Young's modulus, which relates to the elastic properties of the material, and specifically the resistance to deformation and d is the material density.[12] It may seem counterintuitive that sound velocity can decrease in denser materials since intuition might dictate otherwise. Consider how well sound propagates in steel versus rubber. Also recall the observation of the advance notice of an approaching subway train caused by sound energy propagating in the rails of the track.

By definition, a substance of higher density has more mass per unit volume than materials with lower density. Larger molecules typically have more mass. If material A is denser than material B because its molecules are larger, material A will transmit sound slower than material B since it takes more kinetic energy to make large molecules vibrate than small ones. However, this is not the entire story as is evident from (10.6).

A rigid material is composed of atoms and molecules with strong interatomic and intermolecular forces of attraction. Recall Hooke's Law, $F = -kx$, which describes the behavior of a restoring force in response to a displacement. k is the spring constant and x is the displacement from equilibrium. The force is mass times acceleration, and acceleration is the time rate of change of the change in the position of the mass, that is, the second derivative of x with respect to time t.

The sound pressure initially displaces the molecules in the material from their equilibrium position. The intermolecular forces are similar to springs that exert a restoring force in response to the displacement. Particles that return to their equilibrium position quickly can vibrate at higher speeds, and stiffer materials have bigger spring constants.

Said another way, the angular frequency of vibration of the molecules is given by $\sqrt{(k/m)}$. Sound can travel faster through stiffer materials, that is, bigger values of k, than it can through materials that are more easily deformed since stiffer materials have a larger spring constant resulting in a higher vibration frequency but smaller deflection amplitude.

Sound will travel at a slower rate in the more dense material but only if each has equivalent elastic properties as described earlier. The stiffness of a material affects sound velocity more than density. If sound waves were passed through two materials with approximately the same elastic properties such as aluminum and gold, the sound will travel about twice as fast in aluminum (0.632 cm/μs) than in gold (0.324 cm/μs).[13]

Table 10.3 gives the speed of sound for a variety of materials.[14]

The implication of Table 10.3 to information security is that sound can potentially be detected at remote distances from the source within buildings. This is because the energy will travel at higher speeds and travel farther without attenuation in certain building materials. Depending on the attenuation per unit length of propagation, the signal could maintain detectable signal amplitudes downstream from the source.

Building structural elements can potentially support a mode or many modes of acoustic propagation once a wave has been launched. So even if only a small amount of acoustic energy is absorbed after it is incident on a surface, that residual energy could travel significant distances before it attenuates to a level comparable to that of the ambient noise.

That represents a good segue to the issue of attenuation. The velocity of sound is relevant to this attack scenario since the faster sound travels, the greater distance it will cover in a

[13]https://www.nde-ed.org/EducationResources/HighSchool/Sound/speedinmaterials.htm.
[14]http://muller.lbl.gov/teaching/Physics10/PffP_textbook/PffP-07-waves-5-27.htm.

III. THE COMPROMISE OF SIGNALS

TABLE 10.3 Speed of Sound in Various Materials

Material and temperature	Speed of sound (m/s)
Air at 0°C	331
Air at 20°C	343
Water at 0°C	1402
Water at 20°C	1482
Steel	5790
Granite	5800
Wood (varying hardness)	3300–3960

TABLE 10.4 Attenuation of Sound in Solid Materials

Material	Attenuation (Np/m)	Frequency (MHz)
Steel (hardened)	4.94	10
Rubber (natural)	15	0.35
Polystyrene	23	2.5
Concrete	7–13	0.2
Glass (crown)	2	10
Polyvinyl Chloride (PVC)	3.5	0.35

given time interval. But the rate of attenuation of structure-borne sound as it propagates within a specific material must be known to estimate the vulnerability to detection as a function of distance from the audible source.

Table 10.4 lists the attenuation of sound waves in specific solids.[12] Three points are worth noting. First, these values should be viewed as indicative only since many factors will affect the speed of sound in solids. For metals, factors such as texture, cold working, stress, hardening, tempering, and aging can cause significant departures from the values listed here. Properties of plastics vary considerably with molecular weight, additives, and temperature. Rocks or building materials can be equally dissimilar in their physical characteristics.

Second, the units of attenuation are in nepers/meter. A neper is a logarithmic ratio that is similar to the decibel but it is based on natural logarithms rather than base 10.[15]

Third, the table also specifies the frequency of the sound attenuation in megahertz. These values are considerably above the frequencies corresponding to speech, which reinforces the view that the values are merely indicative.

Because of the variability in the data, the table is mostly useful to gain a relative perspective on attenuation. Materials with decreased rates of attenuation increase the vulnerability to remote speech detection because it increases the potential distance the energy can propagate while maintaining a sufficient signal-to-noise ratio.

[15]1 Np = 20/(ln 10) (dB) ~ 8.686 dB. Conversely, 1 dB = 1/(20 log$_{10}$ e) = 0.115 Np.

Anyone who has ever placed his or her ear against a wall to listen in on activity in an adjacent room knows that sound can be detected from direct contact with surfaces. In fact, commercial devices known as accelerometers or contact microphones are used to detect audible signals when no direct air path between the speaker and the sensor exists. Such devices exist for many applications to include replacing microphones in noisy environments, covert surveillance, and guitar pickups.[16,17,18]

One class of contact microphone is based on a piezoelectric transducer.[19] A piezoelectric element is a material, often a crystal, which creates a voltage when it is mechanically disturbed. The disturbance in this case is the audible signal and the voltage is a direct response to this stimulus.

The contact microphone is affixed to the surface that is vibrating in response to a sound source. As one might imagine from the previous discussion, minimizing acoustic impedance mismatches to reduce reflected energy between the surface and the contact microphone is a priority in this scenario.

To optimize energy transfer to the piezoelectric transducer, an impedance matching layer is placed between the active element and the face of the transducer.[20] Optimal energy transfer is achieved by sizing the matching layer so that its thickness is one-fourth of a specific wavelength. This keeps waves that were reflected within the matching layer in phase when they exit the layer and therefore exhibit constructive interference.

For contact-type transducers, the matching layer is made from a material that has a value of acoustic impedance that is between the active element and the material to which it is affixed, for example, steel. The backing material supporting the piezoelectric crystal, that is, the active element, has a great influence on the damping effect of a transducer. The objective is to increase the sensitivity to the audible signal and attenuate extraneous sources of audible energy. Using a backing material with an acoustic impedance that is close to the active element will produce the most effective damping response and thereby increase the signal detected by the active element.

A transducer with this design will have a wider bandwidth resulting in higher sensitivity. As the impedance mismatch between the active element and the backing material increases, the transducer sensitivity is reduced. Fig. 10.6 depicts a piezoelectric transducer and the desired phase relationships of the acoustic waves.[21]

Outdoor Speech Detection: The Parabolic Reflector and Microphone

An outdoor scenario for information compromise is considered next. Specifically, the concern is for an attacker who attempts to detect sensitive conversations in public areas.

---

[16]http://www.knowles.com/eng/Products/Sensors/Accelerometers.

[17]http://www.officer.com/product/10850059/maxsur-wasp-accelerometer-audible-surveillance.

[18]http://www.analog.com/library/analogdialogue/archives/43-02/mems_microphones.html.

[19]A transducer is any device that converts one form of energy into another. A loudspeaker is a form of transducer as it converts electrical signals into mechanical energy, that is, sound.

[20]Note that piezoelectric transducers can be designed to receive or transmit energy and acoustic impedance matching is important in either mode to optimize energy transfer across dissimilar materials.

[21]https://www.nde-ed.org/EducationResources/CommunityCollege/Ultrasonics/EquipmentTrans/characteristicspt.htm.

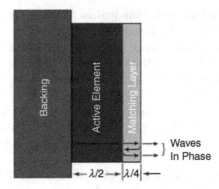

FIGURE 10.6   Piezoelectric transducer (contact microphone/accelerometer) construction.

Of course, there is not much that can be done for individuals who wantonly discuss sensitive information without concern for who else might be in proximity.

One could conceive of an outdoor area accessible to employees that is contiguous with space regularly accessed by nonemployees or even competitors. Conversations about work-related topics would invariably arise in gatherings of employees from the same organization. The question is how to reduce the vulnerability to information compromise in such a scenario.

There seem to be four obvious choices: (1) reduce the speech source intensity or in other words speak more softly, (2) increase the distance between the source and potential nonemployee listeners, (3) increase the background noise, and (4) install a barrier between the source and any potential nonemployee listeners.

Speaking *sotto voce* seems like the simplest solution, but people tend to lapse into their natural speaking voice. In addition, even if one calculated the exact threshold intensity correctly and translated that figure into the proper speaking level, continuously enforcing compliance would be a daunting task.

Increasing the distance between source and listener could definitely work assuming this is practical. Companies usually have limited real estate especially in urban areas, and therefore do not have the luxury of significantly expanding their perimeter. One could restrict areas to be off-limits and thereby create a buffer zone. In this instance a calculation performed later in the chapter would be required in order to more precisely estimate the vulnerability to signal compromise. As always, consideration must be given to the ambient noise across the audible spectrum.

What if a business competitor decides to mount a more aggressive attack? He or she might not rely solely on the human ear as a detection sensor. If close physical access to the location of interest was not possible so that a traditional microphone could not be deployed, the attacker might use a parabolic reflector and microphone system to provide signal gain. How does such a system improve the detected audible signal intensity?

A parabolic reflector and microphone produces gain at audible frequencies by virtue of its shape, which establishes a virtual focal point. This focal point has the following features: (1) equal path lengths for incoming sound waves from anywhere on the dish and (2) the angle at each point on the dish permitting sound waves to reflect exactly to the focal point. These two features allow sound collected by the parabolic dish to concentrate the energy at the focal point where a dynamic microphone is installed.

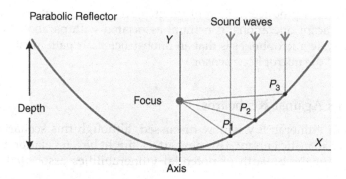

FIGURE 10.7 Parabolic reflector producing signal gain.

Fig. 10.7 illustrates the fact that sound waves hitting the parabolic surface closer to the center axis are bent at proportionately greater angles than those that hit farther from the central axis. The geometry is such that each incoming sound wave is incident at precisely the same point on the axis, that is, the focus. As noted earlier, a traditional audible sensor, for example, a dynamic microphone, is positioned at this focal point to achieve the requisite signal gain.[22]

A more physical explanation is as follows. Sound waves are pressure fluctuations that travel at a speed of about 340 m/s in air at sea level. These pressure fluctuations occur as wave-like motion with a characteristic wavelength. It is the wavelength relative to the shape of the parabolic dish that determines the gain of the dish.

Within a wavelength, the sound pressure increases during half the cycle and decreases during the other half. Therefore, the amplitude of the pressure follows a sinusoidal pattern. Since the entire dish surface is collecting sound energy corresponding to speech, many separate wave fronts are being combined at the focus and at different wavelengths.

The shape of a parabolic reflector results in equal path lengths for each point on the surface. Therefore all wave fronts arrive in phase when the dish is pointed accurately. Intermediate arrival distances will exist between the two extremes, and to achieve reasonable gain all the arrival distances must be within one-sixth wavelength of each other.

If the dish detects the sound from a distant source, each point on the dish will then have to be accurate to one-twelfth wavelength so that all the sound waves add in phase to produce gain. Losses will occur if the microphone location relative to the focal point exceeds one-twelfth wavelength.

If an attacker uses a parabolic reflector and microphone as a detector, the vulnerability to signal detection relative to the naked human ear is increased by the gain of the parabolic reflector:

$$\text{Parabolic Reflector Gain} = \frac{k(\pi R)^2}{\lambda^2} \tag{10.7}$$

where R is the radius of the parabolic dish, λ is the wavelength, and k is an efficiency factor of about 0.55.

[22]http://www.wildtronics.com/parabolicaccuracy.html#.ViXIlihye20.

A 1-ft. diameter dish produces a gain of roughly 1.7 times the intensity detected by the ear alone.[23] A significant operational constraint associated with parabolic reflectors in conjunction with dynamic microphones is that an unobstructed air path must exist between the audible sources and the microphone sensor.

Acoustic Attacks Against Keyboards

A very different vulnerability is now discussed, although this scenario also concerns the compromise of acoustic energy. This next attack might be a revelation to some readers, and is illustrative of the breadth of potential vulnerabilities associated with everyday technology.

As discussed in Chapters 7 and 9 keyboards represent an attractive target for attackers seeking confidential information. This is in large measure because keyboards are used to enter usernames and passwords for computer account authentication. The attacks described in preceding chapters exploited vulnerabilities resulting from electromagnetic emanations from keyboards as well as scenarios where the keyboard was visible to an attacker.

In this case the vulnerability to information compromise resulting from differences in the acoustic signature of individual keystrokes is considered.[24] It has been shown that these differences result from the different key positions and their respective mechanical motion that produce distinct sounds.

This attack also utilized a neural network to classify the familiar clicks that resulted from typing on a keyboard. A personal computer microphone (omnidirectional and manufactured by Radio Shack) was used to detect acoustic energy at close distances or up to 1 m. The now-familiar parabolic reflector and microphone (the "Bionic Booster" manufactured by Silver Creek Industries) was used for greater distances. Fig. 10.8 illustrates the acoustic signature of a single keyboard click in the time domain.[24] The click duration is about 100 ms.

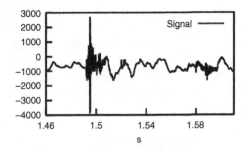

FIGURE 10.8   Acoustic signature of a keyboard click (time domain).

---

[23]The wavelength of a 1-kHz audible tone in air is about 1 ft.

[24]http://www.almaden.ibm.com/cs/projects/iis/hdb/Publications/papers/ssp04.pdf.

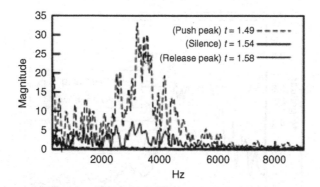

FIGURE 10.9   Acoustic signature of a keyboard click (frequency domain).

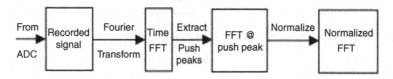

FIGURE 10.10   Acoustic spectral feature extraction for use by a neural network.

One can now see from a frequency domain representation that key clicks consist of a push peak, a silence interval, and a release peak. The frequency distribution used in the attack focused on the push peak given its greater amplitude. Fig. 10.9 illustrates these results.[24]

The JavaNNS neural network simulator was used to build a back-propagation neural network model. The raw signal is not used to analyze clicks. Relevant spectral features derived from the raw data are used to build the neural network model. Input and output nodes for the neural network model correspond to the size of the feature and the number of keys, respectively. Fig. 10.10 indicates the process of spectral feature extraction, where FFT is the acronym for the technique known as the Fast Fourier Transform.[24]

The raw analog signal is first digitized via an analog-to-digital converter (ADC). The resulting time domain signal is Fourier transformed to produce the signal in the frequency domain where the keystroke "push" peaks are again Fourier transformed and normalized.

The neural network was trained to recognize distinct keys based on characteristics of the acoustic signature of the push peak as identified in the frequency domain. However, this attack could visually distinguish keys if a 2- to 3-ms window was used even without aggregating peak features. This effect can be seen in Fig. 10.11.[24]

The neural network was trained to accurately recognize the individual keystroke click signatures. For example, in one experiment 10 "k" clicks and 10 "l" clicks were tested and the neural network correctly identified all 20 clicks. On average, there was 0.5 incorrect recognition per 20 clicks, indicating the potential effectiveness of this technique. It should be noted that detecting keyboard acoustic signals at distances of up to 15 m using a parabolic reflector and microphone produced no diminution in results.

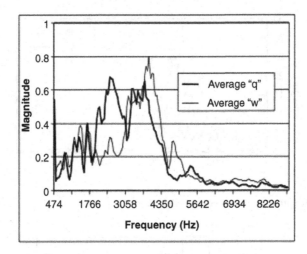

FIGURE 10.11   Normalized average spectra for "q" and "w" keystrokes.

Active Countermeasures

What about general countermeasures to audible information compromises? In the movies, spies and organized crime figures play music in the background to foil government surveillance efforts. Raising the background interference in this way is not going to help against a sophisticated attacker except possibly to interfere with one's own conversations.

An attacker could quite easily subtract this type of interference to produce a comprehensible audible signal. Achieving processing gain in the presence of coherent and spatially localized sources of interference is possible especially if multiple microphones are used.

Ironically, this naïve attempt at hiding the signal could actually make matters worse since speakers might raise their voices above the background thereby enhancing an attacker's signal-to-noise ratio. Recall the positive feedback scenario in the noisy restaurant.

A more effective form of interference might consist of using multiple mechanical objects that can produce spatially diverse, multifrequency, and time-varying sources of interference. Ideally such sources would be numerous and physically separated within a room. Such sources of interference would likely make signal averaging more difficult, but they also might make it difficult for the speakers in the room to hear each other.

With respect to outdoor scenarios, if the interfering source is not physically close to the audible signal, a properly aimed parabolic reflector and microphone will exploit the spatial diversity of the signal and noise sources. The effect will be to increase the intensity of the signal of interest at the expense of the interfering sound. Therefore, any source of interference, preferably a spatially incoherent one consisting of multiple audible frequencies, would be best positioned as close to the speakers as possible.

Various websites offer technology to assist in deterring audio surveillance efforts.[25] These should be scrutinized carefully and tested before relying on their efficacy. In addition, their effectiveness will likely be inversely proportional to the sophistication of the attacker.

[25]http://www.independentlivingnews.com/privacy/privacy-defenses/20397-9-counter-surveillance-tools-you-can-legally-use.stml#.VoiG3yhyc20.

AUDIBLE SIGNAL SHIELDING

Introduction

The vulnerability to signal detection can be quite varied depending on the number and type of reflective and absorbing surfaces encountered along the propagation path. Although little attention is given to the vulnerability of audible information compromise, reducing this risk arguably deserves more attention given the ease with which these compromises can occur and the number of opportunities they present.

Moreover, relevant statistics on information compromises of this type do not appear to be easily attainable.

The airborne attack scenarios discussed in this chapter focused on the vulnerability to overhearing conversations based on proximity to the speaker. The intensity of sound energy propagating in air and in open areas decreases according to the now familiar $1/4\pi r^2$ expression, where r is the distance between the audible source and the listener.

In enclosed areas some of the audible energy will repeatedly be reflected by the higher-density barriers rather than propagating away from the source and dissipated by friction. In one audible scenario analyzed previously in this chapter, the vulnerability to audible information compromise was estimated with and without the presence of noise. Subsequent scenarios involved obstructed and unobstructed paths between the source of audible energy and the detector. In this section, the effect of intervening partial barriers is considered on the vulnerability to information compromise.

Partial Acoustic Barriers

The fourth option in reducing the vulnerability to information compromise is to erect a partial acoustic barrier, that is, a barrier limited in height. In some circumstances, this might be operationally feasible. What specifications for such barriers would be necessary to reduce the vulnerability to audible signal compromise?

Recall diffraction is a process whereby objects that have physical dimensions close to the wavelength of the interacting energy cause that energy to spread out in space. Diffraction applies to both electromagnetic and acoustic waves. Therefore diffraction is used to estimate the attenuation of sound energy caused by a partial barrier inserted between a sound source and a listener at a given frequency.

Consider a scenario where a person purchased a cheap ticket to a concert only to find that he or she is positioned directly behind a structural post within the performance hall. Although the visual experience would be significantly affected, the audio performance can still be appreciated due to the diffraction of the incident acoustic energy around the barrier. This phenomenon is illustrated in Fig. 10.12.[26]

The same phenomenon occurs in scenarios involving partial barriers. This analysis uses the Fresnel number, which is defined as the number of half-wavelengths by which the shortest path of the audible energy grazing the barrier exceeds the straight-line path through the barrier itself.[27]

---

[26]http://hyperphysics.phy-astr.gsu.edu/hbase/sound/diffrac.html.

[27]This is pronounced FrenNEL, named after the French physicist Augustin-Jean Fresnel (1788–1827) who is the same fellow for whom lenses used in photocopiers and lighthouses are named.

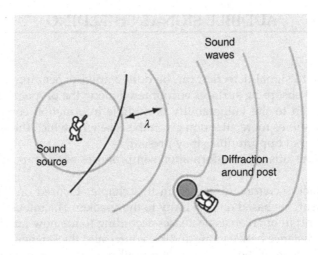

FIGURE 10.12 Acoustic diffraction around a post.

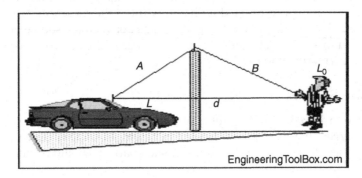

FIGURE 10.13 Geometry of insertion loss for partial barriers.

Referring to Fig. 10.13, the Fresnel number is equal to $2d/\lambda$, where $d = A + B - L$.[28] With the exception of the coefficient, note the similarity of N_f to the expression for the diffraction-limited angular divergence of a circular lens given by (3.7) in Chapter 3. The Fresnel number in this context measures the divergence of the incident wave due to diffraction of the incident acoustic wave around the partial barrier.

Simple geometry can be used to calculate the effect of a partial barrier placed in-line with an audible source [1].

The Fresnel number can also be written as follows:

$$N_f = \frac{A + B - L + d}{\lambda} \tag{10.8}$$

[28]http://www.engineeringtoolbox.com/outdoor-sound-partial-barriers-d_65.html.

where L is the distance from the source to the wall, d is the distance between the listener and the wall, A is the distance from the source to the top of the wall, B is the distance from the receiver to the top of the wall, and λ is the wavelength of the acoustic energy.

The insertion loss (IL) in units of decibels is defined in terms of the Fresnel number as follows [1]:

$$IL = 16 + 10\log N_f \qquad (10.9)$$

The expression for IL indicates how much the sound intensity is reduced due to the presence of the partial barrier. Note the wavelength in the denominator of the expression for N_f. This means that for large wavelengths the IL is reduced for a fixed barrier height. This operational feature has implications to the vulnerability to signal detection. The situation is completely analogous to the hapless concertgoer sitting behind the structural column in the concert hall.

In other words, longer wavelengths or equivalently lower frequencies are more difficult to attenuate than shorter wavelengths. Audible signals consist of many frequencies and the spectral energy density for speech, that is, power as a function of frequency, centers around 3 kHz.

Physical effects relating to the interaction of acoustic and electromagnetic energy with materials often vary with frequency. Therefore an analysis of signal behavior must be performed in several regions of the spectrum to give a complete appreciation of the risk of signal detection and resulting information compromise.

In this case the goal is to quantify the attenuation achieved by a partial barrier pursuant to reducing sound energy on the listener's side of the barrier. This involves calculating the insertion loss due to the barrier for several representative frequencies of audible energy.

Referring to (10.8), the following values are assumed: a barrier height of 4 m, a source located 6 m from the wall, and a listener located 2 m from the wall. A is 6.32 m, B is 8.55 m, and $L + d$ is 14.04 m, at a frequency of 1.7 kHz (wavelength of 0.2 m). Using (10.8) and by geometric arguments, the Fresnel number is calculated to be 8.3, and the IL in this case is 25 dB [1].

What happens at 10 times the wavelength, which corresponds to one-tenth the frequency or 170 Hz? In this case $\lambda/2$ is 1 m so the Fresnel number is 0.83 and the associated IL is calculated to be 15 dB. An increase in the IL would mandate that the quantity $(A + B - L + d)$ in the expression for N_f be proportionally increased. This means that the barrier height would have to be raised to achieve significant attenuation. This again illustrates the difficulty in blocking low-frequency audible signals using partial barriers.

Sound attenuation by a partial barrier as a function of the Fresnel number is shown in Fig. 10.14.[28]

With respect to countermeasures, it is best to position the barrier as near to the source as possible for maximum sound attenuation. This will cause the propagating wave to travel the maximum distance through the air after the barrier, and therefore produces the steepest angle between the audio source and the listener. The second best position is near the listener and the worst position is midway between the source and the listener.

Whatever the position of the speaker with respect to the barrier, a fraction of the acoustic energy will be reflected, a portion will be diffracted, and the remainder will be transmitted to the other side of the barrier. These effects are captured in Fig. 10.15.[28]

III. THE COMPROMISE OF SIGNALS

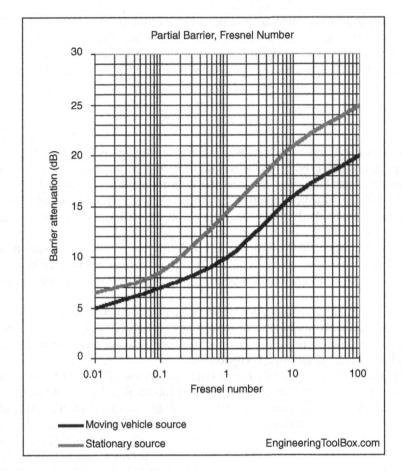

FIGURE 10.14 Fresnel numbers for partial barriers.

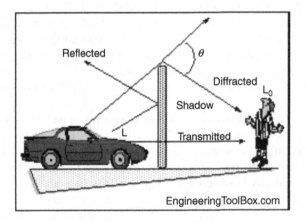

FIGURE 10.15 Acoustic energy and the effect of partial barriers.

III. THE COMPROMISE OF SIGNALS

The effect of floor-to-ceiling walls on the vulnerability to audible information compromise from a contiguous room was discussed previously in this chapter. It was noted that adding mass to such barriers would attenuate sound energy, and the attenuation scales linearly with increasing frequency within specific frequency ranges.

For low-frequency acoustic energy in particular, adding mass to a barrier is an option in mitigating the risk of unauthorized detection. However, this could quickly become impractical unless we have an extremely hefty foundation to support this added weight. Fortunately there is a better way.

Sound Reflection and Absorption

Recall the concept of acoustic impedance mismatch introduced earlier in this chapter. This is relevant when sound energy propagates through materials of different densities. The propagation of sound energy is highly dependent on the medium in which it travels. The reflection coefficient R represents the fraction of propagating sound energy that is reflected, and equals the difference of acoustic impedances divided by the sum of impedances.

Plugging in some numbers into the expression for R revealed that about 99% of the sound energy is reflected back toward the source at an air–wood interface. This implies that 1% of the acoustic energy from the room containing the speaker leaks across the wall into the room occupied by a nosy listener during each reflection of the acoustic wave at the air–solid interface. Denser materials will reflect more energy than less dense materials for energy incident from air because of the acoustic impedance mismatch.

In addition, sound energy that does excite the wood molecules in the wall travels with greater speed than air. Audible energy propagating in stiffer media will travel with greater velocity than those with less stiffness as discussed previously. This is cause for concern in buildings in which space is shared with other tenants. A practical solution to the leakage of energy between the two rooms and the propagation of acoustic energy within building structural elements is to add sound-absorbing material to those elements exposed to audible energy.

The absorption of sound energy results in the generation of heat within the material in which the sound propagates. Heat results from the friction caused by the contact between vibrating air molecules. Recall that the vibrating molecules in acoustically excited materials *are* the sound energy.

There are different types of acoustic absorbing material that can be applied to a surface to reduce the fraction of transmitted energy. Porous absorbers such as mineral wool, fiberboard, or plastic foams have an open pore structure. The vibrating air molecules are forced through the pores, attenuating the vibrations, and the conversion of sound energy to heat energy occurs in the process. Porous materials preferentially absorb high-frequency acoustic energy.[29]

If the thickness of the absorbing material is much less than a quarter wavelength of the incident acoustic energy, the effectiveness of this method is much reduced since the acoustic pressure wave reaches its maximum amplitude at one-fourth of a wavelength consistent with sinusoidal motion.

Recall the discussion on the construction of piezoelectric transducers for use as contact microphones. The design of those transducers called for the inclusion of an impedance

---

[29]http://www.squ1.com/index.php?http://www.squ1.com/sound/absorption.html. This site is no longer accessible online.

matching layer where the thickness equaled one-quarter wavelength of the sound energy. In this way the amplitudes of reflected energy were in phase.

Analogously, displacing the absorbing material between one-fourth and three-fourth wavelengths from the wall will increase absorber effectiveness by affecting the sound energy at its maximum amplitude thereby obviating the need for thicker absorbing material.

Membrane absorbers can exist in the form of flexible sheets stretched over supports or as rigid panels, displaced from the front of a solid wall separating the two rooms. Mounting the material in this way produces an air gap between the absorber and the barrier wall. Air is an excellent absorber of sound energy assuming an impedance mismatch between the air and supporting structures (think of an acoustic-attenuating sandwich). Again, absorption occurs as a result of the conversion of the air vibrations to heat based on the resistance of the sheet to rapid flexing and the resistance of the enclosed air to compression.

These types of absorbers are most effective at the resonant frequency, which is determined by the surface density of the panel M (kilogram per square meter) and the width or depth of the air gap b (meters), where the resonant frequency F is given by the following expression:

$$F[\text{Hz}] = \frac{60}{(M \times b)^{1/2}} \tag{10.10}$$

The harmonic oscillator model was introduced in Chapter 3 and discussed earlier in this chapter. The resonant frequency of this oscillatory system is greater when the effective spring constant, k, is increased. This is because the compressed air in the air gap behind the membrane adds to the restoring bending force. Also, using thin membranes can increase the frequency of oscillation. Membrane absorbers are most effective at low frequencies.

Cavity absorbers are air containers with a narrow neck. The air in the cavity acts like a spring at the resonant frequency of the enclosed air volume. These types of absorbers are highly absorbent but only in a very narrow range of acoustic frequencies that is centered on the resonant frequency.

In the case of cavity absorbers, the resonant frequency F is given by the following expression:

$$F[\text{Hz}] = \left(\frac{340}{2\pi}\right) \times \left(\frac{S}{VL}\right)^{1/2} \tag{10.11}$$

where S is the cross-sectional area of the neck (in meters squared), V is the volume of the cavity (in meters cubed), and L is the length of the neck (in meters).

Perforated panel absorbers combine all three methods into one system. The panel may be composed of plywood, hardboard, plasterboard, or metal, and may also act as a membrane absorber. The perforations in the panel function as cavity resonators augmented by porous absorbing material. Perforated panel absorbers constitute the bulk of the commercially available acoustic insulating materials.

Interposing an air barrier between reflective surfaces can also be effective in reducing the vulnerability to audible information detection and compromise. Adding even a thin layer of air between walls or barriers separating rooms can yield significant attenuation and thereby confine audible energy. One note of caution is that any structural elements or conduits such as studs and/or ducts that physically connect rooms will offer pathways for sound conduction, and these must be addressed using appropriately insulating material.

SUMMARY

The principal form of human communication is speech, and conversations sometimes involve confidential information that is of interest to attackers seeking unauthorized access to this information. The information content affects the impact component of risk and thereby should inform an information security risk management strategy.

Speech consists of modulated acoustic energy that is transmitted via mechanical vibrations in a specific frequency range. The audible frequency range for humans extends from a few hertz to 20 kHz.

The mechanical vibrations of speech are manifest as pressure waves in air and other materials conducting sound energy. These vibrations expand and contract the material in which they propagate consistent with vibratory motion. Acoustic pressure waves are longitudinal, which means the expansion and contraction of the material is in the direction of propagation.

The material encountered by an acoustic signal has a significant effect on propagation and therefore the vulnerability to signal detection. Specifically, the magnitude of the reflection of acoustic energy is determined by the acoustic impedance mismatch between dissimilar materials encountered along the propagation route.

Acoustic impedance is a function of the density of the material and velocity of the pressure wave within the propagation material. Although a significant amount of incident sound energy is reflected at surfaces with dissimilar acoustic impedances, some fraction of the airborne energy excites the molecules in the denser material. The velocity of sound within the material is proportional to its stiffness. Partial and full barriers, for example, walls, attenuate audible signals to varying degrees depending on the characteristics of the barrier, and for partial barriers, the distance between the speaker and the barrier. Acoustic energy propagates quite well through small apertures.

Acoustic sensors that detect audible signals are designed to operate in different media and/or under different operating conditions. Their respective features and performance specifications must be considered in assessing the vulnerability to signal detection along with the relevant parameters in a given attack scenario.

Specifically, dynamic microphones and other microphones with diaphragms are used to detect airborne speech, contact microphones are used to detect structure-borne sound energy, and parabolic reflectors in conjunction with dynamic microphones are used to address outdoor attack scenarios. As in all realistic scenarios, ambient noise must be factored into assessments of vulnerability recognizing that commercial signal processing methods are widely available and can be effective depending on the number and coherence of noise sources.

Various materials have been designed to attenuate audible sound energy. These materials absorb acoustic energy by converting air vibrations to heat. Three types of absorbing materials are often used: porous, membrane, and cavity absorbers. Resonance effects will influence the frequency dependence of each method.

References

[1] Hall D. Basic acoustics. New York: Harper and Row; 1987.
[2] Bolz RE. CRC handbook of tables for applied engineering science. Boca Raton, FL: CRC Press; 1973.

PART IV

INFORMATION TECHNOLOGY RISK

Information Technology Risk Factors

INTRODUCTION

It may be apparent that assessments of information technology (IT) vulnerabilities have largely been ignored in the preceding chapters. The topic is admittedly a bit daunting given the myriad of applications, systems, protocols, services, etc., that affect the risk profile of an IT network, and, by extension, the entire organization. Moreover, subtopics under these general headings could legitimately become chapters in their own right (eg, Windows security, Linux security, VPN security). No single text could adequately address all of the issues that are relevant to IT risk.

Partly for this reason the approach taken in this book differs from traditional treatments of this vast topic. The perspective adopted here is based on the assertion that IT risk is often a manifestation of deeper, more systemic issues. The end game should be to address information security risk on a strategic level across an enterprise. To approach this issue strategically it is necessary to identify and leverage measurements and resulting risk metrics that can provide insights into the root causes of IT risk.

In the approach adopted here, measurements of technology vulnerabilities are used to make inferences about these root causes. Tactical issues that need to be addressed are certainly revealed in the process, but these inferences provide insight into the drivers of information security risk.

Focusing on specific vulnerabilities is sometimes warranted. Tactical measures must be invoked to address critical and time-sensitive vulnerabilities. But in the same way that lifestyle choices are the root cause of many medical health issues, business practices and a lack of security governance are root causes of threats to information.

The approach to addressing the risk of information compromises via the exploitation of technology vulnerabilities is the same for all threats as delineated in Chapter 1:

1. Identify the threats and attack vectors of highest concern.
2. Determine the risk factors that enhance one or more components of risk for those threats.
3. Examine the effectiveness of existing controls in addressing those risk factors.
4. Prioritize mitigation efforts to enhance controls based on the assessed risk in aforementioned 1–3 and in accordance with resource constraints. Apply resources to address priority vulnerabilities. Utilize compensating controls as necessary to explicitly account for all risk factors.
5. Establish metrics that measure the effectiveness of security controls against a risk-based information security policy and accompanying set of technology standards.

With respect to number 5, specific risk measurements and metrics are suggested that are designed to facilitate inferences on the root causes of information security risk noted earlier. There are five measurement types that are designed to facilitate inferences on these root causes as follows: (1) the proliferation of IT vulnerabilities across IT resources, (2) the concentration of IT vulnerabilities across IT resources, (3) trends in the number and distribution of IT vulnerabilities over time, (4) the persistence of IT vulnerabilities over time, and (5) correlations between time series of IT vulnerabilities. Numbers 1–4 have been dubbed "spatiotemporal measurements," borrowing a term from physics that describes the nature of these measurements and the metrics so derived. These spatiotemporal measurements will be discussed in detail in Chapter 12.

A graphic found on the Internet provides a good introduction to the purpose of the IT risk measurements as discussed in this book. Fig. 11.1 shows a percentage of Common Vulnerability and Exposures (CVE) exploited as a function of the number of weeks the exploit occurred following their publication [1].[1] If this same metric was applied to a specific organization, it might be used to assess the requirement for more efficient vulnerability management.

A potentially deeper implication of delays in addressing published technology vulnerabilities is that suboptimal security governance exists across the organization. Perhaps proper resources might not have been allocated to the IT department, and it's possible this condition reflects a culture that does not support that department's mission.

A pervasive view of the IT department as indentured servants might indeed be a root cause of inaction or a nonstrategic approach to remediation at a minimum. Such a condition might explain long-standing technical vulnerabilities that are evidence of pervasive and persistent inertia.

So a CVE metric of this sort is clearly indicative of a significant tactical issue, but also might be indicative of an underlying problem that requires systemic remediation. The bottom line

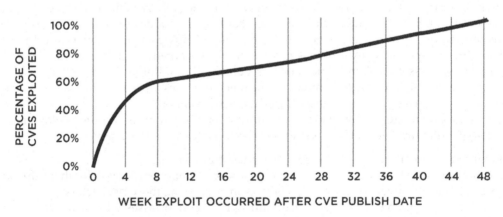

WEEK EXPLOIT OCCURRED AFTER CVE PUBLISH DATE

FIGURE 11.1 Cumulative distribution of dates of exploitation following CVE publication as a function of total CVEs exploited.

[1]https://cve.mitre.org/.

is that a more thorough probe is required to establish the root cause of IT risk, and thereby invoke strategic remediation.

In summary, the net objective of security risk assessments is to facilitate the prioritization of remediation efforts. Absent infinite resources, a risk-based approach to security management is the most effective means of achieving that objective. And identifying the systemic risk factors that drive IT vulnerabilities is the basis for a strategic information security risk management program.

BUSINESS PRACTICES AND ORGANIZATIONAL CULTURE

It seems obvious that IT risk and business practices should be related. Yet the magnitude of that connection is sometimes not appreciated or is just plain ignored. This can be exacerbated by the disconnect that often exists between business and technology types.

IT exists to further organizational objectives by facilitating effective information management and communication. IT departments are responsible for managing that technology, and thereby implement the tools that the organization requires to meet its business objectives.

This does not imply that the IT department does not play a critical role in the organization and in security in particular. But their role is to implement security controls in accordance with the organizational tolerance for risk, and it is the business leaders that define that level of tolerance.

Business practices are closely associated with organizational culture. All successful organizations are mission-oriented, and the ones that have enjoyed sustained success tend to reward creativity, innovation, and flexible thinking. But the *modus operandi* of the security apparatus and businesses is not necessarily aligned. Creativity and adaptive behavior have tremendous value in a business context, but are not necessarily attributes that produce effective security.[2]

The collective will to comply with security practices across an enterprise assumes that the rules and regulations are reasonable, that is, risk-based, and are generally viewed as effective by users. The imposition of silly and/or ineffective controls, also known as "security theater," can actually do more harm than good since it is virtually certain that creative users will do creative things to circumvent such rules.[3]

In addition, the potential fallout from silly security rules is that users lose confidence in the security apparatus and are tempted to circumvent the rules. This was evident in some of the security measures imposed on travelers in US airports over the years. Some of these were seen as both inconvenient *and* ineffective in deterring would-be perpetrators of terrorism.

There are many examples of the relationship between business practices and their effect on security. One might even argue that recognizing this relationship is common sense. However, a natural tension often exists between business and security types in any organization and this tension can produce difficulties that are manifest as security issues.

---

[2]This is not meant to imply security professionals or programs cannot and should not be creative or adaptive. To the contrary a security program must respond to changes in the security risk profile. However, a culture that tolerates or tacitly encourages circumventing risk-based security policies and procedures in the interest of expedience will likely encounter problems.

[3]The origin of this term is attributed to Bruce Schneier.

Specifically, the business needs to get things done, which often involves seamless communications that increasingly depend on IT. The IT department is responsible for ensuring that communications technologies comply with established security policy and/or best practices, which sometimes slow things down. The narrative of information security in any organization inevitably boils down to finding the proper balance between security and convenience.

For example, an academic-oriented institution of considerable renown carried considerable business-driven IT risk. They allowed all staff scientists to maintain local administrative rights on their Windows accounts. The IT staff was supremely competent, and therefore quite aware of the risks associated with this practice. But the scientists ran the show, and they were adamant that they could not perform their duties without the ability to download and install custom software.

Of course, an attacker who succeeded in social engineering one of the scientists would have the same elevated privileges. The scientists also had weak passwords so if attackers managed to access the encrypted password file, it would not have been difficult to access their accounts. Finally, the institution was iconic so hackers might naturally have been drawn to the institution as a target. The situation represented a textbook example of a confluence of risk factors where business practices and organizational culture were the root causes of IT vulnerabilities.

Compensating controls could have been implemented such as rolling out software to manage access privileges and placing privileged accounts into their own subnet with strict inbound/outbound restrictions. But the culture of the institution put a chill on any efforts that dampened interaction among departments and staff. Budgetary constraints on security compounded the problem.

Many organizations have very similar vulnerabilities that are driven by the same types of underlying influences. Superficially these appear to be IT problems. But the insecure implementation of technology is typically a manifestation of the organizational culture at work.

In a related example, facilitating unrestricted access to the various subnets within a network is clearly a technology issue. But the driver behind maintaining this vulnerability, which facilitates one of the principal actions of malware, can often be traced to an artifact of a culture that implicitly mandates "access to anything from anywhere."

Moreover, interviews with IT staff inevitably reveal that they are quite aware of a particular vulnerability but are constrained by cultural norms. Attempts at imposing restrictions to accessing information to only those with a "need-to-know" or implementing compensating controls can meet with disapproval by the organizational culture carriers who pay their salary. In such cases fixing the immediate problem is clearly important, but identifying and addressing the underlying cause is the more strategic objective.

In most cases a security issue can be resolved with the judicious application of compensating controls. Business leaders must mandate that security risks be effectively managed, and acknowledge the potential implications of even one individual engaging in high-risk practices. Furthermore, these same leaders, that is, the ones who establish and perpetuate the organizational culture, must also comply with policy if they expect to achieve broad compliance and maintain a semblance of credibility.

This does not imply that there should be a mindless application of rules without an airing of opinions. A sign of a healthy culture is one that encourages dialogue. Moreover, the outcome of most reasonable security decisions is a compromise where optimal security is not achieved and affected users experience some inconvenience.

The conundrum for any organization is to determine how to adjust the organizational culture to remedy these systemic drivers of security risk without adversely affecting the very attributes that have historically contributed to the organization's success.

SECURITY GOVERNANCE

The lack of security governance is another risk factor for IT risk and information security risk more broadly. It too is often linked to the prevailing culture. Security governance is a useful barometer for how information security is perceived within an organization. If robust information security governance processes exist, it is indicative of a culture where information security is a priority.

Conversely, the absence of security governance increases the likelihood and vulnerability to information security incidents. It is therefore a risk factor for the threat of information compromise and requires measurement and associated risk metrics. Although the importance of security governance might also be seen as common sense, it is sometimes necessary to explicitly convey why processes that add overhead and admittedly some consternation among IT users should continue to exist.

The creation of a risk-based policy and standards is central to security governance, and has outsized importance to the security posture of any organization. A policy and an accompanying set of technology standards are necessary to measure deviations from acceptable practices in accordance with the organizational tolerance for risk.

In previous discussions, information security risk has been compared and contrasted with medical risk issues. Such analogies can be instructive, but it is worth reiterating their differences with respect to risk management. In medicine scientists are able to conduct controlled experiments thereby isolating the effect of a specific variable under test. In general, the controlled nature of these tests coupled with statistically significant samples can yield definitive relationships between cause and effect.

The Framingham heart study is a perfect example. This study began in 1948 with the goal of identifying the risk factors for heart disease. It continues today, and includes many thousands of participants. Furthermore, it has been a significant contributor to understanding the etiology of a major disease [2].

The ability to assess the positive and negative effects of a particular therapy in this way has profound consequences. It enables physicians to make the following statement to a patient: "There is a 90 percent likelihood that this drug will be effective in preventing or controlling this disease." This author has never heard a security professional make such a statement about the effectiveness of a security control and with good reason.

The results of pharmaceutical trials are applicable to the general population based on a large sample space of experiment participants. Implicit in this generalization is the fact that people are physiologically similar or similar enough. Moreover, large population studies enable conclusions about the effectiveness of therapies with quantifiable certitude. In statistical jargon, larger populations translate to smaller standard deviations about the mean, which implies greater certainty in the results.[4]

---

[4]Recall the standard deviation about the mean scales as the square root of the population size as discussed in Chapter 1.

The astute reader might respond by saying, "There are plenty of data generated by security technologies as well as many measurable risk factors. Witness the endless output from Intrusion Detection Systems, Data Leakage Protection solutions, firewall logs, etc. So why is it difficult for IT security professionals to accurately assess risk?"

The answer is that measuring things is the easy bit. Security-related events are not necessarily legitimate security incidents, and, importantly, their risk relevance could vary significantly depending on scenario-specific details. Correlating events with outcomes in order to accurately assess risk in light of the cost (broadly defined) of remediation is much more difficult. This is sometimes true in medicine too as evidenced by the controversy over the effectiveness of mammography and prostate specific antigen (PSA) testing in reducing mortality.

As noted in Chapter 1 and elsewhere in this book, the problem is that security is inherently defensive, adversaries are inconsistent in their adversarial efforts, and the relative importance of risk factors in IT environments can vary considerably with a given scenario. These conditions make it difficult to relate cause and effect with statistical confidence. It also amplifies the requirement for a risk-based security policy and accompanying standards. Why?

Since experiments that can confirm the relationship between cause and effect are not easy to implement in IT environments, a viable alternative is to establish a risk-based information security policy and an accompanying set of IT standards against which compliance is measured. Identified gaps will highlight residual risk, and thereby enable proportionate mitigation that comports with the organization's tolerance for risk. Of course, the policy and standards could be flawed, which would obviously affect the assessment.

Three conditions will increase the probability that information security governance efforts are effective. The first condition is that the IT department should not be responsible for policy creation and/or enforcement. The reasons for this first condition are threefold. First, there is an inherent conflict of interest when those charged with implementing security controls also write the policy that governs those controls.

The second reason is that IT staff members are placed in an invidious position by the business when the latter demand that the former bend the rules that they are charged with enforcing. Typically IT departments create policy by default, as business leaders mistakenly assume that information security is an inherently technical issue.

The third reason for removing the development of security policy from the list of IT department responsibilities is that technologists are notoriously bad at writing policy for nontechnical users. In contrast, the IT security *standard* that links to the information security policy is appropriately written by an IT professional. The standard should link to the policy and dictates the performance specifications associated with security technology implementation.

The second condition that will enhance the effectiveness of security governance is systematic monitoring of compliance with the information security policy. The information security risk profile of organizations can change, and such changes must be reflected in an updated policy document that is eminently readable. Ensuring ongoing compliance with the policy and accompanying standards requires processes that examine the effectiveness and ongoing relevance of security controls.

The third condition to enhance the effectiveness of a security governance program is centralization. Centralization translates to a centrally managed governance entity with the authority and global reach to speak for the organization in a unified voice on security policy issues. The creation of a Security Committee that addresses policy-related issues across the enterprise is a good example of a positive step toward a centralized governance process.

This is especially important for organizations with multiple business units and/or significant geographic diversity. Patterns of bad behavior that affect distinct entities have a better chance of being identified using a coherent oversight process. Moreover, they can be addressed holistically and strategically via the application of consistent controls. Evidence of an enterprise-wide pattern is more likely to be uncovered via metrics that are designed to provide insight into the effectiveness of policy and/or standards-driven controls.

In summary, effective security governance depends on the existence of a well-crafted policy and standards, regular assessments of risk against that policy, and centralized security governance. Furthermore, the lack of security governance is itself a risk factor for information compromises and therefore should be measured pursuant to developing prioritized remediation efforts.

USER BEHAVIOR

It should come as no surprise that the users of information resources represent a source of information security vulnerabilities, and therefore are a risk factor for information compromise. Users handle confidential information and utilize the technologies that facilitate IT account access. There can be hundreds of thousands of users in large organizations. Their individual information access requirements and behaviors can vary significantly while privacy restrictions across jurisdictions enhance the complexity associated with operating a global network.

Some of the IT risk factors associated with user behavior include the history of external sites visited, the breadth of internal resources accessed, the level of access privilege, password selection, and physical access system privileges. The confluence of these risk factors can be used to risk-rank individuals within an organization. This can assist in prioritizing remediation efforts, the *raison d'être* for a risk-based approach to security.

The establishment of user risk profiles will complement the risk profiles of information assets that have been determined via information security risk assessments. It can add a new dimension to the overall information security risk profile where prioritized controls are applied to both users and assets. It is important to keep in mind that a vulnerability associated with a single user can have significant consequence to an IT environment.

The contention is that user risk as manifest in individual behaviors is a significant contributor to the overall information security risk for the organization, and should be addressed as part of a holistic and comprehensive approach to risk management.

Potential metrics that reflect user behavior risk can be derived from data in Active Directory for Windows environments as well as through password cracking efforts. Users with weak passwords inherently represent vulnerable targets. In particular, users with elevated account privileges (eg, local administrators and domain administrators) *and* weak passwords significantly enhance that user's risk profile.

Moreover, a disproportionate number of users who possess all these risk factors elevate the general risk profile of the organization.

THE PHYSICAL SECURITY OF INFORMATION ASSETS

The physical security of information assets is not fully appreciated as a risk factor for information security threats. Although it cannot be proven, part of the reason for this lack of appreciation might relate to the persistent cultural divide between information technologists and physical security types.

The good news is that the increase in networked physical security technologies has moved these two groups closer together. They are even beginning to speak the same language based on the evolving convergence of IT and physical security technologies. The bad news is that although this evolution has benefits, it also carries risk.

Numerous information security attack vectors are facilitated by physical access. Physical security–related attacks associated with virtualization are discussed in Chapter 15, and these represent a mere subset of possible attacks if physical access controls are breached. A malicious individual with physical access to a network port is in a good position to exploit a network-related vulnerability, and an increasing number of devices include such ports.

CCTV cameras and physical access card readers are key physical security devices and they often communicate via the Internet and/or corporate intranets. Specifically, these are the devices that physically monitor and restrict access to critical information assets in data centers and within organizations more generally. It has been estimated that as of 2014, 245 million CCTV cameras have been installed worldwide, and this includes only devices installed by professionals.[5]

Attacks against such devices are not theoretical. In 2013, a distributed denial-of-service (DDoS) attack consisting of an HTTP "Get" flood that peaked at around 20,000 requests/s was successfully launched.[5] Investigation of the relevant IP addresses indicated that compromised assets were networked CCTV cameras, and each of the inspected cameras was accessible via their default log-in credentials.

All compromised devices were running Linux with an application called BusyBox, a package of Unix utilities bundled into a small executable that is designed for systems with limited resources. In the postmortem, malware was discovered that scans for network devices running on BusyBox and looks for open Telnet/SSH services that are susceptible to brute force dictionary attacks. Clearly the importance of password resilience applies to both physical security devices and IT assets.

One important lesson is that CCTV cameras and other key physical security technologies are increasingly networked. Therefore, these devices could have the same vulnerabilities as other networked devices, which can be exploited for broader IT network compromises. This situation clearly has information security implications for the network, but it also directly affects the security of critical information assets. If the physical security devices that protect information assets such as servers and switches are rendered ineffective, this enhances the vulnerability of those assets to attacks, especially by individuals who possess physical access privileges, that is, "insiders."

The bottom line is that physical security infrastructure and processes should be included in assessments of information security risk. Electronic access to technologies such as digital video recorders (DVR) and network video recorders (NVR) should also be part of user risk profiles since individuals with such privileges carry enhanced risk especially if other risk factors

[5]https://www.incapsula.com/blog/cctv-ddos-botnet-back-yard.html.

exist, for example, enhanced access privileges and weak passwords. Finally, physical security devices with network ports should not be installed in publicly accessible places, where analog cameras linked to IP converters would be preferred in such circumstances.

INFORMATION TECHNOLOGY IMPLEMENTATION

Although IT vulnerabilities can point to root causes of information security risk, poor implementation of technology, and in particular technical security controls, represents its own source of risk factors. One certainly cannot discount the possibility that the IT department contributes to IT risk.

Poorly configured networked technologies and/or a lack of rigorous implementation and/ or testing procedures have proven to be the culprit in numerous network compromises. A lack of resources is often cited as a root cause, and this can certainly amplify other problems.

However, there is little excuse for the lack of an IT standard against which performance can be measured. If no such standard exists, or there is only a feeble attempt at conforming to a standard, this is indicative of more systemic information security risk. As an example, one item in such a standard might specify that default settings on network devices should be immediately changed with a procedure in place to check for this condition. Conformity with the standard would be measured annually as part of a regular assessment process.

A standard with such a specification does not guarantee proper procedures will be followed in every instance, but a lack of a standard increases the odds that it will not. An IT department that has not embraced compliance with IT standards contributes to the information security risk profile.

In general, IT departments tend to operate by putting out fires and reacting to crises. In addition, senior executives who often possess little knowledge of technology and/or a concern for security (see the section "Business Practices and Organizational Culture") can make difficult demands. This leaves little room for strategy, and creates an atmosphere of tension with attendant security risks. IT departments regularly straddle the line between facilitating convenience and enforcing security, which sometimes places them in invidious positions. This condition only enhances the need for appropriate security governance by an objective entity with broad oversight and enforcement responsibilities.

Finally, although the performance of IT departments is likely driven by systemic risk factors, the effectiveness of specific technology implementation efforts must be scrutinized. Moreover, the competence, organization, and motivation of those in charge of technology implementation must be assessed as part of a comprehensive information security risk assessment.

INFORMATION SECURITY POLICIES AND INFORMATION TECHNOLOGY STANDARDS

A separate discussion on the information security policy and accompanying standards is warranted due to their criticality to security governance. An information security policy is a manifesto of sorts, and like any good manifesto it should specify the organization's fundamental security principles up front. These principles guide the limits on user behavior and all security requirements and practices should ultimately derive from these principles.

The principles are the information security equivalent of the Ten Commandments. However, unlike the Ten Commandments, the information security policy itself should be a relatively fluid document. It should be periodically reviewed and must evolve as technology changes, unforeseen risk issues arise, and/or the security risk profile of the organization changes. The policy language should be explicit, unambiguous, straightforward, and consist of risk-based, sensible, and useful content to facilitate relevance and broad compliance.

For example, a useful Information Security Policy should include topical issues that directly affect the majority of the user population. These might include issues such as remote network access, Bring Your Own Device (BYOD), use of IT in higher-risk countries, and use of Cloud resources. The risk associated with these issues is dynamic, and therefore the policy governing the use of these technologies should evolve as well.

An effective information security policy should specify a hierarchy of risk categories for the types of information being protected. These might be ranked according to the magnitude of the *impact* to the organization. Such categories should be neither numerous nor complex. High-, medium-, and low-impact designations with accompanying criteria would suffice.

An example of a criterion for the high-risk category is that unauthorized disclosure of the information so designated could have a catastrophic and/or long-term financial and/or reputational impact on the organization.

These categories of information will enable logical, risk-based, and defensible decisions on security issues. For example, an organization might permit storage of low-impact information in the Cloud without further review, but require more due diligence if medium- or high-impact information is being considered for the same type of storage. This is precisely what is meant by a risk-based approach to information security.

Technology standards should be distinct from the information security policy. A standard provides performance specifications for the security controls used to manage information security risk. Therefore, the audience is the implementers of security controls such as the IT and Operations Departments. Documents intended for those audiences should be specific, technical, and will by necessity be ephemeral to reflect changes in risk driven by changes to both technology and the organization.

For example, standards would be expected to specify requirements for password complexity and authentication (eg, two-factor vs single factor). Expected service levels related to the implementation of security controls such as the mean time to resolve high-risk vulnerabilities might also be included in an IT security standard.

In contrast, the security policy would state general requirements about authentication to access IT resources. In other words, the policy would mandate that approved methods of authentication are required to access corporate IT resources. The standard would specify the precise nature of that authentication. As noted above, standards would be expected to change more frequently than a policy since issues such as password complexity would be adjusted in response to changes in threat sophistication and the organization's security risk profile.

In summary, an IT security standard dictates specific security controls and their performance specifications. These specifications are dictated by the organizational tolerance for information security risk as reflected in the information security policy, which in turn should align with the organizational culture. An indicative Table of Contents for an information security policy is provided in Appendix E.

SUMMARY

The explosive rise of the Internet is due to its effectiveness in enhancing communication and providing access to information. Yet this ease of communication is itself a risk factor for information compromise. Moreover, Web-based communications use interconnected software and hardware that interact via services and protocols that are routinely exploited by a veritable army of global attackers with varying agendas.

Effective information security is dependent on information technologies that are designed to help manage the inherent insecurity of networking. It is well known that IT vulnerabilities contribute to the information security risk profile of an organization. The spectrum of potential vulnerabilities is immense due to the scope and complexity of numerous interactive systems.

Although information security vulnerabilities are often manifest as technology issues, the root cause of information security risk often derives from more systemic sources of risk factors. These risk factors include business practices linked to the organizational culture, security governance, user behavior, the physical security of information assets, and IT implementation.

Organizational culture influences risky business practices as well as the effectiveness of security governance. Ultimately it is the organization's culture that drives the attitudes and approaches to information security risk management. Culture is difficult to measure directly, but indirect measurements and inferences based on metrics can be made.

To that end, spatiotemporal risk measurements and metrics have been developed that are designed to facilitate inferences on the root causes of information security risk. These are specified in Chapter 12.

User behavior also affects the information security risk profile of any organization. Risk factors for user behavior include enhanced account access privileges, account access history, physical access system privileges, and password resilience. Organizations typically monitor and assess the security risk associated with devices but not individuals. Assessing the risk associated with both devices and individuals yields additional insight into the nature of vulnerabilities and appropriate remediation across the enterprise.

The physical security of information assets is often neglected in information security risk assessments. The reason is partly due to the silos that typically exist between physical and electronic security entities. Physical security technology is inexorably linked to the information security risk profile in two ways.

First, these devices increasingly communicate via the IT network, and therefore security vulnerabilities affect the overall security of the network. Second, physical security devices protect critical information assets so the effect of their compromise on information security is potentially amplified.

For these reasons the physical security of information assets and the electronic security of physical security infrastructure should be evaluated and included in a comprehensive assessment of information security risk.

References

[1] Verizon. 2015 data breach investigations report. Verizon; 2015.
[2] Jauhar S. The heart disease conundrum. In: The New York Times; November 29, 2015.

Information Technology Risk Measurements and Metrics

INTRODUCTION

Measuring information technology risk in search of the root causes of information security risk is a difficult issue for most organizations. Chief Information Security Officers (CISO) sometimes do not know what to measure and/or how to interpret the results of measurements. Perhaps ironically, there is no shortage of data, which might actually contribute to the problem.

Intrusion Detection Systems (IDS), Data Leakage Prevention (DLP) solutions, firewall logs, etc., can produce gargantuan quantities of data. Security Information and Event Management (SIEM) tools that capture, organize, and correlate events for the purpose of highlighting risk-relevant issues are routinely deployed to assist in risk analyses. Yet somehow data breaches recur with alarming frequency. It is worth speculating on an explanation for this phenomenon.

Maybe organizations are not aware of the metrics resulting from data generated by information security technologies? Possibly organizations are just ignoring such metrics or lack the resources to act on them? An additional explanation might be that existing metrics do not measure the risk factors that drive the *root causes* of information security risk. In this chapter it is presumed that the latter explanation is the explanation in many instances.

The overarching theme emerging from examining multiple IT environments is that each of them has similar information security issues when examined on an enterprise scale. Moreover, the forces that shape information security risk often have little to do with technology. Some frequent observations are noteworthy and provide insights into cultural features that affect information security.

It is quite common to see IT departments with the responsibility for creating and enforcing information security policy. This unfortunate circumstance was highlighted in Chapter 11. The net effect is to place these individuals in invidious positions since it is difficult to say "no" to superiors despite what the policy dictates. Moreover, if IT implementers create the information security policy that governs implementation, it represents an inherent conflict of interest.

Another consistent observation across organizations is that information security issues are typically quite basic. Esoteric phenomena are relatively rare. Therefore, using metrics designed to measure subtle risk indicators will not be an efficient use of resources if improving an information security strategy is the objective.

With respect to strategy, what is missing from the repertoire of security risk measurements is the equivalent of medical vital signs. In medicine, body temperature is a good if incomplete measure of general health. It most certainly would not specify what is happening on a cellular level. But if one's core temperature is significantly above 98.6°F (37°C), then clearly something is amiss and will require further investigation. Note that the converse is not necessarily true: the absence of an elevated body temperature does not by itself imply good health, which is why a routine health checkup includes other tests.

Continuing with the medical analogy, a good medical internist knows the risk factors for various diseases. Moreover, he or she should know when to refer a patient to a specialist. The medical internist is equivalent to the CISO, and the medical specialists are analogous to IT engineers. The medical internist uses vital signs as an initial screening mechanism. The CISO is in need of similar measurements that enable accurate if approximate estimates of systemic security health.

Importantly, such metrics inevitably cannot and would not address every issue. Attempting to measure everything could be as bad or worse than measuring nothing. In fact, the push to capture and analyze everything might explain some of the current security risk management dysfunction. In the next section criteria for *systemic* information security risk measurements and metrics are presented.

INFORMATION SECURITY RISK MEASUREMENT AND METRICS CRITERIA

One criterion IT and systemic information security risk measurements and resulting metrics is that they should be sourced from data that are relatively common and easy to obtain. The resulting metrics will be more intuitive and the assessment process will be more affordable, which will contribute to standardization and broad implementation.

Another criterion for risk measurements is that they should use standard statistical metrics. Analyses based on such metrics can yield surprisingly powerful insights on risk, and their simplicity will only enhance their utility. Specifically, the use of measurements such as averages, standard deviations, and correlation coefficients can identify salient issues and thereby raise questions for further investigation.

Finally, the sources of data for risk measurements should yield enterprise-level risk metrics. Sources for such measurements are given as follows, and the remainder of this chapter is devoted to showing how these sources of risk-relevant data can be measured to reveal security metrics with strategic impact:

1. a file of cryptographic hash values for passwords;
2. vulnerabilities in Active Directory identified through scanning tools, for example, StealthAUDIT;
3. host vulnerabilities based on standard scanning solutions, for example, Nessus and Qualys.

These sources are generally familiar to most organizations. In addition, the data generated by these resources are relatively consistent across environments. Of course, much more information is actually available. Potential sources include firewall logs, IDS data, DLP solution output, etc.

In that vein, there are indeed many parameters that *could* be measured in an IT environment. The challenge here is to measure items that yield insights on a strategic level.

The inclusion of significantly more data might actually be counterproductive depending on the objective. The sheer volume of data associated with sources noted previously might obfuscate the big picture, which is the objective in strategic analyses. Therefore, only the sources of risk-relevant data specified in aforementioned 1–3 are presented in this context, pursuant to measuring information technology vital signs and thereby making inferences on root causes of information security risk.

However, it is possible that organizations might want to leverage more of the unfiltered output from vulnerability scanning than is presented here. Such data could provide additional context, and thereby enhance an understanding of the relevance of the metrics cited later. This context would also facilitate remediation efforts by focusing attention on the highest-risk assets.

For example, what if 60% of the high-risk vulnerabilities were concentrated in 1% of the end points as identified during the vulnerability scan? This metric would be captured by the Concentration of Risk measurement as explained later. The raw data from the vulnerability scan results could provide memory usage associated with the devices containing those high-risk vulnerabilities. This in turn might suggest that a database was stored on that device and thereby lead to prioritizing the vulnerabilities associated with that device relative to others. In general, identifying the intersection of high-impact information assets and the presence of significant vulnerabilities therein is the key to prioritizing remediation efforts.

The final criterion for establishing meaningful if basic information security risk metrics is linking current external threats to specific internal vulnerabilities. Considerable defensive effort is expended on preventing attackers from electronically accessing internal resources. If there are no metrics that incorporate current intelligence on external threats, an important contextual element is missing.

SECURITY RISK DIMENSIONS

As noted earlier in this chapter, truly strategic information technology risk metrics should point to root causes of information security risk. At a high level these drivers can be grouped according to various categories or "dimensions" or broad categories of security risk. Sources of organizational risk factors highlighted in the previous chapter are implicitly included in the following three dimensions:

1. Threat Exposure
2. Vulnerability Management
3. Security Governance

Measurements of Threat Exposure yield metrics that link current external threats to internal vulnerabilities, and, importantly, provide hints regarding the internal organizational forces at work. Such measurements identify specific hosts, for example, end points and servers, with vulnerabilities that are exploitable by known malware kits currently available "in-the-wild." Clearly there is increased risk associated with hosts so affected, and a lax, inefficient, and/or ineffective approach to remediation arguably has significance that warrants strategic fixes.

Vulnerability Management and associated measurements reflect the effectiveness of the IT department in addressing security "housekeeping." Although vulnerability management is traditionally viewed as an inherently technical issue, it might actually reveal risk-relevant features associated with the organizational culture.

For example, a dilatory approach to Vulnerability Management might be directly linked to limited IT Department resources. This condition might ungenerously be ascribed to incompetent IT department management but equally it might be symptomatic of an anti-security culture that starves the IT department of resources. Only further investigation can determine the root cause of the observed phenomenon.

Security Governance is the third dimension or category of information security risk to be measured in this schema. The quality of Security Governance in an organization, good or bad, points to culture as a root cause. The information source for measurements of Security Governance derives primarily from password cracking. Why is this source helpful in identifying root causes of information security risk?

Weak passwords are prevalent across organizations despite the fact that they represent a common and well-known attack vector. If weak passwords are allowed, especially for high-risk accounts such as those with enhanced access privileges, it suggests that convenience is dominant relative to security. Therefore the contention here is that the quality of passwords is indicative of an overarching security governance issue.

Another source of data for measuring Security Governance is Windows Active Directory, noting that most IT environments are Windows-based and use of Active Directory is common as of this writing. Specific features for measurement include the number and duration of stale accounts, which relate to the risk associated with user behavior.

Note that the measurements specified herein might apply to more than one dimension.

For example, measurement of vulnerabilities linked to existing malware kits might equally relate to Vulnerability Management as Threat Exposure. In addition, persistent vulnerabilities that are used to measure the Vulnerability Management dimension might equally relate to Security Governance.

INTRODUCTION TO SPATIOTEMPORAL RISK MEASUREMENTS

At the risk of stating the obvious, one fundamental aspect of risk measurements is the measurement itself. In this case the contention is that measurements of so-called spatiotemporal features are particularly suited to establishing IT vital signs.

The term spatiotemporal implies a relation to space and time. However, "space" in this context is not a physical distance or a region in space. Rather, it refers to the universe of devices in which vulnerabilities reside. In the case of information technology vulnerabilities, the focus is on vulnerabilities within applications, servers, end points, etc.

Specifically, four spatiotemporal measurements are applied to each of the three security dimensions of Security Governance, Vulnerability Management, and Threat Exposure. These measurements are described as follows:

- *Concentration of Risk* is a spatial measurement of the density of vulnerabilities yielding a cumulative distribution of vulnerabilities across information assets. For example, such a measurement might specify that "x" percent of vulnerabilities exist in "y" percent of the information assets in the environment.
- *Proliferation of Risk* is a spatial measurement reflecting the distribution of vulnerabilities and indicates either the absolute or the average number of vulnerabilities across information assets. For example, such a measurement might specify the average number of vulnerabilities per end point (VpE) is "x" or that "z" percent of the assets have at least one high-risk vulnerability.
- *Persistence of Risk* measures the time duration of vulnerabilities across information assets. For example, such a measurement might specify that the oldest vulnerability on an end point that is exploitable by malware as measured by its publication date is "x" months or years.
- *Trending of Risk* measures the time rate of change in the average or absolute number of vulnerabilities. For example, the VpE is measured to be increasing, decreasing, or static.

Spikes in the distribution (proliferation), density (concentration), direction (trending), and duration (persistence) of vulnerabilities are potentially symptomatic of an incoherent, inconsistent, and/or inattentive application of security controls.

A complementary risk measurement is used to provide additional insight into information technology risk. Specifically, correlations between time series measurements yield data on the application of security controls that provide hints on the organizational forces at work. Correlations or anticorrelations in trending might point to inertia or inefficiency embedded in the organization's risk management machinery.

Most importantly, identifying programmatic insufficiencies on an enterprise level facilitates strategic approaches to remediation.

Although risk can seem like a somewhat abstract quantity, the distribution or change in the number of vulnerabilities in space and time provides insightful if indirect data about potential organizational forces at work and thereby enables *inferences* on root causes of information security risk.

SPATIOTEMPORAL RISK MEASUREMENTS AND METRICS

Proliferation of Risk

Proliferation of risk is a spatial measurement. It specifies the number of vulnerabilities across all physical and virtual hosts in the environment. Metrics derived from this measurement can assume two forms: the absolute number of vulnerabilities and the average number of vulnerabilities per endpoint (VPE).

An average figure per end point might be considered the more insightful metric since changes in the number of published vulnerabilities as well as the addition or subtraction of hosts can vary significantly over short time scales. Such swings can greatly affect the absolute number of vulnerabilities without necessarily substantively impacting risk.

However, the absolute number of vulnerabilities is in itself a simple and intuitive metric. It is often a good place to start in specifying enterprise-level risk, and might be reasonably followed by an examination of the concentration of risk across the network, which will be discussed later.

Specific metrics on proliferation are illustrative of this measurement's utility. A privileged account is a risk factor for information compromise since it enables one to download and install software at will. A priority of an attacker attempting to compromise the network would be to compromise the log-in credentials of an account with enhanced access privileges in order to install malicious software at his or her direction and discretion.

Therefore, metrics indicating the proliferation of privileged accounts across the enterprise is an indicator of systemic risk to the organization. Moreover, a disproportionate number of privileged accounts might point to a lack of adequate security governance as the root cause unless a strong business case argues otherwise. Clearly the majority of individuals in most organizations should not have privileged account status.

A key function of any IT department, and often the bane of their existence, is updating security patches. This Sisyphus-like activity is often referred to as vulnerability management. An industry-wide scale for rating the risk associated with vulnerabilities exists and the magnitude is specified according to the so-called CVSS rating.[1] A higher CVSS rating for vulnerabilities translates to increased risk because of their assessed ease of exploitation, the potential impact of the vulnerability, and/or other risk criteria.

A proliferation of high CVSS vulnerabilities across end points indicates something is awry in the ongoing battle to fix published vulnerabilities. Such a condition superficially points to a problem with IT resources and/or the IT department's efficiency. A broad and deep distribution of vulnerabilities, especially if coupled with trending metrics noted later, should precipitate a candid discussion with IT management.

Root causes of information security risk would likely surface as a result of such discussions. As noted earlier, nearly every IT department struggles with vulnerability management. The point of these metrics is to be able to see beyond surface issues and thereby enable broader perspectives on risk.

The average VpE could be considered a core metric. It is analogous to body temperature in that it is coarse, simple, and indicative of the quality of underlying risk management processes. For a large organization with thousands and perhaps hundreds of thousands of hosts, big changes in the average definitely signify something positive or negative is happening depending on the direction.

However, like any average, the number by itself is not extremely informative. A significant spread about the mean can exist so merely quoting an average can be misleading. Nevertheless, it is a good candidate for a vital sign that should precipitate further investigation depending on its value combined with the trend in that value.

[1]"The Common Vulnerability Scoring System (CVSS) is an open framework for communicating the characteristics and severity of software vulnerabilities. CVSS consists of three metric groups: Base, Temporal, and Environmental. The Base group represents the intrinsic qualities of a vulnerability, the Temporal group reflects the characteristics of a vulnerability that change over time, and the Environmental group represents the characteristics of a vulnerability that are unique to a user's environment. The Base metrics produce a score ranging from 0 to 10, which can then be modified by scoring the Temporal and Environmental metrics" (https://www.first.org/cvss).

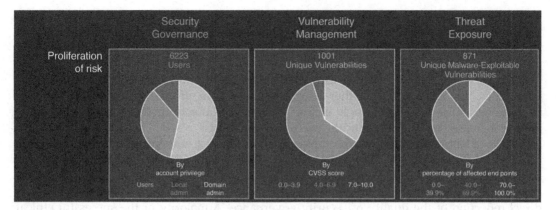

FIGURE 12.1   **Proliferation measurements of information security risk.** *Figure provided by Kate McManus.*

The proliferation risk applied to Threat Exposure is captured by measuring the percentage of end points with unique vulnerabilities that are exploitable by existing malware kits. There is a palpable urgency associated with this metric since a hacker or Script Kiddie who gains access to internal network resources through phishing or another social engineering method has a ready-made weapon at his or her disposal.

The existence of such scripts would obviate the need to develop new code, thereby facilitating the vulnerability to a future attack. Note that this metric explicitly links the current external threat environment to internal vulnerabilities.

Fig. 12.1 summarizes the metrics resulting from proliferation measurements of the Security Governance, Vulnerability Management, and Threat Exposure security risk dimensions.

Concentration of Risk

The concentration of risk applied to Vulnerability Management is a spatial measurement that measures the unevenness in the distribution of vulnerabilities across information assets. This is represented by a cumulative distribution, where the number of vulnerabilities is counted as a function of a percentage of the asset population. Therefore by definition the last data point indicates that 100% of the vulnerabilities are present in 100% of the information assets.

In other words, the concentration of vulnerabilities measures the fraction of vulnerabilities as a function of an increasing percentage of information assets. The concentration measurement for this category of risk speaks volumes about risk management. It is important to note that low concentrations of high-risk vulnerabilities and high concentrations of low-risk vulnerabilities might be indicative of effective (read: prioritized) vulnerability management. A correlation measurement of two time series has been suggested to help determine the implications of such a condition and this metric will be discussed later in this chapter.

Of course, if the condition were reversed, the interpretation would be less favorable. Specifically, a group of priority assets with a high concentration of vulnerabilities could be indicative of inconsistent remediation if not downright neglect. Information about the nature of those assets derived from the vulnerability scan data or elsewhere would help in prioritizing remediation. For example, if the concentration of risk occurred in a server that hosted a high-impact database, that particular server should be prioritized over hosts of lesser value.

Certainly if this metric pointed to a greatly uneven distribution in the concentration of vulnerabilities, it would warrant further analysis. Remediation efforts would again depend on the nature of those assets, and might include isolating the affected assets, intensive patching, and/or increased monitoring of traffic to/from those assets.

Like it or not, passwords are the most common form of authentication used to restrict access to information assets. Although there is a justifiable move away from using passwords as the principal form of authentication, it is still overwhelmingly used in IT environments. Because of its importance to the authentication process, the complexity of passwords is a direct reflection of the quality of security governance. A majority of the successful ethical hacking exercises performed by my company, in addition to many historical attacks, have leveraged password cracking.

In this measurement scheme, the concentration of risk metric for Security Governance is given by the percentage of passwords cracked as a function of the three categories of account privilege in a Windows environment: users, local administrators, and domain administrators. For example, the potential impact of an intruder cracking a domain administrator's password is significantly greater than for an ordinary Windows user. In fact, gaining administrative privilege is likely to be one of the first priorities of a hacker.

Finally, the concentration of risk applied to Threat Exposure is also measured via a cumulative distribution. Specifically, the total number of malware-exploitable vulnerabilities is measured against a percentage of hosts in the environment.

A concentration of information assets with malware-exploitable vulnerabilities greatly increases the susceptibility of those machines to existing threats. As is the case with a concentration of other vulnerabilities, knowing the identity of the assets that harbor the highest concentrations of malware-susceptible vulnerabilities is the context required to prioritize remediation efforts.

Spatial unevenness across information assets suggests that specific assets with a particular function(s) or geographic location are at enhanced risk. Such a finding might be indicative of enhanced risk associated with a particular business unit. For example, unevenness in the distribution of vulnerabilities could reasonably be linked to a corresponding unevenness in remediation efforts. If the group of assets is managed by a specific IT component, the concentration metric could be used to pinpoint organizational deficiencies.

An alternative theory for the data is that remediation has not been implemented for this particular group of assets because of business objections to patching, which speaks to organizational culture as a root cause. It also provides an important datum for both tactical and strategic remediation efforts. Whatever the outcome of the resulting deeper dive, hosts and end points so affected would clearly represent an area of focus for remediation, and the deployment of compensating controls if patching machines were not possible or practical.

Fig. 12.2 illustrates Concentration of Risk measurements across the aforementioned dimensions of information security risk.

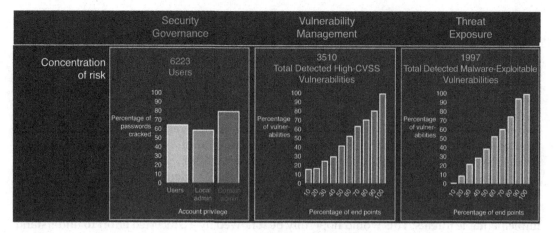

FIGURE 12.2 **Concentration measurements of information security risk.** *Figure provided by Kate McManus.*

Persistence of Risk

The time duration of vulnerabilities is indicative of a persistent risk condition. The vulnerability to exploitation is proportional to the length of time that vulnerability exists. Although the meaning of this risk metric is technically different than the one posited here, companies have a metric that accounts for the increased risk associated with longer time intervals. This metric is called the return period and specifies the probability that a loss will exceed a certain dollar amount as a function of the time interval.

The theory is that the longer the time interval of exposure, the greater is the risk. A persistent risk condition could be indicative of an inherently difficult issue to resolve or alternatively hint at a generally dilatory approach to remediation. These two choices clearly have different implications relative to an information security strategy. The intent of a persistence measurement is to highlight the risk condition to focus tactical remediation efforts as well as initiate an investigation to identify the root cause of the problem.

Specifically, the Persistence of Risk measurement applied to Security Governance entails examining stale accounts. These are accounts that are inactive although still operational. An attacker could discreetly crack the password for that account and masquerade as the legitimate user since the account is dormant and presumably not monitored closely.

The metric associated with the persistence measurement of Security Governance is the average time since the last account log-in as applied to accounts with varying privileges: Windows users, local administrators, and domain administrators. Clearly longer staleness in privileged accounts is indicative of increased risk. The inference is that Security Governance processes are lacking and likely reflect cultural issues that must be addressed on an enterprise scale.

The Persistence of Risk measurement applied to Vulnerability Management focuses on the length of time that published vulnerabilities have gone unaddressed. Recall the CVSS system was introduced earlier in the chapter. Vulnerabilities with CVSS risk ratings of 1–10 (*Note*: 10 is the most severe) are continuously being published for the benefit of the security community. Their presence in IT environments is exposed via the use of standard host vulnerability scanning tools.

This persistence metric here measures the average time since a unique vulnerability was detected as a function of the severity of that vulnerability. Clearly if high-severity vulnerabilities persist after detection, it suggests that Vulnerability Management is less-than-effective. Note that the persistence of vulnerabilities might also have implications to Security Governance.

The persistence measurement applied to Threat Exposure measures the average time since unique, malware-exploitable vulnerabilities were published relative to the percentage of affected end points. This metric specifies the time duration of exposure to external threats versus the percentage of hosts that contain such vulnerabilities.

An organization should use this metric as a stimulus to identify those hosts exhibiting maximal persistence and thereby focus remediation efforts accordingly. There should be some urgency to this effort, as this metric is indicative of the magnitude of exposure to easily implementable threats. This would hopefully be followed by a concerted effort to understand the genesis of any gradients in persistence across all hosts.

Fig. 12.3 illustrates the metrics resulting from the Persistence of Risk measurements applied to the Security Governance, Vulnerability Management, and Threat Exposure security dimensions.

Trending of Risk

Trending of Risk is perhaps the most intuitive measurement among those described herein. Trending in this context indicates the time history of a specific security parameter.

A visual representation of the time history shows changes in the relevant security category or dimension. Such a depiction might be used to gauge the effect of remediation thereby correlating cause and effect. A time history can also facilitate the tracking of remediation efforts.

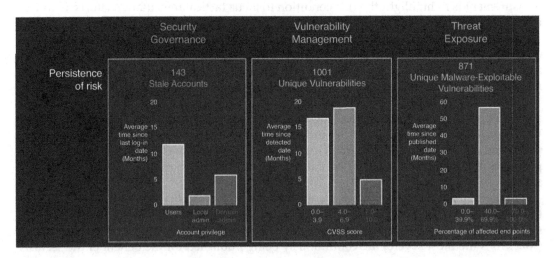

FIGURE 12.3   **Persistence measurements of information security risk.** *Figure provided by Kate McManus.*

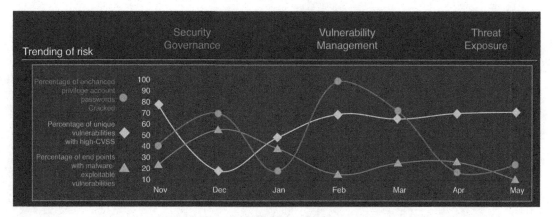

FIGURE 12.4 **Trending measurements of information security risk.** *Figure provided by Kate McManus.*

The specific metrics derived from the Trending of Risk measurements applied to Security Governance, Vulnerability Management, and Threat Exposure are the time histories of the following:

1. the percentage of enhanced privileged account passwords cracked;
2. the percentage of unique vulnerabilities with high CVSS ratings;
3. the percentage of end points with malware-exploitable vulnerabilities.

These are indicative if relatively coarse metrics for each of the three security risk dimensions but each comports with the spirit of a vital sign. Fig. 12.4 illustrates the Trending of Risk metrics for Security Governance, Vulnerability Management and Threat Exposure.

CORRELATION MEASUREMENTS AND METRICS

A fifth measurement that is related to the four spatiotemporal measurements is correlation. Qualitatively, a correlation between two events or variables indicates there is a relationship between them. In other words, the presence of one is associated with the other. However, a correlation does not imply that one event actually *causes* the other. For example, rainfall has traditionally been correlated with the month of April but the month of April does not cause rainfall.

There are relationships between events that are indeed causal. One striking example is the relationship between the number of years an individual smokes and the incidence of lung cancer. Fig. 12.5 shows a rather compelling graphic that indicates the cumulative risk of developing lung cancer as a function of a person's age when he quit smoking.[2]

Identifying a relationship between two variables can be very useful in developing a theory about the root cause of a phenomenon. If there is an increasing/decreasing trend in one variable and a corresponding increasing/decreasing trend in another, one could arguably say something meaningful about the implications of the relationship.

[2]http://topreview-ilonawarf.blogspot.com/2013/11/ilona-warf-blog-day-in-fact-they-able.html.

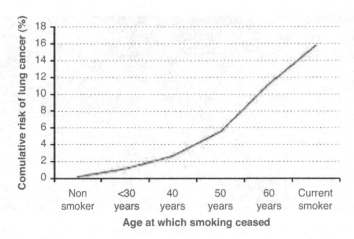

FIGURE 12.5 Cumulative risk of smoking and developing lung cancer among men in the United Kingdom at age 75, according to age at which they stopped smoking.

Furthermore, a tool that quantifies the magnitude of the relationship between two variables might yield data that enables meaningful statements on risk. Moreover, correlations can be subtle and such a metric might identify relationships that are not so obvious. Identifying such quasi-hidden relationships can lead to a better understanding of the root causes of information security risk. More specifically, calculating the correlation coefficient is a quantitative technique that facilitates isolating and identifying a risk factor for a given threat.

The Pearson Product-Moment Correlation Coefficient (PPMCC) measures the degree of linearity between two variables. This coefficient can assume a range of discrete values from +1 to −1. A value of 0 indicates that there is no linear relationship between the variables. A value of the coefficient that is greater than 0 is indicative of a positive linear relationship between two variables. A higher number implies a greater correlation. That is, a positive correlation implies that as the value of one variable increases so does the value of the other variable.

A negative coefficient implies "anticorrelation." In other words, as the value of one variable increases, the value of the other variable tends to decrease. In analogy with positive correlation, the greater the negative number between −0.5 and −1.0, the higher is the anticorrelation.

The PPMCC is denoted by r and is given by the following formula for the variables X, Y, and their sum $X + Y = N$. It may look complicated, but on close inspection the formula merely consists of multiplication and division among X, Y, and N plus a square root operation:

$$r = \frac{\sum XY - \left[(\sum X \sum Y)/N\right]}{\sqrt{\left\{\sum X^2 - \left[(\sum X)^2/N\right]\right\}\left\{\sum Y^2 - \left[(\sum Y)^2/N\right]\right\}}}$$

Let's work an example. Assume we have two arrays of numbers as follows:

Array 1 $(X) = 1, 2, 3, 4, 5, 6, 7, 8, 9, 10$
Array 2 $(Y) = 10, 20, 30, 40, 50, 60, 70, 80, 90, 100$

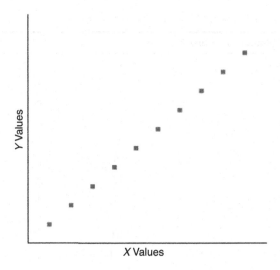

FIGURE 12.6 **Perfect linearity.**

The observant reader will notice that an equation describing the relationship between Array 1 and Array 2 is $Y = 10X$. Fig. 12.6 shows a plot of X versus Y and clearly reflects this perfectly linear relationship.

What would the PPMCC be for these two series X and Y? Although performing the calculation might seem like a superfluous exercise, plugging the values listed for Array 1 and Array 2 into an online calculator yields $r = 1$. Recall a value of 1.0 is the maximum value for the positive correlation coefficient. In other words, the PPMCC confirms there is a perfect linear relationship between X and Y. This is to be expected for $Y = 10X$ since it characterizes a perfectly straight line.

Seeking a more relevant example, the PPMCC can be used to determine the magnitude of a correlation between a security risk factor and another variable of one's choosing. For example, suppose it was hypothesized that there was a correlation between the number of host vulnerabilities that appear each day and the first 20 days of the month.

In other words, the hypothesis is that vulnerabilities increase linearly with increasing days of the first two-thirds of any month. Moreover, it has been suggested that the IT department should not deploy controls in the latter third of the month in order to more efficiently apply resources. A rigorous analysis of the data is required to determine if the hypothesis and recommended strategy have merit.

The PPMCC is now used to test this hypothesis using contrived data. An online calculator will again be leveraged to perform the calculation, thereby saving time and effort.[3] The first step is to create a table of the scores for each variable and the product of the two scores. The first column represents the days of the month up to day 20, and the second column indicates a made-up number of vulnerabilities that appear on the corresponding day of the month. Table 12.1 displays these data.

---

[3]https://statistics.laerd.com/calculators/pearsons-product-moment-correlation-coefficient-calculator-1.php.

TABLE 12.1   Pearson Product-Moment Correlation Coefficient Example

X (day of the month)	Y (number of vulnerabilities)	X^2	Y^2	XY
1	2	1	4	2
2	1	4	1	2
3	3	9	9	9
4	1	16	1	4
5	4	25	16	20
6	2	36	4	12
7	3	49	9	21
8	2	64	4	16
9	2	81	4	18
10	2	100	4	20
11	5	121	25	55
12	1	144	1	12
13	2	169	4	26
14	3	196	9	42
15	3	225	9	45
16	1	256	1	16
17	1	289	1	17
18	2	324	4	36
19	3	361	9	57
20	3	400	9	60
Total = 210	46	2870	128	490

Plugging the numbers in Table 12.1 into the expression for r above reveals $r = 0.058$.

As noted earlier, the correlation coefficient ranges from −1.0 to +1.0. A negative score translates to a negative correlation, that is, the number of vulnerabilities *decreases* with increasing days of the month, 0 corresponds to no correlation, and a positive number is indicative of a correlation.

A correlation coefficient of 0.058 implies that there is only a slight positive correlation between the first 20 days of the month and the number of vulnerabilities that appear on hosts each day. The magnitude of the correlation should refute anecdotal evidence to support this theory and thereby counter any attempts at implementing what will likely be a flawed remediation strategy.

Returning to the search for root causes of information security risk, what would be the implications of a negative PPMCC between two time series, where one plots the number of high-risk vulnerabilities as a function of time and the other plots the number of overall vulnerabilities over the same time period?

A negative correlation coefficient actually might imply completely opposite conclusions relative to the quality of Security Governance depending on how these series were anticorrelated, that is, which time series was trending upward and which one was trending downward. These and other correlations plus their implications to information technology risk will be explored in the next section and applied to an increasingly adopted information security risk framework.

THE NIST CYBERSECURITY FRAMEWORK

Introduction

An information security policy and a set of accompanying security technology standards are a *sine qua non* for a rigorous information security risk management program [1]. The inherently defensive nature of security often precludes measurements of the effectiveness of security controls given the lack of robust incident statistics. Therefore, measurements of the effectiveness of security controls against a risk-based policy and standards are required.

The NIST Cybersecurity Framework referenced in Chapter 1 is an increasingly accepted standard among information security professionals. One positive feature of this framework is that it attempts to characterize the "maturity" of processes and security controls.

In contrast, other information security standards tend to be more prescriptive and merely provide lists of security controls to implement without appropriate context. Assessments based on a checklist can specify *if* controls have been implemented but cannot measure how well such controls are implemented or indeed if they actually should be implemented at all. In addition, they cannot assign weight to specific controls relative to others *based on risk*. In contrast, the NIST Framework can be used to evaluate the approach of enterprise security risk management efforts as well as provide a view of risk on a programmatic level.

With respect to the NIST Framework taxonomy, "Functions" are identified that represent high-level classes of controls. Categories and subcategories of security controls are subsumed under each Function. The Functions are as follows: Identify, Detect, Protect, Respond, and Recover.

The NIST Framework also establishes Tiers that characterize the effectiveness of the Functions. There are four Tiers that are categorized in reverse rank order according to the degree of sophistication. Criteria for these Tiers as quoted from the NIST Framework are as follows:

Tier 1: Partial

- Risk Management Process – Organizational cybersecurity risk management practices are not formalized, and risk is managed in an ad hoc and sometimes reactive manner. Prioritization of cybersecurity activities may not be directly informed by organizational risk objectives, the threat environment, or business/mission requirements.
- Integrated Risk Management Program – There is limited awareness of cybersecurity risk at the organizational level and an organization-wide approach to managing cybersecurity risk has not been established. The organization implements cybersecurity risk management on an irregular, case-by-case basis due to varied experience or information gained from outside sources. The organization may not have processes that enable cybersecurity information to be shared within the organization.
- External Participation – An organization may not have the processes in place to participate in coordination or collaboration with other entities.

Tier 2: Risk Informed

- Risk Management Process – Risk management practices are approved by management but may not be established as organizational-wide policy. Prioritization of cybersecurity activities is directly informed by organizational risk objectives, the threat environment, or business/mission requirements.
- Integrated Risk Management Program – There is an awareness of cybersecurity risk at the organizational level but an organization-wide approach to managing cybersecurity risk has not been established. Risk-informed, management-approved processes and procedures are defined and implemented, and staff has adequate resources to perform their cybersecurity duties. Cybersecurity information is shared within the organization on an informal basis.
- External Participation – The organization knows its role in the larger ecosystem, but has not formalized its capabilities to interact and share information externally.

Tier 3: Repeatable

- Risk Management Process – The organization's risk management practices are formally approved and expressed as policy. Organizational cybersecurity practices are regularly updated based on the application of risk management processes to changes in business/mission requirements and a changing threat and technology landscape.
- Integrated Risk Management Program – There is an organization-wide approach to manage cybersecurity risk. Risk-informed policies, processes, and procedures are defined, implemented as intended, and reviewed. Consistent methods are in place to respond effectively to changes in risk. Personnel possess the knowledge and skills to perform their appointed roles and responsibilities.
- External Participation – The organization understands its dependencies and partners and receives information from these partners that enables collaboration and risk-based management decisions within the organization in response to events.

Tier 4: Adaptive

- Risk Management Process – The organization adapts its cybersecurity practices based on lessons learned and predictive indicators derived from previous and current cybersecurity activities. Through a process of continuous improvement incorporating advanced cybersecurity technologies and practices, the organization actively adapts to a changing cybersecurity landscape and responds to evolving and sophisticated threats in a timely manner.
- Integrated Risk Management Program – There is an organization-wide approach to managing cybersecurity risk that uses risk-informed policies, processes, and procedures to address potential cybersecurity events. Cybersecurity risk management is part of the organizational culture and evolves from an awareness of previous activities, information shared by other sources, and continuous awareness of activities on their systems and networks.
- External Participation – The organization manages risk and actively share information with partners to ensure that accurate, current information is being distributed and consumed to improve cybersecurity before a cybersecurity event occurs.

The rating of each Function is evaluated with respect to the Tier criteria and relative to the totality of security controls. An overall Tier rating can be assigned to the information security program based on the individual Function ratings. The difficulty experienced by many organizations is determining measurements and associated metrics that can be used to rate those Functions according to the appropriate NIST Tier.

The security measurements and metrics specified in this chapter might offer possibilities to partially remedy the situation. Although the metrics cited in the previous section might not apply to all NIST Functions, measurements that can help determine a Tier rating for even a subset of Functions would be useful. This process would provide substantive and repeatable evidence on the status of security program management. Such metrics should not be touted as all-inclusive, but rather as indicative of a rigorous if high-level approach to information security risk management.

Importantly, because spatiotemporal measurements are somewhat intuitive, the metrics derived from these measurements could also help to establish a common language between executive management, security personnel, and information technologists. Gaps based on difficulties in communicating on risk contribute to systemic security issues in acronym-ladened technology environments.

Specifically, the NIST "Identify" and "Protect" Functions align with the metrics derived from the spatiotemporal risk measurements noted earlier. Descriptions of these Functions as stated in the NIST Framework are as follows:

> Identify – Develop the organizational understanding to manage cybersecurity risk to systems, assets, data, and capabilities. The activities in the Identify Function are foundational for effective use of the Framework. Understanding the business context, the resources that support critical functions, and the related cybersecurity risks enables an organization to focus and prioritize its efforts, consistent with its risk management strategy and business needs. Examples of outcome Categories within this Function include: Asset Management, Business Environment, Governance; Risk Assessment, and Risk Management Strategy.
>
> Protect – Develop and implement the appropriate safeguards to ensure delivery of critical infrastructure services. The Protect Function supports the ability to limit or contain the impact of a potential cybersecurity event. Examples of outcome Categories within this Function include: Access Control, Awareness and Training, Data Security, Information Protection Processes and Procedures, Maintenance, and Protective Technology.

Security Governance metrics can be directly applied to the "Identify" Function. Threat Exposure and Vulnerability Management apply to both the "Identify" and "Protect" Functions since the latter involve "Information Protection Processes and Procedures" as well as "Risk Assessments." Details of how spatiotemporal risk measurements can be applied to the NIST Framework are provided next.

Trending of Risk Applied to the NIST Framework

Trends in relevant security parameters can illustrate improvement, deterioration, or stasis in security risk management depending on the presence of an inflection or lack thereof. Trends are illustrated via graphs that plot the magnitude of some variable versus time.

Scientists love graphs since the magnitude and direction of a simple line can tell a powerful story about the relationship between two variables and thereby support or reject hypotheses. In this case that story relates to processes for managing information security risk.

It is relatively easy to use trending data to support the NIST Tier rating scheme. For example, trends in metrics that resulted from measurements of Vulnerability Management, Security Governance, and Threat Exposure can each be used to assess security program sophistication according to the NIST Tier rating scheme. As noted previously, the NIST Tier ratings are specified as Partial, Informed, Repeatable, and Adaptive.

For example, if the Security Governance metric was decreasing over time, but metrics resulting from measurements of the other two security dimensions were increasing over the same time interval, such metrics might support only NIST Identify and/or Protect Function ratings of "Informed."

If all three were seen to be decreasing over a suitable interval, this might arguably be evidence of a "Repeatable" or even "Adaptive" rating depending on the length of the time interval and the rate of decrease. The criteria for a specific NIST Tier rating, for example, the measurement time interval, the magnitude of the change in a metric over that time interval, and the number and type of metric that is collectively used to determine a given rating, will be based on an organization's risk management processes and its tolerance for risk.

Persistence of Risk Applied to the NIST Framework

The Persistence of Risk measurement is indicative of the quality and consistency of security risk management processes. In addition to trending, persistence reveals temporal information that can be used to measure the NIST Identify and/or Protect Functions and therefore be used to specify a NIST Tier rating.

For example, the proliferation of stale accounts and/or hosts with high CVSS ratings would argue that information security risk management processes were less than repeatable. Therefore, the Identify and/or Protect NIST Functions would be rated accordingly. Again, the specific criteria used to justify a NIST Tier rating such as the magnitude of the Persistence of Risk measurement must be determined for each organization.

Concentration and Proliferation of Risk Applied to the NIST Framework

How should one interpret an uneven or extensive proliferation of vulnerabilities across an enterprise? That is what the spatial measurements of Concentration and Proliferation indicate. A credible argument could be made that the proliferation of vulnerabilities, that is, distributed widely across the enterprise, is evidence of less-than-repeatable security risk management processes.

In the same vein, suppose specific assets were afflicted with numerous vulnerabilities. Moreover, if these assets were afflicted with high-CVSS or malware-exploitable vulnerabilities, and compensating controls were not in place, such a condition might suggest a "Risk-Informed" NIST Tier rating at best relative to the Identify and/or Protect NIST Functions. This would be especially true if the assets so afflicted were deemed to be high risk by virtue of the information contained therein.

Similarly, extensive privileged accounts across the enterprise would be potential evidence of ineffective Security Governance unless there was ample business justification for this condition. However, even if there is a business justification for a proliferation of privileged accounts, a lack of compensating controls to offset the risk suggests an immature information security risk management program. This would also imply that a lower NIST Tier rating for the Identify and/or Protect Functions is justified.

Correlation Between Time Series

The PPMCC is a metric that can be used to assess the relationship between spatiotemporal security measurements, and, importantly, make additional inferences on root causes of information security risk. If two security risk metrics are highly correlated or anticorrelated over a sufficient time interval, and are trending in specific directions, the results might say something about the quality of underlying risk management processes. The outcome could be used to determine a NIST Cybersecurity Framework Tier rating.

For example, if the number of overall vulnerabilities is trending higher but the high-risk and/or malware-exploitable versions are trending lower, it might be inferred that the organization is actually addressing higher-risk issues as a priority on a programmatic level. At a high level, and in combination with other metrics, the results of such measurements might suggest that the organization is effective in information security risk management.

In other words, the magnitude and polarity of the correlation could provide a quantitative justification for a particular NIST Tier rating, relative to the Identify and/or Protect NIST Functions. It would also be prudent to confirm that a particular trend in higher-risk vulnerabilities is not due to "random" fluctuations. To that end, longer measurement intervals would tend to dispel or support hypotheses of randomness, and thereby add weight to a given NIST Tier rating.

Examining the magnitude, polarity, and duration of correlations between time series of risk-relevant parameters using the PPMCC would support NIST Tier ratings for the Identification and/or Protection Functions. Examples of such correlations and their implications to security risk management effectiveness ratings are provided next.

- Time series of the average age of malware-exploitable vulnerabilities by *published date* versus a time series of the average age of malware-exploitable vulnerabilities by *detection date*

A high positive correlation between these time series, that is, a coefficient between 0.5 and 1.0, where both are trending higher might infer that the organization is dilatory in vulnerability management and/or security governance.

The assumption is that the longer a malware-exploitable vulnerability has been in the public domain, and the longer it persists in an IT environment as measured by the detection date, the greater is the vulnerability of network resources.

The reasoning is that more malicious individuals would have access to publicly available malware kits, which facilitate attacks that do not require high-level programming skills.

In contrast, if these two time series were correlated and both were trending lower, it might infer that the organization is prioritizing higher-risk vulnerabilities relative to others, and therefore warrants a more sophisticated Tier rating for the Identify and/or Protect NIST Functions.

- Time series of the number of overall VpE versus the number of high CVSS-rated VpE

A high positive correlation and both time series trending upward would be indicative of issues with Security Governance or Vulnerability Management. Such a condition might suggest a depreciated Tier rating is appropriate to the Identify and/or Protect NIST Functions.

A high negative or anticorrelation metric, that is, a coefficient between −0.5 and −1.0, where the high CVSS-rated series was trending lower but the *overall* VpE time series was trending higher, could suggest effective security risk management is at work.

Namely, this condition might infer that remediation of high-risk vulnerabilities is being conducted as a priority. In this case the risk metric would provide quantitative justification for a more sophisticated NIST Tier rating of the Identify and/or Protect NIST Functions.

- Time series of the average VpE (all vulnerabilities) versus the time series for the VpE associated with malware-exploitable vulnerabilities

  The same arguments apply here as those in the bullet immediate above.

- Time series of the percentage of privileged account passwords cracked versus a time series of the percentage of unique vulnerabilities with a high CVSS rating

A high positive correlation coefficient between these time series and both trending upward imply challenged security risk management processes. These conditions might therefore suggest a lower NIST Tier rating for the Identify and/or Protect NIST Functions.

A high negative correlation coefficient plus a condition where either of the time series is trending upward or downward might suggest that these security risk management processes are divorced in the overall risk management program. Such a scenario would likely warrant follow-up to understand why this condition exists.

- Time series of the percentage of privileged account passwords cracked versus a time series of the percentage of end points/hosts with malware-exploitable vulnerabilities

  The same inferences apply here as the bullet immediately above.

- Time series of the percentage of vulnerabilities with a high CVSS rating versus a time series of the percentage of privileged accounts with cracked passwords

A high correlation where both time series were trending upward would infer challenged Vulnerability Management and/or Security Governance with attendant implications to the NIST Tier rating for the Identify and/or Protect Functions.

A high negative correlation between these two time series would be unlikely unless the two processes were owned by different organizational entities. Such a condition might suggest difficulties in security risk management and a correspondingly depreciated NIST Tier rating for the Identify and/or Protect Tier Function.

The astute reader will realize that in some cases, two time series can be highly correlated but trending in a direction that suggests enhanced risk management is warranted. For example, the average VpE might be increasing as well as the average number of high-risk VpE. The correlation coefficient might indicate perfect correlation but this should be cold comfort to the organization since the number of vulnerabilities is increasing over time in both instances. Correlation of two risk-relevant time series by itself does not imply effective risk management.

The discussion on trending direction raises a practical consideration in interpreting the data derived from time series of vulnerabilities. The slope of each time series must be specified in order to make a more informed statement about root causes of information security risk. But the slope of a time series can vary considerably over a given time interval especially if erratic risk management processes exist. Therefore, a simplification has been invoked to facilitate risk measurements recognizing that it represents a gross approximation.

Namely, the direction of the trends for a time series is defined by the value of the graph end points, where intermediate data points are ignored. Therefore, if the last end point in the time series is less than the value of the first end point, the trend is downward irrespective of the values of the intermediate end points. The opposite is true if the polarity is reversed.

FIGURE 12.7 Scenario 1 – both VpE time series positively correlated and trending lower.

FIGURE 12.8 Scenario 2 – both VpE time series positively correlated and trending higher.

To illustrate the difference in inferences that result from differences in polarity of time series, four scenarios have been identified for a given correlation measurement. Similar scenarios should be developed for any correlation measurement between two time series.

For example, let us assume time series A is the average overall VpE, and time series B is the average high-risk VpE. Four scenarios can be constructed from these two time series.

Scenario 1 as depicted in Fig. 12.7 suggests favorable security inferences since both time series of vulnerabilities are trending lower for the selected time interval.

In contrast, Scenario 2 suggests unfavorable security inferences since both time series are trending higher and positively correlated during the time interval. Fig. 12.8 shows the two VpE time series trending higher.

Scenario 3 suggests favorable security inferences since the average VpE time series (A) is trending upward but the average higher-risk VpE time series (B) is trending downward for the selected time interval. Such a scenario would imply that a security risk prioritization process is in effect. Fig. 12.9 shows these two time series where A is trending higher and B is trending lower.

Scenario 4 suggests unfavorable security inferences since the average VpE time series (A) is trending lower and the average high-risk VpE (B) is trending higher for the selected time interval. In other words, the high-risk vulnerabilities are not being addressed while the overall trend is decreasing. Fig. 12.10 shows the two time series trending in opposite directions but reversed from Scenario 3.

The duration of the time interval would provide insight into the consistency of risk management efforts and hence provide additional data to support a given NIST Tier rating. In addition, other features of the correlation coefficient would add weight to a particular NIST Tier rating.

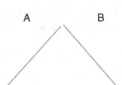

FIGURE 12.9 Scenario 3 – average VpE time series trending higher and average high-risk VpE series trending lower.

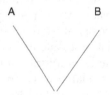

FIGURE 12.10 Scenario 4 – average VpE time series trending lower and average high-risk VpE time series trending higher.

TABLE 12.2 NIST Tier Rating Using Correlation Coefficients for Scenarios 1 and 2

Correlation interval (months)	0.0–0.5 (scenario 1)	0.5–1.0 (scenario 1)	0.0–0.5 (scenario 2)	0.5–1.0 (scenario 2)
3	Repeatable	Repeatable	Repeatable	Partial
6	Repeatable	Risk Informed	Repeatable	Partial
9	Risk Informed	Adaptive	Repeatable	Partial
12	Risk Informed	Adaptive	Partial	Partial

TABLE 12.3 NIST Tier Rating Using Correlation Coefficients for Scenarios 3 and 4

Correlation interval (months)	0 to −0.5 (scenario 3)	−0.5 to −1.0 (scenario 3)	0.0 to −0.5 (scenario 4)	−0.5 to −1.0 (scenario 4)
3	Repeatable	Repeatable	Repeatable	Repeatable
6	Repeatable	Risk Informed	Repeatable	Partial
9	Repeatable	Risk Informed	Repeatable	Partial
12	Risk Informed	Risk Informed	Repeatable	Partial

For example, one might characterize the four scenarios in terms of their relative polarity, correlation magnitude and correlation time interval. This categorization would yield coarse data to support an inference on root cause. Moreover, magnitude, direction/polarity, and duration of the correlation could be used to specify a NIST Tier rating for a given NIST Function.

Tables 12.2 and 12.3 provide a summary of this rating scheme for the NIST Identify and Protect Functions applied to scenarios 1–4. Although the Tier ratings align with the NIST criteria, they are ultimately subjective and will be based on an organization's tolerance for risk and in light of a full compliment of risk-relevant security metrics.

SUMMARY

Measuring information technology risk, which is an important contributor to information security risk, remains a challenge for many organizations. Moreover, current information technology risk metrics mostly point to tactical rather than strategic security risk indicators. An abundance of data derived from information security technology solutions might actually complicate risk assessments.

Measurements of information technology risk are suggested that are based on spatiotemporal features related to IT environments: Concentration, Proliferation, Trending, and Persistence. These are applied to three dimensions, i.e., fundamental categories of information security risk: Security Governance, Vulnerability Management, and Threat Exposure.

These dimensions encompass one or more of the following principal sources of information security vulnerabilities: business practices, security governance, the physical security of information assets, user behavior, and information technology implementation. The metrics associated with the Threat Exposure dimension also link internal vulnerabilities to external threat intelligence.

Basic sources of data are used to calculate these metrics that include the results of host vulnerability scans, Active Directory vulnerability scans, and the results of password cracking efforts applied to the file containing password hash values. The general accessibility of this data across organizations along with the simplicity of the measurements and associated metrics is intended to facilitate insights and broad adoption.

The Pearson Product Moment Correlation Coefficient measurement of time series complements the spatiotemporal measurements and metrics. This additional detail provides further evidence to support or reject theories on root causes of information technology risk and information security risk more generally.

Finally, spatiotemporal and correlation measurements and metrics can be applied to the NIST Cybersecurity Framework to assist in determining a Tier rating for the Identify and/or Protect Functions.

Reference

[1] NIST. NIST framework for improving critical infrastructure cybersecurity, version 1.0. NIST; February 12, 2014.

13

Special Information Technology Risk Measurements and Metrics

INTRODUCTION

There are numerous ways to measure information technology risk and no two organizations will use the same methods. One of the significant lessons of the previous chapters is that risk is contextual. Therefore, risk assessments must be contextual as well. Moreover, addressing vulnerabilities is not without financial and/or operational costs. Although cost is not a component of risk measurements *per se*, it is a principal consideration in decisions on security. Such decisions are affected by an organization's tolerance for risk, which in turn impacts a security risk management strategy.

Although each organization is unique, there is a good deal of similarity across organizations in terms of security controls. Organizations tend to use similar types of IT equipment, which are based on the same operating systems and protocols. However, considerable variability exists with respect to IT implementation, permissible practices, and information security governance.

Chapter 12 presented a set of spatiotemporal measurements and resulting metrics that were intended to facilitate inferences on the root causes of IT risk. In this chapter specific methods borrowed from other scientific and engineering disciplines are suggested in order to develop more sophisticated models of IT risk.

There is admittedly no unifying theme among these approaches except that each is potentially useful depending on the scenario. In addition, each method offers opportunities for identifying quantitative security metrics. Moreover, aspects of each method are well known in science and engineering contexts but have heretofore not been broadly implemented by security practitioners.

The issue of password resilience is part of a ceaseless narrative in information security. The intent in this chapter is to provide quantitative recommendations on length and complexity relative to three significant threat categories. The crux of the discussion is to quantitatively demonstrate that the time required to crack a password increases exponentially with password length for a given source alphabet and attacker, and thereby provide actionable recommendations on password resilience.

A discussion of the physical security risks presented by virtualization technology is included in light of its increasing use in IT environments. This discussion is driven by the concentration of risk associated with virtualization and its wide scale use in data centers. This topic is emblematic of the increasing convergence of information and physical security risks.

Fourier analysis and simple Markov models are applied to security logs in an effort to identify risk factors for information security compromises. These techniques might currently be applied to information security problems but are not particularly well known by security practitioners. Therefore, the contention is they would add value to the suite of existing analytic tools.

A so-called scale-free network is one where the number of links among nodes follows a power law distribution. This model for the distribution of nodes in a network is used to determine the likelihood of viral growth or decay and leads to a metric for resilience to network infections.

Finally, a modestly novel method is presented that is a takeoff on the Monte Carlo method. This has been dubbed "The Probability of Protection" method. Importantly it does *not* predict the likelihood of a future security incident. But it does provide a way of quantifying the likelihood that a security control will be effective. It assumes that a model for the performance of a control can be constructed in terms of risk factors but the precise value of those risk factors is unknown.

METRICS FOR PASSWORD RESILIENCE

For better or worse, passwords remain the most common means of authenticating a user requesting access to an account or resource within a computer system. The consequence of successful authentication is that the authenticated individual inherits the privileges linked to that account.

In modern operating systems, the passwords are kept in a database as a hash value. A hash is a mathematical function, also known as a trap or a one-way function that is applied to the password and assigns a value from which the original password cannot be easily deduced. In addition, there is a one-to-one correspondence between the set of hash values and the set of passwords that have been "hashed." In other words, no two distinct passwords have the same hash value.

MD5 and SHA-1 are common hashing algorithms. The relative benefits of the various hashing algorithms are beyond the scope of this book. But there are many references available because of the importance of hashing to information security.[1]

Two methods for attacking passwords are typically used: dictionary attacks and brute force, and these are often combined. The former consists of creating a list of words, hashing each of them individually, and comparing the output with the hashes. If there is a match, the word from the list is the password. The latter is an extension of this method and consists of trying every possible combination of characters to create words or, more precisely, strings of characters of varying length.

---

[1]A few examples are as follows: (1) Pieprzyk J, Sadeghiyan B. Design of hashing algorithms. In: Lecture notes in computer science. Springer Verlag; 1993; (2) Hoffstein J, Pipher J, Silverman J. An introduction to mathematical cryptography. 2nd ed. Springer; 2014; (3) Smart NP. Cryptography made simple. Springer; 2015.

With the rapid increase in processing speed and the proliferation of Graphical Processing Units (GPU) to perform computations in parallel, the brute-force attack has become an effective means of "cracking" or deciphering passwords. A brief digression on parallel processing as performed by a GPU is provided next. This topic is relevant because enhanced computing power is becoming increasingly accessible to larger segments of the population with attendant risks.[2]

GPUs are multicore machines. For example, the GTX 9800+ (c.2009) consists of 128 cores, where each core is capable of processing a series of instructions. These instructions consist of one 32-bit arithmetic operation per clock cycle. The set of 128 cores is divided into 16 multicores. Each multicore can process eight operations per cycle.

Each of the 16 multicores handles work units, that is, a set of instructions or "threads," in groups of 32. That is, a given multicore issues an instruction to its eight cores over four clock cycles. This instruction represents the initiation of an operation where each operation requires a total of 22 clock cycles. The analogy is that of a wave where the instruction propagates across the cores. Importantly, these "instruction waves" can be launched sequentially, which is one of the ways the system achieves efficiency in processing as described next.

A rhythm of one hundred and twenty-eight 32-bit operations per cycle is maintained so long as there are at least 22 times as many threads available to run, that is, a minimum of 22 clock cycles per operation per core $\times$ 128 cores = 2816 threads, such that the threads can be grouped in packs of 32 identical threads. Each thread executes the same instruction at the same time thereby enhancing efficiency. In practice there are internal thresholds and constraints that require more threads to achieve the optimal bandwidth, up to approximately 4096 threads.

A GPU achieves enhanced performance by using massive parallelism and sometimes involving thousands of cores. This parallelism is accomplished through a process called "pipelining." Each individual operation takes many cycles to run, and, as described earlier, successive operations can be launched in waves while sharing instruction decoding since many cores will run the same instructions at the same time.

For example, a system that utilizes 25 Radeon graphics cards running the Virtual OpenCL cluster platform on 5 Linux servers has been used to crack passwords at unprecedented speeds: 350 billion hashes/s against the ubiquitous Microsoft NTLM algorithm, 63 billion hashes/s against SHA1, and 180 billion hashes/s against MD5. This machine could try every possible Windows password in less than 6 h or in other words 95^8 combinations of passwords in 5.5 h.[3]

If the same Windows passwords are protected by the Microsoft LM (LanMan or LAN Manager) algorithm, which is still used by organizations to ensure backward compatibility with older versions of the operating system, the space of passwords could be cracked in *6 min*.

Although the calculations provided herein and applied to sophisticated attackers do not assume the level of cracking ability associated with such a machine, the increasing accessibility of machines with significant processing power continually moves the goal posts on password resilience.

---

[2]http://security.stackexchange.com/questions/32816/why-are-gpus-so-good-at-cracking-passwords.
[3]Note that typical organizations use passwords of eight-character length, uppercase/lowercase letters, numbers, and symbols as the source alphabet.

Another example of publicly available resources used to crack passwords, is ccl-Hashcat Plus, a free password cracking suite that was running on the aforementioned machine, and has facilitated successful attacks on 44 other algorithms by applying its processing power to dictionary and brute-force attacks. It is available to anyone, and a committed attacker would be expected to be using this tool.

Jean Gobin, a senior engineer at my company, built a custom machine from scratch using a single GPU card that is dedicated to password cracking. It can attempt around 5 billion hash values/s and costs less than $ 5000 to build. The implication is that the technology is within reach of many would-be attackers, perhaps even Script Kiddies, who have the lowest level of sophistication considered in this analysis.

It should also be noted that several vendors, for example, SuperMicro, sell server blades that include GPUs. These servers are more powerful than the one described immediately above, and the estimated cost to build is between 10,000 and 15,000 dollars. The Amazon cloud service offers two types of GPU instances: 2xlarge and 8xlarge. These differ in the number of GPU cards installed, where the former has one and the latter has four. These options reinforce the risk associated with weak passwords since less sophisticated attackers will increasingly have access to more sophisticated cracking resources.

Typically, a password policy will require a minimal password length in addition to mandating at least one uppercase, one lowercase, one digit, and one symbol, that is, a punctuation character or any nonletter and nondigit character present on the keyboard. Let us assume the password policy at an organization is somewhat lax so that the required length is six characters and uses the aforementioned source alphabet.

Calculations confirm that this level of password complexity does not offer sufficient resilience against a hacker with a machine capable of performing 5 billion hash values/s for a given hash algorithm.

Table 13.1 specifies the cracking time required for passwords consisting of a random assortment of characters that were selected from a complex source of characters, that is, uppercase/lowercase letters, numbers, and punctuation marks/symbols such as t^9Q,M$3ka.

This is compared to the time required to crack a more likely construction consisting of one uppercase, followed by several lowercase, a digit, and a symbol, for example, Abnhseuh9! or Password0!.[4] In other words, Table 13.1 compares the time to crack so-called constructed versus random passwords for various password lengths.[5]

Table 13.1 reveals that reducing the information entropy discussed in Chapter 6 leads to a drastic reduction in the time required to crack a given password.[6] For example, for six-character passwords, the cracking time was reduced from nearly 3 min to three-hundredths of a second.

---

[4]Nonrandom choices of password characters increase the predictability, and therefore decrease the entropy of the information source. Password selections are typically not random, and attackers exploit this condition to reduce cracking time. Constructed passwords are considered more likely because of the predictable behavior of humans, which contributes to the vulnerability.

[5]The table and all the following consider the hashing used by Microsoft Windows.

[6]The entropy or Shannon entropy of a message has a strict definition in information theory. Recall this was introduced in Chapter 6. Entropy is a measure of the uncertainty associated with a message source. Recall from the discussion in Chapter 6 the entropy $H = -\sum p_i \log_2(p_i)$ and is measured in bits. So increasing the diversity of the source increases the possible password combinations thereby increasing the entropy.

TABLE 13.1   Time Required to Crack Random Versus Constructed Passwords as a Function of Password Length

Password length	Time required to crack a randomly constructed password	Unit	Time required to crack a nonrandomly constructed password	Unit
6	166.594	Seconds	0.032	Seconds
7	4.489	Hours	0.832	Seconds
8	18.142	Days	21.624	Seconds
9	4.818	Years	9.370	Minutes
10	467.351	Years	4.061	Hours
11	453.331	Centuries	4.399	Days
12	4,397.308	Millennia	114.371	Days
13	426,538.832	Millennia	8.141	Years
14	41,374,266.690	Millennia	211.677	Years
15	4,013,303,868.929	Millennia	55.036	Centuries
16	389,290,475,286.093	Millennia	143.094	Millennia
17	37,761,176,102,751.000	Millennia	3,720.440	Millennia
18	3,662,834,081,966,850.000	Millennia	9,6731.440	Millennia
19	355,294,905,950,784,000.000	Millennia	2,515,017.436	Millennia

The data clearly demonstrates the exponential benefits that accrue from increasing the password length even by modest amounts.

Assume the information technology standard at an organization dictates that the password length must provide resilience from a brute-force attack such that a maximum of 1% of the total password space can be cracked in 90 days. Ninety days is the default period between required password changes in Microsoft Windows. The minimum password length required to satisfy that condition for random passwords is 10 characters. Nonrandom or "constructed" passwords require a minimum of 14 characters to satisfy the same condition.

This disparity in resilience displayed by random versus nonrandomly constructed passwords is illustrated in Fig. 13.1. The vertical axis represents the total size of the password space for a given password length and the horizontal axis represents the password length. Fig. 13.1 specifies the size of the password space as a function of password length for constructed and randomly chosen passwords.

It is important to note that determining password resilience is an inherently statistical process and these numbers indicate the *probability* of finding a given password. There is always a possibility, albeit in some cases infinitesimally small, that an attacker can guess the correct password immediately or after only a few days. The point is that increasing the password space *exponentially* decreases that probability with incremental increases in password length for a given source alphabet.

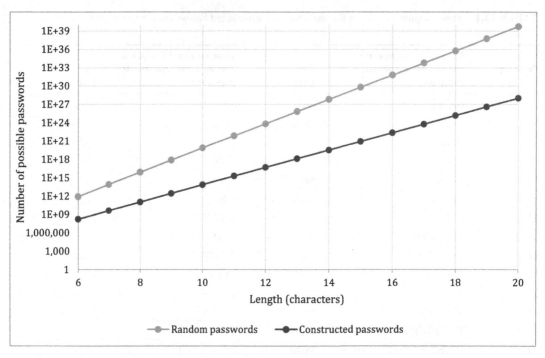

FIGURE 13.1   **Size of password space as a function of password length for random and constructed passwords.**

It is a fact of life that adversaries will have different resources at their disposal in their attempts at password cracking. For example, a Script Kiddy is likely to have limited resources relative to a state-sponsored threat. The latter might have large data centers devoted just to password cracking. The computational power associated with three groups of attackers is estimated in Table 13.2 based on the assumed purchasing power of each group.

Given the appropriate resources, an attacker could process the entire password space defined by a certain password length. Table 13.3 specifies the resilience against cracking for random and constructed passwords relative to these three threats with the computational capabilities assumed previously in Table 13.2.

TABLE 13.2   Estimated Budget and Associated Password Cracking Capability by Threat Type

Threat	Budget ($)	Password cracking capacity (password hashes/s)
Script kiddy	1,000	10^9
Cybercriminal	10,000,000	10^{13}
Nation-state	10,000,000,000	10^{16}

TABLE 13.3 Password Resilience Relative to Password Length and Attacker Type for Randomly Chosen and Constructed Passwords

Password length	Days to crack randomly chosen passwords			Days to crack constructed passwords		
	Script Kiddy	Cybercriminal	Nation-state	Script Kiddy	Cybercriminal	Nation-state
6	0.010	0.000	0.000	0.000	0.000	0.000
7	0.935	0.000	0.000	0.000	0.000	0.000
8	90.711	0.009	0.000	0.000	0.000	0.000
9	8,798.971	0.880	0.001	0.003	0.000	0.000
10	853,500.147	85.350	0.085	0.077	0.000	0.000
11	82,789,514.246	8,278.951	8.279	2.000	0.002	0.000

Note that a password length of six, seven, or eight characters offers limited protection assuming a traditional password change interval of 90 days, even for random passwords. For example, to provide a conservative level of protection against cybercriminals, a password length of at least 11 characters should be chosen assuming completely random password selections. In this case, a cybercriminal could decipher about 1% of the total password space in 90 days. However, given the likely use of constructed passwords, 11-character passwords would provide little protection even against threats possessing limited resources.

Let us define a password to be of sufficient length for adequate protection as before. Namely, a maximum of 1% of the password space could be deciphered by a brute-force attack in less than or equal to 90 days. Table 13.4 shows the length of password that offers that level of resilience relative to the same three threats considered previously. Values in italics indicate adequate resilience based on the aforementioned 1% criterion.

The "Constructed" column could be used as a guide to password length requirements for an organization. The minimum password length required to protect against cybercriminals

TABLE 13.4 Recommended Password Lengths for Specific Threats

Length	Random			Constructed		
	Script Kiddy	Cybercriminal	Nation-state	Script Kiddy	Cybercriminal	Nation-state
12	*80,305,828.819*	*8,030.583*	8.031	0.520	0.001	0.000
13	*7,789,665,395.435*	*778,966.540*	*778.967*	13.517	0.015	0.000
14	*755,597,543,357.185*	*75,559,754.336*	*75,559.754*	351.432	0.387	0.000
15			*7,329,296.171*	*9,137.242*	10.051	0.010
16				*237,568.299*	*261.325*	0.261
17				*6,176,775.777*	*6,794.453*	6.794
18						*176.656*
19						*4,593.050*
20						*119,419.312*

is 16 characters. The minimum password length for nation-states is 18 characters. The caveat here is that the estimate of a government's computational capability is little more than a guess and is likely to be understated.[7]

Adding two characters to the password length is therefore recommended since password constructions such as the consecutive use of uppercase–lowercase–digits–symbols are widely used and can significantly reduce entropy. For this reason, passwords protecting sensitive accounts, for example, access to personal data or privileged accounts, should be at least 20 characters in length based on the aforementioned statistics. The use of passphrases should be encouraged to facilitate memorization.

METRICS FOR NETWORK INFECTIONS: A SCALE-FREE MODEL[8]

Introduction

Computer viruses that propagate via the Internet are an ongoing concern. As noted several times, the computer security literature is chockablock with information on firewalls, virus scanning tools, etc. This book does not address those well-trodden areas. However, there is considerably less information on risk indicators, especially quantitative ones, which presage conditions that are ripe for the growth of network infections.

Given the near-universal dependence on communication via computer networks and the interconnectedness of machines worldwide, the ability to explicitly measure network vulnerability to viruses has been a significant goal of computer security experts. Since the 1960s, there has been increasing attention to problems in network structure and organization. In particular, interest has been generated within the mathematics and physics community aimed at networking theory.

Some of that work has direct applicability to computer networks because of physical models that are applicable to these environments. Specifically, the pattern of machine connectedness that evolves through email traffic lends itself to analysis via mathematical models previously applied to physical problems, and that pattern is believed to have a profound effect on the spread of infections [1].

Scale-Free Networks and Security: Steady-State Network Conditions

The computers of email senders and recipients can be thought of as nodes of a network. These form what is now commonly referred to as a social network. Other examples of social networks include connections between actors as well as the distribution of scientific references in journals. The movie *Six Degrees of Separation* popularized a key characteristic of social networks.

---

[7]The word "reasonable" is admittedly a hedge because the estimate on the computation power available to nation-states is likely low as noted in the text. In addition, Moore's law predicts computation power doubles every 18 months so these figures on the minimum password length should be continuously revised upward.

[8]This discussion closely follows Chang D, Young C. Infection dynamics on the Internet. Computer Security 2005;24(4):280–6.

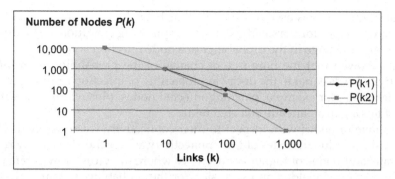

FIGURE 13.2   Scale-free connectivity for two contrived networks.

In social networks, a small number of network members have a large number of connections to fellow members of the network, and a large number of members have a small number of links to fellow members of the network. The topology of networks with this structure is characterized by a so-called scale-free distribution of nodes. In these types of networks, the probability of connectivity $P(k)$ for any node of connectivity k scales as a power law:

$$P(k) = k^{-\gamma} (m < k < k_{\max}) \tag{13.1}$$

Fig. 13.2 shows the probability of node linking in two contrived email networks.

Recall from the discussion on nonlinear functions that the minus sign in the exponent means the function is decreasing and the rate of decrease is greater for increasing values of the exponent γ. So the magnitude of γ determines the steepness of the curve. Typical email networks have been shown to have values of γ between 2 and 4, and in one case a measured value of 1.81 was actually measured [2].

Observe that $P(k_1)$ is less steep, that is, a smaller γ, than $P(k_2)$. Therefore $P(k_1)$ has more nodes with a high number of links, k. The higher number of nodes with more links represents a risk factor for the spread of network infections. What does this condition say quantitatively about the likelihood of infection in the event a computer virus is introduced into the network?

If Person X is in the habit of sending emails to a lot of friends, then clearly the friends of Person X are at risk if he or she becomes infected. In analogy with infectious diseases, the first infected individual is referred to as the index case.

However, if Person Y sends messages only to a few people, the probability that Person Y will infect other network users is lower than it is for Person X. Therefore, the risk of infection by email-borne viruses should be greater for the network node distribution $P(k_1)$ than for $P(k_2)$; the value of γ is an indicator of the risk of infection in the event of a computer virus within a network.

An analysis of the propagation of computer viruses was performed using a so-called "mean field" analysis [1]. Use of the mean field approximation is a form of averaging over many elements of a system and is often used in physics. Viral infections on the Internet were studied and a mean field equation for the time evolution of the probability of viral infection as a function of the nodes connectivity was developed.

Numerical simulation was used to study the time behavior of computer virus propagation and to obtain expressions for the steady-state virus spreading condition. A steady-state condition implies that the change in the probability of a node infection is zero.

The results showed that the time rate of change of the probability of an infected node with connectivity k was equal to the decay in probability of infection resulting from applying network remediation, for example, patching infected nodes, plus a term proportional to the probability of linking to an already-infected node.

A narrow range of nodes with respect to their connectivity was examined. The range of connectivity values included nodes of low connectivity, where the virus decay rate exceeded the growth rate, and nodes of higher connectivity where the virus growth rate exceeded its decay rate. The analysis yielded an expression for the probability Ω that a given node in a scale-free network pointed to an infected node in the steady state:

$$\Omega = \frac{\exp^{-1/\lambda m}}{\lambda m} \tag{13.2}$$

- v is the infection rate of an uninfected node if it is connected to an infected node.
- δ is the remediation rate of infected nodes, that is, the rate of nodes being restored following infection.
- k is the number of connections or links of a node.
- m is the minimum number of nodes available for connection.
- $\lambda = v/\delta$.

One can surmise from (13.2) that zero values of the probability Ω are not permitted for a finite λ. The implication is that a computer virus can reside in a network with finite persistence in sufficiently large networks. In other words, once they have been established, viruses will grow or decay but not remain static under steady-state conditions.

This conclusion contradicted previous work, which supported the belief that viruses died out, that is, exhibited zero persistence, below some threshold infection rate. The explanation for this departure from previous work is that there is an increased statistical likelihood of encountering nodes with higher connectivity in scale-free networks.

However, further analysis of the steady-state condition revealed that a network infection condition can exist under the following conditions[8]:

- When infection growth is larger than infection decay (infection decay implies remediation is applied) for large values of connectivity (k), and when infection growth is smaller than the infection decay for small values of connectivity. The latter case could exist when antivirus software is installed (and that antivirus software recognizes a particular virus!) on end points and expeditious patching has been applied.
- When the infection growth rate is larger than infection decay for all connectivity values. This condition can occur if there are insufficient antivirus controls on end points or remediation in general is lacking.

No steady-state condition is possible when the decay rate is greater than the infection rate for all values of k. Therefore, *a threshold condition does exist for network infection persistence in the steady state, even for a scale-free network.*

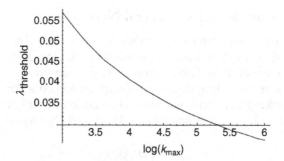

FIGURE 13.3 Variations of threshold with network size.

However, the condition depends on the size of the network through the maximum number of nodes available for connection, k_{max}, and is given by the following expressions:

$$\lambda = \frac{v}{\delta} > \lambda_{threshold} \tag{13.3}$$

and

$$\lambda_{threshold} = m \ln\left(\frac{k_{max}}{m}\right)^{-1}$$

Fig. 13.3 plots the threshold condition for k_{max} (network size) versus $\lambda_{max} = v/\delta$.[8] If $\lambda < \lambda_{max}$, the decay rate exceeds the growth rate and the infection dies out. It should be noted that the logarithmic condition for the threshold dependence applies only for the scaling exponent $\gamma = 3$, considered to be an indicative value for email connectivity.

Fig. 13.4 indicates three regions of virus behavior separated by two curves.[8] Below the lowest curve no persistent infection exists. Between the two curves, infections persist but with smaller probability. The persistence probabilities become vanishingly small as the lower curve is approached. Below the lower curve, there is no persistence in the virus infection.

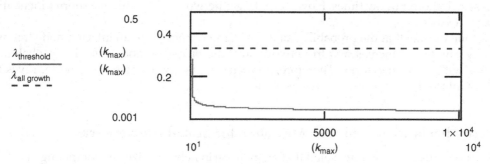

FIGURE 13.4 Boundaries between three regions of virus behavior.

Scale-Free Networks and Security: General Networks

In the previous section, it was determined that persistence of a virus infecting a network is possible for steady-state network conditions. In this section, virus propagation and threshold conditions for the more general case are examined. The assumption is that the virus is introduced into the network at nodes that do not have a specified connectivity.

The probability of linking to an infected node via a node not initially infected can be written in terms of the first and second moments of $P(k)$, D_1 and D_2, respectively:

$$D_1 = \int kP(k)dk \tag{13.4}$$

$$D_2 = \int k^2 P(k)dk \tag{13.5}$$

A general condition for the growth of network infections to a persistent state exists when the following condition holds:

$$\frac{D_2}{D_1} > \frac{1}{v/\delta} = \frac{1}{\lambda} \tag{13.6}$$

Conversely, the condition for nonpersistence of infection is as follows:

$$\frac{D_2}{D_1} < \frac{1}{v/\delta} = \frac{1}{\lambda} \tag{13.7}$$

The probability of infection by nodes that were initially infected continues to grow until it reaches the steady-state condition or persistent value.

It turns out that the size of the network has important security implications with respect to the vulnerability to infection for scale-free networks. (13.7) implies that the larger the network, the lower is the threshold condition for infection persistence. In other words, persistence is easier to achieve for larger networks and therefore a greater vulnerability to infection exists.

For nodes in a narrow range of connectivity that are initially infected, the no-persistence condition will be easier to satisfy for smaller networks than for larger ones since smaller networks have shorter decay times. However, a larger network will result in a shorter incubation time for a virus.

Despite the fact that the probability of a link being connected to an infected node that was initially uninfected increases with network size, the *individual* node infection probabilities *decrease* with larger networks. Therefore, an increase in network size actually improves the odds of infection resilience for a specific node.

Security Implications and Risk Mitigation for Scale-Free Networks

The previous discussion revealed that an increase in network size has competing effects on security. Specifically, the no-persistence condition is easier to satisfy with smaller networks as well as producing shorter infection decay times. But the probability of a particular node being infected actually increases with network size. Infection probabilities are proportional to the node connections that have been previously infected.

Therefore, the most damage is achieved by infecting high-connectivity nodes, which is consistent with intuition. However, if a steady-state condition is achieved, the infection probability is independent of the connectivity of the originally targeted nodes. Adjusting the infection growth and decay rates causes the probability of node infection to change maximally for the highest-connectivity nodes.

The following security conclusions can also be derived from this analysis:

- The larger the network, the lower are the threshold values for λ. In other words, lower threshold values for λ imply it is easier to achieve virus persistence.
- The larger the network exponent γ for a distribution $P(k)$, the higher is the allowable value of λ, that is, the network is more resistant to viral persistence.

The foregoing analysis suggests the following security risk mitigation measures be adopted to enhance resilience to computer infections:

1. Priority quarantine and patch high-connectivity nodes. Other studies have made similar recommendations.
2. Quickly intervene and remediate high-connectivity nodes. Fast action on such nodes will increase the required virus incubation time.
3. Characterize server logs in terms of node connectivity to monitor risk of infection in a targeted fashion.
4. Segment the network according to the number of nodes in a segment.
5. Adopt a network security metric $S = D_1/(D_2\lambda)$. Larger values of S imply an enhanced susceptibility to computer virus infections. In particular, $S = 1$ represents the threshold condition for viral persistence once the virus has been introduced into the network.

METRICS IN FREQUENCY AND TIME: THE FOURIER TRANSFORM[9]

A technique for analyzing periodic functions was briefly introduced in Chapter 3. This technique is known as Fourier analysis and is commonly used in many areas of science and engineering. Fourier analysis involves representing periodic, band-limited functions as a series of sine and cosine functions, and enables representations of data in both the time and frequency domains.

Fig. 13.5 indicates the cosine function, a single pulse, and a pulse train in their respective time and frequency domain representations. These form so-called Fourier transform pairs. Recall each of these had relevance to the discussion of signal compromises in Chapter 7.[10]

---

[9]The author credits Mr. Jean Gobin, Stroz Friedberg, with generating the data and much of the analysis provided in this section.
[10]http://download.ni.com/evaluation/rf/Super_Heterodyne_Signal_Analyzers.pdf.

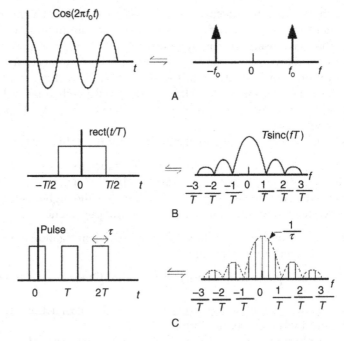

FIGURE 13.5 Representations of a (A) cosine function, (B) a rectangle, and (C) pulses in the time and frequency domains.

What is the relevance of these representations to information security? It is sometimes difficult to appreciate subtle anomalies in data without viewing that data in both the time and frequency domains. Specifically, the security analyst seeks to identify risk factors buried in data relative to specific threats.[11]

For example, firewall logs indicate inbound and outbound network connections to/from external websites. A typical *modus operandi* of malware is to attempt to establish a covert communication channel from an internal network IP address that is commanded and controlled by an external website.

Therefore, a risk factor for malware infection is the appearance of suspicious connections, where the criteria for "suspicious" might include the number of connections, the frequency of connections, the time of day of the connections, and the country associated with the external connection site.

Fourier analysis enables such views, and is a measurement tool that could be leveraged for these types of information security risk analyses. Specifically, Fourier transforms can be applied to firewall log data and thereby view the data in the frequency domain.

---

[11]Note the use of the word "known" in this context. If a method associated with an attack is unknown, then this clearly increases the difficulty of detection since the risk factors would not necessarily be recognized by antivirus software, etc. However, the Fourier transform is particularly useful in revealing risk-relevant behavioral phenomena. Events so detected might reasonably be considered anomalous in any scenario and therefore should be highlighted and investigated as part of an overall network monitoring capability.

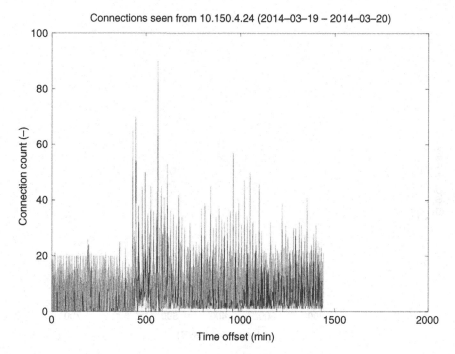

FIGURE 13.6 History of outbound connections for four internal machines as represented in the time domain.

Fig. 13.6 shows outbound connections captured for the following IP addresses within a 2-day interval as represented in the time domain: 10.0.1.104, 10.150.4.24, 10.52.1.21, and 10.150.100.

To reiterate, the mission here is to identify evidence of anomalous outbound connections for an attacker attempting to establish covert command and control over a machine. The data does seem to repeat based on the appearance of peaks signifying the magnitude of connections at specific measurement offset times. Yet the precise nature of these repetitions is difficult to ascertain when the connections are viewed only in the time domain.

However, when the data are converted to the frequency domain, the character of those repetitions becomes readily apparent as shown in Fig. 13.7. Specifically, there are two significant peaks in the connection frequency at approximately 580 per day or once every 2.5 min, and around 290 per day or once every 5 min.

These peaks dominate the spectrum when viewed from this perspective, and would likely be cause for investigation since connection frequencies of this magnitude would be concerning.

This analysis can be used to isolate the connection attempts derived from specific machines and thereby determine the culprit. Fig. 13.8 shows the connection profile for 10.0.1.104 in the time domain.

There do appear to be some connections that repeat. It is noteworthy that this machine was disconnected from the network for about 10 h following the commencement of the measurement period. Fig. 13.9 shows this same data represented in the frequency domain.

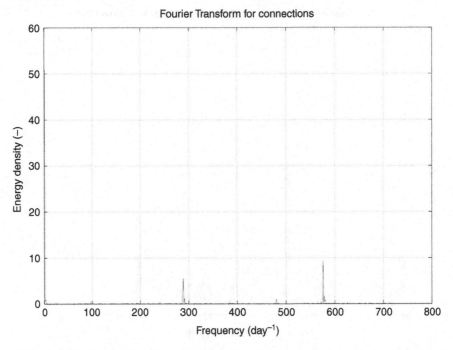

FIGURE 13.7   Outbound connections from four internal machines as represented in the frequency domain.

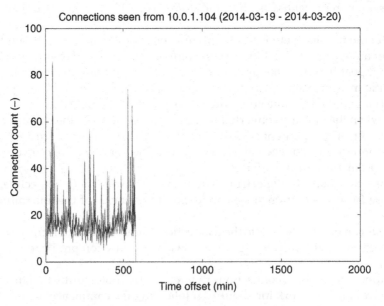

FIGURE 13.8   Time domain representation for connections from 10.0.1.104.

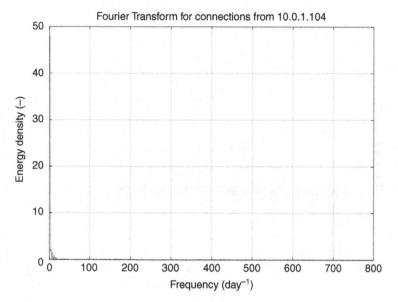

FIGURE 13.9 Connection history for 10.0.1.104 as represented in the frequency domain.

It is clear from this perspective that there is no significant energy concentrated at high frequencies in the spectrum. The presence of energy in that part of the spectrum was not obvious when viewed in the time domain.

The next machine to be evaluated was 10.52.1.21. Fig. 13.10 shows the results in the time domain.

There appears to be an average of 35 connections/min and spikes in the data are immediately apparent in this representation. Moreover, the ratio of the amplitude of the average value to peak value of the signal is quite low, that is, about 1:7 exclusive of the two significant peaks. The ratio never rises above unity.

Therefore, the energy is not concentrated at one particular frequency. Fig. 13.11 confirms this condition. When the peaks corresponding to continuous broadcast energy are removed, no single frequency emerges with significant energy.

The spectrum of 10.150.1.100 is now examined. As usual, the 2-day outbound connection history is first viewed in the time domain. This machine is generating a lot of connections. However, there are a few spikes that appear to dominate all other signals. Fig. 13.12 illustrates the time domain results.

The frequency domain perspective reveals two major spikes at 290 and 190 per day. In addition, a number other spikes exist.

For example, there is a peak at 24 per day. This periodicity suggests that a process is executing at a rate of once per hour. The existence of such a frequency might arouse the suspicion of a curious network security engineer. Figs. 13.13 and 13.14 illustrate these findings in the frequency domain with the continuous frequency component removed and not removed, respectively.

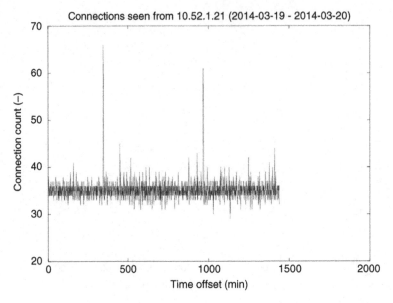

FIGURE 13.10   Time domain representation of outbound connections from 10.52.1.21.

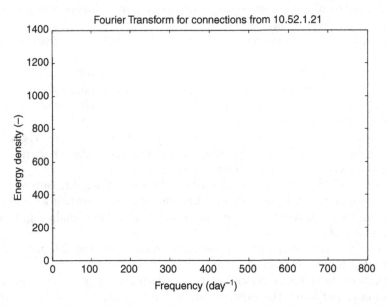

FIGURE 13.11   Outbound connections from 10.52.1.21 as represented in the frequency domain.

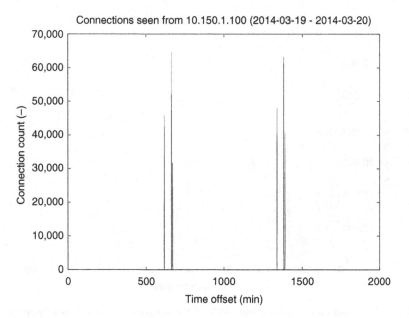

FIGURE 13.12   Time domain representation of outbound connections from 10.150.1.100.

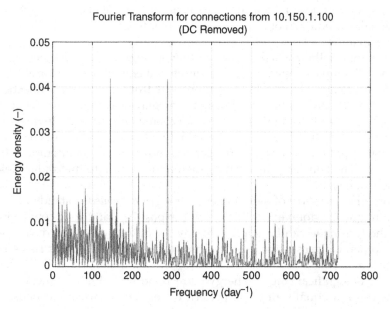

FIGURE 13.13   Outbound connections from 10.50.1.100 as represented in the frequency domain (continuous components removed).

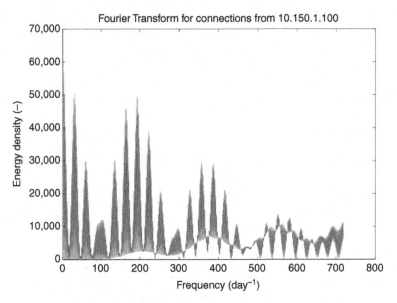

FIGURE 13.14   **All outbound connections from 10.150.1.100 as represented in the frequency domain.**

It is clear from the frequency domain analysis of all four machines that 10.150.1.100 is the most significant communicator. In addition to an abundance of energy at high repetition frequencies, a signal beaconing at once per hour was identified that could reasonably prompt a follow-up investigation.

The power of this method when applied to firewall logs is that machines that repeat connections every "n" minutes appear to have a significant energy despite the absence of a large absolute number of connections. This is not obvious from viewing a connection history in the time domain alone. So in other words, a machine may be communicating only at a rate of once per hour, but it may be doing this every hour thereby producing a frequency peak in the spectrum corresponding to 24 per day. A steady if low-level drumbeat of communications at regular intervals might be the way an attacker communicates in an attempt to fly under the monitoring radar. The Fourier Transform method adds texture to that radar yielding potentially risk-relevant insights.

Furthermore, the accretion of signal energy *at a given frequency* stands out when represented in the frequency domain. In this case, it exposes a pattern of connection attempts. In addition, the technique can be applied to any set of data that records a time history of events. Many other analyses using Fourier Transforms applied to other risk scenarios have been suggested [3].

The existence of significant signal energy corresponding to high-frequency signals might stimulate interest, but equally might a pattern of regular if infrequent ones. A frequency domain analysis of firewall logs will not obviate the need for follow-up to resolve potential false-positives. As always, judgment is required as well as criteria for filtering noise in the data set. The bottom line is that the procedure as outlined here adds another dimension to information security risk analyses.

METRICS TO DETERMINE THE PROBABILITY OF PROTECTION

In Chapter 1 it was stated that there were three components of risk: impact, vulnerability, and likelihood. This book focuses almost exclusively on the vulnerability component. Is it even possible to measure the likelihood component of risk? In other words, one wants to know the probability that a future security incident will occur. Is it possible to make such predictions in the same way meteorologists forecast hurricanes?

As discussed in Chapter 1 and elsewhere, the lack of robust statistical data on incidents represents a significant barrier to this type of metric. Specifically, the absence of stable conditions makes correlations of specific risk factors with security events difficult.

Suppose one could establish a model for the vulnerability to a specific threat. The term model means that a parameter or parameters that affect the magnitude of vulnerability can be identified, which in turn is a function of one or more risk factors. One of the problems in security is that the magnitude of these risk factors is often unknown. One might assume the worst case for a risk factor and plug that value into the expression for the vulnerability parameter. But such an approach is not very subtle, and ideally one would hope to be able to develop a more nuanced view of risk.

Such a view is possible if one assumes one or more of the risk factors are normally distributed random variables or some other probability distribution appropriate to the occasion. More specifically, one might assume that the limits on the probability distribution, which must integrate to unity by definition, are linked to scenario-specific conditions. The vulnerability parameter noted earlier is now characterized in terms of a distribution of risk factor values. In effect, a distribution of risk scenarios has been generated.

If one knows the value of the vulnerability parameter that must be achieved to provide protection against a given threat of concern, that value can now be compared against the normal distribution of vulnerability parameter values. This comparison yields the probability of vulnerability to the threat. In other words, it specifies the probability that the value of the security parameter exceeds the minimum value required to provide protection. Equivalently this metric specifies the probability of protection.

Importantly, this method does "not" say anything about the likelihood of a future threat incident. Moreover, it does not specify that the mitigation method will in fact be effective. There is a presumption of effectiveness, and in the spectrum of possible vulnerability scenarios, it specifies what fraction of those scenarios is successfully addressed by the particular mitigation method. Let us illustrate the technique with the help of some graphics.

Assume a specific security parameter drives the vulnerability component of risk for a given threat. Moreover, this parameter is a function of one or more risk factors, which for physical threats could be distance, time, pressure, etc. Let us further assume one cannot a priori determine the value of this risk factor(s). So by default it is assumed that the risk factor value is a normally distributed random variable.

Furthermore, the limits on this distribution are dictated by scenario-specific conditions. This fact implies that the probability distribution does not extend to plus and minus infinity. Therefore the mathematical nicety of normalizing the distribution is required so that the probability distribution integrates to unity.

Normally distributed random variables are familiar from Chapter 1 and in particular Fig. 1.6. Since in this simplified example the security parameter is a function of a single risk

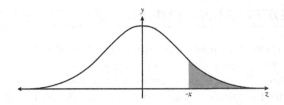

FIGURE 13.15   Normal distribution of (indicative) security parameters and the probability of protection.

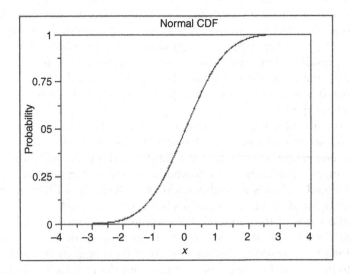

FIGURE 13.16   Cumulative distribution of the security parameter.

factor, the security parameter has been characterized in terms of a normally distributed random variable. Even more impressive is the fact that if the minimum value of the security parameter required to achieve resilience against the threat of concern is known, the probability of protection is also determined.

Fig. 13.15 shows an indicative normal distribution of security parameter values.[12] The shaded portion represents the values of the parameter that do not exceed the minimum value required for protection, x. Therefore the values in the shaded portion of the distribution are those scenarios that remain vulnerable to the threat of concern and the unshaded portion represents the scenarios that are protected.

If the curve in Fig. 13.15 is integrated from the lower limit dictated by the scenario to the beginning of the shaded region x, one arrives at the desired cumulative distribution. The cumulative distribution specifies all values of the parameter that are less than the value required for protection Fig. 13.16 depicts one such cumulative distribution.[13]

[12]http://www2.latech.edu/~schroder/slides/stat/cdf.pdf.
[13]http://www.itl.nist.gov/div898/handbook/eda/section3/eda3661.htm.

It is immediately apparent that this technique is potentially useful in identifying the return on investment for a mitigation method. In this case, the expectation value, that is, the cost of mitigation times the probability of protection, can be determined. The expectation value enables direct comparisons of security controls to yield their comparative value-for-money. In particular, it measures whether the added investment required to achieve incremental protection is justified based on the additional protection it affords, that is, the additional number of scenarios it successfully addresses.

In the first published description of this technique it was applied to the vulnerability to vehicle-borne explosives [4]. In that case the probability of protection afforded by reinforced glass windows was the objective. The overpressure or the pressure in excess of atmospheric pressure, and the impulse, that is, the pressure integrated with respect to time caused by the explosive shock wave, determine the damage to the structures with which it interacts.

The pressure and impulse can each be modeled in terms of two risk factors: the distance between the explosive source and the target structure, and the explosive payload. The distance at which the vehicle detonates its payload cannot be predetermined, but reasonable limits can be established based on scenario-specific conditions. In a similar vein, the explosive payload cannot be known in advance, but practical constraints dictated by concealment and transportation constraints limit an attacker's options.

A given window's performance specification relative to the effect of bomb blasts can be parameterized in terms of overpressure and impulse. Models for overpressure and impulse exist that are functions of two risk factors, distance and payload.

The window specification can therefore be evaluated relative to the distribution of overpressure and impulse values. Normal distributions are used to characterize the possible values of distance and payload that appear as variables in the overpressure and impulse models. From this comparison, the probability of protection is ascertained for a particular window specification. Note that distance and payload are risk factors for the threat of vehicle-borne explosives because they enhance the vulnerability component of risk.

Information security threats are in general more difficult to model than physical security threats. However, one threat that might be amenable to such a model is the denial-of-service attack. Here the flow of packets, a critical vulnerability parameter, is dependent on specific risk factors.[14]

One model that has been posited is briefly considered here. It has been formulated in terms of the total volume of network traffic V. Therefore a possible prescription for applying the Probability of Protection method to ascertain network resilience relative to this threat might be possible [5].

This model incorporates parameters that regulate the amount of packets transferred on each communication link plus the total number of packets transferred during the updating of routing tables. The expression for V in this model is given as follows:

$$V = \frac{T_{sys}}{\Delta t_{sys}} \sum_{i,j=1}^{N} P_i Q_j \qquad (13.8)$$

[14]I credit my colleague, Dr. Chris Briscoe, for the suggestion to apply the Probability of Protection model to DOS/DDOS threats.

where Δt_{sys} is the time of one system clock period; Q_j is the number of packets transferred during one clock period for each channel; N is the number of nodes in the computer network; P_i is the degree of the node that is compromised; T_{sys} is the time to redistribute messages in restoring routes in the event of a topology change for network nodes.

The maximum network capacity can in theory be estimated if the precise values for all the parameters were known. But knowing Q_j would be difficult since it depends on the *modus operandi* of the attacker.

In keeping with the Probability of Protection method, one might assume Q_j and other variables are normally distributed random variables with defined limits, which can be used to establish a distribution for V. More than one normally distributed variable would complicate the mathematics but the basic technique remains unchanged.

If the theoretical limit on V is known, the properties of the normal distribution can be used to ascertain the probability that resilience against a DDoS attack can be achieved for a distribution of values of Q_j. Conversely the method would yield the probability of protection against such an attack for a given Q_j.

Of course, different models will yield different results. The Probability of Protection method is of no help in discriminating good from bad models, and it is not clear into which category (13.8) belongs.

In conclusion, the Probability of Protection method is a relatively simple technique but potential insights on risk derived from its use could be helpful when applied to complex security scenarios. It leverages information on vulnerability to establish the likelihood that a given control provides protection in the event of an incident.[15] One can use these results to make strategic decisions on risk mitigation through a direct comparison of specific controls.

METRICS FOR INTRUSION DETECTION: THE MARKOV PROCESS

Detecting legitimate indicators of network compromise can be a challenging problem. First, attackers intent on intrusion usually do everything possible to remain covert. Complicating matters is that even in a network of modest size there is significant activity, and security logs generate large amounts of data that require significant analytic horsepower to research thoroughly.

Many antivirus packages rely on identifying malicious activity based on signatures of previously identified modes of attack. These work well assuming the attack has been previously identified and reported.

Attacks that have not yet been observed are known as "Zero Day" attacks. Because there is no signature for Zero Day attacks, methods have been developed that are designed to identify anomalous behavior that signifies a risk of infection. Outliers so identified are singled out for potential investigation. Much like insider threats, network intrusion detection is essentially a signal-to-noise problem where there is a lot of noise and often very little signal.

Methods have been adopted from probability theory and combined with pattern recognition to identify anomalous behavior and reduce false-positives. One method of anomaly

---

[15]It is important to reiterate that although a probabilistic statement regarding vulnerability results from this method, it is not equivalent to stating the likelihood of a future threat event.

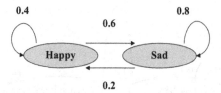

FIGURE 13.17   A simple Markov process.

detection is discussed here, principally because it is well known, and it has been successfully applied to a number of scenarios that include some related to security.[16]

A Markov process is a random process for which the future or in fact the next step depends only on the present state. The process has no memory of how the present state was reached. In more precise terms, for any Markov process, the state of the system at time $t + 1$ depends only on the state of the system at time t. Moreover, transition probabilities, that is, the probability associated with transitions between states, are independent of time.[17] A simple example is as follows.

Assume I can be in one of two states, happy or sad. If I am happy today, the probability that I will be happy tomorrow is somehow determined to be 0.4. Assuming I can exist in only two states, happy and sad, the probability that I will be sad tomorrow if I am happy today must be 0.6 since I am a two-state system and the probabilities of the two states must sum to unity.

On the other hand, if I am sad today, let's say the probability I will be sad tomorrow is 0.8. Therefore, by the same reasoning as before, the probability I will be happy tomorrow if I am sad today is 0.2. The situation is depicted in Fig. 13.17.

The process can be characterized by a transition probability matrix where the rows and columns, p_{ij}, correspond to the probability of going from state i to state j. In this case the transition probability matrix would look as follows, where $P_{i,j}$ specifies the probability of transitioning from state i to state j:

$$P = \left(\begin{array}{cc} P_{11} & P_{12} \\ P_{21} & P_{22} \end{array} \right) = \left(\begin{array}{cc} 0.4 & 0.6 \\ 0.2 & 0.8 \end{array} \right)$$

This general method is now naively applied to identifying anomalous behavior associated with network activity. This is an admittedly simplistic application of the Markov technique, but it is nevertheless illustrative of the general technique.

Suppose one was interested in examining an IT environment for connections to IP addresses that could be indicative of a compromise. Let us assume there is a particular country of concern, and the log activity of a host for outbound connections is to be examined.

It might be quite standard for some hosts to connect to an IP address in China, for example. But for others, sequential connections to that country would be highly unusual and therefore such behavior would warrant follow-up. Recall that attempts to connect to a remote server that is commanding an internal resource are a risk factor for malware.

[16]My colleague, Jean Gobin, applied this technique to security log data in an attempt to detect anomalous outbound connections. I have modified the approach somewhat, although the risk factor is similar, that is, suspicious outbound connections, and the data presented here is completely invented.

[17]This is referred to as the stationary assumption.

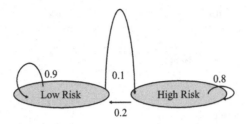

FIGURE 13.18   Transition matrix and associated Markov process.

Suppose the probability of a host connecting to a low-risk IP address immediately following a connection to a low-risk IP address is 0.9. Moreover, the probability of connecting to a high-risk IP address immediately following a connection to a high-risk address is 0.8.

The transition probability matrix and associated Markov process diagram is captured in Fig. 13.18[18]:

$$P = \begin{vmatrix} 0.9 & 0.1 \\ 0.2 & 0.8 \end{vmatrix}$$

Given that a host just connected to a high-risk IP address, that is, the host is in a "high-risk state," what is the probability it will connect to a low-risk IP address two connections hence? This calculation is fairly straightforward, and there are two transition options to consider: (1) the host connects from its high-risk state to a high-risk address followed by a connection to a low-risk address or (2) the host connects from its high-risk state to a low-risk IP address followed by a connection to a low-risk address.

The probability of connecting from a high-risk address to a low-risk IP address is 0.2. The probability of connecting from a low-risk IP address to a low-risk IP address is 0.9. Therefore the joint probability is 0.2 × 0.9 = 0.18. With regard to the second transition option, the probability of connecting to a high-risk address from its high-risk state is 0.8, and the probability of then connecting to a low-risk address is 0.2. The joint probability is 0.8 × 0.2 = 0.16.

Therefore, the total probability of the host connecting to a low-risk state two connections hence is the sum of the two options or 0.18 + 0.16 = 0.34. The transition matrix representation is shown as follows:

$$P^2 = \begin{bmatrix} 0.9 & 0.1 \\ 0.2 & 0.8 \end{bmatrix} \begin{bmatrix} 0.9 & 0.1 \\ 0.2 & 0.8 \end{bmatrix} = \begin{bmatrix} 0.83 & 0.17 \\ 0.34 & 0.66 \end{bmatrix}$$

If the host is currently in a low-risk state, the probability it will connect to a high-risk address in three connections requires another application of the transition probability matrix P as follows, where the sought-after probability is 0.219:

$$P^3 = \begin{bmatrix} 0.9 & 0.1 \\ 0.2 & 0.8 \end{bmatrix} \begin{bmatrix} 0.83 & 0.17 \\ 0.34 & 0.66 \end{bmatrix} = \begin{bmatrix} 0.781 & 0.219 \\ 0.438 & 0.562 \end{bmatrix}$$

[18] An easily understood tutorial on Markov processes can be found at webcourse.cs.technion.ac.il/236522/Spring2007/ho/.../Tutorial05.ppt. The numbers in that tutorial were also used to calculate the examples provided in the text.

As noted earlier, although the example is elementary, it is illustrative of the technique. From a historical record for a specific risk factor such as connection histories, the Markov process can be used to measure the probability of unlikely or anomalous events. For example, an anomaly detection technique has been documented that first develops the normal profile of temporal behavior using a Markov chain model similar to the one described above, learns the Markov chain model from computer log data, and detects anomalies based on the Markov chain model of temporal behavior [6].

The fact that the transition probability matrix and the initial probability distribution of a stationary Markov chain can be learned from the observations of previous system states is notable. The system would be trained to recognize "normal" behavior and flag events that are abnormal based on the probabilities.

The higher the probability, the more likely the sequence of states results from historically normal activities. A sequence of states from intrusive activities is expected to receive a low probability from the Markov model of the profile.

Finally, some of the attributes that could be included in a behavioral model for intrusion detection are listed as follows [7]:

- occurrence of individual events, for example, audit events, system calls, commands, error messages, and IP source address;
- frequency of individual events, for example, number of consecutive password failures;
- duration of individual events, for example, CPU time of a command, and duration of a connection;
- occurrence of multiple events combined through logical operators such as AND, OR, and NOT;
- frequency histogram (distribution) of multiple events, and sequence or transition of events;
- a sequence or transition of events.

SUMMARY

Information technology implementation is one of the principal sources of information security risk factors. Therefore metrics that yield quantitative insights on technology risk are a subject of interest to security professionals. In this chapter various measurements and associated metrics are presented that relate to information technology and information security more generally.

The complexity of passwords is a perennial topic of interest because of their prevalence in authentication, their historic contribution to the vulnerability of information assets, and the frustration exhibited by users when required to enhance password resilience. The risk analysis provided herein contains explicit justification for complexity requirements. Furthermore, it offers recommendations on password length relative to three threat types. A key point is that the benefits of incremental password length accrue exponentially for a given source alphabet.

Specifically, a minimum of 14, 16, and 18 characters is recommended to provide resilience against script kiddies, sophisticated hackers, and state-sponsored adversaries, respectively, assuming the source of characters consists of uppercase and lowercase letters, numbers, and symbols. Significant caveats apply, and added "insurance" of two extra characters in protecting against each attacker type would add exponentially greater resilience that would appear to be prudent given the inherent uncertainties in any such analysis.

Network infections are all-too-common scenarios in IT environments. A so-called scale-free model of network infection is presented, where the network nodes obey an inverse power law corresponding to the distribution of node connectivity. The magnitude of the exponent in the power law conveys quantitative information about the vulnerability of the network to infection.

This analysis unsurprisingly confirms that nodes with the most connections contribute the most to the vulnerability of the network to infection. However, there are competing effects on security with respect to network size such that the risk to the network overall increases for larger networks but actually decreases for specific nodes. Recommendations are provided to reduce the vulnerability of networks to infection, and a threshold condition for viral persistence is specified.

The analysis of security log data also represents an ongoing issue for network security professionals. Although a lack of risk-relevant data would certainly be a problem, an abundance of data presents its own challenges. A well-known technique borrowed from science and engineering is suggested for application to security log data that are captured as a function of time.

This technique is known as Fourier analysis, which mathematically enables representations of periodic information in the time and frequency domains. Here it is applied to firewall logs to show how representing such data in the frequency domain facilitates the identification of risk-relevant features pertaining to outbound connections, and thereby enables insights on the risk associated with known attacks, and in particular malware.

Elementary examples of Markov processes are used to illustrate their utility in identifying risk-relevant network behavior. Specifically, this well-known method is used to highlight anomalous outbound network connections and thereby offers another tool in monitoring IT environments for infection risk factors.

Finally, a novel method to determine the likelihood of the effectiveness of security controls is presented. This is applicable if a threat model is known but the precise values of risk factors within that model are not known or are in fact unknowable. The method involves substituting a probability distribution for one or more risk factors in a threat model to yield the "Probability of Protection." This method is potentially useful in the security risk decision process where the likelihood of the effectiveness of a given control combined with its cost can be quantitatively evaluated against other security countermeasures.

References

[1] Pastor-Satorras R, Vespignani A. Epidemic spreading in scale-free networks. Phys Rev Lett 2001;86:3200.
[2] Ebel H, Mielsch L-I, Bornholdt S. Scale-free topology of e-mail networks. Phys Rev E; 2002;66:035103.
[3] Young C. Periodic behavior and automated money laundering detection. J Money Laundering Control 1994;7(4):295–7.
[4] Chang D, Young C. Probabilistic estimates of vulnerability to explosive overpressures and impulses. J Phys Secur 2010;4(2):10–29.
[5] Shangytbayeva GA, et al. Mathematical model of protection of computer networks against attacks DoS/DDoS. Mod Appl Sci 2015;9(8):106–111. <http://portal.kazntu.kz/files/publicate/2015-06-08-11940_1.pdf>.
[6] Yee N. A Markov chain model of temporal for anomaly detection. In: Proceedings of the 2000 IEEE workshop on information assurance and security, The United States Military Academy, West Point, NY, June 6-7; 2000.
[7] Ye N, et al. Probabilistic techniques for intrusion detection. IEEE Trans Syst Man Cybern 2001;31(4):266–74.

THE PHYSICAL SECURITY
OF INFORMATION ASSETS

Physical Security Controls

INTRODUCTION

In Chapter 1 the physical security of information assets was cited as a principal source of risk factors for the threat of information compromise. Although most security professionals would likely not take issue with increased interaction between physical and IT security entities, it is surprising that these functions are still not well coordinated within most organizations.

It is instructive to be specific about why physical security plays an increasingly crucial role in an information security strategy. First, physical security controls protect against unauthorized physical access to information assets, and unauthorized physical access is a major risk factor for information compromise. The concentration of information is rapidly increasing due to the use of virtualization. Therefore the vulnerability to compromise as well as the potential impact of an individual compromise are increasing.

Second, most physical security technology controls are networked devices and are also Internet Protocol (IP)–enabled. Therefore they are subject to the same threats as other networked devices. The implications are twofold: (1) physical security devices represent attack vectors for the network at large and (2) the vulnerability of the information assets these physical security devices protect is increased.

It is enlightening to see how easy it is to hack modern closed-circuit television (CCTV) cameras. The ease coincides with the public availability of information on hacking these devices. Recall the physical security of information assets was introduced in Chapter 11. In that discussion a botnet infection of CCTV cameras resulting in a successful DDoS attack was recounted. The following simple prescription for hacking CCTV cameras appeared on Facebook[1]:

* Please download the Angry IP Scanner from here http://www.angryip.org/w/Download. This is a simple tool that scans for a range of Live IP Addresses and identifies user specified open ports. (This doesn't require any installation guys. Just download and run it.)

* When you open the tool you can see options to set IP ranges for scanning.

* Just go to Google and Search for your IP Address. You will get your IP address in this links: – www.cmyip.com – www.geobytes.com – www.iplocator.com

* Enter your IP address in the starting field and in the finishing field. This will sure take a lot of time to scan the whole range but will increase the probability of finding more vulnerable cams.

[1]https://www.facebook.com/expertsprogramming/posts/368513023265880

* Next is to specify a Port so that the Angry IP Scanner will ping each IP to find out if that port is open, Go to Tools > Preferences > Ports tab. In Port selection enter the port number you want to scan. I noticed that in my locality most of them are using HIK Vision Digital Video Recorder. This device uses the port 8000. So I'm entered port 8000 in the text box.

* If you want to scan multiple ports you can enter port number separated by commas. After entering the port number go to Display tab. This where you can customize the results displayed. By default All Scanned Hosts will be checked. In this mode all Dead IP will be displayed in Red, Alive in Blue and Open Ports in Green. So I recommend to select Hosts with open ports only so that you need not scroll through the entire ocean of Dead and Alive IPs. Once done click OK.

* Now click on Start button and wait for sometime. If you have selected All Scanned Hosts in Display tab, you would have seen individual IP being scanned and listed.

* If targets are shown. Just right click on the IP Address to copy it.

* Paste the link in the Address Bar of your Internet Explorer and hit Enter. Success!!! It loads the login page. As expected it's the login page of HIK VISION DVR. The reason why we are using IE is that the ActiveX designed to handle these pages can work only with IE. Even in IE sometimes you will have to wait for the prompt to install ActiveX Control for HIK Vision. If your IE blocks the addon, watch this video http://youtu.be/RymqP4uDC9U to enable it. (or Google 'enabling unsigned activex control in IE')

* Here is the trick. Most of the targets after installing their networked DVR, they fail to change their credentials from the default one provided by the manufacturer. So for HIK VISION the default username: admin and the password: 12345

* If you come across a different manufacturer you can just Google the name of the manufacturer with term 'default password' to find out the default credentials.

*Just sharing some of my Movies being Watched now!!! ^^*

The Shed SkatePark 4 cams available around http://120.151.100.155/view/viewer_index.shtml

Villnachen – Aargau – Switzerland 25 cams available around http://91.138.2.129/view/viewer_index.shtml?id=773

6 cams available around GreenHouse Cam http://75.70.54.169:25000/view/viewer_index.shtml

Source : Techno Geek

The Facebook piece highlights several significant vulnerabilities with current CCTV system deployments. Most notable of these is that digital video recorders (DVR), the devices that control CCTV system functionality along with network video recorders (NVR), often operate with their default credentials in place. Moreover, the manufacturer apparently publishes these credentials for global consumption.

The point of sharing this posting is not to tempt the reader into testing his or her hacking skills. Rather it is to highlight the fact that an IT network vulnerability can adversely impact a critical physical security control. Moreover, it is sobering to consider the implications to the information security risk profile of organizations that use Internet-enabled CCTV camera systems or DVRs/NVRs to protect their information assets.

This chapter is devoted to examining high-level *physical security* controls. In some ways these controls mirror those used to prevent unauthorized IT account access, but they also differ in some important respects. In both cases these controls are intended to ensure that only individuals with appropriate privileges can access restricted assets and/or locations.

There are numerous references on physical security technology controls and in particular CCTV systems. The technical details of such controls can be found in cited reference and the fundamental optical principles that govern CCTV functionality such as diffraction, focal length, and field of view are described in Chapters 3 and 9, but many other sources are available [1]. These details are skipped here in favor of understanding the motivation for those controls as they pertain to a comprehensive information security strategy.

Finally, this treatment does not include a detailed analysis of CCTV and physical access restriction technologies, two key physical security controls. Again, many texts provide sufficient details to be conversant in both methods. Moreover, the material presented in Chapter 9 on optical attacks applies equally to CCTV technology, and will provide the reader with the requisite background to understand the fundamentals of CCTV.

There are many technologies that are used to restrict physical access. The specific technology and specification will vary depending on the threat. Detailed analyses of vulnerability to unauthorized physical access yielding quantitative performance metrics for some of the most common methods are provided in another reference for the interested reader [1].

AUTHENTICATING IDENTITY

A prerequisite for managing the risk associated with physical access to restricted space is to authenticate the identity of the individual requesting access. Authentication requires a credential or set of credentials that are uniquely associated with the individual in question. The essential attributes of any authentication process are provided next.

Minimization of Uncertainty

An authentication credential must link the credential owner to the credential with sufficient statistical confidence. A photograph of the credential holder's face is often included on IDs to confirm the identity of the cardholder. A photograph is surely a form of biometric, although it can be less than reliable in this context. Why?

Such photographs can prove difficult in authenticating the identity of the cardholder because of the image quality. Another contributor to ineffective authentication and one that compounds the problem of poor image quality is the fact that those charged with reviewing these pictures are sometimes not sufficiently attentive and/or observant.

More automated and reliable forms of biometric credentials have been developed that rely on sensors linked to computers to minimize uncertainty. It should be noted that uncertainty includes both false acceptance and false rejections. Arguably false acceptance is a more serious security issue since the consequence is unauthorized physical access to restricted space, whereas false rejections will likely result in mere inconvenience.

The level of confidence associated with a particular biometric technique is based on two factors that are incorporated into the performance statistics. The first is the uniqueness of the biometric within the general population, and the second is the capability of the sensor to correctly interpret the distinguishing biometric features.

A biometric system operates in two possible configurations: identification and verification. Identification means the acquired and processed biometric features are compared to all biometric templates stored in the system hoping for a match [2]. In other words, the biometric is presented to a reader and the system searches through its database for a match between the actual biometric and the data stored in the system. This method is typically more processing-intensive depending on the nature of the biometric and the size of the template database.

Verification means that the user registers his/her identity with the system and in the process a biometric feature is scanned. The system compares the previously enrolled reference

TABLE 14.1   Comparison of Biometric Error Rates

Fingerprint	1 in >500
Facial Recognition	No data
Hand Geometry	1 in 500
Speech Recognition	1 in 50
Iris Scan	1 in 131,000
Retinal Scan	1 in 10,000,000
Signature Recognition	1 in 50
Keystroke Recognition	No data
DNA	No data

feature with the feature stored on the ID. If a match occurs, verification is successful. For example, the fingerprint data of a credential owner can be stored on an ID. To implement verification, the system compares the fingerprint stored on the ID against the fingerprint presented by the requester. Verification is typically less complex than identification.

Systems that use a single biometric feature are known as monomodal. When the identification is computed by comparing the matching values between N different biometric features, the system is called multimodal. Multimodal systems are designed to improve the confidence in system accuracy by leveraging the statistical independence of each method.

In other words, if the probability of an error with method one is x, and the probability of an error with method two is y, then the probability that both methods are in error is the product of the probabilities, xy. Since x and y are always less than 1, xy is always less than either x or y by itself.

The most frequently cited biometric features include fingerprint, signature (handwriting), facial geometry, iris recognition, retina scan, hand geometry, vein structure, ear form, voice recognition, DNA matching, odor (human scent), keyboard stroke analysis, and gait comparisons [2]. Table 14.1 compares the error rates (false acceptances and false rejections), for a subset of biometric methods, which reflect their respective uncertainties in performance.[2] Clearly retina scans are the statistical champions according to this reference and as of this writing.

Resistance to Compromise

An important feature of any authentication method is its resistance to compromise. Resistance to compromise is related to the minimization of uncertainty but recognize that these two characteristics are not identical. For example, a method could be statistically robust in terms of the odds of a correct association, but it still could be relatively easy to compromise. This would clearly affect the method's effectiveness over time, and confidence in the one-to-one association between the credential and the credential holder would ultimately degrade.

Multifactor authentication is designed to decrease uncertainty by increasing the resistance to compromise. It decreases uncertainty by combining "something you know" with

---

[2]https://sites.google.com/site/biometricsecuritysolutions/crossover-accuracy.

"something you are or possess." The "something you know" is typically a secret number or Personal Identification Number (PIN) and the "something you are or possess" is a physical ID/card or a biometric. Anyone who has used an Automated Teller Machine (ATM) is quite familiar with multifactor authentication.

Multifactor authentication is not foolproof but it is very effective in thwarting attacks designed to illegitimately access authentication credentials.[3] The theft of an ID is useless to a would-be criminal unless it is paired with the secret number. So the confidence in the validity of the authentication process is high when a valid ID is presented *and* knowledge of the secret number is demonstrated.

But the degree of confidence is based on the assumption that the credential holder is the rightful owner of that credential. That confidence is enhanced when the cardholder enters the correct secret number. Recognize too that such confidence is based on the assumption that the legitimate cardholder has not shared his or her secret number with any other individual.

Uniqueness of Identity

Any method used to authenticate the identity of an individual requesting physical access to restricted areas must ensure uniqueness in linking credentials to credential holders. Authentication features used to ensure uniqueness must persist for as long as access is required.

A trivial example of nonpersistence would be a system that serviced 1,000,000 members but used PINs that contained only 4 digits. In short order PINs must be reused thereby breaking the credential and credential holder uniqueness condition. Another example of a potential persistence transgression is a credential photograph that is no longer recognizable as the legitimate credential holder.

VERIFYING AUTHORIZATION

The identity of an individual requesting physical access might be successfully authenticated but he or she might not possess current access privileges. Although the authorization and authentication controls often go hand-in-hand in a security strategy, they are not identical in terms of their respective validation methods.

Unfortunately the most sophisticated biometric or other mode of authentication reveals nothing about the individual's authorization to enter restricted space. Moreover, in large and complex organizations the authorization can vary considerably depending on the department, connection between departments, and the complexity of department affiliations for employees.

In addition, even for organizations of modest size, an automated physical access control system is required to keep current with dynamic access privilege assignments. Just because Carl Young is a familiar face around the company does not mean his access privileges have

---

[3]We note in passing that multifactor authentication is quite effective at decreasing the risk associated with phishing and spear phishing attacks. These are designed to dupe computer users into submitting their online access credentials, that is, username and password.

Architecture of access control system

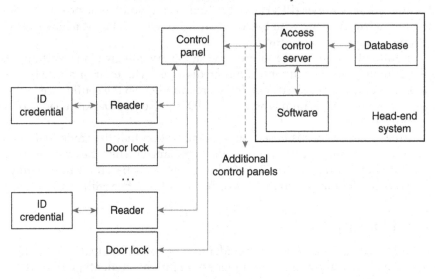

FIGURE 14.1   Physical access control system architecture.

not been revoked that very morning and that the revocation has not been communicated to security personnel tasked with checking IDs.

Therefore, an automated system of authorization is required in order to manage dynamic authorization scenarios. Ideally such a system would consist of credential readers, eg, ID card readers and/or biometric authentication devices, that are linked to a control mechanism with a back-end database of users with privileges linked to their identity.

Fortunately, many such systems exist with varying sophistication. These days they can even be linked to Active Directory to combine physical and electronic access privilege management. A generic physical access control system architecture is depicted in Fig. 14.1.[4]

The database indicated in Fig. 14.1 contains current physical access privilege information relating to the subset of the population authorized to enter a specific physical location. Often a file of specific employees is sent daily via the IT network to a server linked to the relevant set of control panels that is in turn linked to front-end authentication devices.

Two things are clear from this description. First, physical access-related information being sent between the panel and the server must be physically and electronically protected. Various options for secure physical access control system topologies can be found in another reference [1].

Second, the longer the time interval between database updates, the greater is the risk of unauthorized entry. For example, an individual who had been recently fired would maintain his or her privilege to enter restricted areas until the database was updated.

It is important not to assume authentication implies authorization and vice versa. Many organizations allow employees to present an ID credential at the turnstile and mistakenly believe this action satisfies both authentication and authorization control requirements.

[4]http://helpingtext.blogspot.com/2015/03/know-about-access-control-systems-and.html.

It is obvious that without a feature that links a credential to the credential holder there is effectively no authentication of the legitimate cardholder. The individual presenting a credential at a turnstile could have found or stolen the credential. Any individual who uses a valid ID card inherits the access privilege associated with the rightful cardholder.

One can crudely estimate the risk associated with unauthorized entry to restricted space. More precisely, one can assess the likelihood of unauthorized access privilege based on access system enrollment errors. The following is admittedly a very simple statistical model with significant assumptions. However, despite its simplicity, it highlights the complexity associated with physical access administration, and the likelihood of unauthorized physical access if certain operational conditions are assumed.

Using a completely statistical approach to analyze physical access risk admittedly has limitations, particularly for smaller environments. This approach becomes increasingly relevant for more complex physical environments, and this is also where automated enrollment systems add the most value.

Unauthorized physical access to restricted space is a risk factor for numerous threats including information theft. Measuring the frequency of occurrence of a risk factor such as the number of unauthorized physical access incidents, with or without an attendant security incident such as theft, is an indirect measurement of the likelihood of an actual threat incident.

One indicator of risk for both physical and electronic security threats could be the likelihood of an enrollment error in assigning physical access privileges. This would enable unauthorized physical access to one or more restricted spaces recognizing that an individual who gained such privileges in this way might never exploit the opportunity.

As noted earlier, for companies with thousands of employees, maintaining proper access control across disparate groups with varying access privileges can be challenging. A key operational issue is the assignment of appropriate physical access privileges as part of system enrollment. The following definitions and assumptions apply to this simple stochastic model used to evaluate the likelihood of an incorrect assignment of an access role during the enrollment process:

1. *Enrollment errors occur at random* (a critical assumption!).
2. A role is characterized by a unique set of physical access privileges corresponding to specific locations within a facility.
3. There is a unique set of card readers that facilitates physical access to all individuals assigned to that role.
4. Employees are granted physical access privileges based on their assigned role.
5. A physical access incident occurs when an employee is granted a physical access privilege that is not consistent with his or her assigned role and he or she intentionally or unintentionally exploits that error by accessing restricted space.
6. Errors considered here are those where an individual has been assigned an incorrect role and the system grants unauthorized physical access to a restricted space.
7. A card reader that erroneously denies access to a restricted area is not considered to be an error.
8. Each employee must have a role.
9. Each employee can be assigned only one role.
10. Every physically restricted area is protected by a card reader.

If there are N roles in an organization, the probability that a single individual is randomly assigned an incorrect role is $1/(N-1)$.

Note that the denominator is $N-1$ rather than N because one of the N roles is the correct one. In reality, enrollment errors likely do occur as a result of distractions, complexities, and/or miscommunications, although error occurrence is arguably not a random variable.

Note that merely knowing the rate of errors in a physical access enrollment process does not address the risk in this scenario. What is required is the probability that an individual is afforded unauthorized physical access to a restricted area due to an error in the enrollment process. This probability is not precisely equivalent to the probability of an enrollment error as discussed next.

Even though each role is unique and therefore has a correspondingly unique set of card readers linked to that role, some subset of card readers will belong to multiple roles. Therefore, even if an employee has been erroneously assigned a role, some of the card readers that are authorized within the erroneous role could also belong to the correct role. Therefore the employee should legitimately have access to specific restricted areas despite being assigned an erroneous role.

So the actual probability of having unauthorized physical access to a restricted area is given by the probability of being assigned an incorrect role times the fraction of nonauthorized card readers within that erroneous role.

Let N be the total number of roles, T is the total number of card readers, and M is the number of legitimately authorized card readers within an erroneously assigned role. Previously it was explained that the probability of being assigned an incorrect role at random is $1/(N-1)$. The probability of having access to an unauthorized restricted space via a card reader that belongs to that erroneously assigned role is $(T-M)/T$.

Therefore, the probability of being granted unauthorized physical access to a restricted space $p(x)$ equals the probability of being assigned an incorrect role times the probability that there are card readers/restricted areas that the employee should not have access and are related to that erroneous role. That probability is given by the following expression:

$$p(x) = \frac{1}{N-1} \times \frac{T-M}{T} \tag{14.1}$$

Plugging in some numbers, if $N = 100$ roles, $T = 1000$ card readers, and $M = 50$ card readers, the probability of randomly granting unauthorized physical access to an individual at least one card reader is 0.0096 or approximately 1 in 100.

If $N = 1000$ roles, $T = 10,000$ total card readers, and $M = 500$ authorized card readers, $p(x) = 0.001$ or 1 in 1000.

Note that this calculation applies to a single enrollment. What is the probability that at least 1 individual will be granted unauthorized physical access to at least 1 restricted area via a card reader assuming 10,000 enrollments and $p(x) = 0.01$?

That probability is given by $1 - (0.01)^{10,000}$. This number is very close to unity. Therefore the probability of at least one enrollment error is a near certainty with a large number of enrollments. In fact, the larger the number of enrollees, the greater is the probability of an enrollment error across the enterprise. This scenario would also be true if $p(x) = 0.001$.

This model represents a near-worst case scenario. Presumably the enrollment process implemented at an organization has checks in place to ensure such errors do not occur. The worst case relative to the risk of unauthorized access to restricted space would be the intentional misprogramming of the access control system.

To reiterate, this statistical analysis of risk is predicated on the assumptions that an enrollment error is a random variable and unintentional. Intentional enrollment errors are examples of the threat posed by insiders. This is a very different and more vexing security problem, which arguably constitutes the worst case from a security risk perspective.

ASSESSING AFFILIATION

Introduction

Authorized access to a facility or a space within a facility is, at a minimum, predicated on affiliation with the organization that controls that restricted area. Moreover, specific criteria must be established that qualify an individual for the privilege of affiliation with an organization. These should comport with the organization's culture and tolerance for risk.

To cite an extreme example, most organizations with the possible exception of La Cosa Nostra would consider a history of convictions for violent criminal offenses to be a disqualification for employment. Therefore, a felony conviction for murder would typically eliminate one's chances for affiliation with a reputable organization.

Authorized physical access is granted or denied based on an individual's employment status at a given moment in time. So when authorization to pass through a door, turnstile, portal, etc., is granted after presenting a credential to the access control system, successful access implies that the individual who is holding the credential is a member in good standing of the organization at the time of the request.

This process also assumes that the individual presenting a credential is the rightful credential holder. Recognize that such affiliations are ephemeral, and therefore the nature of the affiliation could change over relatively short time scales.

But the previous discussion begs the question of what criteria should be used to determine suitability for affiliation. The decision regarding which criteria are most important and the specific nature of those criteria can be tricky. Ideally, one would use a risk-based approach and thereby determine the criteria that simultaneously reflect the organization's values and those qualities required for successful job performance.

Background Investigations

The privilege of being affiliated with an organization should require passing a background investigation. The theory behind this requirement is twofold: (1) prior behavior is a reasonably good predictor of future behavior and (2) confirming that individuals are who they say they are and have done what they say they have done reduces both security and business risks.

There can be some variation in the criteria for affiliation based on job function, but minimum criteria should be established to determine suitability according to a risk-based standard. The following are discoveries that might disqualify an individual for affiliation if revealed in a preemployment screening program:

- a history of serious criminal activity;
- extreme indebtedness linked to irresponsible behavior;
- lack of permission to work as required by a government;
- erratic, inconsistent, and/or otherwise negative employment history;
- false statements in the application process;
- an inappropriate Internet profile.

In general, investigating criminal history, credit history, and the right to work is less resource intensive than validating employment history. The explanation is that the required information for the former is often accessible via public databases, although this condition might not be true in some jurisdictions outside the United States.

The standard to qualify for organizational affiliation should not be strictly formulaic. Exceptions should be evaluated on a case-by-case basis. Specific standards associated with each criterion, for example, criminal offenses, that are not disqualifiers for employment will be organization-specific, and should be determined through consensus between business leaders, Human Resources, the Legal Department, and security professionals.

Checking credit histories can be controversial and may not even be legal in some jurisdictions. However, there is a correlation between some criminal acts and a history of irresponsible financial behavior. Although one example does not prove the general case, the spy Aldrich Ames claimed that his primary motivation for committing espionage was significant indebtedness. There is evidence to suggest that financial incentives have been a consistent motive in committing espionage, which is the ultimate act of disloyalty [3].

Assessing the risk posed by a history of financial problems is another area where judgment is required. Severe indebtedness because of health care costs is by itself not indicative of irresponsible behavior, but it might tempt people to do dishonest things out of desperation.

In any case, it is preferable to be aware of an issue in advance and thereby make a conscious decision with all the facts prior to a decision on employment. Once an employee is on board, the challenge is to identify an errant insider, which is a far more difficult problem that is discussed in the next section.

With respect to the right to work, a commercial product became available about 10 years ago. It enabled organizations to validate the authenticity of passports issued by many countries. The passport checker application was able to validate certain embedded security features and thereby detect a phony passport.

The right to work in the United Kingdom would clearly be an important criterion for affiliation with companies in that country. The somewhat fluid immigration situation within the European Union resulted in numerous foreign workers seeking employment in the United Kingdom. Confirming the right to work necessitated evaluating the immigration status and associated right to work for individuals from specific countries. This confirmation was predicated on holding a valid passport from those same countries.

Prior to the existence of commercial passport checkers, practical and efficient methods of validating the authenticity of passports were limited if not completely absent. When the method was introduced, Goldman Sachs checked all current contract workers in the United Kingdom.

The result was a not insignificant number of rejects which resulted in termination of employment and notification of the UK authorities.

A candidate's Internet profile is an interesting and evolving risk criterion. Posting inappropriate material on Facebook speaks to issues of judgment at a minimum. Again, part of the decision to hire (or fire) an individual will be based on the organizational culture and tolerance for risk. However, it is worth conducting an exhaustive search of the Internet and viewing online postings prior to employment, and then assess each case individually.

A mentor of mine who was a very senior security figure in the United Kingdom, James A. King, once told me that he would choose a thorough background investigation over bollards any day of the week. Hopefully such a decision would never be required. However, his comment is indicative of the importance of this security control.

The following mantra describes the necessary connection between the elements of a background investigation and the issuance of an ID that confirms organizational affiliation. It is intended to articulate the linkage between an ID and the set of controls that must precede its issuance:

> No physical access will be granted without an ID, no ID will be issued without the creation of identity, no organizational identity will be created without conducting a background investigation, and no background investigations will be complete without criminal, credit and employment-related investigations.

Insider Threats and Affiliation

The preceding sections have focused on criteria needed to qualify for organizational affiliation as well as methods to confirm such criteria. In this case affiliation refers to an official relationship with an organization and the attendant rights and responsibilities that convey with that relationship. The goal of the aforementioned methods is to assess the risk of establishing this relationship *a priori*.

However, such an interpretation is a potentially narrow view of affiliation, especially in the context of security. Individuals who have an official relationship with an organization also maintain a less formal if no less important connection on a personal level. This connection represents a different form of affiliation, and one that may in fact be measurable. Such a version of affiliation relates to feelings of belonging and assimilation manifest by interactions with colleagues, belief in the organizational mission, professional pride, etc.

Alienation resulting in the rejection of affiliation is likely to be a risk factor for information security threats. Moreover, it would be useful to identify individuals who have for one reason or another rejected such an affiliation. That said, it is important to note that most employees will likely fluctuate in their sense of affiliation with anything they love, be it an organization, spouse, religion, etc., and ultimately pose no threat to anyone or anything.

Individuals who experience a more profound alienation and/or are influenced by their personal circumstance are arguably at risk of becoming "insider threats." These are trusted individuals who are predisposed to steal or destroy confidential information to further their own gain and/or hurt the organization. They represent an insidious threat that has historically been very difficult to address.

The theory behind confirming an individual's history with respect to criminal, credit, and employment activities rests on the theory that past and future behaviors are linked. The purpose of a background investigation is to highlight one or more risk factors for bad behavior in advance of employment.

Sometimes these factors constitute an immediate disqualifier. Other times the issue is more nuanced, and involves assessing the likelihood that an applicant will deviate from the straight and narrow after affiliation is granted. The required nuance is amplified if extenuating circumstances exist relative to past indiscretions.

However, once affiliation with an organization is granted, individuals are typically afforded liberal physical and electronic access to internal resources. Their status as full-fledged employees or contractors immediately confers unconditional acceptance and trust. Individuals who develop malicious intent and have been granted physical and/or electronic access privileges are particularly threatening to an organization.

This threat has been a very difficult problem to address as evidenced by the history of successful espionage activity, in both corporate and government settings. Importantly, traditional controls designed to address unauthorized physical access to restricted space have limited effect in addressing insider threats precisely because insiders already have authorized access to enter restricted areas.

Background investigations do not, and probably cannot, identify indicators of a potential for rejecting a personal affiliation with the organization. In addition, conditions change such that an individual can succumb to variable life forces and their behavior changes for the worse. What tools are available to address these scenarios?

One historically unpopular option is to periodically update background investigations. The US government mandates updates for individuals holding security clearances. Such updates constitute a relatively extreme measure due to the expense incurred, especially for a large organization. Also, the organization must be prepared to take action when senior executives are found to have driving while intoxicated (DWI) convictions, delinquent mortgage payments, etc.

There is at least one tool that has been developed specifically to address this problem. It is a commercially available application known as "Scout." It uses psycholinguistic markers present in written communications to indicate risk-relevant behavior. Scout was developed by a former government psychologist, and is based on the results of experiences during interviews as well as scientific research on human behavior.

In the interest of full disclosure, my current employer, Stroz Friedberg, owns the patents on this product and is the only company to market it. It is being presented here because of the lack of viable alternatives in addressing this threat coupled with the scientific principles that underpin its operation. In addition, my company has successfully deployed this software as part of internal investigations. An independent review of Scout and/or a comparison of its effectiveness with other commercial techniques used to identify insider threats is encouraged.

Specifically, the principle behind Scout is based on evidence that an individual's written language changes in predictable ways as a result of his or her emotional state. Moreover, written language of people under stress has specific and predictable characteristics, and people who are about to commit illegal/immoral acts are often under stress. A simple example is multiple uses of the word "I" in certain circumstances. The overuse of this pronoun has been shown to correlate with a particular state of mind, for example, self-righteous indignation, which presages risk-relevant behavior.

Similar linguistic indicators have been identified, and the software has been programmed to examine email traffic from an Exchange server in real time with high processing rates. The spectrum of psycholinguistic markers is identified, weighted, and scored for risk. The publicly available emails associated with the Enron investigation have been used to validate the effectiveness of this method.

However, Scout is not a silver bullet for insider threats; no such silver bullet exists. Clearly many people undergo stress and their language might change or not with little effect on their predisposition to steal information. Its principal value is as a filter in focusing investigative resources. The problem of identifying insider threats is ultimately statistical, where tools that can identify one or more risk factors for insider threats enable the prioritization of investigative resources.

TECHNICAL SURVEILLANCE COUNTERMEASURES

Introduction to TSCM

The vulnerability to information compromise via industrial espionage is a particular concern for companies in highly competitive industries. Competitors are motivated to steal intellectual property in the form of information that would potentially cost millions or even billions of dollars to develop in-house.

Moreover, the threat of insiders or trusted individuals who are authorized to access physical and electronic assets but act maliciously to steal confidential information is a particularly vexing problem. It is exacerbated when companies operate in countries where local governments assist domestic businesses in obtaining information illicitly.

If an intelligence collection device such as an unauthorized audible recorder has been covertly installed in a conference room or any internally restricted area, a breakdown in one or more physical security controls has occurred. Even if it is discovered that an individual who is authorized to access a restricted area is the culprit, something has gone awry in the background investigation process and/or some other internal security control.

Technical Surveillance Countermeasures (TSCM) is a reactive, technology-based control that is intended to backstop other security controls. It is popular with companies concerned about the vulnerability to specific information security threats. These threats are entities that use covert physical surveillance technology to detect, record, and/or transmit confidential at a high level, TSCM is similar to closed circuit television (CCTV) as a control. Both are forms of environmental monitoring although each is monitoring/detecting very different signals.

TSCM enjoys a certain mystique, which has contributed to its allure. Anyone who enjoyed the 1974 movie *The Conversation* is likely to be enamored with TSCM, this author included.[5] After all, it combines the intrigue of espionage with nifty electronic gizmos.

Such gizmos are designed to detect the presence of covert technologies that can capture speech and other signals. The number of confirmed attacks is unknown, so the extent of such activities and their success is difficult to gauge. One such operation that made headlines was the allegation that Air France conducted audio surveillance on its jets to detect conversations between executives of international corporations. The government of France has denied the allegation [4].

---

[5]*The Conversation*, directed by Francis Ford Coppola (1974).

Traditional TSCM

Investigative firms offer TSCM services to clients who are concerned that they might be the focus of an intelligence collection operation. Some of these organizations undergo regular TSCM inspections of their premises. Commercial TSCM practitioners are often advertised as former government employees with relevant experience. TSCM is widely used, yet its capabilities, limitations, and rates of success are not broadly advertised or understood.

Companies sometimes utilize commercial TSCM as the principal means of reducing the vulnerability to corporate espionage. The methods so employed are not subject to testing under controlled conditions and organizations pay handsomely for a service whose historical effectiveness under operational conditions cannot be confirmed.

Unfortunately commercial TSCM is sometimes treated as a perfunctory box to tick in the panoply of security risk mitigation measures. No one wants to be second-guessed if an attack has been exposed and commercial TSCM had not been invoked, notwithstanding the fact that TSCM might not have detected the attack in the first place.

The following questions need to be addressed in order to have confidence in commercial TSCM, or for that matter any security risk management methodology:

1. What is the evidence that commercial TSCM will be effective relative to the attack vectors of concern?
2. Are there alternative inspection methods that might be as effective and/or complement traditional TSCM inspections?

The Effectiveness of TSCM

As noted earlier, it is difficult to accurately gauge the effectiveness of commercial TSCM *in situ*. Reliable statistics on its success are not generally available and some vendors are deliberately fuzzy on this point. It must be noted that TSCM activity is not a regulated industry so in theory anyone can set up shop and start debugging. It is also impractical if not impossible to determine if covert devices were actually missed during an inspection since these have presumably never been discovered.

TSCM can indeed be effective if a targeted strategy is used that accounts for attacker tradecraft, client risks, and the limitations of technology performance based on physical principles.

"Targeted" in this context means that inspection technology is deployed at specific locations and at specified times based on risk to the client. Such a regimen would ideally be complemented by completely random inspections noting that attackers benefit significantly from predictable countermeasures efforts. Lastly, the inspection regimen would incorporate facts about the physical access history to restricted space under inspection plus the physical limitations on the effectiveness of technology imposed by Mother Nature.

One issue that can negate the effectiveness of TSCM is when inspections follow patterns. Whether these are performed at night, on weekends, every 6 months, etc., any hint of regularity constitutes a pattern that can be exploited by an attacker. TSCM vendors are not necessarily at fault here, since corporate executives demand a secure environment but will not tolerate being disturbed or inconvenienced. As a result, only certain inspection times are allowed thereby reducing the uncertainty for an attacker.

An attacker with physical access to sensitive locations and who knows when commercial TSCM inspections will be conducted has a definite advantage. Such knowledge implies that the attacker is aware of when inspections will *not* be conducted. Once an inspection pattern is determined, an attacker could merely remove the device or simply turn it off when the risk of discovery is deemed unacceptably high. A lack of predictability by an inspection team might actually be more concerning to a would-be industrial spy than the specter of sophisticated countersurveillance technology.

It is also important to recognize that a space cannot be considered secure immediately following a TSCM inspection unless physical access to that space is restricted. The inherent insecurity of unrestricted space argues for using commercial TSCM against specific rooms at designated times. For example, Board of Director meetings might qualify for TSCM inspections, but the venue must be physically secured between the time the inspection concludes and the meeting. Ideally the location of the meeting venue would be closely held until just before the meeting occurs.

The good news is that conducting TSCM inspections with sufficient attention to scenario-driven realities, the application of science, a liberal dose of common sense, and the absence of a discernable pattern has the potential to yield operational dividends.

Covert Technology and Operational Risks

Some practical details associated with commercially available surveillance devices are now discussed. The Spy Shop is one well-known purveyor of such devices, although presumably some adversaries have access to more sophisticated technology. Robust transmissions of low-level, radio-frequency signals to remote locations especially in urban areas may appear easy in the movies, but this is not necessarily the case in real life. Moreover, specific operational constraints in a given scenario would likely make the situation more complicated.

For example, radio-frequency signals used to transmit covertly recorded information can be severely attenuated in intrabuilding and interbuilding scenarios. Recall the discussion on the attenuation of electromagnetic signals in Chapter 8. In addition, such signals experience multipath in urban environments due to the presence of multiple reflecting objects.

An attacker would likely be remotely located from the covert device, which in all likelihood would not be broadcasting a strong signal if covertness were the objective. Therefore, an attacker could reasonably be expected to contend with a weak signal-to-noise ratio.

Yet it may not even be necessary for an attacker to resort to radio-frequency transmitters to obtain information being discussed or otherwise communicated within sensitive areas. In fact, a reliance on radio-frequency communications to exfiltrate a covert signal may be operationally and technically ill advised. If an attacker has regular physical access to areas where information is stored, created, and/or discarded, then this opens up a world of opportunities for covert action. In particular, it might obviate the need for deploying technically and operationally risky radio-frequency transmission technologies altogether.

From a technical perspective that has operational implications, broadcasting a radio-frequency signal seems to be an unnecessary risk for the modern industrial spy. The potential for eliminating the use of this technology is due to advances in commercial electronics, and especially electronic storage media and battery technology. Let us examine the specifications

FIGURE 14.2   The Sony PCMD 100.

for a high-end portable recording device that is commercially available and its implications to the execution of a covert attack.

A good example is the Sony PCMD 100. This stereo audio recording device costs about $1000 so it is well within the budget of an organization of any size, and to most individuals as well. It is a high-fidelity device with a frequency response between 20 Hz and 50 kHz or between 20 Hz and 45 kHz depending on the audible format and the sampling rate. Sampling rates between 44.1 and 192 kHz are available. Sixteen-bit Linear Pulse Code Modulation (LPCM), 24-bit Pulse Code Modulation (PCM), or 1-bit Direct Stream Digital (DSD) quantization is also available with a signal-to-noise ratio of 96 or 98 dB.

Importantly, power consumption is 0.75 W and four AA batteries power the device. It is capable of operating for 25 h at the 44.1-kHz sampling rate with 16-bit quantization, 18 h at the 192-kHz sampling rate with 24-bit quantization, or 12 h at 2.8-MHz/1-bit DSD.[6] Each of these specifications would provide full coverage of most meetings.

Device dimensions are 2 ⅞ in × 6 ⅛ in × 1 ¼ in ($w \times h \times d$) so effective concealment would not be trivial. But it is possible if enough preparation time was available and depending on the target room in question. Fig. 14.2 is a photograph of the Sony PCMD 100.[7]

---

[6]Conflicting performance specifications exist on the Internet. For example, sources differed in the recording capabilities for the various modulation formats.

[7]http://www.bhphotovideo.com/c/product/1008089-REG/sony_pcm_d100_portable_stereo_field.html.

The point is that a relatively inexpensive, high-end commercial device is available that could satisfy audio surveillance requirements without resorting to broadcasting a potentially compromising radio-frequency signal. What if a custom device were built with off-the-shelf components? Certainly the cost and expertise would be within the capability of a state-sponsored industrial espionage operation.

Consider the following: widely available memory technology exists in the form of 128-GB flash memory cards, for example, SanDisk UHS I/U3 SDXC Flash Memory Cards. These devices are the size of a matchbook, weigh less than 1 oz, and retail for approximately $95 each, although the price will probably be less by the time you read this book.

Assuming telephone-quality speech is the technical objective along with a 10 kHz audio bandwidth, the Nyquist sampling theorem implies a minimum 20 kHz sampling rate. Let us assume a relatively high-quality device is chosen with 16-bit quantization, a compact disc quality 44.1 kHz sampling rate, and a linear PCM format. These numbers imply an audio storage rate of 705.6×10^3 bits/s or 88.2×10^3 B/s since there are 8 bits to a byte.

Therefore utilizing a single 128-GB memory card could record 16.8 days of continuous speech. If one limits device operation to 8 h/day, this extends the capability to about 50 days. (*Note*: Some covert audible recorders advertised on the Internet record only when activated by speech, thereby saving battery life and memory.) Audio compression would limit the dynamic range, but might extend the record time by a factor of 5–20 or more. Finally, using multiple memory cards would multiply the available memory by the number of cards used.

If image capture is required rather than speech, the storage requirements are more severe. A grayscale image might require 8 bits/pixel. Good resolution and a single frame of 512×512 pixels results in 0.26 MB. A color image would require three times that amount of memory or 0.786 MB because there are three individual color components.[8]

Video is the most data storage-intensive. A high-quality video frame rate is 30 frames/s, although this rate is typically overkill. Informal experiments suggest that anywhere from 5 to 10 frames/s would be adequate to ensure a seamless video experience.

Using the figure cited earlier for the number of pixels per frame yields an estimate of 7.86 MB/s for a black and white image, and 23.6 MB/s for color images. One minute of black and white video requires 472 MB and 1 min of color requires 1.416 GB. Continuing, a 2-h black and white video would require 55.6 GB and the same-length color video would use 170 GB of memory![8]

What about battery life? Let us assume the attacker uses Li-ion batteries with an energy density of 110–160 W h/kg.[9] 3.7-Volt versions are available and rated at 4000 mA h. Using the Sony device as a benchmark, 0.75 W of power consumption is assumed and it operates at 12VDC.

From Ohm's Law, the current drain is calculated to be 0.06 A. The total available current is 4 A h since the four Li-ion batteries are configured in series to achieve the required voltage.

---

[8]Kulkarni S, https://www.princeton.edu/~cuff/ele201/kulkarni_text/information.pdf.
[9]http://batteryuniversity.com/learn/article/whats_the_best_battery.

Therefore our hypothesized device is capable of operating continuously for 4 A-H/ (0.06 A) ~ 67 h or 2.7 days. Features such as voice activation and/or remote on–off capabilities, available in even inexpensive commercial audio surveillance equipment, could extend this figure considerably.

The bottom line is there appears to be little reason to transmit a potentially finicky and less-than-covert electromagnetic signal assuming an attacker has even modest physical access to the target area. Using commercial recording technology or a custom device and periodically dumping the contents of memory would accomplish the intended goal with a lower risk of discovery.

In fact, a colleague once conducted a thought experiment where he imagined a recording device consisting of a microphone, audio and control electronics, 128 Mb memory, and lithium cell power source that was less than 1 mm^3 in volume. The fantasized instrument would provide a full 8 h of sound and would be no bigger in volume than a large grain of salt!

Although it is not realistic to expect that such a device would be commercially available anytime soon, it serves to illustrate the point that broadcasting a radio signal will likely become an increasingly unnecessary risk to an attacker with physical access to sensitive areas.

Scenario-Specific Features Affecting TSCM

A discussion of how radio-frequency signals propagate in and around buildings was provided in Chapter 8. Considerable radio-frequency attenuation should be expected within most buildings and from building-to-building. There is always uncertainty in the link margin for radio-frequency communications over any significant distance unless appreciable signal power is used. Therefore, unless an attacker is willing to broadcast a big signal, which increases the vulnerability to detection as well as increases *in situ* power requirements, the likelihood of a successful broadcast is not assured.

It is important to appreciate that an attacker is subject to the same physical laws as the rest of us. Scenario-specific features will likely affect the required link margin and other risks when planning countermeasures inspections. Such features include the proximity of nearest neighbor buildings, facilities within line-of-sight, the physical location of sensitive areas within a facility, construction materials used in sensitive areas, the frequency of pedestrian traffic in and out of sensitive areas, the proximity to other tenants in the building, etc.

This lesson is sometimes lost on even sophisticated security types:

> Allowing only properly authorized and authenticated individuals to access sensitive areas represents the single most important countermeasure to the threat of information loss.

Proximity to a radiating transmitter significantly reduces the requirement for detection sensitivity by a countermeasures team. An exception to this reduced requirement for signal detection sensitivity at close range occurs when so-called spread spectrum technology is in use. As its name implies, spread spectrum technology is designed to spread the energy over a wide bandwidth, and is used to elude detection and/or improve immunity from interference.

Recall the limits associated with sending information via digital transmission channels dictated by the Shannon–Hartley Law as discussed in Chapter 6. This fundamental law of information theory stated that the encoded communication rate or digital channel capacity, $C = W \log_2[1 + (S/N)]$, where S/N is the linear expression for the signal-to-noise ratio, $\log_2$ is the logarithm in base 2, and W is the channel bandwidth. The units of C are in bits per second. The source of noise is assumed to be White Additive Gaussian noise.

Therefore, the rate of information transfer is dictated by the bandwidth and signal-to-noise ratio of the selected channel. In addition, recall the inverse relationship that exists between bandwidth and signal power for a given channel capacity. Signal covertness can be maintained by reducing power but this must be compensated by increased bandwidth. Table 6.1 illustrated various values of bandwidth versus signal-to-noise ratio for a 1-bit/s channel capacity.

The operational lesson is that it will be less likely to find devices that must transmit high-bandwidth signals via channels that can accommodate only low-frequency transmissions.

The ultimate take-away is that planning a countermeasures strategy must factor in the realities of the physical world. Ultimately it is physics in combination with physical access that dictates what is both possible and practical for any potential attacker. No technology can fool Mother Nature.

Enhancing TSCM Inspection Effectiveness

Allowing physical access to a location where sensitive information is discussed, created, stored, and/or discarded to a less-than-trustworthy individual is a recipe for security problems. It is an obvious risk factor for the theft of physical items and information alike. Common sense dictates that options for concealment grow in proportion to an attacker's unsupervised time on location.

What facts can be leveraged to increase the effectiveness of inspections and what simple methods are available to make life more difficult for an attacker that might attempt to install covert surveillance technology?

Simple visual searches of the premises in conjunction with photography might add value if such searches are conducted frequently and unpredictably. Instruction should be provided on recognizing anomalous features. Of course, careful documentation is also required to recognize subtle changes from inspection-to-inspection.

Unscheduled and frequent inspections by appropriately trained members of the security staff might also act as a deterrent to any potential industrial spy. This form of mitigation could reduce an attacker's confidence that a device can be retrieved or shut down before it is discovered in addition to increasing the chances of catching an attacker in the act.

Inexpensive technology might be leveraged to detect anomalous physical features, especially in countries where traditional commercial TSCM inspection equipment is prohibited, for example, Russia and China. Specifically, commercial stud detectors that can be purchased at a hardware store might be useful in locating hidden and out-of-place objects such as an electronic device concealed in wooden furniture. Readers who are DIY-oriented are probably familiar with such devices.

Stud finders emit a radio-frequency signal to detect dissimilar materials due to the differences in capacitive coupling. The change in capacitance is related to differences in the dielectric constant for different materials.

No special training would be required except to indoctrinate the user on what constitutes an anomalous response and where to focus attention during the inspection. In addition, X-rays of incongruous or entirely new objects could instantly reveal the presence of extraneous and unwanted surprises, although X-ray technology is admittedly more expensive.

The use of poorly shielded cell phones or AM/FM radios to detect the presence of active digital devices might also be useful. Recall the annoying presence of various PDAs (eg, Blackberry) when they are brought in close proximity to some telephones or radios. Portable magnetometers are also an inexpensive option that could detect the presence of anomalous metal objects.

Relatively inexpensive spectrum analyzers or other radio-frequency detection devices could be effective in detecting signals emanating from strange places. If the amplitude mysteriously decreases as you move away from a suspicious location, such a measurement could be a hint that something is awry.

TSCM Revisited

The previous discussion does not imply that standard commercial TSCM inspection equipment cannot be effective when judiciously deployed. For example, nonlinear junction detectors (NLJT) as advertised on the Internet emit a radio-frequency signal and detect the presence of so-called nonlinear electronic components such as diodes.

These are quite useful precisely because they are capable of detecting anomalous features such as the presence of incongruous electronics. Importantly, a hidden device does not have to be powered or radiating to be located using this technique.

There are definitely occasions when sophisticated inspection methods will be required. But equally, value might be achieved by frequent and unscheduled inspections using inexpensive equipment capable of detecting specific anomalous features if used appropriately.

Furthermore, there is inherent value in experimenting with inexpensive and less sophisticated methods. Once a baseline of performance has been established, these can be used as part of an ongoing and unpredictable program of self-inspections. The effectiveness of such methods will improve with regular use and assiduous record keeping. A more focused inspection using traditional techniques could be used to confirm an anomalous finding before tearing the CEO's office apart.

The loss or leakage of information through building design vulnerabilities or by employees who do careless and/or irresponsible things is also a concern. The specter of a compromised conference room was raised in Chapter 1. In that scenario structural building elements conducted acoustic energy to other portions of the building with the potential for information loss. This very scenario was examined in some detail in Chapter 10. The lesson is that a commercial TSCM inspection should identify and report potential channels for information loss such as acoustic pathways.

The existence of a "rogue" local area network is a risk factor for information compromise, intentional or otherwise. Commercial TSCM could be an effective means of identifying such activities since the frequencies of transmission are well known and the signals are anything but covert.

Finally, and on a programmatic level, commercial TSCM inspections should constitute one facet of a comprehensive information security strategy. Such a strategy requires a combination of technical methods, centralized security governance, and training and awareness on threats and risk. The control of physical access to sensitive areas in addition to managing the creation, handling, and destruction of documents and magnetic media represents a key element of an effective information protection program.

SUMMARY

Physical security technologies are used to implement fundamental security controls. These controls include restriction of physical access, environmental monitoring, authentication of identity, verifying access authorization, and assessing affiliation. These controls are central to a comprehensive information security risk management program. Specific security technologies are discussed in this chapter but technical and/or principles of operation are also described in previous chapters as well as other references by this author *et al.*

Authentication of identity is required to confirm that an individual is indeed the person who is authorized to access a particular location. At least three key control features are necessary to ensure the effectiveness of authentication: minimization of uncertainty, resistance to compromise, and sufficient longevity. Technologies used to authenticate identity include biometrics and IDs with photographs.

Robust physical security requires authorization to physically access a restricted space in addition to verifying the identity of an individual so authorized. Access control systems use IDs and card readers on the front end linked to control panels that electronically query a back-end database server. Comparisons are made of the information on the ID with the names of individuals in the database who are authorized to enter restricted space as of the last database update. This argues for frequent database updates over secure communication links.

Affiliation with an organization should be based on satisfying specific criteria. An organization's inability to confirm these criteria is a risk factor for information compromise, etc. Successful passing of a background investigation is a core element of preemployment screening. It is based on the supposition that the nature of past behavior is indicative of the quality of future behavior.

However, affiliation can also relate to an individual's personal identification with an organization, its people, and its principles. Alienation from an organization on a personal level is a risk factor for insider threats. An application exists that measures written linguistic markers that are commonly associated with this form of alienation and/or disgruntlement as well as other precipitators of stress. The name of the application is Scout, and it examines written communications for psycholinguistic risk factors.

Finally, TSCM is a well-known set of technology-based methods that is a form of environmental monitoring and is intended to detect covert surveillance devices. Its effectiveness is difficult to measure but effectiveness likely increases if the technique is judiciously and unpredictably applied. The deployment of low-technology surveillance solutions that complement traditional TSCM measures should be considered. CCTV is the most common form of environmental monitoring that is effective at detecting and deterring risk-relevant incidents.

References

[1] Young C. The science and technology of counterterrorism; measuring physical and electronic security risk. Waltham, MA: Butterworth-Heinemann; 2015.

[2] Gamassi M, et al. Accuracy and performance of biometrics. In: IMTC 2004, instrumentation and measurement conference, Como, Italy, May 18-20; 2004, <http://crema.di.unimi.it/~fscotti/ita/pdf/Scotti14.pdf>.

[3] Herbig M, Wiskoff K. Espionage against the United States by American citizens 1947-2002. Technical report 02-5. Perserec; July 2002.

[4] Air France denies spying on travelers. In: New York Times; September 14, 1991, <http://www.nytimes.com/1991/09/14/news/14iht-spy_.html>.

Data Centers: A Concentration of Information Security Risk

INTRODUCTION

Data centers are facilities that house large numbers of information assets. These can be massive with tremendous power, communications, and cooling requirements. In July 2013, Microsoft estimated it possessed over 1,000,000 servers, although presumably these are not co-located![1]

The rapid rise of virtualization or the ability to run multiple operating systems (OS) on a single physical machine has resulted in exponential increases in server densities within such facilities. Organizations are typically consolidating servers on virtual machines (VMs) at a density of between 4:1 (4 VMs on 1 physical server) and 8:1. This ratio is expected to increase from 10:1 to 20:1 in the near term. With the advent of multicore CPUs, VM densities are expected to approach 50:1 within 2 years.[2]

One implication of this growth is an increase in information security risk due to the greater concentration of information assets. The elevation of risk is driven by the impact of a compromise based on the sheer magnitude of information present on a single machine. Issues inherent to virtualization technology as discussed in this chapter might also affect the vulnerability to compromise.

Data centers often play a critical role in the management of IT infrastructure, and therefore occupy an important place in a security risk management strategy. The ineluctable trend toward Cloud-based resources will drive data center usage for the foreseeable future. Therefore, this final chapter is devoted to discussing data center–related security issues that can affect an organization's security risk profile.

[1]http://www.datacenterknowledge.com/archives/2013/07/15/ballmer-microsoft-has-1-million-servers/.
[2]http://www.cisco.com/c/en/us/solutions/collateral/data-center-virtualization/net_implementation_white_paper0900aecd806a9c05.html.

A (HIGH-LEVEL) DATA CENTER PHYSICAL SECURITY STRATEGY

Chapter 14 identified the most significant physical security controls that should underpin an information security strategy. In this section these controls are examined in the context of data centers. There are essentially two types of data centers: single tenant and multi-tenant. The latter are also known as co-location facilities. The security risk profile for each can be quite different, and therefore facility-specific issues must be addressed as appropriate.

Ensuring effective physical security is maintained in a data center relies on the successful interplay between multiple security controls. These controls are most effective when implemented in a complementary fashion. The benefit of using complementary security controls is actually true for any facility, but the effects are arguably amplified in a data center.

In this analysis, the security strategy of data centers is examined from the vantage of an attacker. A priority for many attackers would be to gain physical access to the IT infrastructure. That infrastructure is most likely protected by physical security technology. As noted in Chapter 14, networked physical security devices can possess electronic vulnerabilities thereby increasing *both* physical and electronic risk.

One of my responsibilities at Goldman Sachs was to develop physical security strategies for data centers in collaboration with IT colleagues. Since these venues housed the proverbial keys to the information kingdom, the first impulse was to embrace the most stringent physical security methods.

Such a strategy typically focuses on extreme perimeter hardening and extensive use of authentication and authorization-type controls to enter restricted internal areas (eg, data fields). Extensive security controls at the perimeter and entrance to data fields are not an incorrect strategy, but it is not obvious that security controls are being applied in proportion to the magnitude of risk. The point is that instead of reflexively applying controls based on an assumption about likely threats, it is necessary to objectively identify such threats and craft a strategy in response. As discussed throughout this book, that approach is the essence of a risk-based security strategy.

For example, one significant attack vector identified by my IT colleagues was the commission of immoral or stupid acts by individuals who were *authorized* for physical entry to the most restricted areas of the data center. Specifically, contractors and vendors with legitimate physical access privileges were responsible for the overwhelming majority of thefts and destruction of property. Historical attempts at unauthorized perimeter and/or data field access and resulting attacks were nonexistent.

The reality is that the most sophisticated biometrics and robust mantraps in the world would have done nothing to address the most significant attack vector. The result of such inquiries offers a valuable lesson on collaboration and the importance of asking customers about the security issues of most concern. This does not mean one should ignore other attack vectors or one's own judgment if it is in direct conflict with the customer. However, customers tend to understand their environments, and their input should always be appreciated if not followed to the letter.

Certainly the perimeter and data fields in data centers must be secured given the impact of a breach at these locations. But the spectrum of threats and associated risk factors should be evaluated relative to each other. Finite resources exist for remediation even at a company like Goldman Sachs. In this case, a rigorous analysis of the spectrum of threats led to the

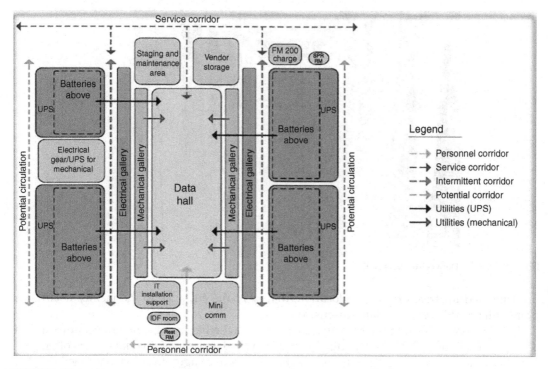

FIGURE 15.1 Indicative data center layout.

selective enhancement of internal security controls in addition to rigorous perimeter and data field defenses.

A digression into the anatomy of data centers is beneficial in order to develop a general physical security strategy. Fig. 15.1 shows an indicative data center internal layout.[3] One of the highest-risk areas is the data field or data hall where servers and other IT infrastructure reside. All other internal areas exist to support the electronic infrastructure located in the data fields.

As noted in the Introduction to this chapter, virtualization is becoming increasingly popular in data centers. This technology results in the consolidation of resources by reducing the number of required physical machines. Changes in the electronic environment have physical security risk implications and exemplify the interrelationship between physical and electronic security risk. The risk associated with physical access to VMs will be discussed later in this chapter.

An effective data center physical security strategy must focus on reducing the vulnerability to unauthorized physical access to the data fields and reducing the vulnerability to malicious or stupid activity by individuals who are authorized to enter the data fields.

Therefore, a logical first step in developing a strategy would be to assess the required security at the entrance to the data fields. However, recognize that the security requirements in this location are impacted by the nature of the authentication and authorization controls

[3]http://fox13now.com/2013/06/06/nsa-data-collection-turns-attention-to-utah-data-center/.

FIGURE 15.2   Data center data field.

implemented upstream from that location, that is, at the entrance to the facility itself. This point will be addressed in a later discussion.

A critical issue affecting the security risk profile is whether a single tenant occupies a data center or if it houses multiple tenants. In multi-tenant data centers, the data fields often consist of individual cages and tenants control their respective cages. In sole-tenant facilities, the data fields are composed of racks containing electronic assets. Anyone with authorized physical access to the data field area has access to all racks, unless these are individually secured. Fig. 15.2 is a photograph of a representative data field.[4]

Requirements for enhancing the internal physical security in the data fields will depend on the physical security at the entrances to the data field and the facility. Other security controls will also influence internal security requirements such as background investigations of contractors and requirements for escorting visitors.

Specifically, physical access to the data fields should ideally require multifactor authentication, such as biometric data stored on a contactless smart card in conjunction with the use of a PIN code. Inbound and outbound card readers linked to an access control system should be installed, and swipe-in and swipe-out requirements enforced. Inbound plus outbound card readers will pinpoint the exact times an individual lingered inside a given area. Authorization to enter the data fields without escort should be predicated on successfully passing a background investigation.

Authentication would be complemented by CCTV surveillance focused at the entrance and activated on motion. The CCTV field of view should cover the entire entrance and the operational requirement for resolution should be facial identification. Chapter 9 discussed the pixel density or the pixels per linear foot specification that applies to megapixel cameras, which is the key technical parameter for measuring resolution. In addition, recall that the camera lens focal length, which enters into the pixel density, and the camera field of view are

[4]http://www.nsf.gov/news/news_summ.jsp?cntn_id=127935.

inversely related. Fig. 9.6 illustrated that concept. Because IP-enabled devices facilitate physical security attack vectors against the network, CCTV cameras on the exterior of the facility should either be analog cameras or at a sufficient height so that they are not physically accessible by the public.

However, one can mandate 10-factor authentication and it would do nothing to address the risk of piggybacking into the data fields. Piggybacking refers to a person authorized to access a facility or an area within a facility who lets another individual enter that space without validating the person's identity and confirming access privilege.

To address this threat, the policy could mandate that authorized individuals challenge those who follow closely behind into the facility or other restricted areas. However, implementing the use of informal challenges is not an effective security control in general. Consider how many times people hold doors open for strangers accessing an ATM machine inside a bank vestibule where the threat is getting robbed!

Most people are inherently polite and nonconfrontational, and it would be a mistake to base a security strategy on inherently countercultural behavior. One should not interpret this as a recommendation against instructing people to politely challenge piggybackers. However, it would be naïve to base a security strategy entirely on this form of security control.

If strict authentication and authorization are performed upstream from the data fields, for example, at the facility entrance, and strict visitor/contractor control is exercised, antipiggybacking measures could be superfluous. However, if entry into the data fields were possible immediately on entering the data center, antipiggybacking measures such as full-height turnstiles at the entrance to the data field would be ideal.

In general, it is possible to manage the risk of unauthorized physical access to the data fields without antipiggybacking technology using compensating security controls. Each case must be evaluated on its own merits relative to the assessed risk, the tolerance for risk, and budgetary constraints.

What compensating controls would be appropriate to reduce the risk of piggybacking or unauthorized access more generally? Authentication and authorization at the data center entrance, escorting of all nonbackground investigated workers/visitors at all times, and pre-registering visitors are a high priority. Locked equipment cabinets or locked and segregated cages inside the data fields of multi-tenant facilities would further reduce the vulnerability associated with unauthorized physical access to the data center or data field entrances.

However, no compensating control will obviate the need for CCTV coverage. Cameras should be installed in each row of the data fields of sole-tenant data centers and ideally within all cages in multi-tenant facilities. Recall that malicious or clumsy individuals were deemed responsible for the vast majority of security incidents at my former employer. It is quite likely this condition is true for most data centers. Deterring and investigating internal risk incidents typically requires the use of recorded CCTV images.

Ideally, authentication and confirmation of authorization for physical access would also be implemented at the entrance to each cage for multi-tenant facilities. Enhanced security would be achieved with an access control system that requires two-factor authentication. The access privilege confirmation process should establish an electronic record of all attempted entries. A card reader linked to a magnetic lock on the cage would serve this purpose. A mechanical lock with strict key control such that key checkout is recorded could suffice but is less than ideal because keys can be copied.

Data centers typically have raised floors to allow for the presence of wires and cables underneath. Because of this configuration, individual cages should extend to the floor slab with ports that allow wires to enter the cage. Such a barrier prevents an individual from crawling into a cage from beneath the raised floor.

In a similar vein, all cages should be enclosed at the top to prevent individuals from gaining unauthorized access by climbing. This may seem like extreme measures, but as Mark Twain presciently remarked, "If you put all your eggs in one basket you had better watch that basket!" This statement represents the essence of effective risk management and should be the mantra for addressing the risk of information loss in data centers.

Although data centers are big business these days, and specifications such as Statement on Standards for Attestation Engagements (SSAE) 16, the successor to Statement on Auditing Standards 70 ("SAS 70"), are intended to provide security standardization, security lapses do occur in facilities that have been rated as secure.

For example, in one instance I observed a magnetic lock leading to the cage area mounted on the insecure side of the door. At another site, cage walls either were insecurely fastened or had no lid. In a number of cases, vendors who had not undergone background investigations had no-escort physical access privileges within the most sensitive areas. Therefore, a particular security designation or compliance with a rating standard does not obviate the requirement for a proper risk assessment.

THE SECURITY OF VIRTUALIZATION

Introduction

The trend in information storage, management, and accessibility is toward the use of Cloud services. Moreover, the use of virtualization by these Cloud services increases the concentration of risk. Although virtualization has definite security benefits, specific vulnerabilities exist and should at least be understood.

In the traditional server architecture, there is one piece of hardware supporting a single instantiation of an OS or application. For example, a corporate email server might be running Windows/Microsoft Exchange. Why is this condition an issue? A software application like Exchange is estimated to use 15% of the processing capacity of a server. This leaves 85% of the processing capacity unused. Virtualization helps to address this inherent inefficiency.

In a virtualized environment, a layer of software known as a hypervisor is inserted between the hardware and the OS. The hypervisor allows for multiple OS/application servers, also called VMs or "guests," to exist on that same physical hardware. This facilitates increased processing capacity of the hardware leading to enhanced resource utilization and efficiency. Fig. 15.3 shows the architecture of a virtual environment.[5]

The hypervisor manages the guest OS access to hardware, for example, CPU, memory, and storage.[6] The hypervisor partitions these resources so that each guest OS can access its own

[5]http://csrc.nist.gov/publications/nistpubs/800-125/SP800-125-final.pdf.
[6]The discussion on security follows arguments provided by the National Institute of Standards and Technology, Scarfone K, Souppaya M, Hoffman P. Guide to security for full virtualization technologies; 2011. NIST special publication 800-125.

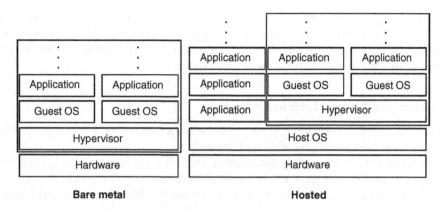

FIGURE 15.3   Full virtualization architecture.

resources but cannot access the other guest OS resources or any resources not allocated for virtualization.

Relevant attack vectors in this context might include infecting a specific guest OS file or inserting malicious code into a guest OS memory. The isolation of guests is one of the principal security benefits of virtualization as it is designed to prevent unauthorized access to resources via partitioning. Virtual configurations also help prevent one guest OS from injecting malware into another. Partitioning can also reduce the threat of denial-of-service (DoS) conditions caused by excess resource consumption by another guest OS that is coresident on the same hypervisor.

Resources may be partitioned physically or logically with attendant security and operational pros and cons. In physical partitioning, the hypervisor assigns separate physical resources to each guest OS. These resources include disk partitions, disk drives, and network interface cards (NIC). Logical partitioning may divide resources on a single host or across multiple hosts.

Such hosts might consist of a collection of resources where each element of the collection would carry equivalent security implications if compromised, that is, an equivalent impact component of risk. Logical partitioning allows multiple guest OSs to share the same physical resources, such as processors and RAM, with the hypervisor controlling access to those resources.

Physical partitioning sets limits on resources for each guest OS because unused capacity from one resource may not be accessed by any other guest OS. The physical separation of resources may provide stronger security and improved performance than logical partitioning. The security risk profile of virtualized machines is strongly dependent on whether physical or logical partitioning is invoked.

As noted earlier, the hypervisor does the heavy lifting in terms of allocating CPU time, etc., across the coresident guest OSs. This configuration requires less hardware to support the same number of application servers. The net result is less money spent on physical servers and supporting hardware as well as the co-location of multiple OSs and applications.

Consider an organization that requires 12 application servers to support its operation. In the traditional model, the organization would purchase 12 physical systems plus associated costs including hardware, OS, and supporting hardware.

If a properly configured virtual server could support 4 application servers, the organization would purchase 3 systems to handle the 12 application servers. The organization would need to purchase the OSs and VMware software, and would probably want to purchase shared storage to leverage other benefits of virtualization.

Virtualization and Physical Security Risk

It is clear that increased efficiency is a by-product of a virtualized environment. However, what are the security implications of virtualization?

Excellent technical reviews of attack vectors targeting virtual technology are available online and are principal sources of information in the following discussion.[7,8]

The focus here will be on VM attack vectors that are facilitated by physical security vulnerabilities or have a physical component. The point is to show how physical security and physical access is relevant to virtualized environments because of the inherent concentration of risk. There are certainly other vulnerabilities inherent to virtual environments that should be understood by information security personnel.[5]

The vulnerability to theft of a physical object from a properly secured data center is likely to be low. It is difficult but not impossible to steal a physical server or other substantial hardware resource from a physically secured data center assuming the spectrum of traditional security controls is implemented.

However, information theft does not require the physical removal of anything these days. VMs are known for their ease of use, and extreme convenience might enhance vulnerability since basic precautions that are routinely implemented on physical machines might be neglected.

This situation appears to be supported by available statistics. It is estimated that 60% of VMs in production might be considered less secure than their physical counterparts as a result of neglecting to use traditional security measures that would likely prevent most attacks on VMs.[9]

The point is that the convenience of VMs contributes to information security risk. For example, there is the potential for a proliferation of disk images, which is a condition known as sprawl. VMs make it trivial to create a new image so unnecessary images may be created and run with attendant physical and electronic security issues. Consider the security implications of a proliferation of images stored on portable flash memory devices. Each new image represents a potential attack vector for information compromise. This scenario is discussed in more detail in the next section.

Compromise of the Virtual Hard Drive and Virtual Files

Physical thefts of information assets can indeed occur in virtual environments. A VM can be encapsulated into a single virtual hard disk (VHD) file. A VHD is a disk image file format for storing the complete contents of a hard drive. The disk image/VMs replicate an

[7]http://www.f5.com/pdf/white-papers/virtual-data-center-security-wp.pdf.
[8]http://www.symantec.com/avcenter/reference/Virtual_Machine_Threats.pdf.
[9]http://www.networkworld.com/news/2010/031510-virtual-server-security.html.

existing hard drive and include all data and structural elements. It can be stored anywhere that the physical host can access so it is easily transportable such as on a USB flash memory device.

An attacker could access a VHD file without entering the data center. He or she could do so by accessing the devices in the host data store. Attackers can access the host with a "Secure Copy" program through client management utilities. Such access would allow an intruder to browse data stores and download files.[10]

It is critical to protect VHD files as part of the information security strategy. Such protection requires three elements:

- limiting access to the host data stores where the VMs reside;
- implementing access logging to know when a breach occurs;
- physically isolating the storage network so that only the storage devices and hosts have access.

Attacks on Backup Repositories and Storage Devices

Another physical attack vector involves access to the backup repositories or network access to VM storage devices. Specifically, an attacker could download the entire virtual disk file from a host to any workstation and copy it to a removable USB storage device. From any secondary location, an attacker could then mount the disk or power on the VM using the same hypervisor software and thereby access the VM contents.

The Holy Grail: Attacks on the Hypervisor

Attacks on the hypervisor through a guest OS consist of using this OS to gain unauthorized access to other VMs or the hypervisor. This scenario is also known as VM escapes or jailbreak attacks since the attacker essentially "escapes" the confinement of the VM into layers that are otherwise unknown to the VM. Such an attack represents one of the more realistic compromises of the hypervisor, since an attacker can often only compromise a VM remotely because the underlying host OS is invisible.[8]

However, since many VMs share the same physical resources, if the attacker can determine how the VM's virtual resources map to physical resources, attacks can be conducted directly on the physical resources. By modifying the virtual memory in a way that exploits how the physical resources are mapped to each VM, the attacker can affect all the VMs, the hypervisor, and potentially other programs on that machine.

The hypervisor is likely to be the principal target on a virtualized machine. Furthermore, attacks on the hypervisor will likely exploit vulnerabilities of the host OS on which the hypervisor runs. In other words, it seems likely that an attack would attempt to exploit the vulnerabilities and security holes inherent to current OSs, and thereby gain control of the host OS as a jumping-off point. Why would such a scenario be likely?

Once the attacker has control of the host OS, the hypervisor is essentially compromised since it is merely a layer running on top of the host OS. The inherent administrative privileges

[10]http://searchservervirtualization.techtarget.com/tip/Virtual-security-New-attack-vectors-new-ballgame.

of the hypervisor will enable the attacker to perform any malicious activities on any of the VMs hosted by the hypervisor.[11]

Physical access controls are required for the hardware on which the virtualization system runs. For example, hosted hypervisors are typically controlled by management software that can be used by anyone with access to the keyboard and mouse. Furthermore, someone who is able to reboot the host computer on which the hypervisor is running could alter some of its security settings. It is also important to secure the external resources that the hypervisor uses, particularly data on hard drives and other storage devices.[6]

Virtual Library Checkout

A large company hosts many virtual servers in its data center. This virtual library of servers consists of all the VMs controlled by the company. Employees check out images of the VMs to perform software upgrades and maintenance on their own machines. Another potential attack that has a physical dimension relates to virtual library checkouts. At a high level, this is when a checked-out VM image becomes infected on another virtual machine monitor (VMM) and is later readmitted to its original virtual library.[12] This type of attack exploits the fact that the guest VMM may not be as secure as the original virtual library.

When the VM image becomes infected on the guest VMM and is readmitted into the virtual library, the infection could potentially spread throughout the entire virtual library as well as to other VMs and hypervisors in the data center or Cloud. The infection dissemination could be accomplished either by using a classic inter-machine communication vector, for example, shared storage and database, or by bouncing off the VMM.

In other words, an attacker entering a VM would infect the VMM and from that point infect all machines on the same hypervisor. The latter attack would be catastrophic since this method bypasses all network security controls.

What does a virtual library checkout precisely mean? A checkout occurs when a VMM fetches a VM's definition and storage from a library and runs it. When the VM is terminated, the VMM copies the definition and storage back to the library. This process allows for the preservation of the state and data of the VM.

Let us consider the following scenario: A VM is stored in a library of VMs. It is moved to an infected VMM where that VM becomes infected. The VM is later readmitted back into the virtual library. From there it can be checked out to another VMM, where it may infect other VMs, which might be stored in other virtual libraries. This process could continue until the entire virtual infrastructure is compromised.

As noted earlier, when the VM image becomes infected on the guest VMM, and is readmitted to the virtual library, the infection could spread through the entire virtual library as well

---

[11]http://www.cse.wustl.edu/~jain/cse571-11/ftp/virtual/#randell.

[12]There are two types of VMMs. A type I VMM is one that runs directly on the hardware without the need of a hosting OS. Type I VMMs are known as "hypervisors." Therefore the difference between a VMM and a hypervisor is determined by where each runs since their functionality is equivalent. A type II VMM is one that runs on top of a host OS and then spawns higher-level VMs. These VMMs monitor their VMs and redirect requests for resource to appropriate APIs in the hosting environment. See http://blogs.msdn.com/b/virtual_pc_guy/archive/2006/07/10/661958.aspx.

as other VMs and hypervisors in the data center. This is an attack that exploits the abuse of implicit trust between the VMM and the VMs.

Therefore, if the VM is not scanned for viruses before being checked-in to the library, it will run "as is" and therefore become a vector for compromises. This is a potentially more significant problem for organizations that utilize a Virtual Desktop Infrastructure since VMs operate as desktops running on personal machines or servers.

Let us consider a related scenario. An attacker hopes to infect a particular VM but lacks direct access to that resource. In an attempt to reach the target, the attacker might infect another VM and instruct the malware to sequentially hop from VM to VMM to VM, etc., as these are repeatedly checked out and checked back in to the library.

In order to implement this attack, he or she gains physical access to an office – not even the data center – and proceeds to check a VM out of the library using a legitimate username and password that has been successfully compromised through phishing.

The attacker then infects the VM now running on a VMM that he or she controls. When the infection is complete, he or she checks the VM back into the virtual library, where it will remain dormant until its legitimate user checks it out. That VM will then infect the VMM being used to run another VM. In fact, any VM run on this VMM will be infected, and the cycle could repeat until the target VM is breached.

Clearly physical access to the employee's machine would facilitate this attack, and, most notably, would not require physical access to the data center thereby emphasizing the importance of physical security controls that protect remote resources.

Migration Attacks

Migration attack vectors are similar to the virtual library checkout attack with one small but important difference: The VM is not stored in a library during its transfer and execution between two VMMs. Instead, the VM is migrated directly between VMMs.

Migration may occur for a variety of reasons to include load balancing and failover. This presents opportunities for information compromise if the migration occurs between machines that are located in less secure environments. In other words, physical and electronic access is available to unauthorized and/or untrustworthy individuals.

Modern VMMs have the ability to globally balance the execution of VMs across several VMMs to avoid depleting a single VMM of its resources. While this represents a significant operational convenience, it also presents a vulnerability as noted earlier.

It should also be noted that the operational objective during migration is to minimize the time a VM is not responsive. Therefore it is migrated while still running. This minimizes the time to conduct security checks prior to resuming operation from its briefly interrupted state. As a result, an infected machine may be migrated to a VMM where it may infect other VMs in operation, in analogy with virtual library checkout scenarios. The net result could be the infection of the entire VM population.

As mentioned earlier, in migration scenarios VMs are moved directly from VMM to VMM, where VMMs are servers. An attacker would have difficulty accessing a VMM directly if he or she does not have the opportunity to check out a VM on his or her own VMM.

However, if the attacker gains physical access to a VMM, he or she might force a migration of all VMs to other VMMs and thereby infect a specific VMM. When this VMM is again available, the centralized manager will detect a VMM with no load, and it will initiate the migration of VMs to it pursuant to its load balancing function. As a consequence, those VMs will become infected, and these in turn may be migrated to other VMMs over time thereby facilitating a widespread infection.

Security Benefits of Virtualization

There are definite security benefits associated with virtualization. Indeed, an attack on a VM would likely require sophistication. Moreover, merely detecting the presence of a VM might be a significant challenge, although some experts believe it to be a difficult but not impossible challenge.[8,13]

Importantly, virtualization allows for the isolation of resources since each guest OS is encapsulated and abstracted from the hardware. Each user accesses separate file systems and memory blocks. In theory, an individual VM compromised by an attacker will not affect the host or other VMs on that host.

Each VM runs without the knowledge of the other VMs controlled by the same hypervisor. Aside from some configurations that allow communication between VMs, if a VM were compromised, it would likely be difficult for an attacker to access other VMs since only the hypervisor knows of their existence.

Cost-effective security can also result from a physical concentration of assets. Most notably, perimeter defenses need to be applied to less numbers of physical machines. Physical security technology costs typically scale with the area required for coverage. So since smaller numbers of physical machines would result from virtualization for an equivalent number of servers, the cost of implementing physical security is reduced. Finally, security appliances can be applied to each VM with software rather than hardware.

Virtualization and Denial-of-Service Attacks

Virtual environments might be attractive to attackers looking to launch a DoS attack. These could be particularly fruitful since such attacks have the potential to consume resources from all VMs on the host.

In VM architecture, the guest machines and the underlying host share physical resources such as CPU, memory disk, and network resource. So it is possible for a rogue guest to initiate a DoS attack against other guests residing within the same system.

A guest machine that consumes all possible system resources would constitute one form of DoS attack in a virtual environment. If such an attack were implemented, the system denies services to other guests that are making request for resources because there is no resource available.[14]

Naively, it would seem that a good approach to prevent a guest from consuming system resources is simply to limit the resources allocated to guest machines. Current virtualization technologies do offer a mechanism to limit the resources allocated to each guest machine in the environment.[15]

---

[13]http://www.cse.wustl.edu/~jain/cse571-09/ftp/vmsec/index.html.
[14]http://www.tml.tkk.fi/Publications/C/25/papers/Reuben_final.pdf.
[15]http://www.cisecurity.org/tools2/vm/CIS_VM_Benchmark_v1.0.pdf.

Although VMs appear to be especially vulnerable to DoS attacks by virtue of their centralized command and control protocol, this vulnerability actually facilitates another security solution: hypervisors can simply prevent any VM from gaining 100% usage of any resource, including CPU, RAM, network bandwidth, and graphics memory.

Additionally, the hypervisor could be configured so that when it detects extreme resource consumption, it evaluates whether an attack is underway and automatically restarts the VM. VMs can usually be initialized much faster than physical machines because their boot sequence does not need to verify hardware.

Physical Theft of Virtual Machines and Virtual Disks

As noted earlier, VMs are not immune to physical theft. The contents of the virtual disk for each VM are usually stored as a file, which can be run by hypervisors on other machines. Therefore attackers could copy the virtual disk and thereby gain unrestricted access to the digital contents of the VM.

It is a useful exercise to think about the security risks associated with a nonbackground-investigated IT technician gaining physical access to a server, and that person is armed with an easily concealed portable flash memory device. The potential consequence of physical attacks places an emphasis on internal security controls in data centers, and, in particular, the use of background investigations as a condition for unescorted privileges. A requirement for stringent background investigations would especially apply to IT workers in multi-tenant facilities.

VMs are inherently not physical, which implies that a physical theft of the host machine is not required to compromise information. To reiterate a point made previously for emphasis, since the contents of the virtual disk for each VM are stored as a file by most hypervisors, VMs can be copied and run from other physical machines. The bottom line is that the need for appropriate internal physical security controls in data centers takes on added significance in light of virtual technology.

Consider the following scenario: A data center is located in a country known to support domestic companies via industrial espionage. The host country has access to internal data center areas via the use of IT technicians hired by the data center. That "insider" could copy the VM to portable storage media and then access this data on their own machine without physically stealing a hard drive.

Once an individual has direct access to the virtual disk, he or she has all the time in the world to defeat security mechanisms. These include the use of standard tools such as password cracking and other offline attacks. Importantly, the attacker is accessing a copy of the VM rather than the original file. Therefore, the VM itself will not show any record of intrusion.

Managing Physical Security Risk in Virtual Environments

The aforementioned discussion emphasizes the need for implementing basic electronic security controls such as the timely installation of patches as well as standard physical security controls applied to data centers. Such controls should include proper background investigations for anyone with unescorted physical access privileges, CCTV coverage of internal data fields and the entrance to those fields, and physical access restrictions to the data center facility, internal data fields, plus individual tenant cages. A significantly more fulsome list of recommended security controls for virtualized environments can be found online.[6]

AN ELECTROMAGNETIC THREAT TO DATA CENTERS

Introduction

In previous sections the vulnerability to information compromise by physical threats against data centers was discussed. In this section a very different threat is considered, although it too has a physical component. Specifically, the threat of a high-amplitude electromagnetic pulse (EMP) that has been detonated in order to damage information assets is analyzed.

As of this writing there is no publicly available evidence to suggest that this threat has been deployed. However, assessing the vulnerability to such threats warrants inclusion in a complete discussion on information security risk. This is based on the potential impact if used against facilities such as data centers that house an increasingly significant number of information assets and in light of global terrorist activity.

One form of pulse generation will be examined: Explosively Pumped Flux Compression Generators (EPFCG). These devices operate by using a conventional explosive to rapidly compress a magnetic field. Maxwell's third equation specifies that the time rate of change of magnetic flux results in electric fields, which in turn generate voltages in conductors. In fact, the collapsing magnetic flux from such an explosion will induce significant voltages in metal objects thousands of feet from the explosive source. EPFCG devices are reportedly capable of producing peak power levels of tens of terawatts (1 TW = 10^{12} W). For reference, the peak power level of a lightning stroke is on the order of 1 TW.

Fig. 15.4 shows the rapid evolution of a magnetic field resulting from the detonation of an EPFCG developed by Los Alamos National Laboratory. (*Note*: The Tesla is a unit of magnetic flux density. 1 T = 1 Wb/m^2 or 10^4 G.[16])

An EPFCG is capable of delivering EMPs that are comparable to those produced by nuclear weapons and lightning strikes. Therefore EPFCGs have the potential to be formidable information security threats.

Consider the scenario where a vehicle detonates an EPFCG in proximity to a data center. On detonation, a powerful EMP is generated that consists of a broad spectrum of frequencies. In theory, an appropriately constructed Faraday cage or a sealed metal box could effectively shield circuits from damaging sources of external electromagnetic energy.

However, electronic devices in data centers require long leads for power and information transfer that preclude complete physical isolation from the external world. As a result, complementary methods are required for an effective mitigation strategy with respect to this threat. Notwithstanding the implementation of these controls, the potential for significant damage exists as detailed later in this section.

---

[16]Mielke, C.H., Los Alamos National Laboratory. Flux Compression Generator.

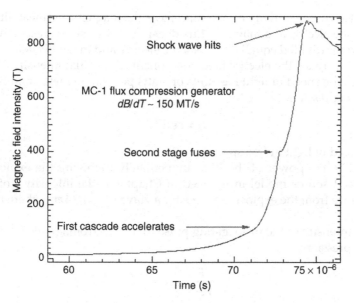

FIGURE 15.4   Time history of the magnetic field resulting from an EMP.

Unshielded Data Centers

In this scenario it is assumed that no electromagnetic shielding exists around servers, routers, and other technical equipment in a data center, and underground cables are not affected by the EMP. Specifically, an EMP generated by an EPFCG directly interacts with the internal circuitry of key electronic components in digital devices. Such circuitry is composed of Metal Oxide Semiconductor (MOS) devices that are sensitive to high-voltage transients.

Power cables and interconnections between electronic circuits will develop electric potentials in response to the changing magnetic flux through induction. This voltage will cause arcing through the insulation that separates the gate from the drain/source elements of field effect transistors (FET). These are the components that make up electronic circuits on computer boards.

The arcing will inevitably result in the breakdown of the device since significant voltage levels would be applied to the gates of the FET, etc. Such devices have maximum operating voltages of about ±20 V. Other electronic components have even smaller breakdown voltages.

Consider an EPFCG that generates 1 TW of electromagnetic power. A rough calculation of the electric field and induced voltage caused by a hypothesized weapon at a distance of 1 km from the pulse source is shown next.

The energy of the pulse is assumed to propagate with equal intensity in all directions. The energy density in free space for electromagnetic fields produced by a dipole charge is given by the following expression:

$$\text{Energy Density} = \frac{1}{2}\left(\varepsilon_o E^2 + \frac{1}{\mu_0} B^2 \right) \qquad (15.1)$$

where ε_o is the electric permittivity of free space, μ_0 is the magnetic permeability of free space, and E and B are the electric and magnetic flux densities in free space, respectively.

The total power is divided equally between the electric and magnetic fields so the intensity can be expressed as twice the electric field component. The initial intensity I_o caused by the pulse traveling at the speed of light has units of watts per square meter, and is thereby equal to the following expression:

$$I_o = c\varepsilon_o E^2 \tag{15.2}$$

where c is the speed of light in free space.

As noted earlier, the power of the EMP immediately following the explosion is 10^{12} W. Based on the point source model introduced in Chapter 3, the intensity I of the EMP as a function of distance from the explosive source for a wave is $I = P/4\pi r^2$, where r is the distance from the source.

Equating the intensity of the propagating pulse to the electromagnetic field density yields the following expression:

$$\frac{P}{4\pi r^2} = c\varepsilon_o E^2 \tag{15.3}$$

The electric field E at a distance of 1 km from the source is now easily calculated. This calculation will yield insight into the effectiveness of physical separation between the device-laden vehicle and the target facility. Note that it might be difficult to establish even 1 km of physical standoff for most facilities in urban areas. Therefore this constraint might strongly affect a risk mitigation strategy that is based exclusively on physical standoff. Moreover, this rough calculation suggests that even this separation distance does not offer sufficient protection.

The distance r is 1 km or 10^3 m. Plugging this value into (15.3) and using $c = 3 \times 10^8$ m/s and $\varepsilon = 8.9 \times 10^{-12}$ F/m, the electric field is calculated to be 5.5×10^3 V/m. Therefore, an internal cable interfaced to a rack of electronics would be vulnerable to kilovolt-level potentials. This greatly exceeds the breakdown voltage of digital circuit components in computers.

Even if this calculation is in error by an order of magnitude, such voltage levels would still exceed the specifications of typical computer electronic components.

Shielded Components in Data Centers

Next it is assumed that the target facility or components within the facility are electromagnetically shielded using a metal enclosure. However, power cables feeding the facility are also factored into this model. In the discussion on shielding in Chapter 8 it was revealed that electromagnetic fields interacting with metal shielding create currents in response to the magnetic and electric field components.

These currents produce fields that cancel the effect of the incident electromagnetic radiation. In this scenario, it is assumed that a Faraday cage has been deployed in order to protect electronics from the effects of externally generated electric fields.

EMP incidents actually occur every day throughout the world. These simulated EPFCG incidents can be used to better understand the effects of a high-amplitude pulse. Namely,

Induced Voltage from a Lightning Strike

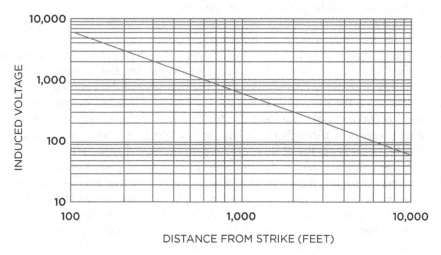

FIGURE 15.5   Induced voltage from a lightning strike.

cloud-to-earth lightning strikes will be examined to gain an appreciation for the effect of an EMPG. A stroke of lightning can produce peak currents ranging from 1000 to 100,000 A with rise times of 1 μs.

Fig. 15.5 shows the induced voltage from a lightning strike as a function of distance from the strike.[17] At 1000 ft. the induced voltage is nearly 1000 V. The intense electric and magnetic fields surrounding a typical 20,000-A lighting strike will induce a voltage of around 2000 V at a distance of 300 ft. in just 3 ft. of wire, and will induce hundreds of volts at a distance of 0.5 mile. Lightning provides a realistic model for the voltages induced by an EMPG.

Despite the presence of shielding, it would be nearly impossible to completely defend against a direct hit by a lighting stroke of this magnitude. An EPFCG source might produce voltages and currents equal to or exceeding those expected from lightning so a similar caveat applies.

As noted earlier in this section, buried cables that lead to and from a data center are vulnerable to an EPFCG attack against an unshielded or shielded facility. Induced voltages on distributed conducting elements are common in lightning scenarios. Experiments have been performed that yield estimates of peak voltages at varying distances from buried cables that supply power to facilities.

In one test, lightning-induced voltages caused by strokes in ground flashes at distances of 5 km (3.1 miles) were measured at both ends of a 448-m, nonenergized power distribution line. The maximum induced voltage was 80 V peak-to-peak [1].

Tens of volts presented to input gates of FET devices would exceed their breakdown voltage. Eighty volts exceeds published operating thresholds, although commercially available surge protection could provide some protection relative to this threat.[18]

---

[17]http://www.surgex.com/library/12001.html.

[18]For example, the drain source voltage and gate source voltage for the BUK7Y12-55B NXP Semiconductor MOSFET are 55 and 20 V, respectively. http://www.nxp.com/documents/application_note/AN11158.pdf.

The point is that shielded devices within data centers are also susceptible to detonated EMP devices because of underground cables that are required for power. The threat posed by an EMP detonated at distances of a few miles from a facility could in theory be mitigated using surge protection and/or isolation transformers.

However, even if it is assumed that electronic devices are contained within shielded enclosures, small openings such as those surrounding wires entering the enclosure will pass electromagnetic energy at wavelengths shorter than the diameter of the opening.

This phenomenon is the same one that allows one to peer inside a microwave oven while electromagnetic radiation cooks the food inside. That is, the shorter wavelengths associated with visible light can pass through the shield, which blocks the longer-wavelength microwaves and therefore prevents the observer from getting cooked along with dinner.

Although information on the bandwidth of EPFCG-derived pulses could not be located, presumably a short-duration pulse could produce energy at wavelengths of a few tenths of 1 mm (microwaves), but this assumption admittedly requires confirmation. These wavelengths are small enough to allow energy to leak into the gap created by wire insulation. The conclusion is that robust electromagnetic shields are required in mitigating this threat, although the effectiveness depends on scenario specifics.

The required standoff distance between an EMP source and a target facility to reduce the risk to manageable levels could be considerable. This conclusion is based on the estimated vulnerability to voltage and current surges generated by direct irradiation and/or electromagnetic signals coupling to underground cables.

A combination of distance, shielding, and surge protection might provide adequate protection against an EMP attack depending on the intensity of the pulse and the distance to the detonated source. A cost–benefit analysis is required to evaluate the potential for such an attack relative to the assessed vulnerability and the cost of risk mitigation.

Standard lightning protection would add value to an anti-EMP strategy. However, a qualified power systems engineer should be consulted to scope the problem for a specific facility as well as to determine the effectiveness of proposed solutions.

SUMMARY

The impact component of risk for information security threats is increasing for data centers due to the high concentration of information stored therein. A high-level physical security strategy based on the security controls introduced in Chapter 14 is presented. These controls include authentication of identity, authorization of physical access privilege, physical access restriction, visitor management, and background investigations.

It has been anecdotally reported that the principal threat to information in data centers derives from individuals who are actually authorized to enter the facility and data fields in particular. Therefore, security controls must effectively address this mode of information loss.

The increasing concentration of risk in data centers is tied to the use of virtual technology. These allow multiple OSs to function within one physical server and therefore promote information density and resource compartmentalization. Physical security–related attack vectors are discussed. These postulated attacks highlight the increased convergence of physical and electronic security risk as well as the relevance of each to a comprehensive information security risk management strategy.

The vulnerability of data centers to high-energy EMPs is analyzed. Although presumably the discharge of a high-amplitude EMP is not a likely threat, the impact to a data center and the information stored therein could be significant if such a threat materialized. The combined use of grounding, shielding, and surge protection could reduce the vulnerability to such threats depending on scenario specifics.

However, a device detonated in close proximity to even shielded devices would likely cause significant damage due to the presence of power cables leading into the facility. These cables would develop tremendous potentials in response to large transients, which would present voltages to the input of electronic devices that would far exceed published breakdown specifications. The physics of lightning strikes provide a natural model for the effects of high-energy EMPs in proximity to data center facilities.

Reference

[1] Schneider K. Lightning and surge protection. Telebyte USA.

Epilogue

Three significant themes emerge from this book, and are therefore worthy of highlighting as follows:

1. A risk-based approach to information security by an organization requires identifying the spectrum of distinct, impactful threats and determining the magnitude of the three components of risk for each of those threats.
2. The vulnerability to a number of information security threats is governed by well-understood physical laws, which should be appreciated in order to develop a comprehensive information security strategy.
3. The root causes of information security risk originate from an organization's culture and and information technology is neither the cause nor the cure for this risk.

Theme number one is fundamental to any rigorous security risk management strategy. Determining the precise threats and attack vectors is the essential first step in that strategy. However, determining what, if anything, an organization should do about it requires an assessment of the impact should the threat materialize, the likelihood that the threat will materialize, and the vulnerability or exposure to information loss as a result of the threat materializing.

In particular, an effective risk management strategy must address the set of risk factors for each threat, which are features or conditions that enhance one or more components of risk. This assessment methodology yields the context that is necessary to articulate the organization's priorities for risk mitigation.

Theme number two is supported by the variety of vulnerability analyses that exist throughout this book. These diverse scenarios range in complexity from the use of a simple telescope to view information displayed on computer monitors and whiteboards or the deployment of commercial microphones to detect airborne and structure-borne speech to sophisticated attacks aimed at detecting electromagnetic signals radiated by computers.

The operational limits for each scenario are dictated by physical phenomena that can be modeled using well-understood Laws of Nature. These limits govern the feasibility of a given attack scenario as well as the effectiveness of countermeasures. Therefore understanding the applicability of these laws can lead to cost-effective and defensible risk mitigation strategies.

Theme number three will be somewhat of an epiphany to many security professionals and they might require some convincing to gain acceptance. The assumption that technology is both the root cause and the exclusive cure for information security vulnerabilities is fairly entrenched. The result is a focus on technical solutions that do not necessarily address the underlying risk issues. The exclusive reliance on such solutions might help explain the recurrence of successful attacks across business sectors despite large investments in information security technology.

Sources of risk factors for information security threats include business operations, security governance, information technology implementation, user behavior, and the physical security of information assets. Metrics are required to measure these risk factors and thereby facilitate inferences on root causes of information security risk. The organizational culture affects each of these risk factors and typically reinforces a philosophy that either endorses convenience or rewards security.

The Divergence and Curl Operators

Maxwell's first two equations appear to be simple but are deceptively profound. These are presented here in integral form but an equally valid representation exists. Namely, one can use a mathematical operator called divergence (div), which turns vectors into scalar quantities by taking the dot product of a differential operator with a vector field.

Chapter 3 described the concept of flux and provided a prescription for calculating the total flux of vector field lines flowing across a surface with a given surface area. Real life typically involves three dimensions so it is useful to expand the scenarios to include calculations involving flux across multiple surfaces, which characterize the source of fields within a volume. The divergence operator is a mathematical construct that enables such calculations.

Some down-to-earth statements on the divergence operator are presented that will help explain the basics of Maxwell's first two equations when written in terms of the divergence operator[1]:

- The symbol for divergence is the upside down triangle for the gradient operator (called del) combined with a dot. The gradient gives the partial derivatives (dx, dy, dz), and the dot product multiplies each component term-by-term and adds the result ($x\,dx + y\,dy + z\,dz$).
- Divergence is the net flux to/from a volume per unit volume.
- Divergence is a single number similar to density.
- Divergence and flux are closely related – if a volume encloses a positive divergence (a source of flux), it will have positive flux.
- Divergence is the rate of flux expansion (positive divergence) or contraction (negative divergence).

In measuring the net flux going through a tiny volume of three-dimensional space, the total flux across each of the x, y, and z dimensions must be measured. Imagine a cube with sides of length dx, dy, and dz. The net flux is measured by examining the following: changes in the X component of flux, changes in the Y component of flux, and changes in the Z component of flux.

If there are no changes, then the result will be the sum of the net fluxes in each direction or $0 + 0 + 0 = 0$. In other words, there is no net flux, and importantly there can be no sources

---

[1]http://betterexplained.com/articles/divergence/

of flux. This last statement has implications to Maxwell's second equation, which states that there are no sources of magnetic charges. Hence, the net flux of a magnetic field across the surface area of any enclosed volume will always be zero.

If there is a change in the vector field through a volume, that is, across the surface area enclosing a volume, a measurement of flux will yield a single number. An example might be if flux is increasing in the X and Z directions but decreasing in the Y direction. The net flux is calculated by adding the results in each direction to yield a single number. This number is the calculated divergence at that point. Note that because the flux across a surface in each of three dimensions is calculated to yield the *net* flux, the flux per unit volume or flux density is what is being measured.

The mathematical representation for divergence is written in terms of partial derivatives, that is, the derivative with respect to one variable with other variables held constant, and is given by the following expression:

$$\text{Divergence} = \frac{\partial F_1}{\partial x} + \frac{\partial F_2}{\partial y} + \frac{\partial F_3}{\partial z} \tag{A.1}$$

F represents a vector field with components F_1, F_2, and F_3 in the X, Y, and Z directions, respectively.

Maxwell's second equation states the following, where div stands for divergence and B is the magnetic flux density:

$$\text{div } B = \nabla \cdot B = 0 \tag{A.2}$$

(A.2) states that there is no net magnetic flux density change and hence no sources of magnetic fields. Said differently, the magnetic equivalent of an electric "charge," also known as a magnetic monopole, does not exist.

The curl of a vector field F is denoted by the following expression:

$$\text{Curl } F = \nabla \times F \tag{A.3}$$

The curl is defined as the infinitesimal area density of the circulation of that field.[2] It is an operation that describes the infinitesimal rotation of a three-dimensional vector field. At every point in the field, the curl of that point is represented by a vector. The attributes of that vector, that is, the length and direction, characterize the rotation at that point.

Quantitatively the curl is written in Cartesian coordinates as follows:

$$\nabla \times F = \left(\frac{\partial F_z}{\partial y} - \frac{\partial F_y}{\partial z}\right)\hat{x} + \left(\frac{\partial F_x}{\partial z} - \frac{\partial F_z}{\partial x}\right)\hat{y} + \left(\frac{\partial F_y}{\partial x} - \frac{\partial F_x}{\partial y}\right)\hat{z}$$

Maxwell's equations in differential form are expressed immediately in the following, where the divergence operator is used in the left side of the first two equations and the curl

[2]https://en.wikipedia.org/wiki/Curl (mathematics).

operator is used in the left side of the last two equations. Both the divergence and the curl operators can be expressed as integrals.

$$\nabla \cdot D = \rho$$
$$\nabla \cdot B = 0$$
$$\nabla \times E = -\frac{\partial B}{\partial t}$$
$$\nabla \times H = J + \frac{\partial D}{\partial t}$$

B

Common Units of Electricity and Magnetism

See Ref. [1].

Quantity	CGS unit	Practical unit (SI)	Relation to CGS unit
Force	Dyne = gm-cm/s^2	Newton	1 N = 10^5 dynes
Work, Energy	Erg = gm-cm^2/s^2	Joule	1 J = 10^7 erg
Power	erg/s	Watt	1 W = 10^7 erg/s
Charge	esu	Coulomb	1 C = 2.998 × 10^9 esu
Charge Density	esu/cm^3		
Current	esu/s	Ampere	1 A = 2.998 × 10^9 esu/s
Current Density	(esu/s)/cm^2		
Electric Potential	statvolt (= erg/esu)	Volt	1 V = (1/2.998) statvolt
Electromotive Force (EMF)	statvolt	Volt	
Electric Field	statvolt/cm	volt/m	(1/29,980) statvolt/cm
Magnetic Field	gauss (= dyne/esu)		
Conductivity	1/s	(ohm-cm)$^{-1}$	
Resistivity	second	ohm-cm	
Resistance	s/cm	Ohm	1 Ω = 1.139 × 10^{-12} s/cm
Magnetic Flux Density	maxwell/m^2	Tesla or Webers/m^2	1 T = 10^4 gauss
Magnetic Flux	gauss-cm^2	Weber	10^8 gauss-cm^2

Reference

[1] Purcell EM. Electricity and magnetism. Berkeley physics course, vol. 2. New York: McGraw-Hill; 1965.

APPENDIX

C

Capacitive and Inductive Coupling in Circuits

There is a capacitance between any two conductors separated by a dielectric, that is, an insulator. The capacitance is a geometric factor that represents a constant of proportionality between the net electric charge in a configuration and the resulting potential.

Specifically, $Q = CV$, where Q is total charge, C is capacitance, and V is voltage; if there is a change in the voltage on one conductor dV/dt, there will be a change in the charge on the other conductor. Therefore a displacement current will flow in the dielectric. A displacement current is a change in the electric flux with time.

According to Maxwell's equations, a displacement current (and/or conduction current) gives rise to a magnetic field. For example, a 1-V/ns rate of change gives rise to displacement currents of 1 mA/pF. Capacitive coupling between circuit elements is one of four mechanisms that result in noise and possible EMI.

Let us calculate the displacement current for a simple, parallel plate capacitor. In this case the area of the plates is A and the separation between the plates is d. Fig. C.1 depicts the capacitor and its dimensions.[1]

As stated earlier $Q = CV$. Therefore differentiating both sides yields the following:

$$i_{\text{disp}} = \frac{dQ}{dt} = C\left(\frac{dV}{dt}\right)$$

where dQ/dt is the change in the charge with respect to time, which is the displacement current across the capacitor. It is clear that the displacement current is directly proportional to capacitance.

Now the capacitance of a parallel plate capacitor is given by $C = \varepsilon A/d$. Therefore substituting this value of C into the expression for i_{disp} yields the following:

$$i_{\text{disp}} = \left(\frac{\varepsilon A}{d}\right)\frac{dV}{dt}$$

[1]http://hyperphysics.phy-astr.gsu.edu/hbase/electric/pplate.html

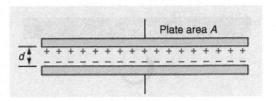

FIGURE C.1 A parallel plate capacitor.

In addition, the electric field E is by definition the voltage divided by distance or $E = V/d$. So by direct substitution the following is true:

$$\frac{dV}{dt} = d\left(\frac{dE}{dt}\right)$$

Therefore the following is the final expression for the displacement current flowing across the capacitor:

$$i_{\text{disp}} = \left(\frac{\varepsilon A}{d}\right) d\left(\frac{dE}{dt}\right) = \varepsilon A\left(\frac{dE}{dt}\right) \tag{C.1}$$

Capacitively coupled noise may be reduced by increasing the conductor separation d to decrease the capacitance but is optimally addressed by shielding.

A conductive and grounded shield placed between the signal source and the affected node will eliminate this noise by routing the displacement current directly to ground. However, it is essential that a Faraday shield be grounded. A floating or open-circuit shield invariably increases capacitively coupled noise.

If changing magnetic flux due to electrical current flowing in one circuit couples to another circuit, it can induce an EMF in the second circuit. This effect explains how transformers work, and is described quantitatively by Faraday's Law. So-called mutual inductance can be a difficult source of noise coupling that causes large changes of current with time. The EMF induced in a second circuit by the first is given by the following:

$$\text{EMF}_2 = -M\left(\frac{dI}{dt}\right) \tag{C.2}$$

where M is the mutual inductance, and dI/dt is the change in current with time. Fig. C.2 illustrates inductive coupling.[2] Note that if circuit 1 is opened and the current in that circuit decreased, the induced voltage in circuit 2 opposes the decrease in the flux density B (Lenz's Law).

As an example, a mutual inductance of 1 nH and a changing current of 1 A/ns (10^{-9} s) will induce an EMF of 1 V.

To illustrate the effect, consider a circuit with a closed loop or coil of area A (cm^2) operating in a magnetic field with a root mean square (RMS) flux density of B gauss. The maximum noise voltage V_n induced in this circuit is given by the following (in CGS units) [1]:

$$V_n = -2\pi f B A \cos(\theta) \times 10^{-8} \text{ V} \tag{C.3}$$

[2]ibid

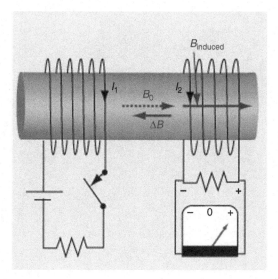

FIGURE C.2 **Inductive coupling.**

(C.3) may appear obscure, but it is merely expressing the fact that the induced voltage results from the time rate of change of the magnetic flux, $d\phi/dt$. This is an example of induction, which is explained by Maxwell's third equation.

Referring to (C.3), f represents the frequency of the fluctuating magnetic field and θ is the angle of the magnetic field relative to the face of the pickup coil of area A. Although it is not apparent from (C.3), the amplitude of the magnetic flux density B is varying in a sinusoidal manner, and the maximum value occurs when the sine function is unity.

(C.3) reveals that inductive coupling can be reduced by reducing the loop area, reducing the magnetic flux density, or changing the angle of incidence. Reducing the circuit loop area requires arranging the circuit conductors so that they are closer together.

Twisting the conductors together reduces the effective loop area. In particular, twisting pairs of conductors has the effect of canceling magnetic field pickup, because the sum of positive and negative incremental loop areas is ideally equal to zero. Parallel conductors are configured as twisted pairs for this reason. Alexander Graham Bell filed the original patent suggesting using twisted pairs of conductors.

However, and as discussed in Chapter 8, the magnetic field intensity due to current loop sources, that is, a low-impedance source, is inversely proportional to the cube of the distance from the source in the near field. Therefore, physically moving a small distance away from the source has a disproportionately large effect on reducing the induced voltage.

Finally, if the circuit is placed perpendicular to the magnetic field, the induced voltage is zero. However, if the circuit's conductors are parallel to the magnetic field, the induced voltage is maximized because the angle of incidence θ is zero and therefore the cosine of the angle between the magnetic field vector and the normal to the surface is unity.

Reference

[1] Purcell EM. Electricity and magnetism. Berkeley physics course, vol. 2. New York: McGraw-Hill; 1965.

APPENDIX

D

Intermediate Frequency (IF) Filtering of Signals

Fig. D.1 depicts a pulsed radio-frequency signal, where T is the pulse repetition time ($1/T$ is therefore the frequency), τ is the pulse width, and T_o is the time between peaks of the carrier signal. f_r and f_o are pulse repetition and carrier signal frequencies, respectively.[1]

The ratio of the target signal pulse repetition rate ($1/T$) to the intermediate frequency (IF) filter bandwidth in the attacker's receiver is important. If the IF filter bandwidth is much smaller than the pulse repetition frequency, only one spectral component of the signal will be in the passband of the IF filter. Fig. D.2 illustrates this situation.[2] Note that the receiver is tuned to the carrier frequency so that the IF filter is centered about the maximum of the main lobe of the impulsive signal.

If on the other hand the IF bandwidth of the receiver is greater than the pulse repetition frequency, many spectral components of the signal will be within the filter passband. Fig. D.3 illustrates the condition where the IF filter is greater than the pulse repetition rate.[3]

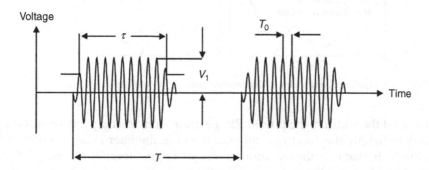

FIGURE D.1 **Digital signal pulses from a targeted device.** Here, τ is the pulse width (at 50% points), $f_r = (1/T)$ is the pulse repetition frequency (PRF), and $f_o = (1/T_o)$ is the carrier signal frequency.

[1]http://ewh.ieee.org/r6/scv/emc/archive/download20001114.pdf
[2]ibid.
[3]ibid.

Information Security Science
Copyright © 2016 Elsevier Inc. All rights reserved.

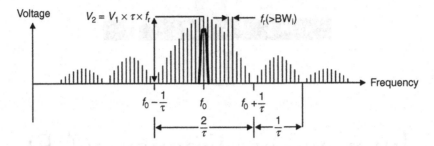

FIGURE D.2   IF filter centered on main signal lobe. The IF filter (heavy black line) is narrower than the pulse repetition frequency.

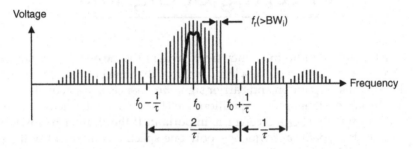

FIGURE D.3   IF filter (heavy black line) that is centered on the main signal lobe and is wider than the pulse repetition rate.

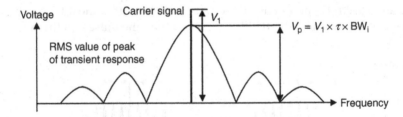

FIGURE D.4   **The impulsive bandwidth and measured peak signal voltage.**

Importantly, if the width of the pulsed RF spectrum from the target machine is larger than the IF filter bandwidth, the spectral components within the filter passband will all have the same amplitude. In that case the maximum voltage of signal transients is proportional to the impulse bandwidth, τ, and the carrier signal voltage.

This condition is valid as long as the resolution bandwidth of the attacker's receiver is much greater than the pulse repetition rate, and the main lobe of the impulsive signal is much greater than the filter bandwidth. Knowing the impulse bandwidth of a receiver is therefore necessary for accurate signal measurements. Fig. D.4 illustrates the situation.[4]

[4]ibid.

An Indicative Table of Contents for an Information Security Policy

Index

Printed in the United States
By Bookmasters